THE POLITICAL ECONOMY OF COLLECTIVE ACTION, INEQUALITY, AND DEVELOPMENT

THE POLITICAL ECONOMY OF COLLECTIVE ACTION, INEQUALITY, AND DEVELOPMENT

William D. Ferguson

Stanford University Press
Stanford, California

Stanford University Press
Stanford, California

Printed in the United States of America on acid-free, archival-quality paper

Library of Congress Cataloging-in-Publication Data

Names: Ferguson, William D., author.
Title: The political economy of collective action, inequality, and
    development / William D. Ferguson.
Description: Stanford, California : Stanford University Press, [2020] |
    Includes bibliographical references and index.
Identifiers: LCCN 2019049300 (print) | LCCN 2019049301 (ebook) |
    ISBN 9781503604612 (cloth) | ISBN 9781503611979 (ebook)
Subjects: LCSH: Equality—Economic aspects. | Economic development. |
    Political development.
Classification: LCC HM821 .F47 2020 (print) | LCC HM821 (ebook) |
    DDC 320.01/1—dc23
LC record available at https://lccn.loc.gov/2019049300
LC ebook record available at https://lccn.loc.gov/2019049301

Cover image: iStock

Cover design: Rob Ehle

Typeset by Newgen in 10/14 Minion Regular

Dedicated to my wife, Claudia Beckwith; my children, Caitlin and
Taylor Beckwith-Ferguson; and to the memory of my parents,
Audrey I. and Allen R. Ferguson.

Contents

Preface

Sapiens and Neanderthals

Thanks to their ability to invent fiction, Sapiens create more and more complex games, which each generation develops and elaborates even further.

—*Yuval Noah Harari,* Sapiens: A Brief History of Humankind *(2015)*

According to historian Yuval Noah Harari (2015), from about 70,000 to 30,000 years ago, *Homo sapiens* vied with *Homo neanderthalensis* for dominance in areas of Europe and the Middle East. The Neanderthals were larger, stronger, better adapted to cold climates, and had larger brains. They also used tools and knew how to care for their sick. Neanderthals could dominate in one-on-one combat. Yet, Sapiens ultimately prevailed. Indeed, they exterminated the Neanderthals. Sapiens triumphed because they had developed collaborative cognitive abilities that Neanderthals simply lacked. Specifically, Sapiens developed the ability to tell stories, not just about lions in bushes, but also about each other—that is, to gossip. This capability permitted forms of cooperation that Neanderthals could not achieve; it fostered organizing cooperative activity among individuals, resolving some collective-action problems. Concurrently, Sapiens developed the ability to talk about things not present, "things they have never seen, touched, or smelled. . . . Only *Homo sapiens* can speak about things that don't really exist, and believe six impossible things before breakfast" (Ibid., 24). Sapiens learned to share legends, myths, gods, and other abstract concepts (relevant later on) like nationhood. They shared stories that could forge common purpose, identity, and ideologies: "Fiction has enabled us to not merely imagine things, but to do so *collectively*" (Ibid., 25; emphasis in original). Collective storytelling facilitated rapid social adaptation to changing environments. To alter group behavior, Sapiens could change shared stories—a process much faster than genetic evolution. This cognitive revolution ushered in the triumph of *Homo sapiens* over *Homo neanderthalensis.*

Before 10,000 years ago, Sapiens spread across the planet and survived as foragers. In terms of leisure and, arguably, quality of work, they achieved relatively high standards of living. Normally, work did not exceed 35–40 hours per week, and it involved multiple stimulating tasks. Foragers ate varied and balanced diets and exercised substantially. Children who survived their first few years had good prospects of living at least until age 60, sometimes age 80. With multiple sources of food, deprivation of one type rarely led to starvation.

Starting about 9,500 years ago, however, Sapiens began to develop agriculture. The agricultural revolution unfolded over the next 7,000 years, extending across the globe via simultaneous invention. Cultivating crops was not the idea of a single person or group but rather an adaptation to roughly similar environmental conditions encountered around the globe. The agricultural revolution, which Harari calls history's greatest fraud, vastly improved food productivity, permitting substantial population growth. It also brought more labor, more disease (transmitted between humans and domesticated animals), lower life expectancies, additional reasons for territorial conflict, graver consequences to losing such conflicts—such as starvation, which might also arise from drought or insects—and dimensions of inequality and social hierarchy that Sapiens had not previously experienced. Whereas this shift in production benefited the species as a whole (the gene pool), most individuals—except those at the top of the hierarchy—experienced more deprivation. Adaptive human activity—sensible in multiple relevant contexts—fostered more work for mere survival, more disease, and so on. From the viewpoint of the peasant masses, the agricultural revolution introduced many new collective-action problems. How might they work together to escape toil, disease, instances of starvation, and the often cruel authority of those at the top of social hierarchies?

Acknowledgments

I wrote the bulk of *The Political Economy of Collective Action, Inequality, and Development* during a series of academic visits, most of which occurred during my 2017–18 sabbatical. The following institutions provided office support with extensive opportunities to interact with scholars, attend and present my work at seminars, workshops, and various lectures, while writing the basic manuscript: The Effective States and Inclusive Development Research Centre (ESID) of the Global Development Institute, University of Manchester; the Institute for New Economic Thinking (INET) at the Oxford Martin School, University of Oxford; the Political Science Department and Amsterdam Institute for Social Science Research (AISSR), University of Amsterdam; the Berlin WZB Social Science Center; and the Economics Department at University College London.

I want to thank the following individuals for arranging these visits: Kunal Sen, Julia Brunt, and Kat Bethell at Manchester's ESID; Eric Beinhocker and Susan Mousley at INET Oxford; Brian Burgoon and Geoffrey Underhill at the University of Amsterdam; Steffen Huck at WBZ Berlin; and Wendy Carlin and Frank Witte at University College London.

I offer special thanks to Brian Levy and David Booth for their support and comments and for putting me in contact with ESID's Kunal Sen and Sam Hickey. A special thanks also goes to Rob Axtell, who has consistently supported my work, offered me comments, and who introduced me to Eric Beinhocker.

The ESID visit and workshops contributed decisively to my understanding of the concept of political settlements. I especially thank Tim Kelsall and Matthias vom Hau, whose basic approach to political settlements underlies mine. Brian Levy and David Booth introduced me to the concept. I benefited substantially from conversations, workshops, and seminar sessions with scholars including Pritish Behuria, Abhishek Chakravarty, Ralitza Dimova, Sam Hickey, David Hulme, David Jackman, Thomas Lavers, Diana Mitlin, Dilip Mookherjee, Kate Pruce, Antonio Savoia, Nicolai Schulz, Kunal Sen, Maya Tudor, Matthias vom Hau, and Pablo Yanguas. I thank Tim Kelsall and Kunal Sen for their comments on several chapters. ESID also offered me the honor of delivering the 2017 Adrian Leftwich Memorial Lecture, about my book, on November 29.

At Oxford, I benefited from conversations and seminars with scholars including Eric Beinhocker, Richard Bailey, Enresto Carillo, Rita Maria del Rio Chanona, Paul Collier, Stefan Dercon, Doyne Farmer, Ian Goldin, Robert Hahn, Francois Lafond, Penny Mealy, Sharun Mukand, Brian Nolan, Kevin O'Rourke, Lars Osberg, Anton Pichler, Karthik Ramanna, Huei-chun Su, Vilhelm Verendel, Rupert Way, Martin Williams, and Peyton Young.

At Amsterdam's AISSR, Abbey Steele and Imke Habers contributed to my understanding of subnational political dynamics. Joost Berkhout contributed to my understanding of policy dynamics. I also benefited substantially from conversations and seminars with scholars including Maarten Bavinck, Arnoud Boot, Jeroen Bruggerman, Brian Burgoon, Ursula Daxecker, Sijeong Lim, Nicky Pouw, Kris Ruijgrok, Seiki Tanaka, and Geoffrey Underhill.

At WZB Berlin, I learned from conversations and seminars with scholars including Hande Erkut, Steffen Huck, Macartan Humphreys, Levent Neyse, Justin Valasek, Pauline Vorjohann, and Michael Zürn.

At University College London, I benefited from conversations and seminars with Wendy Carlin, Martin Cripps, Philippe Jehiel, Imran Rasul, Vasiliki Skreta, Ran Spiegler, Marcos Vera Hernandez, and Frank Witte.

I gleaned useful ideas from several Political Science and Political Economy seminars at the London School of Economics and from conversations with Tim Besley, Richard Bronk, Lloyd Gruber, Bob Hanke, and Waltraud Schelkle. I thank Bob Hanke for his comments on several related papers.

I thank Peter Hall for his comments on several preliminary papers related to this project. Conversations with Leigh Anderson, Sam Bowles, Lukas Brun,

Karla Hoff, Wade Jacoby, Mushtaq Khan, John Morrow, Dani Rodrik, Hilton Root, and Michael Woolcock informed my approach.

I thank Grinnell College and the Committee for Support of Faculty Scholarship for my sabbatical leave and financial support. Nicholas Haeg, Mukand Kalani, Terran Mott, and Takshil Sachdev provided useful research assistance. I especially thank (former) Dean Mike Latham for his consistent support of this project. My colleagues Janet Seiz and Eliza Willis offered useful comments on a draft prospectus. I appreciate consistent support from (former) Economics Department Chair Keith Brouhle. I thank my colleagues Mark Montgomery and Jack Mutti, who, as always, encouraged my work.

I offer special thanks to Margo Beth Fleming, my first editor at Stanford University Press, who, following a brief conversation at an economics conference, encouraged me to write my 2013 Stanford book and who subsequently supported this second book through its prospectus and contract. I thank Stanford's current senior editor, Steve Catalano, and Sunna Juhn for their assistance on this project.

I appreciate comments on this book's prospectus from Kaushik Basu and an anonymous reviewer. I also received very useful comments from two anonymous reviewers of the draft manuscript.

I extend a special thanks to my graduate school professors Sam Bowles and Herb Gintis, who have inspired my entire research career, and to my ninth grade (public school) Civics teacher, Patricia Rudy, for inspiring my interest in politics and social science.

I extend heartfelt thanks to my son, Taylor Beckwith-Ferguson, who, in the midst of his international travels, provided editorial comments on the entire draft of the manuscript. I especially thank my wife, Claudia Beckwith, for her consistent loving support during the, sometimes arduous, writing process.

THE POLITICAL ECONOMY
OF COLLECTIVE ACTION,
INEQUALITY, AND
DEVELOPMENT

Introduction

Toward a Framework for Development Theory

The power of a theory is exactly proportional to the diversity of situations it can explain.

—*Elinor Ostrom,* Governing the Commons: The Evolution of Institutions for Collective Action *(1990)*

WHY DO SOME SOCIETIES ACHIEVE high standards of living, with broad access to education and quality health care, serviceable infrastructure, predictable and largely impersonal legal procedures, along with relatively accessible avenues to peaceful political expression, while others stagnate with guarded islands of extravagant wealth, surrounded by oceans of poverty, corrupt autocratic systems, and simmering conflicts—or even full-blown civil wars? Why did South Korea, with an authoritarian patronage-oriented regime that faced a devastating war from 1950 to 1954, whose 1960 gross domestic product (GDP) per capita was half that of Mexico and twice that of India, have, by 2015, a per capita GDP that exceeded Mexico's by a factor of 3 and India's by a factor of 17? By that time, moreover, South Korea had become a functioning democracy. These two questions lead to a third. How might a society trapped in stagnation initiate and sustain processes of economic and political development?

In the Americas, the resource-rich areas first colonized by Europeans had, by the twentieth century, experienced substantially less growth in per capita output than the later colonized, resource-poor, and less desirable areas (Engerman and Sokoloff 2002). Following its 1994 brutal civil war and genocide, Rwanda developed a successful government that, although authoritarian, instituted stability and economic growth. That same year, South Africa elected Nelson Mandela as president, signifying the end of its repressive apartheid regime. Since 1979, under the political monopoly of its Communist Party,

China, on the one hand, has attained an average annual rate of GDP per capita growth of 8.5%. Burundi, on the other hand, increased its per capita GDP at an average annual rate of 0.13% since 1961.

Development is not just a matter of achieving adequate rates of saving, building capital, and acquiring technology; nor is it just a matter of getting the institutions right—at least not in a superficial sense of importing constitutions, legislation, and concepts of property rights from developed countries. These two prescriptions speak to often necessary conditions that affect development, but they do not begin to establish sufficient conditions for development because the political economy of development is more complicated. The first prescription ignores power entirely. The second fails to adequately consider how configurations of power operating within specific social contexts shape the creation, evolution, and demise of institutions, and, perhaps more critically, how such configurations shape degrees of enforcement and implementation of institutional prescriptions within such contexts. Argentina's "electoral law of 1853, which purported to allow popular participation in the political process, from the beginning proved itself a sham. Elections were invariably ritualistic parodies, staged-managed by lackeys of the powerful, with only a minute fraction of the electorate participating" (Rock 2000, 129; quoted in Acemoglu and Robinson 2006, 5).

Indeed, development has multifaceted economic and political components. At a simple level, economic development connotes sustainable, steady increases in average living standards, especially for the lower half of the income distribution. More comprehensively, it involves widespread realization of basic human capabilities by arranging for adequate health care, education, other public services, and infrastructure. At an institutional level, economic development connotes the evolution of mutually understood and expected informal and formal procedures for circumventing multiple forms of free riding that accompany public goods, common resources, and externalities; and for mitigating conflict, protecting universal (as opposed to selective) property rights, and enforcing production and exchange agreements. Political development connotes a similar evolution with respect to creating and enhancing the effectiveness, legitimacy, and sustainability of informal and formal political institutions that foster capacities to deliver public services, broad participation, and that, simultaneously, protect basic civil rights. In both cases, development requires reform of existing formal arrangements, along with a complementary evolution of informal institutions. It involves enhancing state capacity, balanced—over time—with broad avenues for political input and limits on concentrated private and public power.

Political and economic inequalities permeate developmental processes, both as conditions that shape their evolution and as developmental outcomes. Unequal access to power, decision arenas, knowledge, wealth, productive resources, and positions within exchange processes create large asymmetries with respect to basic capacities, opportunities, barriers, and ensuing outcomes—such as distributions of income, wealth, and political authority. Myriad social conflicts follow. These effects, in turn, influence and constrain future developmental prospects. A society's often tenuous ability to resolve sets of associated collective-action problems, therefore, shapes its political and economic evolution—its prospects for development.

The complexity of political economy poses a core dilemma for social scientists: We know, for example, that institutions both facilitate and emerge from processes of economic and political development. Yet, why do functional institutions emerge in some places and not others? Why do institutional forms that appear to work well in some settings utterly fail in others? How can we systematically analyze phenomena that exhibit such intricate interactions, so many routes of causality, and so many instances of idiosyncrasy that emerge from unique combinations of social ingredients? Might we exhaust ourselves merely trying to list specific instances, inputs, relations, and outcomes, or do so by merely recounting anecdotes?

Biologists face similar, if not greater, complexity. There are myriad species, subspecies, genera, and phyla; so many possible competitive, symbiotic, and accidental interactions; so many mechanisms of transfer, locomotion, propagation, and reproduction; so many niche and environmental influences. Biologists address this complexity with a mix of theory—such as evolution, genetic transmission, photosynthesis, and predator-prey dynamics—along with description and categorization that draws distinctions among phyla, genera, species, components of cells, environmental conditions, and so forth.

In this text, I adopt an analogous approach. I construct a conceptual framework for development theory that integrates concepts of causality and techniques for categorization that integrates three related components, five core developmental hypotheses, a typology of political settlements, and an analytical approach based on the concept of collective-action problems. The developmental hypotheses address interactions between public goods, coordination of productive activity, power, institutional evolution, credible commitments, and a potential role for organizational and institutional innovation to relax political constraints. *Political settlements* are shared understandings, relationships, and arrangements held among powerful parties to use politics, rather than violence, as their primary method for resolving disputes. Political settlements underlie social order and shape the configuration of social orders. *Collective-action problems* (hereafter, CAPs) arise when, within a given social context, individual and group pursuit of inclinations and interests generates undesirable outcomes for one or more groups. Pollution, crime, and excess conflict are examples. CAPs are ubiquitous in human social interaction. Indeed, achieving economic and political development entails resolving multiple CAPs. CAPs, moreover, both condition and arise from the relationships specified in each of the core hypotheses, and the most foundational developmental CAPs concern limiting organized violence—by forging some form of a political settlement. Furthermore, classifying political settlements in terms of underlying social foundations and configurations of authority facilitates developmental inquiry by designating core attributes of developmental contexts; specific types of settlements imply specific sets of CAPs that condition developmental prospects.

The point here is to provide an analytical framework that permits tractable navigation of such complexities: one that allows traversing the difficult theoretical terrain stretched between relatively simplistic hierarchies of causality (e.g., geography or a combination of preferences and technology as ultimate causes), on the one hand, and idiosyncratic case studies on the other.

Here, I employ the straightforward concept of collective-action problems accompanied by game-theoretic reasoning as the principal analytical lenses for examining multifaceted interactions between inequality, power, and economic and political development. Although the idea of CAPs frequently appears in the literature, my approach adds nuance. I distinguish between first- and second-order CAPs. First-order CAPs involve multiple forms of free riding—letting others do the work, take the risks, pay the costs. Typically, they involve some form of distributional conflict. Who makes the coffee at work, lifts his head to oppose the dictator, or cuts her carbon consumption? In principle, negotiated agreements can resolve such CAPs, but why should anyone believe a mere promise to honor an agreement when cutting corners is easier or more profitable? Should we believe a firm's promise to deliver a safe, high-quality product or not pollute, a politician's promise to respect minority rights, a warring party's promise to lay down arms if the other side does so first? Second-order CAPs involve arranging mechanisms (or relations) of coordination and enforcement that render agreements which (in principle) could resolve first-order CAPs, credible, implementable, indeed meaningful.[1] And the enforcement component of second-order CAPs, which always involves power, links economic and political processes and agreements; second-order CAPs underlie political economy. This two-sided concept of CAPs thus offers an analytical lens for examining a huge variety of developmental issues. Humans, after all, are simultaneously individuals and social beings. Individual activities and beliefs both respond to and influence group beliefs and interactions, and vice versa. Competition, co-operation, conflict, and incomplete or skewed understandings abound. CAPs thus permeate economic, political, and social dynamics.

Analogously, strategic behavior permeates human societies, occurring whenever one person's or one group's actions affects others. Game-theoretic reasoning permits systematic analysis of myriad strategic interactions. It fosters *vicarious problem solving*, wherein investigators attribute material and/or social goals to individuals or groups, along with possible actions and various obstacles and constraints (Schelling 1978). On this basis, one can infer (predict) likely behavior. Game-theoretic reasoning requires only an assumption that humans seek goals and that agents' actions influence outcomes for others (Gintis 2009), hence its breadth of application—here, application to the political economy of development.

In the social sciences, a *conceptual framework* provides a platform for drawing distinctions, explaining core avenues of causality, and, often via extensions, predicting outcomes of social interactions that operate in various specific contexts (Jenkins-Smith et al. 2018). Conceptual frameworks provide vocabulary, sets of categories, and sets of causal principles that facilitate subsequent analysis. By designating and fostering avenues for inquiry, they create foundations for entire research programs. Although, given such breadth, many elements of a specific framework are, at best, difficult to test empirically, frameworks point to coherent bodies of complementary theory that may guide subsequent research, including multiple, more focused theoretical models with more precise conceptual and operational specifications. Multiple testable hypotheses may then follow.[2]

Despite its breadth, this book does not attempt to explain long-term historical origins of developmentally functional institutional systems. For example, it does not sort out the degree to which geographical differences have conditioned distributions of power and institutional evolution over centuries—a question posed by Stanley Engerman and Kenneth Sokoloff (2002). The present focus is more contemporary, primarily though not exclusively concentrating on the twentieth and early twenty-first centuries, and it pays considerable attention to short- and medium-term time horizons; the latter might extend a few decades. Even so, this approach addresses foundations of institutional development in a manner that is consistent with many historical accounts of institutional evolution.

This text employs the nation-state as its primary unit of analysis, but many of its principles apply to specific geographical and topical policy domains (addressed in Chapter 6), industrial sectors and various subnational regions including municipalities (addressed in Chapters 8 and 9), and supranational regions and organizations such as the European Union (EU) and the African Union. Indeed, the discussion of political settlements in Chapter 8 invites subnational distinctions within at least two of its four designated categories.

My proposed framework also merges several intellectual traditions. It utilizes a broad and flexible interpretation of economic and rational choice institutionalism—a variant on methodological individualism that employs a broad and minimal conception of rationality as goal-oriented behavior (Ostrom 1998; Gintis 2009). It adds a complementary emphasis on game-theoretic reasoning as a systematic method for conceptualizing ubiquitous strategic interactions among various agents, which may be individuals, organizations, or coalitions. As such, this framework offers multiple avenues for vicarious problem solving that analysts may apply to specific developmental contexts. It also incorporates social conflict theory. Distributions of power shape institutional formation, and asymmetric distributions of power generate commitment problems. To classify underlying developmental contexts, this approach considers discrete types of political settlements. Distinct configurations of these shared understandings, relationships, and arrangements among powerful parties that establish politics, rather than violence, as their key method for resolving disputes underlie distinct configurations of social orders. Finally, this approach frames processes of institutional evolution within a punctuated equilibrium dynamic, an addition that renders its premises compatible with historical institutionalism and punctuated equilibrium theory (PET) in policymaking.[3]

Because their concept of social conflict underlies two of this text's core hypotheses, a brief comparison to Daron Acemoglu and James Robinson's approach (2006, 2008, 2012) permits further elaboration.[4] In their discussions of the economic origins of dictatorship and democracy, the uses of elite power, and the comparative economic success of nations, these authors utilize seven basic principles:

1. They start with an economic foundation, meaning that individuals use well-defined (broad) preferences (such as a desire for more income) to evaluate social outcomes. Corresponding economic incentives affect political attitudes, and individuals behave strategically, as in game theory.

2. They focus on social conflict among various groups of political actors who can affect economic and political outcomes through collective organization and access to resources (sources of de facto power) and, more generally, through exercises of both de facto and de jure power.[5]

3. They address the role of political institutions in designating decision-making authority (de jure power) and, more generally, the impacts of distributions of power on the evolution of both political and economic institutions.

4. The authors focus on commitment problems related to the typical inability of powerful parties to credibly signal that they will refrain from using their power for their own benefit—a condition that undermines the credibility and feasibility of potential agreements. By designating the distribution of relatively permanent de jure political power, however, political institutions can (sometimes) resolve such problems.

5. They pay attention to distinctions among various sources of income and wealth, notably that between the political incentives implied by land ownership as opposed to ownership of productive resources that rely on physical and human capital.

6. They apply a Schumpeterian approach to political development as constituting fair elections and broad political participation. This approach underlies the Acemoglu-Robinson distinction between authoritarian and democratic forms of governance.

7. They employ the concept of a political equilibrium in which powerful parties do not encounter sufficiently strong incentives to invest resources in acquiring (additional) de facto power for the purpose of altering existing institutional configurations.

Using these principles, Acemoglu and Robinson (2012) distinguish between *extractive* and *inclusive institutions*, with attention to the stability of each. Whereas extractive institutions sometimes foster short- to medium-term growth by transferring resources from relatively unproductive to productive sectors—for example, from agriculture to heavy industry in the USSR starting in the late 1920s—they cannot achieve sustained growth because extractive institutions stifle technological innovation and creative destruction. By contrast, inclusive political and economic institutions, when sufficiently stable, foster long-term growth.

My approach retains this emphasis on the importance of strategic reasoning and economic incentives—though with more leeway for shifts in preferences arising from social influence. It also retains a focus on social conflict, the significance of political incentives conferred by distinct sources of wealth, the impact of distributions of power on institutional evolution, the critical role of commitment, and a potential for institutions to establish credible commitment. Indeed, commitment problems reflect unresolved second-order CAPs, and, for complex exchanges, institutions underlie feasible possibilities for resolution.

Yet, there are differences. Rather than focus inquiry on distinguishing democratic from authoritarian paths of development, and corresponding concepts on inclusiveness and exclusiveness (important though they are), my approach adds dimension and nuance by directly considering categories of political settlements. The contours of political settlements, which depend on their social foundations and configurations of authority, influence the evolution of institutions and, consequently, corresponding economic and political development. They do so, moreover, in manners that do not necessarily rely on a democracy/dictatorship dichotomy. Even so, the notion of a political settlement (developed in Part III) does bear resemblance to the Acemoglu-Robinson concept of a political equilibrium. The implications of distinct types of political settlement, however, extend beyond an exclusive/inclusive dichotomy—relevant though that is. I also place more emphasis on second-order CAPs—especially those related to enforcing institutional prescriptions. Such CAPs interfere with attaining sufficient implementation and social mobilization for rendering nominally inclusive political and economic institutions inclusive in practice. Moreover, my approach does not require that political inclusion guarantee or lead to economic inclusion, and vice versa.[6] Additionally, I include a richer concept of political development that extends beyond a Schumpeterian notion by also stressing state capacity, the rule of law, legitimacy, and social mobilization.

In many respects, this text offers a sequel to my 2013 book, *Collective Action and Exchange: A Game-Theoretic Approach to Contemporary Political Economy*. That book addresses the same basic proposition: development requires resolution of CAPs, but it does so with more micro foundation and less attention to macro-level interactions and processes of development. My 2013 text begins with micro foundations that address the ability of small and large groups to develop and implement cooperative agreements related to myriad types of free riding (first-order CAPs) as well as methods for rendering such agreements credible by establishing requisite coordination and enforcement (second-order CAPs). A key implication follows: resolution via enforcement requires exercises of power. The discussion proceeds to complicate the analysis by successively discussing the sources, instruments, and dimensions of power; social preference theory, especially the concept of intrinsic reciprocity; and bounded rationality, which then establishes foundations for conceptualizing institutions. Next, it turns to institutions as conduits for the transmission of motivation, information, and, more fundamentally, cognition. Informal and formal institutions and institutional systems thus act as social coordination devices—foundations of social choreography (Gintis 2009). This discussion proceeds to address the compatibility of informal and formal institutions (or lack thereof), with implications on relationships between local self-governance, third-party enforcement, social norms, formal institutions, and complex exchange. These are foundations of governance and economic development. After considering social networks and the political economy of policymaking, my 2013 text closes at the macrolevel: location, information, growth, power, commitment, and development.

My new text expands on these final topics.

I FOUNDATIONS

PART I DEVELOPS FOUNDATIONAL concepts for the remaining argument in this text. Chapter 1 sets the stage for interactions of agency and structure. It addresses the difficulties of achieving cooperation among individuals, noting two basic types of collective-action problems (CAPs). It proceeds to develop the contextual concepts of informal and formal institutions, noting links to bounded rationality. It proceeds to the larger-scale concepts of institutional systems, social orders, and political settlements, with attention to implications on resolving CAPs. Chapter 2 addresses the following multifaceted concepts: economic development, with attention to growth, distribution, and foundations of productive and other economic capabilities; political development, with attention to capacities, rules, accountability, social mobilization, and legitimacy; various dimensions of political and economic inequality; and how inequality and development interact.

1 Collective-Action Problems and Institutional Systems

Institutional failures, weak accountability mechanisms, and missed opportunities for cooperative problem solving constitute the running themes of our story of economic underdevelopment. The institutional framework of an economy defines and constrains the opportunities for individuals, determines the business climate, shapes the incentives and organizations for collective action by local communities in resolving their common problems, and encompasses the structures of commitment and accountability that the political authority of a society provides.

—*Pranab Bardhan,* Scarcity, Conflicts, and Cooperation: Essays in the
Political and Institutional Economics of Development *(2005)*

ZAMBIA ACHIEVED INDEPENDENCE from Great Britain in 1964. The new government adopted nominally open institutions that prescribed broad political and economic access. Yet, Europeans retained the best jobs, 60–70% of marketable agriculture, and ownership of valuable copper mines. Despite the shift in political control, "rents remained principally in the hands of the preexisting elites, with their control over those rents supported by the bequeathed economic institutions" (Levy 2013, 119). Moreover, lacking a shared concept of national purpose and identity, the pre-independence unity of the anticolonialist coalition that had formed the new government quickly fragmented. Regional and ethnic conflicts emerged, and organized labor, especially the miner's union, staged multiple strikes. For the 11 years between 1961 and 1971, Zambian GDP per capita grew at an average annual rate of 0.3%. In 1972, the United National Independence Party (UNIP) consolidated its power, forming a one-party state (Ibid., 120). Even though the new regime provided some stability, it could not adapt to declining copper prices and other economic problems. For the next 18 years, GDP per capita declined at an average annual rate of −1.84%.[1] Over these years, the UNIP government presided over "crisis, response, backtracking, and deeper decline" (Ibid.).

The post–World War II Philippines faced similarly daunting problems. Gabriella R. Montinola elucidates:

> From 1946 to 1972, the country was dominated by a coalition of elite families and foreign capitalists who controlled access to economic and political power. The major source of wealth at independence was agricultural land, but this source was soon augmented by industrial policy-induced rents. The ruling coalition used these rents to secure loyalty and to defuse periodic violence from non-elite groups. The strategy was unsustainable, however, because the rent-creating policies did not produce enough resources to satisfy the increasingly restive non-elite groups. The threat of disorder and violence enabled Ferdinand Marcos to install himself as dictator in 1972. (2013, 149–50)

Why did Zambia's initially open political and economic institutions fail to generate reasonably shared substantial economic growth and democratic institutions? Why was the Philippines unable to create more accessible and responsive institutions?

Many approaches to economic development stress the rate of growth of GDP per capita as the single most important developmental variable. Some proceed to focus on *proximate* causes of economic growth, such as physical capital, human capital, and technology, with attention to immediate antecedents. Associated policy prescriptions might then include promoting savings, research and development (R&D), and enacting policies aimed at protecting property rights or encouraging the free movement of labor and capital. In this text, however, I strive for a deeper and more comprehensive approach. As a work in political economy, this text addresses both political and economic development, with attention to their interactions, overlaps, conflicts, and complementarities. Its broad concept of development—namely, sustained widespread improvement in human economic and political capabilities—focuses attention on both barriers and opportunities. Using a set of related developmental hypotheses, this approach moves beyond proximate causes of growth and their policy or institutional antecedents to deeper interactions between collective action, cooperation, coordination, and sources and exercises of power that shape institutional development. At a yet deeper level, this text's conceptual framework addresses how distinct configurations of understandings and arrangements for restraining the organized use of violence—that is, political settlements—influence prospects for achieving some balance of political and economic conflict, competition, and cooperation that may then foster accessible and accountable political participation, along with broadly distributed economic capabilities, growth, and access.

Accordingly, this book addresses three intertwined themes. First, economic and political development requires resolution of underlying CAPs. CAPs arise whenever individuals, pursuing their own interests in given contexts, generate undesirable outcomes for one or more groups. Crime and pollution are examples—as is providing for physical, educational, technological, and health infrastructure; achieving reform; and forging arrangements that can settle disputes without resorting to violence. Widespread improvements in human capabilities thus require removing barriers posed by CAPs, including sources of deprivation, in addition to the more traditionally considered routes to opportunity. Development thus entails interacting economic and political components, including sustained improvements in living standards; widespread provision of public goods and services such as health care, education, and basic infrastructure; continuously strengthening institutional arrangements that protect economic, political, and civil rights; and simultaneously fostering widespread economic and political access and participation. CAPs permeate myriad efforts toward such achievement.

Second, a society's prospects for resolving fundamental CAPs—and therefore its potential set of developmental trajectories—depends critically on the underlying political-economic context. Such contexts involve power relationships and institutional configurations, which themselves emerge from previous attempts to resolve CAPs—notably those related to constraining the use of organized violence among parties with such potential via some form of mutually understood political settlement.

Third, inequality infuses the relevant processes—doing so as an outcome, an impetus, and an impediment to development. Multiple inequities emerge from economic and political processes—whether conducive to development or not. Concurrently, unequal distributions, relationships, and access shape the basic characteristics of developmental CAPs, as well prospects for resolution. Although political and economic inequities sometimes offer impetus for action, they also underlie multiple deprivations that serve as barriers to development; and excessive inequity fosters political instability. Inequality generates its own set of developmental CAPs.

Turning to specifics, this chapter discusses the core concepts of CAPs, institutions, institutional systems, and political settlements. Section 1 addresses CAPs in more detail, distinguishing first-order CAPS of free riding from second-order CAPs of arranging mechanisms (or relations) of coordination and enforcement that render agreements, which (in principal) could resolve first-order CAPs, credible, implementable, meaningful. Second-order CAPs often pose subtle and difficult political and economic barriers to development as they merge and intertwine the political and economic components of development processes, beginning with micro-level exchange agreements. Institutions can facilitate resolution. Section 2 discusses institutions (rules), organizations (a type of actor), and institutional systems (mixes of both). After defining institutions, the discussion turns to micro-level underpinnings, using concepts of bounded rationality and cognition that draw attention to the importance of mental models (conceptual frameworks), noting that institutions are in fact a type of shared mental model. Discussion proceeds to three key channels through which institutions condition behavior (motivation, information, and cognition) before more fully addressing distinctions between institutions and organizations. Complementary combinations of both entities form institutional systems, which then coordinate understandings and activity across multiple agents—what we later call social choreography. Section 3 addresses how institutions and institutional systems both resolve and create CAPs. It discusses how informal and formal institutions interact, with attention to manners through which institutions and organizations jointly foster social coordination (choreography) that tends to follow a punctuated equilibrium dynamic—resolving some CAPs and creating others in the process. Moving to foundations, Section 4 introduces the concept of political settlements—the chief component of this text's conceptual framework. As shared understandings and arrangements that limit organized exercises of violence, political settlements underlie the formation of institutions and institutional systems. They establish requisite conditions for economic and political development. In their absence, development does not occur. Because the social bases and configurations of authority within political settlements condition developmental CAPs, precise specification of these relationships provides a conceptual framework for analyzing the political economy of development. Section 5 presents the plan of the book.

Section 1: First- and Second-Order Collective-Action Problems

A society's prospects for development depend on its ability to resolve multiple underlying CAPs. CAPs arise when the pursuit of individual inclinations and self-interest, within given social contexts, leads to socially undesirable outcomes for one or more groups.[2] Relevant groups include nations, cities, communities, tribes, clubs, companies, nonprofit and religious organizations, colleagues, friends, and combinations or subsets therein. Examples of CAPs include the difficulties of achieving cooperation among individuals or groups related to the following types of issues: addressing climate change at international, national, and local levels; reducing international conflict; deciding who makes the coffee at work or who washes dishes at home; reducing crime, pollution, and traffic jams; providing basic public services such as potable water, roads, parks, disease control, R&D, and adequate education and health care; resolving disputes; and achieving political reform.

CAPs are ubiquitous in human social interactions. Indeed, the concept of CAPs offers a relatively simple, intuitive lens for analyzing myriad complex social problems. Because they permeate developmental processes, CAPs serve as a unifying analytical concept for this book. There are two basic types: first-order and second-order.

First-order CAPs involve multiple manifestations of free riding and social conflict related to the provision of public goods, promotion of positive externalities, reduction of negative externalities, and limiting the use of common resources—all broadly defined. For example, adjudication of disputes is a type of public good, as are the social benefits of opposing repressive regimes; excess conflict generates negative externalities; and within organizations, such as government agencies and private firms, managerial time is a common resource. Developmental first-order CAPs include how to provide and arrange for transportation, communication, health care, and educational infrastructure, and related social services; how to reduce pollution or ameliorate its effects; and how to provide for public safety.

In principle, resolving first-order CAPs involves forging implicit or explicit arrangements—among parties whose interests usually differ—for distributing the associated costs and benefits. Here, specific parties often bear the costs, such as time, effort, risk, and money; whereas benefits, such as a reduction of disease prevalence, are frequently nonexcludable (publicly available). Even so, the Coase Theorem asserts that, in the absence of transaction costs, affected parties can negotiate agreements about distributing costs and benefits, and that any associated distribution does not affect efficiency.[3] Yet, effective agreements require credibility, and perceived inequities within agreements often foster conflict. Indeed, many conceivable arrangements that, in principle, could resolve CAPs—and even imply Pareto improvement—never emerge, or they unravel under the stress of anticipated or ensuing conflict. Will the relevant parties have sufficient motivation, ability, information, and understanding to honor their side of a possible agreement?

Second-order CAPs involve arranging the coordination and enforcement that renders possible agreements, plans, or promises to resolve first-order CAPs credible—and hence implementable.[4] In fact, the anticipation of problematic coordination or enforcement often undermines the will to negotiate or even consider any resolution—and so impedes economic and political development. Second-order CAPs themselves arise from a combination of divergent interests and incomplete information. This mix creates opportunities for strategically manipulating information, via selective revelation, distortion, or outright lying. Indeed, these second-order coordination and enforcement CAPs—rather than simpler matters like costs of transportation to meetings—are the chief source of the ever-present transaction costs of forging credible agreements.[5]

Generally speaking, information-bound second-order CAPs may operate either before parties negotiate agreements, implying problems of adverse selection, or afterward, implying problems of moral hazard.[6] *Adverse selection* arises from a tendency of parties to withhold or misrepresent private information concerning the attributes of items, services, or persons (including themselves) that affect the nature or value of a subsequent exchange or agreement. For example, sellers of used cars may overstate a car's true value; job seekers may exaggerate their qualifications; potential employers may fail to reveal workplace hazards; borrowers may exaggerate their creditworthiness; and potential coalition partners may overstate their desire to cooperate or their political influence. Involved parties thus encounter obstacles to credibly communicating or discovering information about relevant characteristics of, say, used cars, job applicants, or potential coalition partners. Unless they devote resources to credibly providing or adequately discovering relevant information, potential exchange partners will lack potentially important information related to appraising the desirability of possible agreements or exchanges.

Adverse selection thus imposes transaction costs, such as those related to offering warranties and acquiring job credentials, and its existence influences exchange prospects and outcomes. Some purchased used cars actually are lemons; some new hires or elected officials are just not qualified. More fundamentally, the presence of high costs to signaling or screening and/or the possibility of undesirable outcomes can preclude potentially beneficial exchanges and agreements. Because they cannot credibly signal quality worthy of a good price, sellers of good used cars may withhold their vehicles from the market (Akerlof 1970). Brilliant graduates from third-rate universities may not even apply for sophisticated jobs. Potentially viable coalitions do not form. Development suffers.

Referring more specifically to second-order CAPs, adverse selection undermines coordination among potential parties to exchanges and agreements. For economic exchanges, the relevant markets cannot sufficiently match quality-conscious buyers and sellers. Market failure ensues because the parties lack a full understanding of the de facto property rights subject to exchange. Does a certain price entitle a buyer to a car that will run for 5,000 miles or 50,000 miles? Likewise, potentially effective coalition partners may not be able to credibly signal good intentions. The ensuing barriers to and difficulties of conducting myriad economic and political exchanges often truncates developmental prospects. Successful development requires at least some prior resolution.

Moral hazard problems also impede development, but via different information channels. *Moral hazard* refers to possible opportunistic behavior occurring only *after* making agreements or signing contracts. It arises when at least one party to an agreement undertakes actions (or opts for inaction) and/ or provides (or fails to provide) information in a manner that benefits that party and harms other parties. Moral hazard arises under three conditions: (i) at least partial divergence of interests (nearly ubiquitous in economic and political exchanges), (ii) perceived gains from some sort of exchange or cooperation (typically a requirement for exchange), and (iii) activities of one or more parties that cannot be observed perfectly and without cost by others affected (Milgrom and Roberts 1992).

Principal-agent problems offer an important and commonly discussed form of moral hazard (the "canonical form"; Bowles 2004, 250). A principal contracts with an agent to perform services and/or provide information. Moral hazard conditions (i)–(iii) apply, where (iii) specifically refers to the principal's inability to costlessly and perfectly observe the agent's activities. Labor contracts offer a standard example. Employers (principals) hire workers (agents), but labor contracts cannot fully specify the details of on-the-job effort and diligence. Workers prefer levels of effort and diligence that may not maximize the employers' profits (divergence of interests). Employees at computer screens, for example, may spend time reading private e-mails.

Monitoring is costly (supervisors require pay) and imperfect (they overlook things; they lack sufficient time). To enhance worker diligence, employers can pay workers more than their reservation wage and/or engage in some form of profit sharing. Similarly, in credit markets, lenders are principals and borrowers are agents. After securing a loan, borrowers may want to pursue activities that pose undue risk of default. Collateral requirements reflect efforts to address this problem.

More complicated varieties of moral hazard involve multiple principals and agents, with some parties playing both roles, depending on the circumstances. Overall, and more colloquially, since fully honoring contracts usually involves costs, parties have incentives to cut corners if they believe others will not notice. Equivalently, it is not possible to write fully enforceable contracts. Stated commitments may then lack credibility. Second-order CAPs of enforcing agreements emerge.

Moral hazard problems generate four basic implications:

- Exchange parties themselves must engage in enforcement activities. They cannot rely on the state, at whatever level of development, to fully enforce (necessarily incomplete) contracts.
- Such internal enforcement is costly—a major component of transaction costs. The greater the difficulty of observing postcontractual activity (i.e., the more asymmetric the information and the more costly the monitoring), the greater the transaction costs.
- For economic exchanges, internal resolutions to moral hazard problems prevent full market clearing: even in equilibrium, the quantity supplied does not equal the quantity demanded. Even without unions and minimum wage laws, employers striving for diligent effort must often pay wages that, when aggregated across a market, generate involuntary unemployment. Lenders face analogous incentives to charge interest rates that lead to credit rationing.[7]
- Internal (endogenous) enforcement implies exercises of power that operate within exchange processes themselves (Bowles and Gintis 1992, 1993).

The first two items point to the importance of crafting methods for credibly delivering on specific terms of agreements. Moreover, they imply a key role for informal mechanisms of trust building that can supplement formal mechanisms of contract enforcement. The last two items point to micro-level conflict and power relationships that infuse economic and political exchange. In terms of broad theory, second-order CAPs bridge economic and political dynamics because credible agreements underlie even basic economic exchanges, and enforcing agreements involves exercising power.

To sum up, the existence and anticipation of adverse selection and moral hazard pose significant second-order CAPs that often undermine developmental prospects. Coordination problems of adverse selection both preclude exchange and diminish its outcomes. Anticipated or actual transaction costs from moral hazard also undermine exchange (why sign a contract that one suspects will lack enforcement?) or generate undesirable results (high collateral for loans, excessive supervision of employees). In this regard, economic historian Douglass North states:

> One cannot take enforcement for granted. It is (and always has been) the critical obstacle to increasing specialization and division of labor. . . . [W]ithout institutional constraints, self-interested behavior will foreclose complex exchange, because of the uncertainty that the other party will find it in his or her interest to live up to the agreement. The transaction cost will reflect the uncertainty by including a risk premium, the magnitude of which will turn on the likelihood of defection by the other party and consequent costs to the first party. Throughout history the size of this premium has largely foreclosed complex exchange and therefore limited the possibilities of economic growth. (1990, 33)

This same principle also applies to the transaction costs that accompany adverse selection.

Returning to CAPs in general, Mancur Olson (1971) asserts that in the absence of selective sanctions individuals will not contribute to the provision of collective goods.[8] Small groups, however, often resolve such CAPs by applying selective social or material sanctions. In such cases, sufficiently powerful intrinsic reciprocity—a human willingness to sacrifice (some) material gain to reward apparently kind or fair behavior and punish unkind or unfair behavior—can foster resolution of both first- and second-order CAPs. Group members may regard contributing to collective well-being as kind or fair, inducing social rewards; defection can engender scorn or sometimes violent reprisal. Mutual awareness of such inclination renders enforcement credible. Because face-to-face contact strengthens reciprocal inclinations, small groups can often resolve internal CAPs via such sentiment.[9]

Resolution among larger groups—wherein infrequent contact renders reciprocal inclinations weak or nonexistent—requires more sophisticated social mechanisms. Such mechanisms must not only influence motivations to contribute, they must also convey information and even shape participants' understandings of pertinent relationships. Informal and formal institutions, along with complementary organizations, can foster cooperative resolution, though often introducing a new set of CAPs related to attendant undesirable outcomes, such as highly inequitable distributions of power. Resolving one set of CAPs often begets another. Accordingly, the resolution of developmental CAPs requires not only the creation of institutions and, on a larger scale, institutional systems and social orders; it also involves achieving methods for addressing their failures and for modifying, reforming, abolishing, and replacing them. Section 2 addresses these concepts.

Section 2: Institutions, Organizations, Institutional Systems, and Social Orders

Institutions interact with complementary organizations to form institutional systems and, on a large scale, social orders. These combinations resolve substantive developmental (and other) CAPs and simultaneously create others—notably those related to accomplishing reform. The involved evolutionary processes tend to follow a *punctuated equilibrium* dynamic, marked by relatively long periods of stability that succumb to rapid bursts of dramatic change or disruption. Development responds to the creation, reform, disruption, and replacement of institutions and social orders—with myriad attendant CAPs.

Simply put, institutions are the rules of the game in a society (North 1990, 3). More specifically, an *institution* is a combination of mutually understood and self-enforcing beliefs, decision rules, conventions, social norms, and/or formal rules that jointly specify or prescribe behavioral regularities in specific or varied social contexts. Institutions are technologies (analogous to blueprints) that signal social coordination and prescriptions for managing conflict; they allow society and individuals to pursue long-term goals—even in the face of changing circumstances (World Bank 2017). From a longer-term perspective, institutions are outcomes of prior social games that, in turn, establish key parameters (rules) for multiple subsequent interactions (Aoki 2010).

Before addressing types of institutions, institutional functions, and their relationships to CAPs, a micro-level discussion of the cognitive origins of institutions provides relevant background.[10]

The concepts of bounded rationality (Simon 1955, 1983, 1985) and mental models (Kahneman 2003; Denzau and North 1994) offer insight into micro-level underpinnings of institutions and their relationship to CAPs. Undergraduate economics classes, however, typically associate individual rationality with utility maximization based on self-regarding material preferences over outcomes. Individuals seek to maximize their own actual or expected material gains, given their resources (budget constraints). By incorporating (known) probabilities and corresponding expected values, such maximization can account for risk (a manifestation of imperfect information) and even the asymmetric information that underlies adverse selection and moral hazard. Yet, broader approaches to rationality offer additional developmental insight.

The concept of *substantive rationality* retains individual maximization of expected values but augments material-based utility with social preferences. *Social preferences* add two elements: (i) *other-regarding preferences*, meaning concern for the well-being of others (e.g., family, friends, members of one's community, colleagues); and (ii) *process-regarding preferences*, meaning subjective evaluations of processes themselves that are independent of the outcomes generated by such processes (Bowles 2004). Citizens may value election outcomes or pay raises, in part, by considering the fairness or impartiality of the involved procedures. Much of the logic of adverse selection and moral hazard models, mentioned in Section 1, arises from incomplete information concerning another's preference rankings of alternative outcomes and processes. Even so, assuming an understanding of the relevant probabilities, substantively rational utility maximization can still occur.[11] Individuals choose actions as they seek to maximize their expected utility based on both material and social preferences, given the expected activity of others. But what happens if individuals do not know the relevant probabilities?[12]

The yet broader, albeit more complicated, concept of bounded rationality facilitates a deeper understanding of social behavior and adaptations to social context. Bounded rationality theory rests on two minimal assumptions: (i) individuals have goals—they pursue goal-oriented behavior, and (ii) they learn (often imperfectly) from experience. Combined with the idea that individual preferences adapt to social contexts—that is, endogenous social preferences—one can relate individual adaptive behavior to institutions, CAPs, and development processes.[13]

More specifically, bounded rationality implies both limits on and costs to cognition itself. Individuals have limited understandings of how to achieve their goals—rendering strict maximization of values and expected values, impossible in complex situations. Moreover, systematic analysis requires costly cognitive effort and time (both scarce resources). Yet, goal-oriented individuals use available information and understandings as they seek good outcomes. And they learn from experience. Individuals economize on costly cognitive effort by combining intuitive (often knee-jerk) heuristics (System 1 [S1] processes—thinking fast) with doses of reasoned calculation (System 2 [S2] processes—thinking slow; Kahneman 2003, 2011). S1 heuristics respond to social contexts. For example, the heuristic called *attribute substitution* implies judging a person's character by her or his appearance (dress, age, race, etc.), and interpretations of appearance often reflect social norms and other elements of pertinent contexts. Wearing formal clothes to a job interview may generate a distinctly different first impression than wearing jeans. S1 processes also exhibit framing effects: they respond to the manner in which ideas or events are presented. The wording of questions in opinion polls, for example, influences responses (Shuman and Presser 1981). In contrast, S2-reasoned calculation involves analytical strategic thinking, including estimating strategic trade-offs. To the degree possible, S2 processing approaches substantive rationality.[14] A person's relative use of S1 and S2, in turn, depends on the difficulty of the problem at hand and the perceived value of a good resolution (to the degree that either are known or predictable). This mix, particularly its S1 elements, can lead to systematic or accidental errors with many unintended and some quite unfortunate outcomes.[15] When she called for the June 2017 general election, British Prime Minister Theresa May, for example, had anticipated a rather different outcome (the Conservative Party lost its majority in Parliament). Yet such cognitive limits lend a social dimension to cognition that contributes to both resolving and creating CAPs.[16]

To process information and reach conclusions, boundedly rational actors use *mental models*—that is, cognitive frameworks that define and utilize social or environmental categories (e.g., liberal, conservative; old, young), along with conceptions of causality (e.g., payment precedes ownership). Mental models mix S1 and S2 reasoning to produce judgments. They behave much like Thomas Kuhn's (1962) scientific paradigms operating at an individual level. Mental models underlie individual understandings of social environments. For example, a mental model related to economic development may generate the following hypothesis: food subsidies given directly to women (a social category) are more likely to improve child nutrition than the same subsidy given to men (a causal relationship).

Individuals use mental models to engage in two types of learning: hypothesis testing and reevaluative learning (Kahneman 2003). The former uses existing mental models to evaluate propositions. Given her understanding of business conditions, an entrepreneur expects a modest positive return from a specific investment. In contrast, *reevaluative learning* reconfigures mental models—a process that requires considerable mental effort. Yet, success may require an entirely new approach to business. Accordingly, reevaluative learning typically occurs only after individuals have experienced multiple inconsistencies with existing models. Did the failed coup in Turkey, the passage of Brexit, and the election of Donald Trump fundamentally alter understandings of Turkish, British, and US politics? On a lighter note, professors often hope to induce reevaluative learning among their students.

Two additional points link mental models to institutional theory. First, the two types of learning create their own punctuated equilibrium dynamic. For long stable periods, existing mental models structure basic understandings; learning occurs via hypothesis testing within that framework. Punctuation occurs when multiple inconsistencies induce rapid reevaluative learning. New understandings displace and replace prior mental models with new categories and conceptions of causality. Second, mental models reflect both individual experience and social influence. In particular, narratives—stories of causation—transmit mental models across groups. For example, the political debate surrounding climate change responds to and transmits stories related to ultimate causes (human induced or not), responsibility (developed nations or all nations), and consequences (minimal or dramatic). These stories can reflect and convey radically different interpretive frameworks—that is, radically different mental models.[17]

This narrative element of mental models fosters sharing. Stories can embody and convey mental models. Indeed, shared mental models underlie what sociologists call the social construction of knowledge. For Arthur Denzau and Douglass North (1994), there are two fundamental types of shared mental models: ideologies and institutions. *Ideologies* combine social categories and stories of causality into shared visions of society (or community) with ethical

content. Libertarian economics, for example, utilizes a sharp distinction between markets and government (two social categories) and laissez-faire theories of market mechanisms (causation) to generate a vision of a (largely)
unregulated economy as a foundation for prosperity and individual liberty
(ethical content).

Institutions, as mutually expected behavioral prescriptions, are also a
type of shared mental model. They convey common understandings of social
categories (e.g., who should or should not perform specific actions, such as
pay taxes) and causal relationships, sometimes with normative content. We
expect shoppers to pay for their goods, and failing to meet this social expectation often appears unethical.

Broadly speaking, there are two basic types of institutions: formal and
informal. *Formal institutions* (formal rules) arise from specified collective
decision-making processes and are typically, though not always, written. Examples include constitutions, legislation, regulations, and other formally decided government or corporate rules, such as personnel policies. By contrast,
informal institutions are mutually expected informal behavioral patterns, conventions, and especially social norms that emerge (roughly) spontaneously
from repeated social interactions and informal decision procedures. *Social
norms* are mutually understood and expected behavioral prescriptions with
ethical content and unspecified but generally understood social enforcement.
Examples include norms against cutting in line or for doing one's fair share.

Two additional categories of institutions relate directly to development.
Political institutions are mutually understood and expected behavioral prescriptions for allocating decision-making power; they are formal and informal rules that designate positions and procedures for collective decision
making. *Economic institutions* are mutually understood and expected informal and formal prescriptions for allocating resources among competing uses.
They specify property rights; mechanisms for contract enforcement; procedures for coordinating exchange; and processes for addressing market failures
related to public goods, common resources, externalities, incomplete information, and macroeconomic instability.[18]

As shared mental models, informal and formal institutions, whether political or economic, perform three basic functions:

1. They motivate certain types of behavior—either directly or indirectly.
    They directly motivate behavior by providing social and material

incentives, such as anticipated social praise, for contributing to a community project or the additional cost of taxes on gasoline. Less directly but more fundamentally, institutions (especially norms) shape the evolution of individual preferences that, in turn, underlie goal-oriented decision making.[19] Individuals who believe in (i.e., internalize) normative prescriptions, such as not littering or stealing, usually follow such prescriptions—even if nobody would notice.

2. Institutions affect available information in two fashions: their prescriptions provide information about socially expected behavior that apply to specific types of actors in specific contexts. For example, we know that we are not supposed to cut in line. Additionally, rules and norms channel flows of information (e.g., only the CEO receives the unabridged treasurer's report; only a few see the unredacted *Mueller Report*).

3. As shared mental models, institutions provide cognitive frameworks that shape agents' understandings of present and future social interactions, as well as interpretations of past actions and interactions. Again, there are two levels. First, institutions influence expectations about others' behavior in specific strategic interactions. We expect most people to follow prevalent norms and rules. In a store, we expect most people to pay for merchandise. Second, at a deeper level, institutions shape basic understandings of pertinent social categories and causal relationships. The institutions of indentured servitude, sharecropping, social castes, and corporate hierarchies fundamentally shape understandings of individuals, groups, possible actions, interactions, and relationships among them. As such, institutions provide cognitive foundations on which individuals base hypotheses (suppositions) about their social environments.

Ultimately, institutions underlie goal-oriented, rational behavior. They coordinate understandings, expectations, and activity across broad groupings of individuals. They render complex social interactions at least somewhat predictable by actors who have limited cognition and limited time. They underlie decision making in social contexts (North 1990; Greif 2006). Institutions provide motivational, informational, and cognitive guidelines that coordinate various premises, expectations, and incentives across multiple parties in a manner that, in turn, can coordinate their decisions and activity. In other words, by focusing expectations on specific outcomes or relations—among myriad possibilities—institutions orchestrate a broad *social choreography* (Gintis 2009). In India, for instance, everyone knows that everybody drives on the left-hand side of the road, and everyone does so.

It is important now to distinguish between institutions and organizations. *Organizations* are structured groupings of individuals—often with differing interests—who nonetheless jointly pursue sets of negotiated goals using evolving decision rules (their own microlevel, internal institutions) to coordinate key expectations and activities among their members (Cyert and March 1963).[20] In fact, one may regard the same entity as both an organization and an institution. As an organization, an economic firm, such as Hyundai, produces output. As an institution, it constitutes a set of rules concerning hiring or sales procedures, pay structures, and so forth. As relatively coherent groups, organizations operate as actors (agents) within institutional contexts. In game-theoretic terms, institutions are the rules of the game that establish the contexts within which organizations (and individuals) act as players.

Institutional systems are relatively stable configurations of formal institutions, informal institutions, and organizations that generate social regularities. Whereas institutions prescribe or signal behavioral regularities, institutional systems—by also incorporating organizations—actually generate such regularities. For example, laws prescribe that shoppers shall not take merchandise without first paying for it. In countries with a rule of law, the social outcome of rare shoplifting follows not just from laws but from a combination of laws against theft, norms (theft is bad), and complementary organizations—such as police departments and courts that can enforce institutional prescriptions. In this regard, there are two basic types of transactions: core transactions, such as exchanges of goods for money or trading political favors, and *auxiliary transactions*—namely, transactions that arise only under certain conditions pertaining to specific core transactions (Greif 2006). For shoplifting, the auxiliary transaction of apprehending shoplifters arises only if a shopper has been observed (or is believed to be) stealing merchandise. Within institutional systems, organizations perform key auxiliary transactions that facilitate resolving second-order CAPs, rendering institutional prescriptions credible. By maintaining a credible threat of apprehending reported shoplifters, police departments, as organizations, resolve a second-order CAP that might otherwise leave a formal institutional prescription against shoplifting poorly enforced.

Institutional systems thus structure governance at various, often nested, levels of aggregation ranging from neighborhoods, villages, towns, and cities to provinces, nation-states, or larger regions, such as the EU. *Social orders* are macro-level institutional systems that persist as social equilibria.[21] At any of these levels, the relevant political-economic equilibria usually follow a punctuated equilibrium dynamic, with long periods of relative stability interrupted by rapid bursts of change, which lead to substantially different equilibria—often following a (sometimes prolonged) period of conflict. Prior to punctuation, stable-phase equilibria can be either self-reinforcing or self-undermining, reflecting the evolution of their capacity to withstand external and internal shocks that may then usher in punctuation.[22]

Section 3: Institutional Systems and Collective-Action Problems

Institutions and institutional systems both resolve and create CAPs. As shared mental models, as rules of the game, and as social choreographers, institutions coordinate understandings across numerous individuals, sometimes millions. By augmenting such prescriptions with an understood potential for auxiliary transactions via associated organizations, institutional systems foster otherwise unattainable compliance, coordination, and cooperation. Yet, in resolving multifarious CAPs, institutions and systems simultaneously create others related to excessive compliance (undue obedience) and from conflicts that follow asymmetric distributions of costs, benefits, power, unaligned interests, and disjointed perceptions. Institutions create CAPs that arise from the difficulties of adjusting understandings, prescriptions, and behavioral patterns to changing environments, along with the typically daunting prospects of achieving substantive reform. Within such dynamics, organizations not only address second-order CAPs via their potential to conduct auxiliary transactions, they also participate in the creation, reform, maintenance, and demise of institutions. Institutional systems thus provide multiple capacities for and obstacles to development; and the associated punctuated social equilibria operate at both meso- and macrolevels.[23] Consequently, political and economic development entails creating, strengthening, reforming, and destroying various institutions and institutional systems and, on a larger scale, social orders.

Within such complex dynamics, formal institutions, informal institutions, and organizations each play distinct and interacting roles. Formal institutions, as deliberately decided rules of the game, play three key roles—though their ability to do so depends critically on underlying factors that influence institutional strength. Such factors include the perceived legitimacy of institutional prescriptions and associated governance arrangements, as well as the motivation and ability of relevant actors (often organizations) to implement designated prescriptions. Details on the three roles follow.[24]

First, as already stated, the (usually) written prescriptions of formal institutions coordinate behavior across multiple actors. They do so by transmitting mutually understood signals related to coercive power (fines and jail terms), promised rewards (subsidies for R&D), and focal points for coordination (e.g., driving on the left-hand side of the road in India, Japan, and the United Kingdom). Moreover, formal institutions sometimes offer avenues for legitimizing various behaviors and prescriptions, such as a socially acceptable excuse for wearing a motorcycle helmet and a conformity inducement for voluntary acceptance of rules against indoor smoking. Focal points and avenues for legitimization reinforce each other. Accordingly, in efforts to influence their reputation, individuals can signal their type (e.g., a willingness to cooperate) by conforming to prescription—by following (or disobeying) the law (Posner 2000; Sunstein 1996). In this latter sense, strong (or legitimate) formal institutions acquire normative characteristics: the law becomes *expressive* (Sunstein 1996)—as in the concept of law-abiding citizens.

Second, formal institutions provide relatively durable frameworks for ordering power relationships—though with large variation in the degree and extent of such ordering. Here, they define the de jure elements of governing by designating positions of authority, such as the Minister of Defense or a corporate CEO, along with designated powers, limits on power, and resources, such as staffing and budgets. In so doing, formal institutions assign roles for making and implementing policy. They allocate forms of authority. They point to associated relationships among various positions (president and cabinet minister), agencies (the housing authority), branches (legislative, judiciary), and levels of government (national, regional, village-level), as well as relationships between governmental entities, the private sector, civic organizations, and the population at large. Even in societies with weak institutions, where many formal rules remain suspect and arbitrarily enforced, formal institutions provide (signal) structure that coordinates at least some expectations—such as who to fear or who to bribe.

Third, formal institutions designate rules for making, amending, and abolishing other rules. At a foundational level, constitutions often play this role: who belongs to a sovereign community, which kinds of actors legislate, and so on. At intermediate levels, laws and regulations, as collective-choice rules (Ostrom 2005), allocate decision-making authority among various bodies and agencies. For example, the US Congress designates and revokes certain rule-making authorities to various departments, such as the Environmental Protection Agency.

Informal institutions, notably social norms, also play the first two roles, but in a less structured, more ambiguous fashion that may, nonetheless, confer greater legitimacy, moral authority, and reputational consequence.

Regarding the first role, as mutually understood behavioral prescriptions with ethical content, norms coordinate behavior across large groups. They point to socially expected, context-specific actions and prohibitions for which nonadherence can signal not only a lack of conformity but questionable moral standing.[25] Norms imply a series of informal, often ambiguous but typically expected social sanctions for violators. Sanctions range from quizzical or seemingly dirty looks on the part of possibly random observers to violent confrontation from the deeply offended. These informal sanctions, moreover, do not rely on formal law enforcement or expenditure. Norms thus can efficiently resolve second-order CAPs. More fundamentally, norms create internalized ethical prescriptions for at least some portion of the relevant population. For such parties, adherence—within limits—not only follows voluntarily without need for observation or sanction from others, internalization also fosters inclinations to sanction nonadherence. Norm internalizers may sanction norm violators. Furthermore, as shared mental models, norms offer common cognitive frameworks for interpreting current and future actions of oneself and others (e.g., constructive, destructive; good, bad; moral, immoral).[26] By mixing these influences, norms create social (and sometimes material) incentives for adherence to their prescriptions. Like laws, norms create incentives to signal one's type via appropriate action (or inaction), and they do so with socially conditioned moral authority (a characteristic laws may or may not possess) that can influence one's reputation.[27] Social norms thus coordinate vast arrays of understanding and activity across large groups. People expect others to follow established norms, such as shaking hands when greeting a stranger, and most extend their hand.

Regarding the second role, norms also order power relationships. They do so without formality, with ambiguity, and yet with considerable effect and adherence. Norms can allocate decision-making authority within families, workplaces, or communities. They may do so by gender, race, religion, age, social class, experience, credentials, and/or ethnicity. Patriarchy rests on social norms. Given their power, certain individuals, *normative entrepreneurs*, endeavor to change norms (Posner 2000; Sunstein 1996). Such parties interpret, modify, and even create social norms—with varying degrees of success or failure. They publically announce that certain actions are, in fact, signals that do or do not confer normative (moral) acceptability. For example, a nationalistic normative entrepreneur may broadcast that duty to one's country implies joining the army, saluting the president, or hiring only nationals. A rural leader may proclaim that contributing labor to a community irrigation project signifies that one is a valuable (deserving, cooperative) member of the community. When successful, normative entrepreneurs exercise a type of power (power3; see Chapter 5).

Formal and informal institutions *coevolve*: they interact in a manner that influences their mutual functioning and development. Both types of institutions simultaneously order power and coordinate behavior by mixing expectation, conformity pressure, signaling, reputation, internalization, conceptualization of social context, and interpretation of one's own and others' behavior. They do so across distinct and overlapping groups, with varying degrees of complementarity and disjuncture. On the one hand, laws that violate prevalent normative prescriptions often remain unenforced. The prohibition amendment to the US Constitution (the Eighteenth, adopted in 1919 and repealed in 1933) offers a painful example. On the other hand, when laws complement norms, both gain legitimacy and impact, as is usually the case for laws against shoplifting. Indeed, the notion of a law-abiding citizen may become a social norm. Exhibiting their expressive function, laws may then transform or reinterpret norms, particularly in instances when competing norms operate simultaneously. In such cases, the law can become a focal point for adherence. Sometimes, social mobilization in opposition to existing rules and norms favors legislation that subsequently alters norms. The Civil Rights Act of 1964 and Voting Rights Act of 1965, in large part responses to the civil rights movement, played a significant role in undermining prior norms that favored overt racial segregation in public spaces, such as buses, restaurants, and parks.[28]

Analogously, social norms often complement laws and other formal insti-tutions, enhancing their ability to resolve CAPs. Norm enforcement does not require organized auxiliary transactions because internalization and concern for reputation often enforce normative prescriptions. Complementary norms can then reinforce inclinations to signal good citizenship, congeniality, or one's community membership through law-abiding behavior. Norms, such as those against shoplifting, significantly reduce the need for (and costs of) or-ganizational enforcement of formal prescriptions—often rendering enforce-ment, via a mix of formal and informal mechanisms, feasible and effective.

> Conformity [to institutional prescriptions] achieved through the coordination of expectations or the internalization of norms . . . may not be very costly, as in the case of driving on one side of the road or the voluntary compliance with tax laws in some countries. However, where conformity to a society's institutions is secured primarily through governmental coercion or privately deployed sanc-tions, the resource costs may be substantial. (Jayadev and Bowles 2006, 333)

Accordingly, coercive mechanisms usually involve devoting resources to organizations.

Operating within institutional systems, organizations contribute deci-sively to the social choreography of actual behavior. As stated in Section 2, re-solving second-order CAPs that surround the implementation of formal rules usually entails at least some organized action, or a belief that such action will occur when needed. Equivalently, resolution requires the credible possibility of auxiliary transactions conducted by organizations. More generally, by in-corporating their own sets of informal and formal rules, organizations offer structured, relatively predictable manners for boundedly rational individuals to combine efforts in pursuit of common goals. Organizations resolve multi-ple internal CAPs, allowing individuals to act collectively in fashions that—unlike spontaneous crowd activity—persist for some time. More specifically, organizations operate as

i. arenas for action (A great deal of social activity occurs within organi-zations. Firms are arenas for production. Political parties are arenas for political mobilization.); and

ii. crucibles, laboratories, and conduits for developing distinct internal informal and formal institutions (e.g., rules of promotion, organiza-tional culture).

As such, organizations

    iii. reinforce (or undermine) certain beliefs and norms (The internal oper-
        ations of a government agency or a large firm may, for example, either
        confirm or challenge beliefs about citizen participation in government
        or proper behavior at work.); and

    iv. affect agents' beliefs about relationships between feasible actions
        and consequences—an important element in their ability to resolve
        second-order CAPs of coordination and enforcement via the credible
        possibility of auxiliary transactions.

Combining these attributes, organizations act as players in complex social, political, and economic games, with various possible impacts. On the
one hand, by creating a potential for auxiliary transactions, organizations
resolve second-order CAPs associated with implementing institutional prescriptions. Courts enforce laws, and professional associations enforce rules
of professional conduct. Political parties may discipline their own members.
Gangs enforce internal codes of conduct. On the other hand, organizations
can block the implementation of policies and institutional rules. Firms file
lawsuits to overturn policies that threaten their interests. Gangs and militias
subvert government enforcement of laws. In these and related endeavors, organizations become conduits and agents for creating and transforming institutions. Political parties strive to change laws and regulations. Labor unions
endeavor to change rules about pay, working conditions, labor relations, and
management. Private lobbies try to initiate, alter, or abolish economic regulations. Ethnic organizations seek social, political, and economic recognition.

By combining prescriptive and organizational processes, then, institutional systems resolve multiple CAPs—as they create others. Informal institutions, notably social norms, not only designate desired and prohibited
behaviors, they often achieve relatively low-cost enforcement through the
combined influence of internalization and an understood potential of somewhat unspecified social sanctions for violation. Norms of fair contribution
motivate members of large groups of strangers to sacrifice material benefit for
the good of the group. Formal institutions designate less ambiguous, more
specific, and more nuanced behavioral prescriptions, often with specific procedures for adjustment that provide cognitive and sometimes motivational
platforms for amending their very rules—frameworks within which certain
types of institutional evolution may operate. These formal and informal so-

cial mechanisms coevolve. By harnessing social sanctions and internalization, complementary social norms ease burdens and costs of formal enforcement. Formal institutions, notably laws with expressive elements, can reinforce, re-interpret, and alter norms, especially when competing norms point in different directions. Disjunctures between normative and legal prescriptions, how-ever, render the latter weak and often illegitimate, with arbitrary, minimal, or no enforcement.

In either case, mixes of informal and formal institutions, with multifar-ious degrees of effectiveness, coordinate behavioral expectations and order power. They shape motivation, information, and cognition across multiple individuals, conveying or signaling shared understandings, perceptions, ex-pectations, and obligations. Formal institutions designate positions of au-thority, often with resources, such as budgets. Norms also signal position and resource access, doing so more ambiguously but with ethical content (obliga-tion) that often legitimizes such allocation and a corresponding obedience to power relationships. Institutions thus achieve a sophisticated social choreog-raphy of mutually understood incentives and social expectations—resolving formidable first-order CAPs that mere individual material incentives and small-group reciprocity could not begin to address. Yet, absent a credible potential for organizational auxiliary transactions, substantial second-order enforcement CAPs impede effective realization of formal legal and regulatory prescriptions, even when accompanied by complementary norms. Accord-ingly, institutional systems also rely on organizations.

When credible prospects of organizational auxiliary transactions interact with informal and formal prescriptions, institutional systems move beyond prescription: by addressing second-order CAPs, they actually generate behav-iors that correspond to institutional prescriptions.[29] Realized social chore-ography follows. Such systems, moreover, operate at multiple, often nested, levels, ranging from villages to nation-states and international bodies, such as the EU.

These dense interactions generate a punctuated equilibrium dynamic for institutions and institutional systems wherein deeply embedded, often nor-mative, motivational and cognitive mechanisms interact with distributions of power and organizational potential. At a given point in time, existing con-ditions generate shared cognitive and behavioral patterns that reproduce and persist via correlated patterns of thought and activity. Accompanying resolu-tions to otherwise intractable first- and second-order CAPs lend durability to the underlying social choreography, fostering the stable phase of a punctuation cycle.

Unfortunately, this social choreography may adapt slowly or not at all to changing conditions. It may foster inefficient allocations of resources; inefficient production; and highly inequitable distributions of wealth, income, and output. Moreover, obedience to norms, rules, and corresponding social patterns often leads to repression and exploitation of individuals and specific groups (e.g., women; the poor and disadvantaged; ethnic, racial, and religious groups). Indeed, undesirable institutions, such as norms of patriarchal, ethnic, and racial privilege and systems of inequitable economic-political access and participation, create substantive CAPs that accompany the work and risks of attempting reform or social change—especially for those who lack power and resources.

Here, the evolutionary logic of substantive institutional change—that is, punctuation—follows directly from the dynamic logic of individual mental models: reevaluative learning is difficult. On a far greater scale, dramatic change of institutions and systems requires coordinated and often near simultaneous reevaluative learning and reconfiguration of practices across large groups. And powerful status quo beneficiaries, including organizations whose livelihood depends on extant institutions, often oppose change. Indeed, institutions are fundamentally conservative, resistant to change, and slow to adapt (Fukuyama 2014). Such institutional and social stability, moreover, implies path dependence. Initial patterns repeat and shape future patterns.[30] Yet, once change gathers momentum, once it crosses a critical-mass threshold, shifts in shared understandings, power relations, and processes of social imitation can facilitate dramatic change. Eastern European communism persisted with little anticipation of fundamental change, especially after the 1968 Soviet Army overturned the brief Prague Spring, until the events of 1989–91 punctuated the social equilibrium. Chapter 6 elaborates on processes of institutional change.

Returning to our basic theme, development entails widespread and steady augmentation of human capabilities via multiple political and economic interactions and exchanges. Whereas small-group reciprocity can establish self-enforcing mechanisms that facilitate simple exchanges among members, larger-scale complex exchanges, be they economic or political, require institutional mechanisms of social coordination—namely, institutional systems that can resolve myriad underlying CAPs of cooperation, coordination, and enforcement. Within these complexities, moreover, the creation, maintenance, alteration, and abolition of institutions and their corresponding systems relies fundamentally on political relationships. Functional political relationships emerge from some form of political settlement: the next topic.

Section 4: Political Settlements and Limiting Organized Violence

Institutional systems, and by extension a society's ability to resolve large-scale CAPs, rest on foundations of political settlements. As a relatively new element of the political economy literature, the concept of political settlements remains a work in progress. Chapters 7 and 8 elaborate in some detail. For now, we can consider a relatively simple definition: a *political settlement* is a mutual understanding held among powerful parties that establishes politics, rather than violence, as the primary social mechanism for handling disputes, which possesses sufficient sustainability to persist over medium-term time horizons. Political settlements address, however imperfectly, a host of first- and second-order CAPs related to managing conflict. They set boundaries. They limit the exercise of organized violence. By restraining violence, political settlements permit the development and maintenance of institutional prescriptions, along with arrangements for coordination and enforcement that enable their implementation. Political settlements thereby shape the creation and evolutionary trajectory of institutions, institutional systems, and social orders. As such, they underlie political and economic development. In their absence, development simply does not occur. Societies that lack political settlements include Sierra Leone between 1991 and 2002, Somalia between 1991 and 2011, Rwanda between 1990 and 1994, and most of Syria between 2011 and 2018.

Political settlements arise from, incorporate, and shape institutions. Indeed, institutions are antecedents, components, and outcomes of political settlements. Regarding antecedents, a settlement's core mutual understandings emerge from political contestation within preexisting social contexts conditioned by preexisting institutions. Regarding components, the shared understandings that constitute political settlements are a form of behavioral prescription. Political settlements are a type of institution—specifically, an informal or formal constitutional-choice rule (Ostrom 2005) that shapes basic allocations of authority. Consequently, the configuration of institutions responds to the constituent elements of political settlements. The dynamics and structure of political settlements thus shape institutional evolution.

Yet, to become a sustainable medium-term equilibrium, a settlement's corresponding institutional system must deliver policies and (net) political and economic benefits in a manner that at least minimally meets the goals of powerful actors and also reflects and reproduces underlying distributions of power. Concurrently, settlements must foster—usually via a far more detailed set of prescriptions and procedures from emergent institutional systems—the organizational and group dynamics that deliver the requisite coordination and enforcement.

Accordingly, the characteristics of political settlements, such as their social foundations, respond to and shape context-specific configurations of CAPs, institutional evolution, and, by extension, political and economic development. Classifying political settlements on the basis of their key features thus informs the political economy of development. Part III elaborates.

Section 5: The Plan of this Book

Chapter 1 addresses foundational concepts—specifically, first- and second-order CAPs, institutions, organizations, institutional systems, social orders, and political settlements, with commentary on relationships and interactions. Chapter 2 continues in this vein by discussing the concepts of political and economic development, utilizing Amartya Sen's (1999) capability approach. Political development entails establishing usable state capacity, the rule of law, accountability, legitimacy, and social mobilization. Economic development involves growth and distribution related to income, consumption goods, capital, and technology, as well as other foundations of economic capability such as health care, education, infrastructure, and functional institutions for defining and enforcing universal (as opposed to selective) property rights, providing public goods, and mitigating negative externalities. Inequality—itself a multidimensional concept involving both individuals and social groups (distinguished by factors such as race, gender, religion, status, class, and ideology) is both an outcome of and condition that shapes economic and political development, via the influence of myriad embedded CAPs.

Part II proceeds with five key developmental hypotheses, which often appear separately in the literature. By relating these five hypotheses to important categories of developmental CAPs, Part II creates a platform for Part III's conceptual framework. More specifically, Chapter 3 addresses CAPs of market failure and political development. Applying basic economic theory,

it discusses the first hypothesis (H1): Development requires establishing social arrangements that deliver key public goods and services and that concurrently mitigate important negative externalities. A few simple game models,
some in the spirit of Olson, illustrate types of relevant CAPs. A more involved
game-theoretic logic, largely derived from Tim Besley and Torston Persson
(2011), describes a set of CAPs specifically related to establishing and utilizing
state fiscal and legal capacity—key foundations of political and, by extension,
economic development. Chapter 4 addresses economic roots of developmental inequality. It incorporates the following concepts: Paul Romer's (1990) endogenous growth theory, spatial location or agglomeration theory noted by
Paul Krugman (1995), social influence theory noted by Steven Durlauf (1996),
O-ring theory of Michael Kremer (1993), and the production externality theory of Alfred Marshall ([1920] 1979) and Paul Rosenstein-Rodan (1943). H2
follows: Inherent complementarities that emerge from the nonrival properties of knowledge, skill matching, social imitation, and production externalities generate uneven locational and sectoral agglomerations of production,
knowledge acquisition, innovation, and growth. Stark inequalities, including
centers of innovation and poverty traps, thus emerge from basic developmental processes—unless policy successfully alters such trajectories. The ensuing
unequal access to economic foundations of capability, production, innovation, income, wealth, and physical and knowledge infrastructure, along with
a host of associated conflicts, create CAPs that shape developmental prospects
and processes.

Chapter 5 addresses institutional formation. Referring to social conflict
theory from Jack Knight (1992) as well as Acemoglu and Robinson (2008),
it discusses H3 and H4.[31] In this logic, H3 offers the core proposition. H3:
Unequal distributions of power shape the creation, evolution, and demise
of economic and political institutions. Because economic institutions affect
distributional outcomes, involved parties have conflicting interests. Because
powerful parties tend to dominate such conflict, they shape the formation,
modification, and demise of economic institutions, and do the same for political institutions. CAPs of unequal access follow. This chapter's background
discussion considers sources, dimensions (or faces), and exercises of power,
incorporating concepts from Kaushik Basu (2000b), Samuel Bowles (2004),
Robert Dahl (1957), Václav Havel (2015), Steven Lukes (1974), and Georg
Simmel (1971), with attention to both dyadic and triadic interactions. Discussion proceeds to interactions between power, organizations, and institutional

evolution. H4 extends this logic to CAPs of creating credible commitment. H4: Powerful parties, left to themselves, cannot credibly commit to refrain from using their power for their own future benefit. Consequently, a society's developmental prospects depend on its ability to create and maintain provisions that credibly limit the ability and desire of powerful parties (private and public) to seize the gains from others' efforts and investments. Jointly, H3 and H4 imply that unequal distributions of power generate enormous developmental CAPs whose resolution relies on establishing credible commitments and restraining exercises of power.

Chapter 6 addresses H5: Policy innovations sometimes relax political and commitment constraints from H3 and H4, as well as free-riding and coordination CAPs from H1 and H2. Novel arrangements can enhance capacities for resolving various embedded CAPs in a manner analogous to the influence of technological advances on production.[32] This chapter's background discussion draws on concepts of social capital from Amy Poteete, Marco Janssen, and Elinor Ostrom (2010), along with ideas about institutional change and reform from Peter Hall (2005) and James Mahoney and Kathleen Thelen (2009). Next, drawing on ideas from Frank Baumgartner and Bryan Jones (1993), John Kingdon (2003), and Paul Sabatier and coauthors (1993, 1998, 2007), it summarizes key elements from the policy process literature—a literature that traditionally focuses on the United States and Western Europe, whose principles can apply to development. Noting foundations in Simon's (1955) bounded rationality theory and linking the concept of a domain-specific policy subsystem with this text's concept of meso-level institutional systems, and also noting similar application of a punctuated equilibrium dynamic, this chapter applies policy process theory to developmental CAPs. It concludes with several ideas on how specific types of CAPs relate to certain types of innovation. Jointly, Chapters 3–6 create foundations for Part III's discussion of political settlements.

Part III develops this text's new conceptual framework for development theory. It applies the logic of Part II's five hypotheses to a typology of political settlements to illustrate how specific combinations of social foundations and configurations of authority influence a set of corresponding CAPs that underlie and shape developmental prospects. Chapter 7 discusses several existing approaches to political settlements and social orders. After comparing a few definitions of political settlements, it summarizes developmental typologies of social orders and political settlements, with some attention to foundations of economic activity. More specifically, it summarizes work by North, Wallis, and Weingast (2009); Brian Levy (2014); Mustaq Khan (2010, 2013, 2017); and Lant Pritchett, Kunal Sen, and Eric Werker (2018), with commentary on relationships among their approaches. Chapter 8, with reference to Chapter 7, first discusses characteristics of political settlements. Incorporating ideas from Tim Kelsall and Matthias vom Hau (2019), it constructs this text's typology of political settlements. The typology specifies how a society's political-economic context, manifested in specific combinations of social foundations and configurations of authority, engender distinct categories of political settlements that, in turn, underlie institutional systems and social orders—all of which operate with punctuated equilibrium dynamics. Drawing on ideas from Richard Doner, Bryan Ritchie, and Dan Slater (2005), this chapter also considers how the presence or absence of resource constraints and mutually understood compelling threats influences a ruling coalition's motivation to resolve a complex set of CAPs associated with H1–H4. Operating within contexts of distinct political settlements, these features shape a society's prospects for achieving or failing to achieve political and economic development.

Chapter 9 more directly considers business-state interactions and extends Chapter 8's largely macro-level political settlement approach into meso-level, subnational interactions. Combining relevant typologies with game-theoretic logic, it presents a systematic method for conceptualizing a series of complex developmental CAPs. More specifically, drawing on work from Pritchett, Werker, and Sen, it directly addresses economic transactions as both outcomes of and influences on political settlements. This chapter incorporates typologies of meso-level market configurations and micro-level agreements (or deals) to address both the credibility of economic agreements and various demands that businesses place on the state. The core analysis revolves around a relatively simple game model that specifies four basic conditions for generating credible economic agreements (deals). This discussion notes the developmental importance of H4 credibility CAPs, with attention to H1, H3, and especially H2. Moreover, specific elements (variables) within the four basic conditions respond to (depend on) attributes of the social context reflected in Chapter 8's categories of political settlements. And the presence or absence of resource constraints and mutually understood compelling internal or external threats influences such dynamics. These factors jointly condition sectoral, regional, and national abilities to address pertinent H1–H4 CAPs. Because credible agreements underlie economic and political development, Chapter 9 cements this text's conceptual framework in a manner that implies numerous modeling and empirical extensions. Lastly, the Conclusion summarizes this text's core arguments and suggests a series of theoretical and empirical extensions.

Overall, this approach offers a method for classifying key context-specific elements of political settlements that shape configurations within institutional systems, along with a host of context-specific CAPs. These CAPs both reflect and reinforce inequities with respect to fundamental capabilities, the breadth of political and economic participation, and, ultimately, developmental prospects and outcomes. This broad, yet focused approach offers a set of complementary lenses for analyzing developmental processes, prospects, and policies. Its systematic manner of merging analytical perspectives establishes the groundwork for interpreting numerous developmental case studies and for designing more specific models and hypotheses that can then motivate extensive empirical investigation and policy analysis.

2 Economic Development, Political Development, and Inequality

Every normative theory of social arrangement that has at all stood the test of time seems to demand equality of something—something that is regarded as particularly important in that theory.

—*Amartya Sen*, Inequality Reexamined *(1992)*

The interest of the landlord is always opposed to the interests of every other class in the community.

—*David Ricardo, "An Essay on the Influence of a Low Price of Corn on the Profits of Stock" ([1815] 2010)*

IN 1912, FEARING LABOR UNREST, the Argentine government enacted the Sáenz Peña Law, establishing universal male suffrage by secret ballot. In 1930, the military took power in a coup, followed by a series of fraudulent elections, with another coup in 1943. In 1946, Juan Domingo Perón, initially a member of the military junta, won the presidency on a pro-labor populist platform. In 1955, another coup deposed Perón, soon followed by a nominally civilian government, which lasted from 1958 until yet another coup in 1966. After substantial unrest on the part of workers, students, and the urban poor, as well as guerilla activity, Perón returned to the presidency in 1973, succeeded by his wife, Isabel, in 1974. In 1976, another coup led to the notorious regime that "disappeared" tens of thousands. After that government's failure in the Falklands War and substantial unrest, an elected government returned in 1983.[1]

In the Philippines in 1955, 0.36% of the population owned 41.5% of agricultural land, with 0.01% (221 families) owning 9% (Simbulan 2005, cited in Montinola 2013, 151). In the predominant *kasama* (sharecropping) system, the owner allocated land access and provided seed, animals, and implements for a share of the crop. Owners also provided loans, some medical services, and protection in return for compensation, usually in the form of return services, including votes and support for owner-preferred candidates (Lande 1967, cited in Montinola 2013). Accordingly, the Philippine ruling coalition included landowners; local bosses called *caciques*, who controlled access to other resources; and foreign capitalists, who dominated agricultural exports.

Regarding Central America, Klaus Deininger writes:

> In El Salvador and Guatemala, large landowners depended on a repressive labor regime to remain economically viable, and the boom led to land expropriation and the massive concentration of land in the possession of a few, to the detriment especially of indigenous communities. Landlords held a monopsony on power in the labor market, which allowed them to pay their workers the bare subsistence minimum, thereby eliminating any incentives for human capital accumulation. By contrast, in Colombia and Costa Rica, which are characterized by small-scale landholdings, elites depended on trade rather than on large-scale agriculture, and the coffee boom led to the emergence of a smallholder coffee economy. (2004, 2)

By contrast, South Korean land reform, conducted primarily between 1950 and 1956, "created an unusually equal distribution of income and wealth" that facilitated a rapid expansion of education and other preconditions for South Korea's emergence as a successful developmental state between 1960 and 1987 (You 2013, 296).

Chapter 1 has established a groundwork for subsequent discussion by introducing the concepts of CAPs, institutions, institutional systems, and political settlements. I now augment these foundations with concepts of political and economic development, dimensions of inequality, and interactions between inequality and development.

This book's approach to economic and political development draws on Amartya Sen's (1999) capability approach. For Sen, human functionings (e.g., walking, reading, etc.) constitute a person's well-being, and development "is the process of expanding human freedoms" (Ibid., 36). Capabilities generate functionings; capabilities underlie the potential to create, shape, and choose among possible states of living. Human capabilities both enable and constitute effective freedom of choice.[2]

This capability approach to development addresses interactions between achievements (outcomes that affect human well-being) and capability sets (foundations of human agency).[3] Achievements arise from applications of agency to processes embedded within social (and other environmental) contexts. Relevant achievements include material outcomes—the levels and distribution of income and wealth (types of prosperity)—along with broader components of well-being, such as life expectancy, mortality rates, and the prevalence or absence of disease. Developmental achievements also have political dimensions, such as established rights of political expression and participation.

Capabilities play a dual role in development. As platforms for the exercise of human agency, capability sets are ends (goals) of development; as instruments of achievement, they are means of development.[4] Capability sets create developmental achievements. Enhancing capability sets requires both widespread provision of opportunities—avenues for the exercise of human functionings— and the steady removal of social, economic, and political barriers to exercising agency (e.g., racism). Providing opportunities requires creating and widely distributing important means of achievement, such as income, wealth, education, and health care.[5] The economic concept of a budget constraint illustrates. The budget constraint of a poor person offers far less freedom for choice among activities, goods, and services than does that of a rich person—by orders of magnitude. Wealthy individuals face vastly larger opportunity sets. Moreover, investments in education and other foundations of achievement, such as available quality health care, relax budget constraints by enhancing labor productivity, employment opportunities, and earnings. Yet, the realization of apparently available opportunities may fall victim to prevalent attitudes, norms, and rules regarding race, gender, ethnicity, and/or social class. Such realization may also suffer from a simple lack of resources. Schooling uses time that families might need for earning basic sustenance. These elements of social contexts often limit capabilities; they obstruct choice; they are barriers to realizing potential.[6]

A combination of resource deficiency and various social barriers deprives poor individuals, groups, and communities of developmental opportunity. Poverty is deprivation. Moreover, barriers that emerge from racial, ethnic, gender, income, and class discrimination, as well as a lack of "acceptable" cultural capital, deny individuals and groups avenues for building and utilizing capabilities. Because deprivation impedes and negates capability, development requires systematically reducing economic and political deprivation. Development thus entails poverty reduction, removing barriers to participation, and achieving some degree of equity.

At a society-wide level, expanding developmental capabilities and achievements involves simultaneously creating and strengthening economic and political institutions. It involves defining and enforcing universal, as opposed to selective, property rights—an outcome of political processes. It involves establishing procedures to provide public goods and services—also a political outcome. Developmental success requires enhancing functional state capacity, balanced—over time—with broad avenues for participation and limits on concentrated private and public power. Consequently, the political economy of development always involves alteration, reform, restructuring, and/or abolition of existing formal and informal economic and political institutions—and addressing a host of attendant CAPs.

Because capabilities, as foundations of agency, both arise from and transform social contexts, development signifies widespread and steady improvements across multiple dimensions of economic and political achievement, along with steady expansion of underlying capability sets.

This chapter's discussion proceeds as follows. Section 1 addresses political development noting five key elements: building state capacity, establishing a rule of law, achieving public accountability, attaining social mobilization, and establishing legitimacy. The first three directly affect governance; the last two involve transformations of social contexts. Section 2 addresses economic development, with attention to dimensions of achievement and underlying capabilities. Specifically, it considers growth; elements of distribution including deprivation, poverty, and broad inequality; structural transformation; and the configuration of institutions. Section 3 addresses the two-way causal pathway between inequality and development.

Section 1: Political Development

Thousands of years ago, Aristotle noted that humans are social creatures. Because it entails and facilitates the exercise of human agency across groups, political development lies at the foundation of human social capability.

Political development implies effective governance, along with widespread and functional participation. *Governance* "is the process through which state and nonstate actors interact to design and implement policies within a given set of formal and informal rules that shape and are shaped by power" (World Bank 2017, 41).[7] *Policies* are decisions (often sets of decisions, including decisions to do nothing) made by informally or formally designated officials or bodies (a tribal council, a parliament, a dictator, an agency, a board of directors) that establish plans of action, with an intent to affect behavior as well as outcomes for some group or groups.[8] Policies endeavor to resolve CAPs, but they do so with tremendous variance in rates of success and failure. Political development, and by extension effective governance, thus entails creating, modifying, and abolishing various informal and formal social mechanisms for resolving sets of CAPs that surround the construction of policies, procedures, rules, various means of coordination and enforcement, and the selection of governing officials. Indeed, these activities underlie human social functioning. They are ends in themselves—in addition to instruments of development.

As a basic human capability, political expression draws attention to the goals and needs of participating parties. At the individual level, such expression develops cognition regarding interactions between goals and specific social contexts—enhancing the capabilities of those involved. Across groups, political expression fosters social learning and shapes policies.[9] At a deeper level, it conditions the forms and exercise of governance and the rules that structure governance—namely, political institutions. Political institutions—themselves outcomes of myriad prior exercises of political expression, governance, and corresponding policies—signal avenues for and barriers to individual and group expression; they identify limited conduits for creating and modifying policies and methods for implementation. As informal and formal rules of the political game, political institutions shape environments within which exercises of political engagement occur or fail to do so.[10] As outcomes of previous political development, political institutions shape the current manifestations and future evolution of such development.

More fundamentally, political settlements—as mutual understandings held among powerful parties that establish politics, rather than violence, as the primary social mechanism for handling disputes—underlie the evolution of functional capability. They underlie governance, institution building, and ultimately the evolution of functional institutional systems and social orders—and hence political and economic development.[11]

Given some form of political settlement, and drawing on Frances Fukuyama's work (2014), political development involves the steady enhancement of three desirable, though often conflicting, dimensions of governance, along with two elements of social mobilization and transformation.

Regarding governance, political development entails establishing three relevant domains of capability:

1. *State capacity*: the degree to which a community can concentrate power into a governing authority to provide public goods and services, enforce laws, maintain internal peace (domestic tranquility), and provide defense from external aggression. Note that the term "state" extends beyond the apparatus of the public sector; it includes "a set of social relations that establishes a certain order, and ultimately backs it with a centralized coercive guarantee over a given territory" (O'Donnell 1993, 1356). States also serve an important ideological function by claiming to represent the good of the community (or nation) as a whole. Ultimately, states provide order—the supreme collective good—fostering generalized social predictability.

   Fukuyama (2013) notes that building state capacity involves establishing an efficient, merit-based bureaucracy with an ability to provide services and collect revenue, as noted in Max Weber's (1978) *Economy and Society*. Organizationally, however, such capacity need not imply Weber's strict hierarchy. Functional capacity entails some bureaucratic autonomy over pertinent areas of discretion—a source of innovation and experimentation, a notion that Weber does not address.

   Furthermore, the implementation dimension of state capacity— that is, the ability to translate policy directives into actual practice— requires acquiring information and motivating relevant parties to execute directives and enforce provisions in pertinent social contexts. Creating effective state capacity thus extends well beyond merely establishing best-practice institutions and training bureaucrats. It entails creating and employing a mix of formal and informal mechanisms that can address multiple first- and second-order CAPs related to attaining sufficient organizational coherence to provide needed services and collect revenue.[12]

2. *The rule of law*: the degree to which all participants in political and economic relationships—whether members of an elite or not—adhere to broadly accepted and impersonal rules—as opposed to relying on personal characteristics (charisma) and connections (e.g., common ancestry, friendship, clientelism). Establishing the rule of law involves creating processes of adjudication that operate independently from

an executive branch of government. At an intermediate developmental level, a *rule by law* signifies impersonal rules and procedures that apply to portions of society other than top governing officials and possibly other powerful agents. Gradations of rule by law relate to the distinction between enforcing universal as opposed to selective property rights. Chapter 3 elaborates.

3. *Accountability*: the degree to which governing officials work for and respond to the common good. There are two elements: *substantive accountability* means responding to the general public interest. *Procedural accountability* involves public oversight in the selection, tenure, and behavior of public officials, as well as creating avenues for input. It entails creating participatory and transparent governing processes, such as democratic elections and open committee meetings. Intermediate levels of procedural accountability allow such participation from a select oligarchy or limited class (e.g., the Athenian oligarchy or white male property owners in the early US republic). Intermediate political development may also involve either type of accountability on its own; neither, by itself, guarantees the other.

Establishing any one of these three components of political development entails resolving a series of challenging first- and second-order CAPs. Moreover, these three elements of governance inherently conflict—implying a set of higher-level (meta) CAPs related to balancing their various influences. Resolution of state-building CAPs requires motivating agents and establishing an administrative machinery with an intellectual division of labor that can channel specialized expertise among an agency's members, and doing so independent from political pressure. Relevant civil servants and bureaucrats need the capability and discretion to apply their specific mix of human capital and contextual experience to appropriate and always evolving contexts and problems (Fukuyama 2013). To accomplish their mission, scientists at the US Centers for Disease Control (CDC) need the autonomy to perform their own experiments and draw their own conclusions. Yet, formal rules and procedures (consistent with a rule of law) often limit bureaucratic discretion, inhibiting context-specific adaptation—and even the use of common sense. Likewise, political accountability can generate inefficient and conflicting mandates for governmental agencies that respond to shifting demands from distinct interests and constituencies. Popular discontent with law enforcement in the

United States, for example, has led to three-strikes legislation that compromises judicial discretion by mandating minimum sentences for people convicted of certain types of offences at least three times.

Excessive bureaucratic autonomy, however, can undermine both the rule of law and public accountability—top bureaucrats may effectively become exempt. The utter lack of accountability for the Prussian military bureaucracy contributed to the precipitation of two world wars (Fukuyama 2014). Furthermore, conflicts between a rule of law (or by law) and accountability arise when majorities (not so infrequently) demand suppression of minority rights, and, conversely, when regulations limit access to political expression. Political development, then, requires resolving a series of meta-level CAPs that accompany establishing a relatively stable dynamic balance across these three elements—a long, varied, complex, and fundamentally context-specific process. Part III addresses these issues in more detail by relating them to basic categories of political settlements.

Political development also involves two social components:

4. *Social mobilization*: the creation of new social groups and the evolution of interactions among them. Groups become conscious of themselves in terms of identities and shared interests.[13] They develop a potential to engage in collective action (resolving organizational CAPs). Fukuyama (2014) links social mobilization to modernization, especially industrialization and urbanization. Over generations, social identities change—breaking with village or tribe—as new identities emerge (working class, professional, nation, etc.). Social mobilization is both an outcome of and antecedent to the social transformations that accompany political and economic development.

The final component of political development, operating a cognitive-normative level, speaks to perceived relations between ruling coalitions and the broader population.

5. *Political legitimacy:* an evolving set of understandings of a system's political institutions and associated allocations of decision-making authority that implies their widespread acceptance as reasonably fair, reliable, and appropriate for the relevant society (or segment within). A strong sense of political legitimacy held among the public, civil servants, and other key groups, facilitates resolving many second-order

CAPs that otherwise would inhibit governance—notably, policy implementation. Accordingly, legitimacy influences a system's ability to function, adapt, and withstand crisis.[14]

The extent of legitimacy awarded to a given system depends on how the values it promotes align with the core values of the public and relevant constituencies—and on the manner and degree to which key historically divisive issues have been resolved. For example, the symbolism and values of the (pre-Hitler) German Weimar Republic conflicted with core values of the army, civil service, and aristocracy. Moreover, the prolonged prior denial of political access to the German lower classes enhanced their propensity to accept extremist doctrines. This development subsequently increased the desire of the upper strata to reject nonelite political participation. These reinforcing dynamics undermined the Weimar democracy (Lipset 1959).[15]

As a component of political development, the evolution of legitimacy implies increasing acceptance of broad participation in political mechanisms (i.e., increasing accountability) and the protection of civil rights, especially for disadvantaged groups (a component of the rule of law). To illustrate, Fukuyama (2014) points to the influence of Enlightenment concepts of the "rights of man" on the French Revolution and the "rights of Englishmen" on the rise of the British Parliament and the gradual increase in political participation in those countries during the nineteenth century.

Overall, political development requires creating formal institutions with a complementary evolution of informal institutions and relevant organizations, and a compatible balance of power in relevant domains. It involves enhancing state capacity balanced with universally applicable impersonal rules, broad avenues for participation, and limits on concentrated private and public power—all with broad legitimacy and broad-based, inclusive social mobilization. For its part, economic development influences and interacts with these political dynamics. These two forms of development (or lack thereof) often complement each other, though not in any simple, linear, or necessarily enduring fashion.

Section 2: Economic Development

Economic development connotes a steady improvement in the levels and distributions of key economic achievements (e.g., living standards), the allocation of available resources to productive activities, and widespread enhancement of human capability sets related to production and consumption. Because underdevelopment is deprivation (Sen 1999), developmental progress implies particular focus on reducing poverty and, more generally, improving living standards and enhancing capabilities at the lower ends of the distributions of income and wealth.

There are three basic, interrelated domains of economic development: growth, distribution, and institutional development.[16] Within each domain, development involves specific achievements—specific levels of relevant attributes attained at a point in time—along with associated capabilities that both underlie and flow from such achievements. This section's discussion begins with growth and its proximate causes related to physical capital, human capital, technological change, employment, and structural transformation—all of which influence human capabilities—followed by attention to distribution, and finally the more foundational concept of institutional development.

Factor Endowments, Structural Transformation, and Growth

A society's average standard of living depends on achieved levels and rates of growth of output and productivity. Such achievements establish foundations of capability for a host of human activities related to or involving consumption and production. How does growth arise? It often comes about through some combination of available factors of production, technology, and structural transformation occurring within receptive environments. Available growth fundamentals, notably physical and human capital and technology, directly impact the level and growth of output as proximate determinates. Structural transformation (defined later) can induce rapid though not necessarily sustainable growth by enhancing the efficiency of a given set of factors. A mix of both elements can achieve sustainable growth, but as Chapters 3–9 illustrate, a series of CAPs can hinder or preclude the attainment and influence of either or both.

Many traditional approaches to economic development focus on growth and define economic growth as steady improvement in average standards of living, usually designated by per capita income or output (gross national income [GNI] or GDP).[17] GDP per capita also serves as a basic measure of the average labor productivity within a country (or specific regions). A more precise measure, *labor productivity* connotes output per worker or hour worked. Key related achievements include attaining certain levels of per capita income—as in the distinction between low-, middle-, and high-income countries, and the potential to move along that spectrum depends on attained rates of growth of GDP, GDP per capita, and labor productivity—and their sustainability.

Despite their limitations as measures of overall welfare, growing levels of per capita GNI and GDP increase average living standards, relax economic constraints, and augment capabilities. Incomes finance education and health care. Steady growth in per capita output thus permits positive-sum gains, as shown by an outward shifting production possibilities frontier. In contrast, stagnant or declining GDP per capita intensifies zero-sum trade-offs—a source of political conflict.[18] "Higher levels of living standards are the most direct route to achieving improvements in social and human indicators" (Hausmann, Rodrik, and Velasco 2005, 1).

Over time, output growth also augments wealth (the net value of assets at a point in time), another category of economic achievement that can foster capabilities. Attained levels of financial capital may finance domestic accumulation of physical and human capital, new technology, and consumption, although if invested abroad, the contribution to domestic development is indirect at best.

Growth, nevertheless, is not automatic. Many developing countries experience episodic growth with periods of acceleration, deceleration, or stagnation (Hausmann, Pritchett, and Rodrik 2005). Highly variable growth tends to undermine capabilities. Referring to earlier growth literature, Kunal Sen states, "Their focus on rates of average growth of per capita income has obscured the fact that most countries observe dramatic fluctuations in growth of per-capita income . . . growth accelerations followed by growth decelerations or collapses" (2013, 71). For example, between 1950 and 2007, Ghana and the United Kingdom had nearly identical average rates of growth. For the United Kingdom, however, annual growth (for nearly all years) varied within a narrow range between 0 and 4% per year, whereas Ghana experienced periods of very rapid growth (above 6% per year) and collapse (below −2% per year). Ghana experienced rapid growth from 1965 to 1972, followed by collapse and stagnation into the 1990s, with rapid growth after 1999. Development theory should thus address growth accelerations, decelerations, and methods for achieving stable long-term growth (Pritchett and Werker 2012).[19] CAPs condition these processes.

Achieving sustained, rapid economic growth requires achieving a combination of two, often interacting, basic (yet still proximate) elements that often appear separately in the literature:

i.   Enhancing *growth fundamentals*, a concept addressed in one-sector neoclassical and endogenous growth models, means that growth arises from combining technology with factor endowments in labor, physical capital, human capital, and infrastructure. Steady augmentation of fundamentals can generate steady growth.

ii. Processes of *structural transformation*, a concept addressed in two-sector, dual economy models, involves shifting resources from low- to high-productivity activities (Rodrik 2013; Lin 2012).[20] In cases of large productivity differences (gaps) between sectors or activities, sectoral transformation can substantially augment growth, though often with diminishing returns.

Considering both elements, several patterns are possible. Rapid structural transformation combined with low investment in fundamentals can achieve early growth accelerations that may lift a country out of poverty. High investment in fundamentals combined with slow transformation can achieve more durable, slow but steady growth. Rapid sustainable growth involves both rapid structural transformation and large investments to augment fundamental capabilities (Rodrik 2013).[21] Early industrializers, such as the United Kingdom and the United States, combined relatively slow and steady improvements in both features. For many developing countries, however, rapid structural transformation has initiated rapid growth that reduced poverty—but not always in a sustainable fashion. Mixing both conditions, somewhat in sequence with structural transformation leading, Vietnam has achieved rapid, enduring growth (so far). Each element merits further discussion.

Regarding fundamentals, technology, physical capital, and human capital underlie multiple individual and organizational capabilities. Adequate housing, for example, facilitates myriad human functions. Increases in the stock of physical and human capital enhance labor productivity. For given levels of physical and human capital, available technology determines labor productivity.[22] As an indicator of the efficiency of work, a given level of labor productivity signifies the potential (realized or not) for paying wages. Similarly, total factor productivity (TFP), accounts for the efficiency of combined labor and capital. Enhancements in any of these factors allow for positive-sum gains—though their distribution may be quite unequal.

More generally, steady augmentation of productive capabilities involves shifting the overall *endowment structure* of a society by increasing the capital/labor ratio, including human capital, along with improvements in both hard infrastructure (e.g., roads, school buildings) and soft infrastructure, meaning "institutions, regulation, social capital, value systems and other social and economic arrangements" (Lin 2012, 22).[23] Countries at different levels of development have different endowment structures. Labor-intensive economies, for example, exhibit limited economies of scale and typically have rudimentary infrastructure (Ibid.). Better endowments facilitate (but do not guarantee) incorporating newer technologies into existing industries and diversifying production into new, more capital-intensive areas. Serviceable roads, sewers, communication infrastructure, school buildings, and so on, foster individual and organizational activity and production. Locations that lack such infrastructure rarely attract substantial investment. Regarding soft infrastructure, improving economic institutions facilitates resolving CAPs related to organizing and coordinating production and exchange (the end of this section elaborates).

At a more detailed level, specific productive outcomes influence future capabilities. Educational attainments underlie available human capital. Health outcomes, such as achieved levels of life expectancy or infant mortality, facilitate human productive capability (and general human functioning). The global number of people newly infected with HIV and the number of deaths from AIDS have been declining in recent years (UNAIDS 2012). Conversely, 870 million people suffer from hunger (International Food Policy Research Institute [IFPRI] 2014). Malaria has not only caused one million deaths per year in addition to neurological disorders among survivors, it lowers productivity and economic growth (Gallup and Sachs 2001; Cole and Neumayer 2006).

Levels of employment, another factor of production, also mark developmental achievements that underlie capabilities. High employment/population ratios and low rates of unemployment facilitate greater per capita production. A society's performance in generating employment, especially in relatively high-paying formal sector industries, underlies productive capacities, as well as household incomes and often a sense of individual well-being related to the use of one's time. Moreover, the distribution of employment across different types of production influences such outcomes. The percentage of employment devoted to the formal, informal, and household sectors, along with shares of employment within broad sectors—agriculture, industry, and services—or more narrowly defined industries, affect both output produced and productive potential. Development usually involves increasing participation in the formal sector, along with a declining agricultural share of employment: two types of structural transformation.

More precisely, *structural transformation* means transferring resources from low- to high-productivity sectors and activities—notably away from agriculture and other forms of traditional production—along with product diversification and increasing product complexity (Hausmann, Pritchett, and Rodrik 2005; McMillan, Rodrik, and Verduzco-Gallo 2014; Sen and Tyce 2018). This resource transfer may operate at several levels: between broad production sectors (e.g., agriculture and manufacturing); between sectors defined on the basis of organization—namely between informal and formal sectors; between industries within sectors; between traditional and modern production processes and products; and/or within sectors, industries, and even firms moving resources from low- to high-productivity operations. Structural transformation affects both attained living standards and rates of growth. When the productivity gaps between affected activities are large, such as typical gaps between agricultural and manufacturing productivity, structural transformation can lift countries out of deep poverty, as it did in much of East Asia. Maintaining and repeating this experience, however, may be difficult. Growth outcomes may not endure, opportunities for transformation may shrink, and sectoral productivity gaps may diminish, reducing net gains.

Many discussions of structural transformation focus on shifts across the broad productive sectors: agriculture, manufacturing, and services; or somewhat finer distinctions across about 10 sectors (e.g., construction, transportation and utilities, business services, retail/wholesale, financial services).[24] Throughout much of the nineteenth and twentieth centuries, developed countries established what one might call the classic pattern. These countries experienced relatively slow long-term shifts in sector shares of employment and value added from agriculture to manufacturing and then services (Singelmann 1978), with corresponding steady, slow growth in GDP per capita. This pattern appears in regressions of log GDP per capita on shares of employment and value added. Over long time spans, however, the shares of manufacturing employment and (to a lesser extent) value added exhibit an inverted U-shape

relationship; a downward trend emerges in late industrialization, with corresponding accelerated growth in service-sector shares. In the United States, for
example, the manufacturing share of employment peaked at about 25% in the
1950s. For the United Kingdom, the peak occurred in the 1970s at about 33%
(Rodrik 2016).

More recently, many developing countries exhibit a truncated version of
this pattern. They show much shorter periods of shift, lower peak levels of
manufacturing employment shares, and a smaller final decline (Herrendorf,
Rogerson, and Valentinyi 2013). Moreover, the later the onset of industrialization, the more truncated the patterns—a phenomenon Dani Rodrik calls
premature deindustrialization (2016). Declining peak manufacturing shares
can limit the potential for broad structural transformation to improve living
standards (Ibid.).

Whatever the case, a procedure called *shift-share* analysis illustrates the
potential (realizable or not) for broad structural transformation to improve
living standards. This procedure holds sectoral productivity levels constant
and hypothetically applies advanced economy employment shares (across
nine sectors) to poor countries. Such (conjectured) industrial structure could
(in principle) enhance productivity as follows: twofold for India; sixfold for
Ethiopia, and sevenfold for Malawi (McMillan et al. 2014). Indeed, the growth
experience of Vietnam testifies to such influence. In the late 1980s, agriculture absorbed 75% of Vietnamese employment but produced only one-third
of Vietnamese GDP. Meanwhile, manufacturing exhibited four times greater
labor productivity. Over the next two decades, agriculture's employment
share declined 20%, while the manufacturing and service shares increased,
respectively, from 8% to 14% and from 19% to 32%. Correspondingly, Vietnamese GDP per capita tripled, and national labor productivity grew at an
average annual rate of 5.1% per year between 1990 and 2008 (Rodrik 2013).

On a smaller scale, and for a given set of factor endowments, shifting resources from low- to high-productivity uses, often by moving from informal
to formal organization, can enhance within-industry productivity—reflecting
finely tuned structural transformation. For example, between one-third and
one-half of the manufacturing TFP gap between India and China, on the one
hand, and the United States, on the other, would close by removing excess
variance in plant-level productivity within industries.[25]

Structural transformation and growth fundamentals can reinforce each
other. Vietnam's rapid, sustained growth followed from a combination of

structural transformation that reallocated employment across industries—in part an outcome of export-oriented industrial policies—with significant institutional change that enhanced growth fundamentals. Vietnam transitioned from state-owned to largely private enterprises, and it liberalized trade and rules on investment. The government also increased formal registration of family farms and businesses (an increase in regulation that may have facilitated structural transformation within that sector). These changes encouraged foreign investment and enhanced competition among private businesses, generating revenues that could finance education, health care, and infrastructure.[26]

This relatively rapid route to achieving impressive growth, however, may not be available to many low- and middle-income countries—even setting aside a set of CAPs that arise from distinct types of political settlements (see Part III). The combined influence of new international trade regulations that restrict the use of industrial policies, along with the now higher human capital requirements in manufacturing (an outcome of technological advance) diminish prospects for productivity-enhancing structural shift (Rodrik 2013). Indeed, most non–East Asian developing countries are experiencing premature deindustrialization. Compared to early industrializers, their manufacturing employment shares peaked at lower levels and correspondingly (much) lower levels of income per capita. For Western European countries, the manufacturing share of employment peaked at a per capita income of $14,000 in 1990 dollars, whereas for India and most sub-Saharan African countries, it peaked at about $700 per capita. Furthermore, for the relevant countries, the declining share of manufacturing employment occurs almost entirely in low-skilled jobs—the main source of productivity and earnings enhancement for rural migrants who leave even lower-productivity employments. Rodrik concludes: "Developing countries are turning into service economies without having gone through a proper experience of industrialization" (2013, 2).

More specifically, Rodrik finds "premature" declines in employment and output shares (both real and nominal) for sub-Saharan Africa (excluding Mauritius, a manufacturing exporter) and for Latin America, but no declines in these shares for Asian countries. These results "apparently reflect the sizable shift in global manufacturing activity in recent decades towards East Asia and China in particular. . . . On the output side, it appears that the brunt of globalization and the rise of Asian exporters has been borne by other developing countries, rather than the advanced economies" (2016, 16).

Premature deindustrialization thus signifies the closing of a key route to rapid early growth via shifting employment from agriculture to manufacturing—a significant component of the successful export-oriented industrialization strategies employed by China, South Korea, Taiwan, and Vietnam.

This closure thus implies distinct and more substantial CAPs related to improving standards of living and associated capabilities. Although service-led growth is possible, it poses another set of CAPs because many dynamic and tradeable service industries, such as finance, tend to employ skilled labor. Consequently, formal-sector service production cannot absorb much labor from the rapid rural-to-urban migration experienced by many developing countries. Indeed, the productivity-reducing (or neutral) structural transformation observed in Latin America reflects a movement from agriculture into informal rather than formal sector employment (Rodrik 2016; Diao, McMillan, and Rodrik 2017).[27]

Another complication arises from the implications of improvements within low-productivity industries (from either endowments or transformation) on between-industry productivity gaps. Declining gaps imply less growth potential from shifting employment to higher-productivity sectors. Indeed, the rural-urban productivity gap, like manufacturing's employment share, follows an inverted U-shaped relationship when graphed against time (or GDP per capita) because late industrialization often improves agricultural productivity (McMillan et al. 2014). This outcome may reflect Jane Jacobs's (1984) concept of balanced regional growth generated by innovative cities— whereby urban development fosters rural development—itself a good outcome. Nevertheless, this narrowing gap limits potential future growth arising from the industrial-shift component of structural transformation.

Sub-Saharan Africa offers a mixed case in these regards. Since the early 1990s, structural shift (measured across 10 sectors) and rising agricultural productivity have jointly contributed to rising aggregate productivity and high per capita growth but with little contribution from manufacturing. This outcome suggests some potential for service-led growth, but productivity growth in sub-Saharan African nonagricultural sectors has been declining— implying limited potential for productive sectoral shift (Diao et al. 2017). Even though agricultural productivity remains below nonagricultural productivity, the small (and closing) productivity gap limits potential growth arising from rural–urban migration. Furthermore, in these countries, the main impetus for rising nonagricultural employment has come from in-creased demand derived from external transfers and the income effects from growing agricultural productivity. Neither offers long-term growth prospects.

In contrast, successful East Asian countries that instituted industrializa-tion a few decades earlier, experienced both productivity-enhancing sectoral shift and innovation-induced manufacturing productivity growth—a more sustainable combination that generated productive employment for rural mi-grants (Rodrik 2016; Diao et al. 2017).[28] Hence, the combination of prema-ture deindustrialization and small, declining productivity gaps has enhanced the CAPs—notably H2 CAPs of coordination—that confound achieving complementary combinations of structural transformation and growth fundamentals.

Perhaps more optimistically, Ricardo Hausmann and Dani Rodrik (2005) discuss a related developmental prerequisite that effectively merges elements of structural transformation and capability fundamentals: self-discovery concerning how to incorporate new production ideas into local contexts. For Taiwan, South Korea, and Chile, the acquisition of capabilities in an expand-ing range of nontraditional activities has driven growth. Such achievement, however, requires addressing information, coordination, and labor-training externalities—in other words, a set of H1 and H2 CAPs, discussed in Chap-ters 3 and 4.[29] Chapter 5 offers some perspective on how policy and organi-zational innovation—types of self-discovery—might improve prospects for resolution. With this background, we now turn to distribution.

Distribution and Equity

Inequality is simultaneously an outcome of development (or lack thereof) and an ever-present feature that shapes its evolution—as both impetus and constraint. Unequal relationships create and condition developmental CAPs, as well as prospects for resolution. From a capability perspective, economic development entails avoiding and reducing excess inequality—especially that related to the provision and accessibility of the underpinnings of economic capability, ranging from income and wealth to services, such as education and health care. Indeed, deprivation, as the key symptom of underdevelopment, both reflects past and implies future patterns of highly inequitable distribu-tions of the means of achieving capabilities. Moreover, the distribution of economic resources within and across societies shapes corresponding abilities to remove economic barriers to agency. Individuals, households, and social groupings—whether designated by gender, race, economic status or other criteria—who occupy the lower ends of relevant economic distributions undergo relative, often severe deprivation. Economic development, therefore, requires reducing deprivation for the most affected segments of various populations and societies.

The Complexity of Inequality

There are multiple interrelated spaces within (or along) which one may conceptualize degrees of inequality. In addition to the economic distributions just mentioned, one might consider various distributions of access to political input, to neighborhoods, to the internet—or distributions of political or civil rights. Along each of these dimensions, one might conceptualize (and depending on data availability, measure) various degrees of equity or inequity with respect to both attainment and access.

The ensuing trade-offs are complicated because more equality along one dimension often creates less along another. Explicitly or not, many policy approaches to achieving equal opportunities or outcomes specify or (more often) assume some *basal* level of equality: a key dimension valued above the others. Proponents may then justify more inequality of one type with less inequality along some explicit or implied basal dimension (Sen 1992). For example, libertarians argue that equality of opportunity justifies certain inequities—such as an unequal distribution of income and wealth. Such diversity of equity spaces reflects different perspectives on types of asymmetric advantage, reflecting a deeper diversity of values. Equivalently, a more precise evaluation of inequity depends on purpose.[30]

Yet, regardless of one's favored dimensions and purposes, a concern for equity demands a type of impartiality—some form of equal treatment. Moreover, such implied fairness explains the political appeal of multiple conceptions of equity—be they socialist or libertarian—because concepts of fairness lend legitimacy to policy arguments and ultimately to various types of political and economic arrangements.

Numerous measures can represent degrees of economic inequality as an outcome of prior development. Relevant distributional measures include various percentile indexes of income and wealth that specify the shares attained by, say, the bottom half, quartile, or decile of the relevant distribution—or by the top 1%, 5%, 10%, and so on. Percentile ratios (e.g., share of the top 5%

over that of the bottom 20% or top 20%/bottom 80%) more directly compare different portions of the relevant distributions. Similar measures can apply to education and health care, and types of employment, though pertinent data may be less available. Alternative measures can specify the percentage of a population that falls below a specific level of income (e.g., poverty rates) or wealth. Additionally, one might consider population shares employed in the informal sector, shares with less than a secondary education, or with a life expectancy below, say, 10 years.

Returning to capabilities, relative access to income and wealth critically influences the opportunities (choice sets) of individuals, households, and groups—affording far less opportunity at the lower ends of any distribution. The distribution of wealth (or its negation, debt) conditions relative access to key conduits of capability, such as credit and other means of financing investment in human capital, physical capital, infrastructure, and health care.[31] Inequitable access not only shapes individual and household capabilities, it does so for organizations, communities, localities, regions, and nations.

Poverty and Inequality

Poverty signifies deprivation, both relative and absolute. A capability approach to development thus prioritizes reducing poverty, especially extreme poverty. For a nation or community, basic poverty arises from a combination of the average per capita income (or wealth) and, for any given level, how it is distributed. Poverty—whether measured in terms of income or wealth and whether applied to individuals, households, groups, or societies—truncates capability sets by restricting access to food, housing, education, health care, employment, and other means of production and consumption.

Alternative distributions among the poor, moreover, signify degrees of deprivation. Relevant measures include metrics of extreme poverty, such as a count or percentage of households or individuals who fall below a designated level of income of $1.25 or $2.00 per day (adjusted for purchasing power parity [PPP]; World Bank 2017). Somewhat more comprehensively, the total poverty gap and average poverty gap (APG) assess the amount of income needed to, respectively, bring all impoverished or the average poor person up to the poverty line.[32] A person just below the poverty line may lack the means to purchase reasonable shelter but not suffer malnutrition, whereas a person at half that level may also suffer malnutrition. The squared poverty gap, as shown in the Foster-Greer-Thorbecke (FGT) index (with $\alpha = 2$) offers an approach to measuring poverty deprivation.[33] This index specifically assesses the impact of severe poverty. Moving a person from one-half of the poverty line up to the line has five times the impact on consumption as the same adjustment for someone at 90% of the poverty line (Todaro and Smith 2015). Measures of multidimensional poverty also incorporate levels of education and health care. The Human Development Index (HDI) offers a weighted combination of per capita GNI, schooling, and life expectancy. The Multidimensional Poverty Index (MPI) measures the percentage of a population that is poor, accounting for three dimensions of capability deprivation, with several measures for each dimension. These include six measures of the standard of living (e.g., lack of electricity, unsafe drinking water), two measures of health (death of a child and whether any household member suffers malnutrition), and two measures of education (whether any household member has five years of schooling and whether any school-age child is out of school for grades 1–8). In addition, the MPI accounts for interactions between dimensions, allowing capability along one to partially compensate for low capability along another, but only within limits. The MPI also accounts for the multiplicative harm from multiple deprivations experienced by more than one household member.[34] The United Nations Development Programme (UNDP 2013) reports Mozambique's relatively high MPI (2007–11) at 0.512. By contrast, Vietnam's is 0.017. This report finds nearly 1.6 billion living in multidimensional poverty—several hundred million more than those reported as having incomes below $1.25 per day.

Ultrapoverty connotes high deprivation (e.g., income below $0.54 per day in 1993 dollars) over long periods (chronic poverty) along several dimensions (e.g., illiteracy and malnutrition), a condition that creates multiple reinforcing poverty traps (Todaro and Smith 2015, 247). Methods that can address less extreme poverty, such as microfinance, often fail to reduce ultrapoverty. The IFPRI (2007) reports more progress in addressing poverty just below $1.00 per day than for poverty below $0.50, implying a trap at ultra-low levels.[35]

Skewed distributions of economic resources across locations and social groups create systematic inequities of capability. Most extreme poverty is rural. In Africa and Asia, about 80% of "target poverty groups" reside in rural areas; 50% for Latin America (World Bank 2010, cited in Todaro and Smith 2015, 250). Yet, most poverty programs have an urban focus. Rural poverty underlies and interacts with patterns of urban–rural migration. Multiple H1– H4 CAPs apply; Chapter 4 addresses rural–urban migration.

In all societies, women suffer relative deprivation. Most adults living in poverty are women, and the ultrapoor disproportionately live in female-headed households. The Gender Inequality Index (GII) measures women's achievement losses arising from gender-based inequities with respect to reproductive health, empowerment, and economic status reflected in the labor market.[36] In 2015, Scandinavian countries and the Netherlands reported the lowest values (lowest losses) at about 0.05; Korea showed 0.067; Vietnam, 0.337; Rwanda, 0.343; Mexico, 0.345; and Ghana, 0.547.

Gender-specific barriers contribute to such inequity. More specifically, various informal and formal restrictions and biases limit women's access to nutrition, clean water, sanitation, health care, education, formal-sector employment, household income, credit, assets, inheritance, and social security. Legislation and/or social norms prevent women in some areas from owning property and signing contracts. Accordingly, much work performed by women receives no pay. When employed, women are overrepresented in low-wage, unstable informal-sector jobs with little or no regulatory protection. In many urban areas, recent women migrants provide a disproportionate share of the informal labor supply. For any type of employment, most women face gender-based earnings and promotion differentials (a disproportionate share of dead-end jobs). In rural areas, especially in Africa and Asia, women produce a large share of agricultural output, especially subsistence farming. They also suffer from time poverty. Women provide 60–80% of agricultural labor in Africa and Asia (about 40% in Latin America)—often unremunerated—in addition to extensive household responsibilities (Todaro and Smith 2015, 459). Lack of time effectively precludes women's efforts and investments that could improve their overall well-being.

Within households, women often suffer from unequal bargaining power and ensuing unequal distributions of household income, assets, and consumption items, including food for themselves and frequently for children, especially girls.[37] Men typically control earnings from commercial crops, and women often have little say in how men's income is spent. Increased commercialization of agriculture often diminishes the portion of assets controlled by women (Todaro and Smith 2015, 458–62; Udry 1996). In households with relatively high female income, girls suffer less discrimination and women can more readily meet their own needs and the needs of their children. When women receive cash transfers, child nutritional outcomes improve (Duflo 2003). Finally, in Asia and Africa, over 100,000 women are "missing" due to gender mortality bias, including sex-selective abortions (Sen 1990, 2003; Klasen and Wink 2003).

Ethnic, racial, and religious minorities also face persistent, systematic disparities and obstacles arising from informal and formal barriers to agency, access, and participation—ranging from formal segregation, as in pre-1994 apartheid South Africa, to discriminatory social norms; group-based habits of hostile reciprocity along ethnic, religious, or racial fault lines; and individual habits of prejudice. For example, indigenous populations face the greatest deprivation with respect to all components of economic development. In Mexico, 80.6% of the indigenous population is poor, compared to 17.9% of the nonindigenous population. The corresponding figures for Peru are 79% and 49.7% (Todaro and Smith 2015, 255; citing Psacharopoulos and Patrinos 1994).

Development-related inequities also have environmental dimensions, especially regarding the distribution of damages across social groups. Disadvantaged social groups, such as the poor, ethnic and religious minorities, and women suffer most. For example, deforestation disproportionately harms poor farmers and tenants, especially those residing on marginal land; it increases the workload for women who collect firewood and displaces indigenous groups. Erosion and increases in extreme weather from climate change similarly inflict the greatest harm on the most vulnerable populations.

Finally, inequities—especially those associated with group social characteristics such as race and ethnicity—transmit across generations. The family into which a child is born affects her or his inherited wealth, knowledge, skills, financial support, educational opportunities, adopted norms, social connections, and even learned personality traits and habits that, in turn, influence labor market outcomes (Groves 2005). Inherited group membership—for example, race—affects intergenerational economic mobility (Hertz 2005). These factors create path-dependent inequities. For example, in the United States— often considered as a country with much social mobility—gaps between high- and low-income families can persist for decades (Mazumder 2005).[38]

The CAPs of deprivation and unequal development compound those of economic growth. In this regard, Kaushik Basu (2011) offers a simple developmental goal that combines growth and distribution into a simple metric, *quintile growth*—that is, the average per capita growth of the bottom quintile of the income distribution. As a measure of developmental success, quintile growth offers several advantages: it is simple; it focuses on reducing deprivation; it sets a moving target (as opposed to a static target such as reducing poverty to a specific level); it combines reductions in absolute and relative poverty; and the per capita income of the bottom quintile is likely more closely tied to foundations of capability (e.g., access to nutrition, housing, health care, and education) than is average GDP per capita.

Along any of these multiple dimensions of inequality, CAPs of deprivation and asymmetric access, as well as those related to attaining sustainable growth outcomes and capabilities, arise from and shape institutions and institutional development. Institutions condition prospects for enhancing growth fundamentals, prospects for achieving structural transformation, and the trajectories of multiple dimensions of inequality.

Economic Institutions and Economic Development

At its foundation, economic development requires creating, strengthening, adjusting, and maintaining economic institutions. The potential for conducting multiple exchanges underlies economic development; and the range and complexity of a society's economic exchanges depends on the strength of its institutions. A capability perspective implies that economic institutional development should achieve two related objectives: (a) the creation, provision, and activation of avenues for economic activity (opportunities) and, simultaneously, (b) the reduction and removal of barriers to such activity. Institutional development establishes foundations for achieving these objectives by facilitating progress along two related dimensions:

1. establishing rules of exchange, finance, and production that circumvent or minimize myriad forms of free riding related to basic market failures (notably the provision of public goods and services) limiting the incidence and impacts of negative externalities, and limiting the use of common resources; and

2. establishing and enforcing basic economic rights at a universal—as opposed to selective—level, including property rights that grant relatively equal access to productive activities and finance, along with procedures for enforcing economic agreements (contracts).

Regarding item 1, note that basic infrastructure is often a public good, education and health care have significant public-good attributes associated with positive externalities, and that the overuse of existing infrastructure and services can generate common-resource problems. Arranging for provision and maintenance thus suffers from free-rider and enforcement CAPs, which viable economic institutions sometimes resolve. For example, enforceable tax legislation can facilitate funding potable water, public education, disease control, and other provisions of health care. Functional central banks can stabilize financial systems, limit inflation, and reduce the length and severity of recessions. Regulations or taxes that reduce pollution can enhance capability sets by improving health outcomes.

Item 2 requires elaboration. A capability approach to development entails more nuance than a simple statement that property rights underlie exchange. First, some background. Property rights both provide opportunities (e.g., securing gains from one's efforts) and establish barriers (only owners have access). Indeed, property rights are themselves a type of economic regulation. The balance between opportunity and barrier is complex since many opportunities require barriers. Patents limit uses of technologies, yet provide incentives for R&D. Hence, different configurations of property rights engender distinct approaches to the involved trade-offs.

A political economy approach invites placing economic rights, notably property rights, within political contexts. Successfully defining property rights requires resolving multiple first-and second-order CAPs—many related to free riding, distributional conflict, and coordination—that surround the social allocation of returns to productive activity, as well as the ownership of goods, services, financial assets, and the means of production. Defining property rights is, therefore, an intricately political process.[39]

Merely defining property rights, however, is not sufficient. Enforcing property rights involves addressing substantive second-order CAPs—a political process that underlies prospects for economic exchange. Moreover, universal property rights are themselves a type of public good. Private producers may prefer selective rights that would grant them monopoly power. Selective property rights (a type of club good)—such as rights conferred to a dictator's supporters or exclusive monopoly licenses—pose barriers to production and exchange for those not designated—at least in the formal sector. Universal property rights thus imply a type of equity because they more broadly distribute production and exchange opportunities, with fewer barriers. Even so, a capability approach requires a more precise statement.

The development of functional, capability-enhancing economic institutions involves creating access and removing barriers to exchanges of the three main factors of production—labor, capital, and land. Classical economists Adam Smith, David Ricardo, and Karl Marx address this point. Along these lines, Robert Heilbroner (1992) identifies the commodification of land, labor (time), and capital as the principle development in the emergence of capitalism.

Removing barriers to the exchange of labor is most fundamental. Inclusive development requires universal (adult) ownership of marketable labor power. Slavery and, to a lesser extent, indentured servitude, deny individuals the possibility (the freedom) to refuse work and to exchange their labor time for remuneration. Related restrictive arrangements include serfdom, debt peonage, and child labor (a barrier to education and hence to future employment). Additional developmental obstacles arise from multiple informal and formal barriers to women's entry into labor markets or portions therein—as well as similar barriers that apply to various ethnic, racial, religious, or national groups. These impediments to labor exchange truncate the capability sets of individuals, families, communities, social groups, and entire societies with respect to earning income, producing output, and—in terms of human functioning—exercising agency over the use of one's own time, often with enduring impacts.[40] For example, Melissa Dell (2010) finds that the *mita* labor system, which operated in Peru between 1573 and 1812 and required indigenous communities to send one-seventh of their male labor force to work in silver mines, undermined long-run capabilities. In particular, current-day communities that were previously subject to that system have, compared to other Peruvian communities, systematically lower levels of consumption (25%) and more incidences of stunted growth among children.

Restricted access to capital markets, notably to small-scale finance, also undermines prospects for attaining productive capabilities. Credit market imperfections inhibit financing potentially beneficial investments by small firms and individuals who possess little or no wealth (Galor and Zeria 1993). Multiple forms of discrimination create additional, often insurmountable gender, racial, religious, and ethnic barriers. Various microfinance agencies, such as the Grameen Bank, endeavor to reduce such barriers by creating new avenues for lending without collateral—a type of institution building.

Concentrated land ownership, as a condition that often fosters serfdom and debt peonage, frequently undermines the productive use of land, labor, and capital by restricting access to land. Highly unequal societies at the onset of colonialization tended to establish institutions that reproduced such inequality by restricting the political and economic access of nonelites (Engerman and Sokoloff 2002). Concentrated land ownership also undermines motivation, truncating rural laborers' returns to labor by denying them any claim to a surplus in cases of wage labor and debt peonage, or reducing such claims (usually by 50%) in cases of sharecropping. Additionally, concentrated land ownership limits capital markets when large landowners control tenant access to finance. Land markets are thin because limited credit and land collateral requirements prevent small farmers from buying land (Bardhan 2005, 33), and landholders' credit monopolies can convert sharecropping into debt peonage. The post-Reconstruction sharecropping system in the US South, in which local merchants, who often also owned land, were the only source of credit, constrained small, especially black, farmers to debt peonage (Ransom and Sutch 2001).[41]

In contrast, West Bengal's post-1977 partial land reform increased agricultural productivity (Banerjee, Gertler, and Ghatak 2002). Comprehensive land reform programs in Japan, Korea, and Taiwan contributed dramatically to economic development by offering a substantial portion of the rural population the means and incentives to engage in their own production. Indeed, these examples point to the complications of property rights: redistributing land often does not coincide with honoring or enforcing previously established property rights.

Finally, note that the two aforementioned dimensions of institutional development may conflict with each other. Some property rights foster market failures, such as pollution. Restrictive patents may slow the transmission of technological knowledge and block competition that could significantly lower consumer prices in industries such as pharmaceuticals.

Overall, economic development involves systematic removal of economic deprivation. It entails widespread enhancement of living standards (achievements); improving aggregate levels of production and technology; shifting resources to highly productive activities; and a steady expansion of basic economic opportunities via adequate public health, educational services, and infrastructure. It also involves reducing and avoiding excess inequality, with specific attention to those on the lower end of relevant distributions of income, wealth, employment, health, and education—across individuals, households, and social groupings distinguished by gender, race, religion, and ethnicity, as well as across communities, regions, and nations. Furthermore, economic development entails creating institutional rules and procedures for defining and enforcing universal property rights; resolving CAPs of market failure; and, simultaneously, removing gender, racial, ethnic, religious, class, and other barriers to the exchange of labor, land, and capital and, more broadly, to exercising economic agency.

From a slightly different angle with some forward-looking reference to the hypotheses that appear in Chapters 3–6, economic development has five basic elements:

1. Resolving H1's CAPs that accompany the provision of basic public goods and services and limiting large negative externalities;

2. Resolving H2's CAPs of coordinating innovative and productive activity in a manner that does not engender excessive inequality;

3. Resolving H3's CAPs of undue influence of powerful parties on access to production, exchange, and the definition and enforcement of economic institutions, including property rights; such influence often creates participation barriers for less powerful parties;

4. Resolving H4's CAPs of creating credible commitments that investments in effort, knowledge, and human and physical capital will not be seized by powerful parties—private or public—often a component of enforcing universal property rights; and

5. Incorporating innovative ideas (H5) into the creation and functioning of economic processes and institutions—an element of self-discovery.

Section 3: Development and Inequality

Any given level of inequality, of whatever type operating within a social context, arises from prior developmental processes—or lack thereof. Furthermore, inequality constitutes a key aspect of the social environment that conditions prospects and directions for future development. Inequality affects allocations of capabilities, opportunities, and barriers across individuals and groups. This two-way causality, exhibited by manifold dimensions of inequality and development, implies multiple complex interactions and relationships; many go beyond what this text can address. Numerous studies, however, focus on less complex relationships between inequality of income and/or wealth and the growth of GDP per capita—sometimes with attention to underlying factors. This section's discussion highlights a few key points from that literature before briefly considering a broader political economy perspective on inequality and development as capability.

The Kuznets curve offers the classic approach to treating inequality as a function of economic growth—or more accurately as a function of the economic transformations that underlie achieving successively higher levels of GDP per capita. An inverted U-curve, with GDP per capita on the horizontal axis and the Gini coefficient on the vertical axis, traces this relationship (Kuznets 1955). Low levels of per capita GDP coincide with low inequality, a characteristic of economies dominated by agriculture. Early industrialization, which offers high returns to wealthy investors and low wages to unskilled labor, instantiates GDP growth with rising inequality. Later industrialization, however, reduces inequality because urbanization and an increasing share of employment in manufacturing reduces the proportion of workers earning low rural wages, and the spread of education reduces the wage premium for the highly educated. Concurrently, public demands for redistribution increase, and the return on capital decreases.

This inverse U-pattern appeared to hold for most countries that belong to the Organization for Economic Cooperation and Development (OECD) and Latin America until about 1975 or 1980. For the OECD countries, inequality peaked in the mid- to late nineteenth century (Great Britain) or the early twentieth century (United States), later for others. Inequality continued its decline or held steady through the third quarter of the twentieth century (Milanovic 2016). Subsequent events, however, undermined the Kuznets pattern. Inequality (measured by the income share of the top decile) has steadily increased in the United States, the United Kingdom, Australia, Canada, Argentina, South Africa, and Asia (notably Russia, China, and India); moderately in Europe and Japan; and it stabilized at high levels in the Middle East, sub-Saharan Africa, and Brazil (Piketty 2014; Alvaredo et al. 2016, 2018).[42]

To explain this overall pattern, Branko Milanovic (2016) proposes a more complicated relationship: Kuznets waves.[43] The first wave, which follows Kuznets's original argument, ends circa 1980, after which time the second begins. Milanovic, moreover, contends that continuously rising inequality is not sustainable; it must end through some endogenous mix of benign and malign factors that reverse the trend. More precisely, he adopts Kuznets's explanation for the initial rise in inequality from early industrialization, augmenting Kuznets's explanation for decreasing inequality during late industrialization with attention to both benign and malign factors. Regarding benign inducements that reversed the first wave of rising inequality, Milanovic (like Kuznets) points to urbanization and spreading education, along with political pressure for redistribution. The latter, he notes, arose from the unionization of industrial workers, middle-class progressivism, and various socialist political movements, along with a need for broad domestic support to resist the threat of communism.[44] The malign inducements for the first wave's reversal include two world wars. Citing John Hobson ([1902] 2005) and John Maynard Keynes ([1936] 1964), Milanovic asserts that World War I, which prompted the Russian Revolution and later World War II, was an endogenous response to an inequality-induced "competitive struggle for markets" via colonialism (2016, 95). This rivalry fostered unstable international relations among contending colonial powers (an increasingly fragile punctuated equilibrium). The outcome, two world wars, subsequently drove a reduction of inequality by destroying large fortunes and creating a compelling need to retain domestic support, especially from industrial workers, reinforcing political incentives for redistribution.[45]

After 1980, however, interactions between globalization and skill-biased technological change, along with endogenous policy responses (e.g., lower marginal tax rates on high incomes), have precipitated rising inequality—initiating a second Kuznets wave within many OECD countries. More specifically, the entry of inexpensive Chinese labor into the global market has enhanced the value of (and hence demand for) cheap labor-saving technology—an endogenous response of technology to shifting factor prices.[46] These developments have fostered widespread displacement of less-skilled (largely manufacturing) workers in rich countries, simultaneously lowering their wages. The associated reduction in their bargaining power has augmented the rents going to capital. Additionally, increasingly powerful wealthy parties have successfully promoted policy changes in their favor, such as tax cuts focused on the upper ends of income and wealth distributions. Milanovic (2016; note the date) concludes by predicting greater political instability.[47] In this text's framework, high inequality creates substantial H3 and H4 CAPs, discussed in Chapter 5.

Milanovic also discusses between-nation inequality, contending that such inequality creates a "citizenship premium" for those lucky enough to be born in rich countries (Ibid., 131). In 2016, national income per adult, in PPP euros, was €50,700 in the United States/Canada, €7,000 in India, and €5,100 in sub-Saharan Africa (distributed unequally within each; World Inequality Lab 2018). A Japanese newborn can expect to live nearly twice as long as one from Zambia, Angola, or Swaziland. In Iceland and Singapore, infant mortality is 3 per 1,000 but more than 150 per 1,000 in Sierra Leone. Most neonatal deaths, moreover, result from diseases for which cures are known and inexpensive (Milanovic 2016, 273). For any given comparison between countries, however, the size of the citizenship premium differs across ranges of the respective income distributions—a factor that affects incentives to migrate. Those at the bottom deciles in developing countries stand to gain more from moving to, say, Sweden, than do those at the top. While international migration is not a key focus of this book, it exerts some influence on Chapter 4's H2 CAPs related to skill matching and more generally to CAPs of political instability.

Comparing income and wealth inequality across nations, Milanovic attributes four key developments to post-1988 growth, globalization, and technological change. First, an equalizing influence has emerged from dramatically increasing relative incomes between the 40th and 60th percentiles of the global distribution—primarily an outcome of rapid growth in China, India, Thailand, Vietnam, and Indonesia. Second, stagnant incomes for the 80th to 90th global percentiles—equivalent to the lower middle class in the United States and Western Europe—have decreased their income share. Third, the global top 1% (equivalent to the US top 12%) have experienced rapid income growth. Fourth, the hyper-rich (billionaires; adjusting the definition of the included group for inflation) have enjoyed a fivefold increase in their wealth share. In 2013, the world's 1,426 billionaires controlled 2% of world wealth, more than 6% of global GDP and more than the entire wealth of Africa (Milanovic 2016, 43–44). Correspondingly, the wealth share of the top 1% increased from 28% in 1980 to 33% in 2017, while that of the bottom 75% stayed close to 10% (World Inequality Lab 2018).[48] More dramatically, in a report for the World Economic Forum, Oxfam (2019, 6) reports that the top 26 billionaires "own as many assets" as the poorest 50% of the world population.[49]

The first of these four developments implies a benign equalization of capabilities across much of the world (notably between the OECD and listed Asian countries), but this convergence may not last as East Asian countries face low-wage competition from other developing areas. The latter three developments, as Milanovic predicts, may prompt greater political instability within and even across nations. In any case, stagnant incomes and rising inequality present substantial H3 and H4 CAPs.

Inequality as a Causal Variable
Reversing the direction of causality, inequality affects prospects for growth and development. Many discussions of such impacts offer two contrasting (though not necessarily contradictory) perspectives, the latter of which has

gained increasing prominence. Much traditional economic literature asserts that unequal distributions of income and wealth create incentives to work and invest. Merit pay offers an example. An expectation of high returns to investment encourages entrepreneurship and growth (Chaudhuri and Ravallion 2006). Writing near the end of the first Kuznets wave, Arthur Okun (1975) proposed a trade-off between income equality and growth, but with a specific focus on redistribution via taxes and transfers: pursuing equality through these specific policy mechanisms compromises growth by undermining incentives to work and invest. Alternatively, many recent studies—without necessarily disputing Okun's point on redistribution policy—contend that high inequality interferes with growth. This relationship operates on two principal levels: capital markets and broader political economy.

Capital market imperfections—a feature of all developing economies and to a lesser degree all others—interact with inequality in three key fashions: First, as the large literature on moral hazard asserts, loan contracts cannot fully specify—and lenders cannot costlessly observe—borrowers' post-loan behavior, notably the degree of risk they are willing to undertake.[50] Enforcing terms of repayment thus becomes a second-order CAP, even in societies with well-established legal systems. Consequently, lenders (usually) require collateral—a percentage of an agent's assets—as a condition for extending loans. Collateral contributes to contract enforcement (a type of endogenous enforcement within exchange; Bowles 1985) by giving lenders an incentive to repay. Yet, this requirement limits credit access for asset-poor borrowers, curtailing their ability to finance human capital and entrepreneurial activity.[51] Along these lines, Jonathan Ostry and François Bourguignon (2016, 138) report a negative correlation between income inequality and secondary school achievement. Similarly, Richard Wilkinson and Kate Pickett (2009) associate higher inequality with low performance across a range of social indicators.

Second, reviewing relevant literature, Philippe Aghion, Eve Caroli, and Cecilia García-Peñalosa (1999) assert that those with the most access to capital (wealthy investors) face greater diminishing returns than others would. Due to imperfect capital markets, there is no aggregate production function for capital, but rather many individual functions. With diminishing returns, the marginal productivity of capital is lowest for the wealthy. Similarly, greater access to productive capital affords greater opportunities for learning by doing, and such activities also face diminishing marginal returns. Unequal wealth distribution thus discourages growth.

Third, the moral hazard problems of lending reduce borrowers' incentives to engage in labor effort because the lender claims some of the residual. Parties whose individual wealth exceeds some threshold (W_i^*) need not borrow. Because such parties can retain the full residual of their efforts, they encounter relatively strong incentives to work diligently. A more equal distribution would then enhance aggregate productivity by reducing the proportion of borrowers (i.e., generate more parties with $W > W_i^*$; Aghion et al. 1999).[52]

Regarding political economy, a large literature asserts that excess income and wealth inequality interferes with economic development by limiting investment opportunities and granting unequal political influence, inducing conflict and eroding the legitimacy of government and various institutions. Highly unequal early colonial societies in Latin America led to unequal political power, which granted unequal access to suffrage and schooling (Engerman and Sokoloff 2005, 2006). India's postcolonial development offers a consistent example. Areas wherein British colonialists awarded property rights over land to landlords, with a correspondingly unequal distribution, have experienced lower postcolonial agricultural investment and productivity, along with less investment in health and education, than areas where colonialists awarded cultivators such rights. Similarly, the former areas experienced greater political conflict and comparatively lower state development expenditures in agriculture, education, and health care (Banerjee and Iyer 2005).

For contemporary societies, the World Bank's *World Development Report* (2017) notes three sources of inefficiency that arise from the political economy of inequality:

i. In countries with weak institutions, inequality is both a cause and consequence of corruption and clientelism. Economic prospects suffer from required or implied bribes for service, inefficient work habits, absenteeism, unaccountable officials, and inadequate provision of key public goods, often biased toward political supporters. Opportunities for short-term gain undermine long-term objectives. Elites may capture funding for education, health care, and other services intended for the poor.

ii. Powerful parties oppose potentially efficiency-enhancing reforms that could harm their interests.

iii. Inequality reduces the willingness of multiple parties to cooperate for public benefit.

Along similar lines, William Easterly (2007) finds evidence that *structural inequality*—related to the distribution of factors of production—compromises development. Focusing on unequal land ownership (using an instrumental variable technique), his analysis supports the Engerman-Sokoloff (2002) hypothesis that unequal factor endowments (notably land) generate inequalities and corresponding political dynamics that foster weak institutions, low investment in human capital, and overall underdevelopment.[53] In 1977, West Bengal's left-wing government passed the West Bengal Land Reform Act and began Operation Barga. These measures effectively implemented India's, otherwise largely dormant, Land Reform Act of 1955 in that particular state (unlike others). The West Bengal act stipulated that landlords could demand no more than a 25% crop share from tenants and that registered tenants would have inheritable tenancy rights to the land provided they pay their share. The new policy enhanced tenant bargaining power, the security of tenant land tenure, and agricultural productivity (Banerjee et al. 2002).

A complementary argument from Arjun Jayadev and Samuel Bowles (2006) focuses on conflict, property rights, and appropriation. They note a correlation between inequality and the deployment of *guard labor*—that is, labor that endeavors to protect property rights and/or increase distributional shares in situations with nonexistent or incomplete contracts (as in capital and labor markets). While often necessary, guard labor does not directly contribute to producing goods and services. It is unproductive "in the classical sense" (Ibid., 335). Accordingly, these authors assert that resources devoted to the maintenance of economic institutions, including guard labor, counts as a type of depreciation expenditure. Such expense does not contribute to net national income. This approach fits an appropriately adjusted concept of Fisherian income from William Nordhaus (2000).[54] For a given GDP, rising inequality reduces net national income by demanding more guard labor.

Returning to the theme of growth, Ostry and Bourguignon (2016) report that a combination of capital market imperfections and inequality-induced political distortions has reduced the duration of growth spells for developing countries. Andrew Berg, Jonathan Ostry, and Jeromin Zettelmeyer (2012) find that a 10-percentile decrease in income inequality increases the expected length of growth spells by 50%.[55] Ostry and Bourguignon conclude, "The key result from the joint analysis is that income distribution survives as one of the most robust and important factors associated with growth duration" (2016, 141). Along similar lines, Easterly (2007) contends that countries with more structural inequality grow more slowly. Likewise, social cleavages reduce the average value of public goods within a community (Alesina, Baqir, and Easterly 1999).

Regarding this last point, Henrik Jordahl (2007), who reviews literature on economic inequality and trust, concludes that inequality reduces trust (i.e., lowers expectations of cooperative behavior) primarily through its effect on social ties. Social ties create familiarity and corresponding incentives for trusting one's close connections. Many social ties form within socioeconomic groups. Inequality increases the social distance between groups, reducing the likelihood that their members share ties and norms (Coffé and Geys 2005). Correspondingly, the likelihood of establishing trust declines. More generally, distinct social networks with unequal degrees of connection transmit cultural capital, which then shapes access to multiple forms of economic, political, and social participation, such as invitations to political or social meetings and degrees of familiarity with procedures like applying for jobs, filling out forms, answering questions from officials, finding lawyers, and so on. On average, the poor have fewer pertinent connections and thus fewer avenues for opportunity. In this regard, Sen quotes Adam Smith on the importance of the ability to "appear in public without shame" (1999, 71).

Angus Deaton (2002, 2003, 2013) focuses specifically on relationships between health outcomes and various forms of inequality. Because health is a critical underpinning of human capability and indeed functioning, his analysis merits a brief summary. Deaton reviews literature and data with some initial attention to whether income inequality affects health, and then a broader approach that considers two-directional causality, in which health also affects inequality. He stresses the importance of early childhood, along with influences of education, social factors including gender and race, and political inequality.

Despite numerous high correlations between income inequality and health, after accounting for other factors, Deaton finds no direct verifiable causal link per se. He nevertheless makes several points:

- Much evidence points to a poverty hypothesis, whereby low income limits access to care. More generally, health outcomes (mortality in particular) follow a concave gradient with respect to income—a move from low to moderate income has greater impact than a move from moderate to high income.[56]

- Education improves health outcomes. In particular, parents' education influences their children's health and educational outcomes. Credit constraints, however, limit access to education for the less wealthy—especially for women and girls—with likely negative consequences on health.[57]
- A capability perspective also implies a reverse causality—poor health impairs ability to earn income. Poor childhood health reduces adult earning prospects, "even conditional on adult health" (2013, 267).

Turning to political economy, Deaton notes interactions between political power, social position, and health outcomes. He reports on large racial disparities in health outcomes. For example, in the United States in 2006, life expectancy for African Americans was 4.1 years lower than that for European Americans (Ibid.). Moreover, exposure to environmental hazards differs by race; 61% of black mothers and 41% of white mothers live within 1,000 meters of a site listed in the Environmental Protection Agency's (EPA) Toxic Release Inventory (Currie 2011). Social interactions between races also affect health outcomes. In the United States, racial disparities that emerge within encounters between providers and patients affect the treatments offered (Smedley, Stith, and Nelson 2002).

More comprehensively, political inequality compromises public health because a lack of political power undermines the provision of public goods to the poor. Deaton notes several examples:

- Prior to 1965, hospitals in the US South were segregated. In 1963, the Supreme Court outlawed "separate but equal" public facilities. Congress passed the Civil Rights Act in 1964 and the Voting Rights Act in 1965. The Medicare Act of 1965 denied Medicare funding to segregated hospitals. Between 1965 and 1971, black neonatal mortality rates declined substantially (Almond, Chay, and Greenstone 2007). Even so, African Americans still experience underprovision of public goods, including (contrary to much public opinion) welfare benefits (Alesina and Glaeser 2004).
- Before the passage of the British Reform Acts of 1832, 1867, and 1884, British cities failed to allocate their abundant water supplies to improving access and sanitation in poor communities. These three acts, however, gradually expanded the franchise, fostering the formation

of coalitions that successfully pushed for better urban sanitation (Szreter 1988).

- Raghabendra Chattopadhyay and Esther Duflo (2004) find that the 1993 constitutional mandate in India requiring that women comprise at least one-third of village council members increased the local provision of public goods favored by women in the two districts they studied.[58] The authors note that Rohini Pande (2003) finds a similar result on ethnic representation and distribution of transfers. They conclude that the identity of policymakers influences policies enacted.

- The introduction of voting machines into poor areas in Brazil improved health outcomes. Moreover, the locational pattern of the new machines matched the locational pattern of subsequent improvements on public health, prenatal care, and fractions of low birth-weight babies (Fujiwara 2015).

To sum up, the capability approach to economic development encompasses all of these perspectives on inequality: development both responds to and affects inequities along multiple dimensions. Whereas nonextreme inequality of income can incentivize work and investment, many dimensions of inequity, including that of income and especially wealth, both constitute and reinforce various forms of deprivation and capability-limiting outcomes for the lower portions of the relevant distributions. Political, social, and economic inequities create barriers to agency for the less well provided, even in affluent societies. Economic and political inequities unevenly distribute abilities to purchase multiple private goods and services, such as food and housing. Inequities unevenly distribute the provision of and access to public goods and services, such as clean water, education, and health care, along with social access that often confers economic (and other forms of) status—doing so via social networks that underlie access to multiple social relationships and a corresponding transmission of cultural capital.[59] Ensuing educational and health outcomes both reinforce existing inequities and create new ones, such as those related to lifetime earnings potential. All such inequities apply to individuals, households, and social groups differentiated by gender, race, ethnicity, religion, social class, region, and nation.

Across these various dimensions, political and economic capability sets serve as a basal space for the analysis of inequality. Echoing Sen (1999), Deaton (2003) notes that a reduction in any one dimension of deprivation not only generates benefits in its own right; it also reduces deprivation along other dimensions.

Ultimately, development entails steadily enhancing multifaceted political and economic capabilities across broad populations. At a simple level, economic development involves steady increases in average living standards—sustainable economic growth, though with particular attention to the lower portions of the income and wealth distributions. More comprehensively, it entails widespread provision of basic proficiencies of production and consumption—defined broadly to include elements of human experience—and doing so by arranging for adequate health care, education, other public services, and infrastructure; by limiting excess inequality; and especially by reducing extreme poverty. At an institutional level, economic development connotes the evolution of mutually understood and expected informal and formal procedures for circumventing free riding, mitigating negative externalities, channeling economic conflict into productive competition, protecting universal (as opposed to selective) property rights, ensuring broad access to economic activities, coordinating activity, and enforcing agreements. Political development entails a similar evolution: building state capacity that can provide public goods and services, mitigate conflict, and enforce agreements; establishing a rule of law that systematically allocates decision-making authority, limits concentrated private and public power, and protects civil rights; forging multiple avenues for public accountability; encouraging inclusive social mobilization; and creating a sense of legitimacy for associated institutions and processes.

These elements of development interact. Growth and distribution are inseparable, as are economic and political development—as implied by their mutual attention to public goods and reliance on enforcement. Jointly and separately, these components of development involve myriad CAPs that accompany creating, reforming, and abolishing formal economic and political institutions, along with concurrent social mechanisms of coordination and enforcement, with complementary informal institutional evolution.

Moving forward, Part II's five hypotheses offer systematic avenues for inquiry into five principle categories of developmental CAPs. These concern providing public goods and limiting externalities and conflict (from H1); coordinating innovation and production within and across locations (H2); addressing disproportionate influence of powerful parties on institutional development (H3); creating restraints on exercises of power that underlie credible commitments (H4); and adopting policy and organizational innovations that can enhance the prospects and efficiency of resolving these basic CAPs (H5). Part III extends this logic with a typology of political settlements that facilitates identifying distinct foundations of institutional social orders and corresponding sets of binding and nonbinding constraints related to fundamental CAPs of development.

II FIVE KEY DEVELOPMENTAL HYPOTHESES AND ASSOCIATED COLLECTIVE-ACTION PROBLEMS

BUILDING ON PART I'S CONCEPTS, Part II provides foundations for Part III's typologies of development. The next four chapters discuss and apply five related developmental hypotheses, derived from separate segments of the literature, unifying their implications by linking each to important categories of developmental CAPs. Chapters 3 and 4 address two hypotheses related to developmental preconditions and associated CAPs. H1, discussed in Chapter 3, is obvious, yet fundamental and universally applicable: Development requires establishing social arrangements that deliver key public goods and services and that concurrently mitigate important negative externalities. In Chapter 4, H2 explicitly addresses spatial and sectoral inequities: Inherent complementarities that emerge from the nonrival properties of knowledge, skill matching, social imitation, and production externalities, separately and in combination, generate uneven locational and sectoral agglomerations of production, knowledge acquisition, innovation, and growth. Neither H1 nor H2 directly address social conflict, but their logic often implies social conflict. Accordingly, Chapter 5's two hypotheses directly apply social conflict theory to development. H3: Unequal distributions of power shape the creation, evolution, and demise of economic and political institutions. H4: Left to themselves, powerful parties cannot credibly commit to refrain from using their power for their own future benefit. Finally, Chapter 6's hypothesis addresses possible avenues for resolution. H5: Policy innovations can relax some of the political constraints that follow from H3 and H4, as well as coordination and free-riding constraints from H1 and H2. Chapter 6's conclusion traces relationships among these five hypotheses, offering both rationale for integrating them and conceptual foundations for Part III's typology of development.

3 Public Goods, Externalities, and Collective-Action Problems of Governance

A tourist's casual observations of the quality of infrastructure can distinguish underdeveloped from developed economies.
—*Allen R. Ferguson, personal communication (1998)*

FOLLOWING SIGNIFICANT DISCONTENT, the one-party (UNIP) government of Zambia called for elections in 1991. The opposition Movement for Multiparty Democracy (MMD) won and instituted an economic reform program, including extensive privatization. As the former leader of the miner's union, the new president, Frederick Chiluba, lent credibility to these policies. Whereas the previous UNIP government had maintained support by distributing rents to stable constituent groups, the MMD distributed benefits to individual entrepreneurs, conditioned on "winning access to the president's (revolving) inner circle through the continual forming, unforming, and re-forming of political coalitions under the MMD umbrella" (Levy 2013, 124). In this process, insiders circumvented the formal rules of privatization. They acquired former parastatal enterprises, tourist lodges, manufacturing firms, and trade enterprises at low prices.[1] Even though the new regime achieved stability and some growth (5–6% per year between 2003 and 2009), it suffered from a weak bureaucracy, an inability to provide public goods—public investment below 6% of GDP—and weak contract enforcement. Cotton production increased 10-fold between 1994 and 2005, but side deals to independent traders undermined institutional arrangements and economic performance (Ibid.). Why, despite economic growth, was Zambian public good provision inadequate?

This chapter addresses a set of CAPs associated with the first developmental hypothesis:

H1: Development requires establishing social arrangements that deliver key public goods and services and that concurrently mitigate important negative externalities.

These terms apply broadly. Public goods, for example, include mechanisms for resolving disputes and items such as the nonrival benefits that often accompany technological advance. Negative externalities arise not only from pollution but also from the overuse of common resources, such as managerial time within a firm or an established court system and the pricing behavior of monopolies.

Discussion proceeds as follows. Section 1 develops H1, relating it to basic first-order CAPs and then to corresponding second-order CAPs that underlie credible resolution. A few simple games—prisoners' dilemma, pure coordination, battle (of the sexes), and chicken—can illustrate archetypal patterns of divergence between individual incentives and beneficial group outcomes. Identification of these patterns, with attention to underlying causal relationships, permits systematic analysis of avenues for and barriers to resolving identifiable sets of CAPs whose resolution, in turn, usually requires developing some form of governance, often at multiple levels. Accordingly, Sections 2 and 3 consider governance. They discuss factors that condition the ability and willingness of state agents to address such CAPs. When achieved, resolution reflects two components of political development: state capacity and the rule of law.

More specifically, Section 2 relates H1 CAPs to the creation and utilization of state fiscal capacity, which then enables public good provision. Here, political contestation between possible governing coalitions generates additional first- and second-order CAPs that preclude, distort, or at least complicate such provision. Section 3 follows a similar approach to issues of developing and utilizing state legal capacity. It focuses on the degree to which a governing coalition's actual use of such capacity generates or fails to generate a rule of law—often a precondition for resolving multiple second-order CAPs. Although this discussion focuses on developing two dimensions of state capacity, the same principles apply, usually less formally, to other forms of governance. Militias and gangs, for example, develop their own versions of fiscal and legal capacity, as do private firms.

Section 4 concludes with commentary on capacity traps. These are self-reinforcing combinations of low fiscal and legal capacity, which undermine development by posing nearly insurmountable second-order coordination and enforcement CAPs.

Section 1: Public Goods, Externalities, and Developmental CAPs

H1 is obvious, fundamental, and universal. A failure to provide minimal public goods and simultaneously mitigate the most basic and extreme negative externalities signifies a failure to remove enormous barriers to developing economic and political capabilities. Yet, removing such barriers requires confronting a series of substantial first- and second-order CAPs that preclude, distort, or inhibit creating social mechanisms that can provide items like the following: sanitation, potable water, transportation, communication, education, R&D, and technology infrastructure, along with support for and regulation of economic transactions, contract enforcement, dispute resolution, and containing the spread of disease. Indeed, markets themselves are public goods—as is creating macroeconomic stability and insurance against various political and economic risks. Likewise, development rests on creating and utilizing social mechanisms for avoiding or mitigating numerous negative externalities that accompany private predation and extraction, such as murder and theft, along with unsanitary practices, monopolistic overreach, resource depletion, and multiple forms of environmental degradation.

China, for example, faces dire health consequences of particulate air pollution that compromise both personal and productive capabilities. Various tropical regions in Brazil and elsewhere face a *deforestation trap* within which poverty and environmental degradation reinforce each other. Small farmers clear patches of forest for cultivation, but nutrient-poor rainforest soil only supports crops for a few years. Subsequently, large farmers buy the land for cattle grazing, and small farmers clear adjacent land. The process repeats. In a related manner, rapid urbanization in Port-au-Prince, Haiti, has accelerated deforestation in adjacent areas because wood provides fuel for cooking. Only 2% of Haiti's land remains forested (Roc 2008).

These issues pose substantive CAPs, rather than mere difficulties that technical or individual solutions could remedy. Resolutions are thus political, requiring some type of governance—be it informal or formal. A few simple game models illustrate the logic of conflicting incentives that underlie these (and other) CAPs. This logic provides a foundation for systematic analysis of

TABLE 3.1 First-Order CAPs as a Prisoners' Dilemma

		Pablo	
		Cooperate (C)	Defect (D)
Maria	Cooperate (C)	$a1(3), b1(3)$	$a3(-2), b2(8)$
	Defect (D)	$a2(8), b3(-2)$	$a4(0), b4(0)*$

LEGEND: $a1$, $b1$, etc. = variables; (3), (8), etc. = hypothetical values; * indicates the Nash equilibrium.

types of problems and relationships between underlying incentives and possible solutions.

Consider a set of first-order CAPs that surround forging agreements to provide public goods, limit negative externalities, limit the use of common resources, and/or enhance activities that create positive externalities. Table 3.1's two-player prisoners' dilemma game points to how material incentives encourage free riding, *ceteris paribus*.

Farmers Maria and Pablo each choose to either cooperate (C) on some costly but mutually beneficial project—or defect (D). Suppose that contributing to a public good such as constructing a common irrigation canal (strategy C) creates a nonexclusive benefit of 8 at a total cost of 10 (5 each if shared; so that variables $a1$ and $b1$ = 3, etc.).[2] Here, D is the dominant strategy for both players—preferred regardless of what the other does. The Nash equilibrium occurs at strategy combination DD. If both players follow their material incentives, they never build the canal. This same logic applies to limiting the use of a common resource or reducing production of a negative externality (costly to limit or reduce; others benefit) or to increasing production of a positive externality (costly to provide; others benefit). Accordingly, small farmers in rainforests (a common resource) encounter material incentives to clear land. Doing so depletes the resource and imposes negative externalities on other farmers and society.

A few simple alterations to Table 3.1 can depict variants of this social dilemma. Pablo, for example, may face higher contribution costs (let $b3 = -4$). Players M and P might represent groups, coalitions, firms, and government officials or agencies. To illustrate civil conflict, let C signify negotiate and D signify fight, steal, or lie. More generally, each of the variables ($a1$, etc.) can depend on specific conditions in the political-economic environment that additional variables could represent. For example, if Maria is a rainforest farmer, her expected returns to clearing land ($a2$ and $a4$) may depend on her expected revenue from selling crops (R), the size of her family (F), and so on. Moreover, the difference between payoffs $a2$ and $a4$ depends on how Maria expects Pablo's choice of C or D to affect her outcomes, and his payoff to each strategy depends on a similar set of variables. Specification of such functions offers considerable opportunity for analyzing how social context influences a set of strategic trade-offs associated with public goods, externalities, and so forth. As long as the game retains a prisoners' dilemma structure, its logic implies that material incentives pose obstacles to resolving these first-order CAPs.[3]

A second avenue for generalizing such games involves increasing the number of players. A multiplayer prisoners' dilemma game usually implies more intractable (larger-scale) versions of the same basic dilemma. Equation (3.1) illustrates a marginal player's payoff to strategies C and D in a public good game with N players:

$$(3.1) \quad y_i = q_i - c_i + \alpha \sum_{j=1}^{N} c_j.$$

Here, y_i is player i's material payoff; c is the cost of contribution to a public good (G); q_i is the value of player i's endowment, representing the return to private production without G; $\alpha < 1$ is the marginal benefit from a single contribution; and i is a member (any member) of group j of size N. The condition $\alpha < 1$ gives the game its prisoners' dilemma structure: each agent's cost of contribution (c) outweighs the marginal gain (αc). Moreover, as a rule, a larger N lowers the value of α, reducing the incentive to contribute for any given expectation concerning strategies of the other ($N-1$) players.[4] All else equal, large groups face more potential free riding, augmenting CAPs of collective-good provision (Olson 1971). We may interpret public good *provision* to include paying the costs to reduce the negative externalities that accompany one's actions (e.g., burning coal).

In principle, agreements to share the various costs and benefits of cooperation among the involved parties could resolve these CAPs, but only if such agreements are credible: only if each party expects the others to abide, not cut corners, and not cheat. Indeed, successful private exchange typically requires dependable informal or formal agreements or contracts. Likewise, adherence to an adopted policy prescription hinges on whether the relevant agents (e.g., bureaucrats) have incentives to actually implement the policy—a process that is often costly and which often requires coordination with others. Both private and public agents, therefore, face second-order CAPs of coordination and enforcement that create barriers to the realization of potentially beneficial political and economic exchanges.[5]

Now suppose that Maria and Pablo understand the benefits of cooperating, yet each prefers that the other bear the costs. A Coasian logic (zero transactions costs to negotiating credible agreements) might suggest that, prior to play, they make an agreement that each contributes a specific amount. Yet, if Table 3.1's payoffs represent everything the players care about, the agreement will lack credibility: agreement notwithstanding, both parties have incentives to defect, and each should expect the other to do so even if she or he abides by the agreement! Economic and political agreements (formal or not) face this very problem: implicit or explicit promises to undertake one's share of costly contract adherence or policy implementation often appear suspicious. Maria and Pablo could, for example, represent government agents who understand the benefits of a new health-care policy but prefer that the other bear the political costs of putting the policy into practice. Alternatively, these players could represent two firms who may question the other's devotion to an agreement concerning a joint venture.

With slight adjustment, Table 3.1 can illustrate this problem. Here, strategy C signifies full adherence to an agreement; D signifies cheating on the agreement. Again, both players do better by choosing D regardless of the other's choice: they face a second-order enforcement CAP. Anticipating this outcome, they may not even bother to negotiate. Equation (3.1) illustrates a similar second-order logic if we interpret the variable c to represent the cost of actually delivering on a stated commitment. Second-order enforcement CAPs thus interfere with economic and political development by undermining the credibility of otherwise possible contracts, agreements, and policies.

Reliable public and private agreements, especially those involving many parties, also require forms of coordination. The timing and location of action, for example, may affect outcomes. Second-order CAPs of coordination often have public good elements: if one agent undertakes the costs of orchestrating coordination, another might free ride. Versions of Table 3.1 and equation (3.1) thus apply.[6] Moreover, as the name suggests, such CAPs also involve issues of pure coordination. Table 3.2 shows a simple two-player version.

Suppose that paths A and B are distinct methods for implementing a public or private policy prescription.[7] The players, perhaps bureaucrats in different agencies, decide their paths independently. If they both choose the same

TABLE 3.2 Pure Coordination Game

		Pablo	
		Path A	Path B
Maria	Path A	1, 1*	0, 0
	Path B	0, 0	1, 1*

* indicate the two Nash equqilibria.

TABLE 3.3 Game of Battle

		Pablo	
		Path A	Path B
Maria	Path A	2, 1*	0, 0
	Path B	0, 0	1, 2*

* indicate the two Nash equqilibria.

path, the policy succeeds and each receives 1; zero otherwise. The game has two pure-strategy Nash equilibria (AA and BB) and one mixed-strategy Nash equilibrium (both play A and B with probability 0.5). Because they cannot predict which pure-strategy equilibrium is more likely, they may opt for the (suboptimal) mixed strategy (each chooses randomly), in which case each has an expected payoff of 0.5. Achieving coordination among larger numbers of players enhances this difficulty, usually exponentially. Chapter 4's discussion of H2 presents a series of such larger coordination problems, with relevant equations and a multiplayer game diagram.

To complicate matters further, the players may have different interests regarding the manner of coordination. In Table 3.3's game of Battle, both players benefit from some form of coordination, but Maria prefers path A, whereas Pablo prefers B.

Again, there are two pure-strategy Nash equilibria, but Maria prefers AA, and Pablo prefers BB. Absent coordination, a mixed strategy (playing one's preferred strategy with probability 2/3), yields a suboptimal equilibrium with expected payoffs (2/3, 2/3). Worse still, if both insist on their own path, they both end up with zero.[8] Many policy implementation problems have this characteristic. Rival business partners may face the same dilemma. If both parties stick to their guns in the hopes that the other will yield rather than face the prospect of receiving zero, the game transforms into chicken.

A fourth game, a simple version of chicken (Table 3.4), illustrates cases in which agents' insistence on their preferred options leads to mutual disaster.

TABLE 3.4 Game of Chicken

| | | Pablo | |
		Insist on B	Accept A
Maria	Insist on A	−1, −1	2, 1*
	Accept B	1, 2*	0, 0

* indicate the two Nash equqilibria.

Again, there are two pure-strategy Nash equilibria (AB and BA) with no reason to expect one over the other; the mixed-strategy equilibrium generates suboptimal expected payoffs (1/3, 1/3). In the worst-case scenario, both insist, and both lose (equivalent to "drive straight" in the classic description of chicken).[9]

For these last three games, as in Table 3.1, the numerical payoffs could be variables that represent a range of values, each of which depends on additional variables that reflect or respond to specific social contexts, such as an anticipated public reaction to a policy choice. Alternative configurations or changes among the underlying variables could shift the game structure from, say, coordination to battle (due to local conformity pressure, each prefers a different way to coordinate) or from prisoners' dilemma to chicken (high costs to defecting as when resource depletion undermines food supplies).

Because of first- and second-order H1 CAPs, deforestation continues in Brazil (with massive fires in August 2019) and, considerable government effort notwithstanding, pollution in Beijing remains hazardous. Climate change poses truly daunting global CAPs along all of these dimensions. Meanwhile, Haiti has poorly developed transportation, communication, and educational infrastructure. Many developing countries that rely on primary product exports fail to develop (costly) infrastructure that could enhance productive capabilities by accommodating more diversified production. Civil war continues in Yemen.

Section 2: Governance, H1 CAPs, and Fiscal Capacity

Recall that governance signifies the process through which state and nonstate actors interact to design and implement policies, and that policies offer (usually imperfect) attempts to resolve CAPs. More specifically, addressing H1 CAPs requires developing and maintaining configurations of institutions—

both informal and formal—with complementary organizations that can foster governance at both public and private levels, with some degree of legitimacy. The state, with its various institutions, policy prescriptions, and organizations (e.g., bureaucracies) fundamentally shapes a society's ability to addresses such CAPs, as do any governance arrangements within their realms of operation. From a capability perspective, political development implies that states (and other governance mechanisms) both develop and utilize abilities to provide public goods, mitigate negative externalities and conflict, coordinate activity, enforce agreements, and protect rights. In doing so, they must, at a minimum, develop and utilize pertinent administrative capabilities, where such development entails resolving a prior set of first- and second-order CAPs.[10] Indeed, the complexity of these CAPs can generate a capacity trap whereby ineffective implementation becomes part of a political equilibrium that constrains or truncates general economic and political capabilities.

These issues notwithstanding, Francis Fukuyama asserts that the political science literature rarely considers productive uses of state power:

> Overwhelming emphasis in comparative politics has been on democracy, transitions to democracy. . . . [E]veryone is interested in studying political institutions that limit or check power—democratic accountability and rule of law—but very few people pay attention to the institution that accumulates and uses power, the state. (2013, 348)

If governments intend to adequately provide public goods and mitigate negative externalities (mitigation itself is a public good), they need to develop and utilize both fiscal and legal capacity. Fiscal capacity underlies financing the provision of public goods. Legal capacity facilitates resolving disputes, enforcing contracts, and enforcing property rights and rights of economic and political access. Success for either requires addressing two basic tasks:

1. developing adequate state capacities in relevant domains—that is, creating effective administrative capabilities for funding, crafting, adopting, revising, and implementing applicable policies across relevant territories;[11] and

2. motivating agents (e.g., bureaucrats) to utilize such capacities in order to create, adjust, and especially implement policies.

This chapter's discussion of fiscal and legal capacity addresses both tasks. The treatment of task 1 is direct and transparent. Task 2, however, involves the motivations and corresponding political and economic incentives of governing coalitions (or elites within), with attention to political institutions. Pertinent details unfold as the argument progresses through variations of its basic models.[12] Accomplishing either tasks 1 or 2 involves addressing both first- and second-order CAPs that accompany policy decisions and policy implementation. Regarding the two types of state capacity, fiscal capacity primarily addresses a society's first-order CAPs, and legal capacity primarily addresses second-order CAPs. In terms of Chapter 2's discussion of political development, both fiscal and legal capacity are elements of state capacity, but legal capacity also underlies (but does not determine) the degree to which a society achieves or fails to achieve either a rule of law or a rule by law.

The discussion that follows summarizes and applies concepts and models of fiscal and legal capacity developed by Timothy Besley and Torsten Persson (2011). This treatment offers a set of necessary, though not always sufficient, conditions for effective governance that can resolve H1 CAPs.[13] The remainder of this section focuses on fiscal capacity. Section 3 addresses legal capacity.

Besley and Persson (2011) develop a model that represents an incumbent governing coalition's decisions related to allocating government revenue across three purposes: providing public goods, allocating transfers, and investing in future fiscal capacity. The model also considers the degree to which a coalition decides to actually utilize any existing state fiscal capacity. For present purposes, the model illustrates relationships between political incentives and H1 CAPs of public good provision. It generates three basic outcomes: common-interest states largely resolve H1 CAPs and thus experience relatively favorable developmental prospects; redistributive states experience mediocre H1 performance and can fall into middle-income traps (Eichengreen, Park, and Shin 2013); and weak states fail to address H1 provision and often land in poverty traps.

Here is a summary of the model. Appendix 3A offers more detail. The state has access to tax revenue and resource rents. There are two competing political coalitions (A and B), one of which governs in each time period. In the simplest case, coalitions A and B have equal economic resources (e.g., wealth), equal power, equal membership, and there is no political polarization—meaning that both place the same utility value on public goods. Even so, H1 CAPs arise. There are two periods, t_1 and t_2. Coalition A is the t_1 incumbent. With probability γ (representing political instability), B governs in t_2. The governing coalition decides the following:

- In t_1: whether or not to allocate scarce revenue to investing in fiscal capacity (I_F), defined as administrative tax-collection infrastructure (τ). For a given initial tax capacity (τ_1), the level of I_F determines the t_2 capacity, τ_2.
- In both t_1 and t_2: how to allocate (residual) revenue between public goods (g) and transfers (υ). Public goods create value αg, where α (the marginal value of g) takes on either a high or low value, respectively, α_H and α_L; α_H occurs with probability $\varphi \in [0.1]$; υ funds consumption with a per-unit value of 1.
- When relevant, the incumbent also decides how to allocate υ between coalitions A and B. Here, the cohesiveness of political institutions (parameter $\theta \in [0, 1]$) determines the degree to which an incumbent coalition skews the distribution of transfers ($\sigma\upsilon$) in its own direction: $\sigma = \sigma(\theta) \in [0.5, 1]$; θ reflects underlying political norms, in addition to more formal rules that may, for example, set formulas for allocating transfers. Cohesive political institutions ($\theta \to 1$) imply equal shares of transfers ($\sigma \to 0.5$).[14]

In either period, the incumbent (I) receives utility u_{It}:

(3.2) $u_{It} = (1 - \tau_t)\omega_t + \sigma(\theta)\upsilon_t + [\sigma\alpha_H + (1 - \sigma)\alpha_L]g_t$;

and the opposition (O) receives

(3.3) $u_{Ot} = (1 - \tau_t)\omega_t + [1 - \sigma(\theta)]\upsilon + [\sigma\alpha_H + (1 - \sigma)\alpha_L]g_t$.

Here, $\omega =$ the wage (or income) and the other terms remain as previously defined. In both periods, the incumbent faces a government budget constraint (no borrowing) in which the sum of tax revenue and resource rents limits the sum of government expenditure:

(3.4) $R + \tau_t\omega = g_t + I_{Ft} + \upsilon_{At} + \upsilon_{Bt}$,

where R is the government's per-period resource rent, which does not change; subscripts A and B signify values for each coalition; and $I_{F1} \geq 0$ and $I_{F2} = 0$. In t_1, $\upsilon_A = \sigma(\theta)\upsilon$ and $\upsilon_B = [1 - \sigma(\theta)]\upsilon$. With probability γ, these transfer proportions reverse in t_2.

Given the budget constraint, coalition A's decision on funding I_F involves comparing its t_1 losses from lower expenditure on g and $\sigma\upsilon$ against future gains from higher revenue $\tau_2\omega$. The allocation of remaining revenue between

g and v depends on the marginal gains from increasing g (α_H or α_L) compared to σv, where α_H is greater than σv, and α_L can be greater than or less than σv. Here, the probability (φ) of attaining α_H can depend on prior institutional development and other factors, such as the presence of a compelling external threat.[15]

The model generates three basic outcomes. Each offers distinct implications on resolving H1 CAPs—even in this simple case. All three, moreover, inform Chapter 8's discussion of political settlements:

1. The *common-interest state* (S1) occurs whenever

    (3.5) $\alpha_L > \sigma(\theta)v$; or $\varphi = 1$.

    This condition requires sufficiently high marginal valuation of g and a relatively high value for θ, which pushes σ toward 0.5. If so, expenditure on g offers incumbents more benefit than distributing transfers to their own members. Hence, the t_2 incumbent (A or B) allocates all revenue to g. In t_1, anticipating this outcome, coalition A expands fiscal capacity ($I_F > 0$ and $\tau_2 > \tau_1$), because τ_2 can fund additional high-value g. Note that in this case, the level of political instability (γ) does not affect the outcome since either coalition would devote all t_2 revenue to g.

    Even here, however, greater access to resource rents (R) lowers I_F by relaxing the budget constraint, reducing the importance of τ. A specific type of resource curse that affects S1 applies in the following cases: the resource is not sustainable; R is subject to price volatility from international market trends; R generates a Dutch disease appreciation of the real exchange rate, reducing the competitiveness of manufacturing (or other traded) sectors; or the presence of R weakens institutions ($\partial\theta/\partial R < 0$).

2. A *redistributive state* (S2) occurs whenever (3.5) fails and

    (3.6) $\varphi\alpha_H + (1 - \varphi)\{(1 - \gamma)\sigma(\theta)v + \gamma[1 - \sigma(\theta)]v\} > 1$

    Here, coalition A's expected t_2 gains from the expected expenditures on $g + v$, accounting for α, φ, γ, and σ, exceeds the value of its tax-induced foregone t_1 consumption. In this case, coalition A expects to retain power with a sufficiently high probability (low γ) and high enough σ to justify I_F, in order to augment its expected t_2 receipt of σv by achieving $\tau_2 > \tau_1$.

In a redistributive state, greater political stability (lower γ) incentivizes I_F by extending A's (expected) time horizon. Perhaps counterintuitively, however, as long as $\gamma < 0.5$, more cohesive institutions reduce A's incentive for I_F because a higher θ would reduce σ, lowering $\sigma\upsilon$ in t_2.

Redistributive states can be stuck in a political equilibrium that, despite $I_F > 0$, allocates relatively little government revenue to g. Such mediocre H1 performance can relegate S2 societies to a middle-income trap. Additionally, as in S1, a resource curse can follow the same principles, noting that R can finance skewed distributions of υ to incumbent coalition members. Furthermore, with sufficient political stability, between-coalition inequality increases over time, creating additional CAPs. Greater instability (larger γ), however, increases the likelihood of moving from S2 to S3.

3. A *weak state* (S3) fails to meet both conditions (3.5) and (3.6). There is no common interest, and excessive instability undermines any incentive for spending on I_F or g. Moreover, with any positive rate of depreciation (see Appendix 3A), fiscal capacity will decline over time. Larger H1 CAPs and CAPs of inequality follow.

These large CAPs often confine weak states (or populations within) to poverty traps. Such outcomes can become sustainable when R funds transfers to incumbent coalition supporters—another manifestation of a resource curse.

Several additions to the model complicate the H1 CAPs in S1 and S2, reduce the likelihood of attaining S1, and increase the likelihood of S3. First, in either S1 or S2, adding a fixed cost of creating fiscal capacity reduces spending on I_F, reflecting a hurdle to attaining any expected benefits. This addition also increases the likelihood of S3.[16] Second, introducing polarization between coalitions A and B undermines A's S2 incentives to fund I_F and increases the likelihood of S3. In this model, *polarization* means uncorrelated coalition valuations of public goods: A and B ascribe different valuations (α_H and α_L) to specific public goods. For example, A could be an urban coalition that values public expenditure on urban streets and public transportation, whereas rural coalition B may prefer government expenditure on irrigation projects. Alternately, religious and secular coalitions may differ over public funding to religious schools. For given levels α_H and α_L, the degree of polarization (ζ) signifies the extent of such noncorrelated valuations. Specifically, let $(1 - \zeta) = $ Prob. $\{\alpha_{At} = z | \alpha_{Bt} = z\} \leq 1$ (subscripts A and B denote coalition-specific valuations, and $z \in [0, 1]$ indicates a specific probability value). A high ζ thus signifies high polarization. Now assume $\zeta > 0$. In S1, with $\alpha_L >$ $\sigma(\theta)\upsilon$, both coalitions would still spend on g in t_2 (despite different α valuations); consequently, A still spends on I_F. By contrast, in S2, before investing, coalition A, in addition to the aforementioned trade-offs, considers the following: if B attains power in t_2 and if B values α at α_H, what is the likelihood that A will also value α at α_H? The higher ζ, the less likely this outcome and the lower A's incentive to spend on I_F. Furthermore, whenever greater polarization leads to more political instability γ [$\gamma = \gamma(\zeta)$, and $\partial\gamma/\partial\zeta > 0$; a plausible scenario], the likelihood of S3 increases.

Third, adding between-coalition economic and political inequality complicates these H1 CAPs. Assume that one coalition is rich and the other poor: $\omega_J/\omega_K > 1$ (where J is either A or B, and K is the other). As Chapter 5's discussion implies, a rich coalition's greater resource access grants it more political power, *ceteris paribus*. In order to reduce the impact of taxes on its members, a rich, powerful incumbent underutilizes existing fiscal capacity, setting actual utilization of fiscal capacity $(t_x) < \tau$. This action tightens the budget constraint on all types of expenditure. Moreover, a powerful incumbent likely enjoys a higher σ, increasing its incentives to favor υ over g.[17] I_F also suffers, since a rich coalition would not fully utilize a higher τ_2 (why then invest?). In contrast, a poor incumbent coalition fully utilizes τ and faces the previously discussed trade-offs between g and υ that operate in S1 and S2. Yet, if a poor coalition A faces a high γ, it minimizes I_F, realizing that once B attains power, A will receive few if any benefits.

Furthermore, a high degree of inequality, *ceteris paribus*, reduces prospects for S1 because highly valued public goods and cohesive institutions need not guarantee common interest. Specifically, because the marginal cost of taxes on the rich is greater than 1, the condition $\alpha_L \geq \sigma\upsilon$ [from (3.5)] no longer assures an S1 outcome. Even with a relatively high α_L and θ, a very rich coalition A may not fund I_F and g because the tax price to its wealthy members would be too high.[18]

Alternatively, with moderate inequality, a somewhat rich coalition A will spend on I_F and g if α_L is sufficiently high to generate S1 [i.e., higher than (3.5)'s $\sigma\upsilon$]. This latter (often stringent) condition provides insight into why (mutually understood) external threats, which can enhance the perceived value of public goods (e.g., defense), can motivate state building (as in Tilly 1985). Chapter 8 returns to this point, relating it to distinctions among types of political settlements that condition prospects for resolving CAPs and, by extension, to developmental prospects.

Finally, consider a case with unequal coalition sizes. One coalition represents a small group of elites and the other a broad population. The likelihood of S1 again declines because, with higher per capita taxes for the elite coalition, $\alpha_L \geq \sigma\upsilon$ no longer denotes a sufficient condition for S1. Furthermore, the product $\sigma\upsilon$ now understates the per capita benefits of distributing transfers to a small coalition. Given σ and υ, a coalition's per capita transfers decrease in its size. The likelihood of S1 thus declines if either A or B represent elites. Furthermore, in S2, incumbent elite incentives often encourage narrowly focused clientelism that disproportionately deploys existing fiscal capacity to benefit coalition members, and prospects for S3 increase. Enhanced H1 CAPs and CAPs of inequality follow, along with a possible resource curse, whereby R can sustain large transfers to elites, even in the absence of economic development.

Overall, governing coalition incentives to invest in and utilize state fiscal capacity and allocate revenue to public goods depend on the value of public goods, the cohesiveness of political institutions, fixed costs to investing, degrees of coalition polarization, between-coalition inequality, and the relative size of coalitions. These factors critically influence a society's type of fiscal governance—S1, S2, or S3—and consequently its capabilities for resolving H1 CAPs, which then affect developmental prospects, such as those implied by middle-income traps in S2 and poverty traps in S3. Table 3B.1 (in Appendix 3B) summarizes these fiscal capacity outcomes.

Section 3: Legal Capacity and Second-Order CAPs of Enforcing Agreements and Rights

State legal capacity also conditions development. Government legal agencies act as third-party enforcers for a host of private activities, including exchanges, agreements, and contracts. As such, they mediate disputes, enforce multiple specific contract provisions, and protect various rights—both economic and political—from incursion by various private and public parties. Functional legal capacity can offer substantial public benefits and mitigate multiple negative externalities. Yet, governments develop and apply legal capacity with widely varying degrees of selectivity, bias, and effectiveness—including abject failure.

Even in societies with a well-established rule of law, however, incomplete contracting in markets involving complex exchanges, notably labor and capital markets, limits or precludes third-party enforcement of specific elements of contract and exchange agreements. As noted in Chapter 2, due to the presence of asymmetric information, employment and finance contracts cannot fully specify—and thus third parties cannot fully enforce—the degree of mental concentration that workers place on the execution of specific tasks or the degree of risk that borrowers undertake after securing loans. Enforcing provisions thus involves private (second-party, endogenous) mechanisms, such as monitoring workers and requiring collateral for loans.[19] Even so, third-party mediation and enforcement shapes relevant contexts and addresses a host of additional second-order CAPs, such as limiting theft. In systems with a functional rule of law, legal institutions and associated governance agencies achieve some legitimacy (public acceptance). Accordingly, third-party arrangements often underlie and complement a host of informal, internal, private dispute resolution and enforcement mechanisms or practices, including complementary social norms.[20] Furthermore, the need for formal third-party mechanisms increases with the complexity of exchange.[21] The underlying dynamics, naturally, are deeply political, influenced by inequities, and permeated with CAPs.

Achieving reliable public mediation and enforcement entails developing and utilizing state legal capacity. A state's *legal capacity* is its ability to mediate disputes, enforce provisions of contracts and agreements, and protect rights across or within relevant territories. The development and utilization of state legal capacity constitutes a key realm of political development because it conditions the degree to which states establish a functional rule of (or by) law. Indeed, state legal capacity facilitates enforcing and thereby implementing myriad behavioral prescriptions specified by economic and political institutions. Successful application of legal capacity then resolves numerous second-order CAPs that would otherwise undermine the credibility of potentially beneficial economic and political exchanges. The development and utilization of legal capacity thus conditions economic as well as political development.

Such development, however, is not automatic. As Section 1 implies, the enforcement of rights and mechanisms for resolving disputes are public goods—that is, when universally applied. When selectively applied, however, legal enforcement is a club good—as in a rule by law. In either case, the values achieved may differ significantly among specific parties (e.g., contesting sides in legal disputes). The attainment of legal capacity thus involves both free-riding problems and political conflict, posing complex political trade-offs and substantial H1 CAPs.

This section applies the concept of legal capacity to economic exchange, growth, and distribution, doing so with some attention to elements of political development. Discussion focuses on how legal capacity may or may not effectively protect economic production and exchange from private as well as public predation—that is, how exercises of legal capacity universally enforce, selectively enforce, or fail to enforce property and exchange rights; these rights underlie economic activity.[22] The conclusion briefly relates these principles to political rights.

Basic One- and Two-Sector Models of Legal Capacity
Substantial first- and second-order H1 CAPs hinder developing and utilizing a state's legal capacity. Two basic models from Besley and Persson (2011), one with one sector and the other with two, augment Section 2's fiscal capacity model by adding legal capacity. These models illustrate relevant CAPs by pointing to strategic trade-offs regarding the development and application of legal capacity, which then affect the selectivity or universality of rights enforcement. Implications on growth and distribution follow. The one-sector model largely replicates Section 2's conclusions with respect to how state outcomes S1, S2, and S3 condition investment, now applied to legal capacity. This first model also suggests location-specific variation in developed legal capacity—an outcome that directly relates to Chapter 4's discussion of H2's location-oriented CAPs. The two-sector model indicates additional CAPs related to rent-seeking opportunities that influence how incumbents apply a state's existing legal capacity. Selective application connotes a rule by (rather than rule of) law. Inequality, both between and within coalitions, reinforces this outcome, creating possibilities for class-based politics, corruption, state predation, and fiscal-legal capacity traps—a likely characteristic of poverty-trap equilibria. Details follow.

The one-sector model adds three elements to Section 2's model of coalition fiscal decisions:

1. an existing period t_1 level of legal capacity (π_1), determined by nature (i.e., past history);

2. a potential for the t_1 incumbent (A) to invest some state revenue in building legal capacity ($I_L \geq 0$); whenever $I_L > 0$, $\pi_2 > \pi_1$; and

3. a provision that, during both t_1 and t_2, the incumbent coalition decides how much existing legal capacity to apply to enforcing economic rights of each coalition; here, $L_{Jt} \leq \pi_t$, for $J \in [A, B]$.[23]

Besley and Persson (2011) note that legal and fiscal capacity are (nearly always) complements because fiscal capacity can fund developing legal capacity, and the use of legal capacity increases national income, relaxing budget constraints.[24]

In this formulation, the total income received by members of coalition J (y_{Jt}) depends positively on the amount of legal support (L_{Jt}) provided by the incumbent. Consequently, each period's GDP depends on the legal support provided to both coalitions [$Y_t = y_{At}(L_{At}) + y_{Bt}(L_{Bt})$]. Thus in t_1, coalition A considers, in addition to Section 2's fiscal trade-offs, how much government revenue to allocate to I_L, noting that such expenditure enhances t_2's tax base (τY), which can fund more g and/or υ.

In the simplest version of this model, both coalitions fully utilize existing legal capacity π to protect rights for both ($L_{Jt} = \pi_t$ for $J \in [A, B]$ for t_1 and t_2). Four outcomes follow.

1. *Taxes and growth*: Due to fiscal-legal complementarity, increasing taxes (within a range) enhances growth by facilitating better legal enforcement.

2. *States and legal investment*: The type of state, S1, S2, or S3, shapes the incentives that underlie I_L, as it does for I_F in Section 2. In S1, coalition A spends on I_L because increasing π increases τY, financing more highly valued g, which either t_2 incumbent will provide. In S2, with sufficient political stability (low γ) coalition A expects that I_L's positive impact on τY will augment its ability to allocate t_2 transfers to itself [$\sigma(\theta)\upsilon$]. As in Section 2 and somewhat counterintuitively, whenever $\gamma < 0.5$, less cohesive political institutions (a lower θ) allow for a higher incumbent transfer share (σ), which encourages I_L ($\partial I_L/\partial \theta < 0$, since $\partial \sigma/\partial \theta < 0$). In S3, $I_L = 0$. Furthermore, if π depreciates over time, S3 noninvestment becomes self-reinforcing, signifying increasingly difficult H1 CAPs of exiting S3—a form of political decay.

3. *Endogenous growth*: Because high incomes motivate spending on I_L (more revenue and value to protect), factors that increase per capita

GDP—such as human capital—encourage I_L, which then increases Y. Effective legal capacity thus fosters a type of endogenous growth, via institutional improvement (Ibid., 115–16).

4. *Locational inequality*: Areas with high legal capacity (cet. par.) grow more rapidly than others do. As Chapter 4's discussion of H2 shows, productive capacity emerges in highly unequal locational agglomerations. We thus expect correspondingly unequal distributions of legal capacity—an outcome that reinforces location-based productive inequalities and correspondingly unequal distributions of economic capabilities and benefits. The associated CAPs complement each other.

A two-sector model, in the spirit of W. Arthur Lewis (1954), reinforces outcomes 1–4, with complications arising from imperfect capital markets. Specifically, this model addresses interactions between legal capacity, private uses of capital, and the condition of capital markets. Here, imperfect capital markets offer rent-seeking opportunities for distribution-conscious governing coalitions, potentially reducing their incentives for spending on I_L and, more dramatically, creating incentives for selective application of existing legal capacity. Additional CAPs thus shape developmental trajectories.

Consider an economy with two sectors: modern and traditional. The latter connotes either an agricultural or an informal sector. The modern sector earns a higher return on capital ($r_M > r_T$). If we initially assume perfect capital markets, the (efficient) modern sector utilizes all capital, and coalition A's period t_1 investments in expanding legal capacity increase incomes for both coalitions—another form of institutional endogenous growth. Pecuniary externalities follow, since A does not receive the full benefit of its investment (B receives some). As Chapter 4 asserts, sector-specific pecuniary externalities generate H2 coordination CAPs.

Adding imperfect capital markets to this model more clearly illustrates how expected distributional outcomes—notably potential rents—affect the provision and utilization of legal capacity, with corresponding implications on growth, as well as distribution. Imperfect capital markets arise because loan contracts cannot specify a borrower's postcontractual willingness to undertake risks of default. To enhance prospects of repayment, lenders require collateral (a percentage of a borrower's assets) before issuing loans. The prospect of losing collateral usually motivates loan repayment; it can (endogenously) enforce loan contract provisions. As noted in Chapter 2, however, collateral requirements limit or eliminate financial access for the less wealthy. Even so, courts and legal procedures can improve contract enforcement. Consequently, increasing legal capacity can enhance access to credit by reducing collateral requirements. Greater legal capacity thus not only enhances growth by improving general contract reliability, it also loosens constraints on modern-sector acquisition and use of capital. Total factor productivity correspondingly increases. This form of institutional enhancement thus augments per capita growth in a fashion analogous to an improvement in technology (Besley and Persson 2011, 126–27).[25] Location-based inequities between high- and low-capital areas, however, may increase.

Furthermore, because capital market imperfections limit credit access, they generate an excess demand for credit, with corresponding rents accruing to modern-sector capital (Stiglitz 1987).[26] Rent-seeking prospects then influence incentives for applying legal capacity to each coalition. Incumbents can often increase their members' incomes with selective property-rights enforcement—that is, by underutilizing existing legal capacity for members of the opposition.

Two variations of this two-sector model follow. In the first, all members within a coalition are equal: each has the same chance of becoming a leader. In the second, each coalition has its own elites and followers, raising the question of the degree to which ruling elites follow an economic rule of law.

The equal-member version yields five additional results, all of which imply substantial H1 CAPs:

5. *Rising Inequality.* When not constrained by coherent institutions ($\theta < 1$), an incumbent coalition selectively utilizes legal capacity to enhance its rents at the expense of the opposition ($L_{It} = \pi_t > L_{Ot} \geq 0$; subscript I signifies incumbent and O the opposition).[27] Incumbent incomes grow more rapidly. As long as an incumbent retains power (relatively low γ), inequality increases over time. This dynamic reinforces Section 2's inequality outcomes for I_p, $\sigma(\theta)\upsilon$, and the utilization of τ.

6. *Class-based policy*: An unequal distribution of capital between coalitions fosters class-based policy preferences. The capital-rich coalition is a net demander of labor; the other a net supplier. An increase in legal capacity confers larger benefits to the rich coalition, whereas more fiscal capacity favors the poor coalition (greater relative benefit from g and lower per capita taxes). A capital-rich incumbent also encounters

a greater incentive to bias legal support in its own direction (again as constrained by θ), reinforcing inequality.[28]

7. *The "genius of taxation"* (Ibid., 131–36): Greater fiscal capacity reduces a rich coalition's incentives to bias its application of legal capacity. Above (below) a fiscal-capacity threshold τ^*, rich incumbents favor universal (selective) legal support. In S1, high fiscal capacity not only fosters growth by funding (valuable) g, it also facilitates funding I_L, increasing π, which then increases the tax base, facilitating additional g. Normally, only an S1 state crosses the τ^* threshold.[29]

8. *Class and the fiscal-capacity threshold*: In S2 and S3, a rich coalition's selective employment of legal capacity generates a self-reinforcing dynamic that enhances inequality, holding $\tau < \tau^*$. Yet, in S2, a poor incumbent coalition that retains power for long enough (a low enough γ) can push τ above τ^*.

9. *State-capacity trap*: A low τ, by reducing incentives for I_L, can create a downward spiral in which low incomes generate low revenue and thus low (or zero) I_F, which then reduces incentives for I_L, and vice versa. Any biased utilization of π ($L_1 > L_O$) enhances this effect. The likelihood of S3 thereby increases. Lacking investment, both τ and π deteriorate. Growth stagnates. Inequality increases or remains high. Weak institutions (low θ) and high instability (high γ) create and reinforce incentives for short-term focus on distorted redistributive transfers. When present, a high R resource curse reinforces these tendencies.

Now, by adding within-coalition inequality between elites and followers, the second variant of this model illustrates additional opportunities for corruption and predation.

Elites, Corruption, and Government Predation

Although corruption and government predation imply a dysfunctional or nonexistent rule of law, a legal-capacity approach offers more nuance. Sometimes, corruption coincides with a type of rule by law that involves selective provision of public goods and selective enforcement of property rights. This qualification matters because, as Chapter 8 asserts, within certain political settlements, these features can generate a type of political stability that permits some forms of development. The 1870–1910 early Mexican industrialization offers an example.

To model such possibilities, we designate a small portion of each coalition's members as elites (e) who dominate its policy decisions and claim any rents it receives.[30] To retain minimal legitimacy within their own coalition, incumbent elites usually extract rents from the other coalition. Adding elites to the model yields two additional implications, both of which compound the previous CAPs.

> 10. *Yet greater inequality:* The ability to focus coalition rents on small-group e increases incumbent incentives for unequal application of existing legal capacity, compounding the inequities and CAPs from results 5, 8, and 9. Furthermore, the τ^* threshold under 7 increases, perhaps to an unattainable level. The presence of elites may also complicate result 6 with the prospect of within-coalition class dynamics (not pursued here).

This consideration of elite rent extraction introduces another institutional parameter that represents the degree to which elites must adhere to an economic rule of law (hereafter EROL; parameter ψ). More precisely, $\psi \in [0, 1]$ depicts the degree to which rules impose transactions costs on rent extraction; as $\psi \to 1$, elite gains from rent extraction vanish. The final implication follows:

> 11. *Rule by law, oligarchic, and predatory states:* The EROL parameter ψ exhibits two thresholds, implying three possible equilibria (Ibid., 152):
>
>   a. *Economic rule of law* (large ψ)—With high costs to extracting rents, incumbents fully utilize π for both coalitions.
>
>   b. *Oligarchic rule by law* (intermediate ψ)—Application of π favors the incumbent coalition, as in (most of) the prior discussion, but now elites claim most rents. Inequality, both within and between coalitions, increases.
>
>   c. *Predatory state* ($\psi \to 0$)—Incumbents do not apply any existing legal capacity beyond narrow elite circles. Ruling elites extract rents from members of both coalitions.

Despite apparent similarity and some positive correlation, the three gradations of ψ do not directly correspond with fiscal states S1, S2, and S3. The respective distinctions concern different variables and arise from different parameters (θ vs. ψ). Whereas in an S3 state, $\theta \to 0$, $I_F = I_L = 0$, τ and π

diminish, and $g \to 0$; in a predatory state $\psi \to 0$ and $L \to 0$. Both S2 and S3 could be predatory but need not be. Even S3 states could enforce property rights across incumbent coalition members (to the degree that $\pi > 0$ from prior history), whereas predatory states always limit enforcement to a small set of elites (often informally).[31]

Table 3B.2 (in Appendix 3B) summarizes the legal capacity outcomes.

Section 4: Summary and Conclusion

This chapter addresses H1: Development requires establishing social arrangements that deliver key public goods and services and that concurrently mitigate important negative externalities. Both terms apply broadly. Social mechanisms of coordination, mediation, and enforcement, for example, have public good attributes. Hence, both first- and second-order CAPs fall under H1.

Section 1 utilizes several simple game-theoretic models to illustrate archetypal patterns of deviation between individual incentives and group outcomes that characterize both first- and second-order CAPs. The prisoners' dilemma game offers the most direct illustration of first-order H1 CAPs of free riding related to public goods, externalities, and common resources, as well as second-order CAPs of creating social mechanisms for coordination and enforcement that, in turn, render possible agreements on first-order CAPs credible, implementable, and worth negotiating to begin with. The pure coordination, chicken, and battle games can represent second-order coordination CAPs, and the latter two directly represent myriad associated conflicts. All of these games facilitate analysis of H2–H4 CAPs of Chapters 4 and 5. More generally, resolution of such CAPs underlies fostering the social capabilities that constitute economic and political development.

To address these fundamental developmental CAPs, societies must establish effective mechanisms of governance that follow from creating and utilizing state fiscal and legal capacity. While framed in terms of states, this logic also applies to less formal governance mechanisms, such as procedures that foster discipline within corporations and gangs. Effective use of fiscal capacity facilitates providing public goods and services; functional legal capacity underlies credible exchange commitments, protecting rights, instituting a rule of law, and fostering accountability. Both types of capacity signify important elements of political development that, nevertheless, often suffer from abuse.

Establishing either capacity, moreover, entails resolving a set of substantive H1 CAPs, as discussed in Sections 2 and 3.

A society's ability to resolve H1 CAPs of creating fiscal and legal capacity depends on the strength of its institutions, the value of relevant public goods, its political stability, and the availability of resource rents. Section 2's fiscal capacity model and Section 3's legal capacity model represent these influences as parameters. Specifically, we have the following: θ, the cohesiveness of political institutions; α, the value of public goods (combining α_L, φ, and α_H); γ, political instability; R, the availability of resource rents; and ψ, the extent of economic rule of law. Distinct values of these parameters yield distinct incentives for governing coalitions. These, in turn, imply distinct types of state governance (S1, S2, and S3), as well as the extent or even presence of an economic rule of law. These factors condition the resolution of multiple H1 CAPs that accompany the creation and utilization of fiscal and legal capacity. Tables 3B.1 and 3B.2 (in Appendix 3B), respectively, summarize the logic and outcomes of these fiscal and legal capacity models.

Both models have basic and amplified versions. The basic fiscal model yields three types of states: common-interest, redistributive, and weak. Each implies distinct CAPs. In a common-interest state (S1), high values of θ and α induce incumbents to spend on public goods (g), and the t_1 incumbent (A) invests in fiscal capacity (I_F). Even so, these processes operate under constraints from prior fiscal development, reflecting CAPs of prior institutional development, which generate location-based inequities—a topic pursued in Chapter 4. In a redistributive state (S2), lower values of θ and/or α combined with high political stability (low γ) pose more substantial fiscal CAPs. Even though incumbents spend on I_F, they focus remaining expenditure on transfers (v) that favor their own members because low θ allows them a disproportionate share ($\sigma > 0.5$). Middle-income traps may follow. In a weak state (S3), a high γ and low θ eliminate incentives for I_F and g. Insecure incumbents spend on transfers to their constituents; fiscal capacity erodes over time. These H1 problems induce self-reinforcing poverty traps. Finally, for all three states, high levels of R create a resource curse that undermines incumbent motivations for I_F (in S1 and S2) and g (in S2), often contributing to conflict that can increase instability (γ). S3 becomes more likely. Resource rents can render S3 sustainable by funding sufficient transfers despite low fiscal capacity.[32]

Section 3's legal capacity models augment fiscal capacity with complementary legal capacity (π), signifying the ability to enforce economic agreements and rights. A higher π enhances income, relaxing fiscal budget constraints. The basic (one-sector) case, in which incumbents fully utilize π to protect economic rights of both coalitions, duplicates the fiscal model's S1, S2, and S3 investment outcomes—now applied to I_L. Two additional results follow. First, fiscal-legal complementarity leads to an institutional version of endogenous growth. Utilized fiscal and legal capacities induce growth, in a manner analogous to technological advance in endogenous growth models (e.g., Romer 1990). Indeed, implemented fiscal and legal capacities constitute types of organizational technology—a topic more fully addressed in Chapter 6. This endogenous growth logic also implies an unequal locational distribution of legal capacity and, by extension, growth. Chapter 4 relates locational inequities to coordination CAPs.

In the amplified fiscal model, additional parameters and variables yield additional H1 CAPs. With fixed costs to investment ($F > 0$), incumbent incentives to spend on I_F and g decrease (in S1 and S2), and the likelihood of S3 increases. Similarly, polarization between coalitions (ζ) reduces S2 incentives for I_F and enhances the likelihood of S3 if, as is often the case, ζ fosters instability (γ). Now, if we add between-coalition inequality, rich coalitions underutilize fiscal capacity (τ) and devote little spending to I_F because they face higher per capita taxes. More dramatically, condition (3.5) no longer guarantees achieving S1. Unless constrained by coherent institutions (a high θ), rich incumbents focus spending on (clientelistic) distributions of transfers (υ) to their own. Poor incumbents, however, behave as in the basic model, except that political instability (γ) now exerts a larger negative impact on I_F and g.[33] Because between-coalition distributional conflict often enhances γ, the likelihood of S3 poverty traps increases. Finally, if a small coalition represents only elites, all of these CAPs become more pronounced. Moving slightly beyond the present models, elite coalitions may also spend on "guard labor" (Jayadev and Bowles 2006) in efforts to enhance and defend their wealth, transfer shares, and maintain (monopolistic) access to R—draining resources from more productive activities.[34] Access to high resource rents (R) allow elite coalitions to maintain S3, increasing the likelihood of poverty traps. Part III relates clientelism and resource availability to political settlements.

Regarding legal capacity, an amplified model with two sectors (modern and traditional) uncovers additional sources of distributional conflict. The modern sector earns higher returns ($\rho_M > \rho_T$). A relatively simple case, with equal members within coalitions, adds four points. First, imperfect capital markets generate rent-seeking opportunities in the modern sector that, when not constrained by θ, foster selective enforcement of property rights ($L_O < \pi$). Aggregate growth suffers and a rising disparity between coalition incomes reinforces the basic model's inequality outcomes. Second, class-based politics follow because wealthy coalitions usually benefit more from legal capacity (more value to protect), whereas poor coalitions usually benefit more from fiscal capacity (lower per capita taxes and greater benefits from g). Third, in S1, a sufficiently high fiscal capacity ($\tau \geq \tau^*$) can motivate equal application of π from either coalition because protecting another's rights generates income that can fund valuable g. Even in S2, if a poor coalition can retain power long enough (low γ), spending on I_F might facilitate crossing the τ^* threshold. The mid-twentieth-century policies promoted by the British Labour Party and Nordic Social Democrats illustrate this principle. Fourth, a combination of weak institutions, political instability, and resource rents (when present) reinforce incumbents' short-term focus on skewing transfers to themselves, while denying legal protection to opponents. An S3 fiscal-legal *capacity trap* follows.

Finally, adding a distinction between elites and followers within coalitions reinforces the previous proclivities toward inequality, strengthens associated CAPs, and introduces a final institutional parameter that facilitates closer analysis of the rule of law. An EROL parameter (ψ) reflects the degree to which institutions limit elite abilities to seize rents by imposing high transactions costs on rent-seeking behavior. Equivalently, ψ denotes the degree of universal as opposed to selective property-right enforcement. Three pertinent EROL distinctions based on levels of ψ follow: an *economic rule of law* (high ψ) whereby elites respect both coalitions' rights; an *oligarchic rule by law* (intermediate ψ) with selective legal protections focused on elites and their coalition followers; and a *predatory state* (low ψ) in which incumbent elites protect only their own property rights and prey on all nonelites. Predatory states can coexist with either S2 or S3. Chapter 9 more fully considers relationships between selective enforcement and economic development.

This discussion has taken the parameters (θ, ψ, φ, α_L, γ, and R) as given. Following a punctuated equilibrium logic, these terms could serve as quasi parameters that respond to internal and external developments over long time horizons. A more complicated model, for example, could make γ a function of social conflict, which may then respond to factors such as social cleavages, inequality, coalition investments in building violence capacity, resource rents, and the presence of external threats.[35] Likewise, the institutional parameters, θ and ψ, may respond to the presence or absence of mutually understood external or internal threats and to the cumulative impacts of coalition actions, such as spending on g and υ, that may shift distributions of resources within or between coalitions. Similarly, the public good parameters, α_H, α_L, and φ, which may exhibit shorter-term fluctuations, can depend in part on prior institutional development (including θ and ψ), as well as shared perceptions, including the legitimacy of current institutional arrangements—and the presence or absence of mutually understood internal or external threats.

I close with a few additional comments on *capacity traps.* These are equilibria characterized by weak institutions, underutilization of (low) existing state fiscal and legal capacity, little or no investment in either, and allocations of transfers and selective rights enforcement that favor incumbent coalitions, especially elites (Besley and Persson 2011). In a capacity trap, low fiscal and legal capacity becomes a self-enforcing and reinforcing equilibrium. In such cases, governing coalitions may bolster their positions with appeals to ethnic, racial, or religious superiority, nationalism, and other—typically divisive—claims to legitimacy. These appeals can undermine any proclivities among nonelites and opposition coalitions to resolve a substantial set of CAPs related to challenging an existing social order.[36] Governments, for example, may adopt the formality—but not the reality—of best-practice institutions, such as constitutions that prescribe limits on executive power and laws that prescribe equal protection of property and civil rights. Yet, insufficient state fiscal and legal capacity combined with multiple disincentives to utilize and equally allocate any existing capacity precludes implementing such practices. Second-order coordination, enforcement, and credibility CAPs remain unresolved—often to the benefit of powerful parties. Lofty prescriptions remain inert. Even so, the "isomorphic mimicry" of so-called best practices can lend legitimacy to existing arrangements and corresponding inequities (Andrews, Pritchett, and Woolcock 2013, 324–5). Such (faux) legitimacy can reinforce the skewed mechanisms of S2 and S3 states, notably those with an oligarchic rule by law.

Subsequent chapters develop these themes. Chapter 4 addresses a large set of related CAPs of coordination. Chapter 5's analysis of social conflict implies that deliberate efforts to construct legitimacy for weak, unenforced institutional prescriptions constitute exercises of power. Chapter 6 addresses legitimacy in more detail, relating it to the potential for policy innovations to relax certain political constraints. Chapters 8 and 9 relate the likelihood of the dysfunctional outcomes, such as capacity traps, to the characteristics of political settlements that underlie a society's social order.

4 Economic Foundations of Unequal Development

Knowledge, Skills, Social Imitation, and Production Externalities

In order to reach an "optimum size" of the industrial enterprises, the area of industrialisation must be sufficiently large.

> —*Paul. N. Rosenstein-Rodan, "Problems of Industrialisation in Eastern and South-Eastern Europe" (1943)*

The lack of interdependence and linkage is of course one of the most typical characteristics of underdeveloped economies.

> —*Albert O. Hirschman,* The Strategy of Economic Development *(1958)*

The increasing returns story of poverty traps says that poverty is a failure of coordination.

> —*William Easterly,* The Elusive Quest for Growth: Economists' Adventures and Misadventures in the Tropics *(2002)*

BETWEEN 1983 AND 1999, real GDP in Ghana grew at about 4.3% per year, accelerating to about 6.5% per year between 2000 and 2012. Over this period, agriculture's share of employment declined and the service share increased. Yet, Ghana failed to achieve structural transformation—that is, it failed to achieve substantial shift of resources from low- to high-productivity sectors because the labor that left agriculture moved to low-, rather than high-, productivity services (Osei et al. 2018).

At the turn of the twentieth century, the Uruguayan government's home-steading policy had allocated land to many independent farmers and ranchers.

In 1911, wages were high, and Uruguay began assembling a generous welfare state. Relatively prosperous conditions continued until the early 1950s, when France started protecting its meat and wool markets and other countries succeeded in marketing and exporting traditional Uruguayan exports: meat, wool, and leather. In response, the Uruguayan government instituted a program of import substitution industrialization (ISI) that involved constructing steel, textile, shoe, and electrical equipment factories. Commenting on the outcome, Jane Jacobs writes, "The scheme could not have worked because Montevideo itself lacked the ranges of skills, the symbiotic nests of producers' goods and services, and the practice at improvising and adapting necessary to make import-replacing a practical economic endeavor. Montevideo . . . had no foundation for the kind of versatile production that was now desperately needed" (1984, 62).

In 1973, South Korea started implementing the second phase of its industrial policy, an export-oriented *big push*, driven by security fears that accompanied the large US troop withdrawal from Asia. Prior developments had created necessary preconditions. Korea's early 1950s land reform increased agricultural productivity and facilitated substantial educational gains (You 2013). The 1960–72 first-wave industrial policy had focused on textiles, footwear, and wood, with attention to earning foreign exchange via exports, combined with extensive investment in education (Doner, Ritchie, and Slater 2005; Sen 2013). The post-1973 policy shifted resources to capital-intensive industries (steel, metals, shipbuilding, machinery, electronics, nonpetroleum chemicals) and generated benefits for nontargeted forward-linked (downstream) industries by lowering prices for downstream buyers. Complementary export promotion allowed the targeted industries to import intermediate inputs, which increased competition among upstream suppliers. South Korea's prior development of state capacity contributed to the success of the policy (Lane 2017). In these endeavors, the state coordinated interests, monitored firm performance, and "maintained sufficient autonomy from private interests to impose reciprocity" (Doner et al. 2005, 346).

Why did Ghana and Uruguay, unlike South Korea, fail to achieve both structural transformation and growth?

Development requires a mix of multidimensional individual and group capabilities, along with sufficient coordination to utilize them. Unfortunately, underlying properties of knowledge, productive skills, social imitation, and various spillovers and production externalities engender significant coordination problems that pose CAPs of unequal and uneven development. The second hypothesis follows.

H2: Inherent complementarities that emerge from the nonrival properties of knowledge, skill matching, social imitation, and production externalities, separately and in combination, generate uneven locational and sectoral agglomerations of production, knowledge acquisition, innovation, and growth.

Centers of innovation (Silicon Valley) and poverty traps (rural Kentucky, Sierra Leone) operate at multiple levels: national, regional, local, and sectoral. This contrast exists even within relatively small areas, such as neighborhoods within New York City, Cape Town, and Mexico City. These patterns reflect unresolved coordination CAPs and, concurrently, generate CAPs of unequal development, often with excess conflict.

This chapter develops H2 by utilizing endogenous growth, spatial location, skill clustering, social imitation, and production externality theory. It merges four basic assertions from the literature.

1. From spatial location theory (the new economic geography; e.g., Krugman 1991): Because complementary, nonrival knowledge generates increasing returns, locations with established knowledge can innovate and grow more quickly than others. Distinct locational economic equilibria, often with growing inequity among them, follow. This assertion helps explain instances of growth divergence across nations, regions, locations, and sectors.

2. From skill clustering or O-ring theory (Kremer 1993): Skill complementarities in production processes generate incentives—on both sides of the labor market—for matching highly skilled workers with similar workers, leaving residual low-skill matches. An ensuing clustering of productive human capital generates uneven sectoral and locational distributions of productivity, remuneration, and growth.

3. From social imitation theory (e.g., Durlauf 2006): Group-based proclivities for social imitation—conformity effects that emerge from intrinsic reciprocity and complementary social norms—generate unequal social incentives for investment in human capital. This pattern reinforces both skill clustering and knowledge agglomeration, exacerbating tendencies toward distinct unequal locational and sectoral distributional equilibria.[1]

4. From theories of inter- and intrasectoral production externalities (e.g., big push theory, as in Rosenstein-Rodan [1943] and linkage theory, as in Hirschman [1958]): Externalities that arise from complementarities of production generate distinct production equilibria—notably, the simultaneous presence of modern (complex) and traditional production equilibria. Achieving the former requires resolving a series of coordination CAPs across producers.

These four principles reinforce each other. Operating simultaneously at micro-, meso-, and macrolevels, they imply that developmental processes of innovation, skill matching, social imitation, and coordinating production inherently create, or lead to, starkly uneven patterns of distribution and growth. Centers of innovation and poverty equilibria emerge at multiple scales—regions, nations, provinces, cities, and even neighborhoods. A host of coordination CAPs follow, as do multiple CAPs that underlie and emerge from such economic inequity.

This chapter's discussion proceeds as follows. Section 1 develops assertions 1–3. It uses a relatively simple model of location- or sector-based technological innovation to illustrate how knowledge complementarity, increasing returns, skill complementarities, and patterns of social imitation affect regional and sectoral rates of innovation. CAPs of unequal development, including poverty traps and innovation centers, follow. Section 2 addresses the fourth assertion. It opens by discussing the pecuniary externalities of the big push theory and then adds complementary factors, such as imperfect capital markets. These interactions create additional impetus that reinforces Section 1's unequal developmental outcomes. Section 3 considers how rural–urban migration influences these locational dynamics. The chapter closes by reiterating its primary implications: fundamental production processes related to knowledge, skill, social interaction, and a set of corresponding complementarities and externalities generate stark economic inequities—that is, unless policy successfully alters economic outcomes. CAPs of unequal access and distribution, with associated social conflicts, thus permeate development processes on global, national, regional, and local scales.

Section 1: Knowledge, Skill Clusters, Social Imitation, and Agglomerations

This section addresses the knowledge, skill matching, and social imitation assertions (1–3) in order.

Assertion 1: Nonrival Knowledge and
Agglomerations of Innovation

The growth literature, both neoclassical and endogenous, puts forward the proposition that technological advance, as it interacts with labor, physical capital, and human capital, offers the key (proximate) source of economic growth (e.g., Solow 1957; Romer 1990). The knowledge that permeates these interactions has both social and individual dimensions. *Technology*—that is, knowledge concerning processes of production—is social; it is shared across various groupings of individuals within and/or across production teams, firms, regions, nations, and so on.[2] Furthermore, technology has both technical and organizational dimensions. The former concerns the science and engineering that underlie processes of physical production; the latter concerns structuring and motivating the social interactions that accompany human labor as the most complicated input into production processes—how to organize teams of human beings to accomplish sequences of specific tasks. The individual dimension of productive knowledge resides in *human capital*— that is, the accumulated stock of knowledge that individuals gain through education and experience relevant to production. As a property of individuals, human capital, unlike social knowledge, is excludable. Economists often consider the aggregate or average human capital of some group and available technology as prerequisites for enhancing productive capability.

Endogenous growth theory builds on the concept of nonrival knowledge and its interactions with human capital. Nonrivalry implies that the costs of creating knowledge need only be borne once; imitators may adopt ideas (though not necessarily practices) at essentially no cost.[3] Consequently, knowledge spills over; people emulate good ideas. Furthermore, new knowledge complements existing knowledge, and complementarity confers increasing returns to investments in knowledge (Romer 1990).

Existing knowledge emerges from interactions between human capital and preexisting, nonrival technological knowledge. Innovation follows this same logic. A simple model illustrates. The current level of technological knowledge (A_t) depends on both the current level of human capital (H_t) and preexisting knowledge (A_{t-1}) so that $A_t = A_t(H_t, A_{t-1})$.[4] The rate of technological advance (the growth of A) can be written as

$$(4.1) \quad \partial A/\partial t = \varphi HA.$$

The rate of (macro-level) technological change is the product of parameter φ, human capital—especially that related to R&D—and the existing stock of technological knowledge. Two statements follow. First, the rate of technological advance depends in part on the availability and allocation of human capital. Second, knowledge complementarity implies that knowledge builds on itself. Before developing the theory of relativity, for instance, Albert Einstein had thoroughly absorbed Newtonian physics and calculus.

Spatial location (agglomeration) theory applies knowledge complementarity to geography, operating at both macro- and mesolevels. Interactions between human capital and existing knowledge not only establish foundations for technological advance, they also foster an extraordinarily uneven geographic distribution of production, strikingly unequal standards of living, and similarly unequal rates of growth (Krugman 1991, 1995). This logic follows from two related propositions: First, knowledge spills over; it spreads. People copy good ideas; they imitate successful procedures. In economic terms, knowledge generation confers enormous (often positive) externalities—via nearly costless transmission. Second, knowledge spreads unevenly. Knowledge spillovers occur through networks of unequal quality and dimension—transmission requires some form of connection.[5] Moreover, knowledge spreads only to those who have the capacity to absorb it: those who have acquired sufficient levels of relevant human capital. Most children do not understand relativity. Cognitively limited (boundedly rational) individuals can absorb only so much knowledge, but adaptive learning (acquisition of human capital) improves such capacity. Assertion 1 follows: nonrival knowledge spreads unevenly across groups, generating distinct locational and sectoral equilibria—often with growing inequity among them.

Assertion 2: Skill Clustering

Gary Becker (1971) and Gregory Mankiw, David Romer, and David N. Weil (1992) stress the importance of human capital for advancing productivity and growth, but again, associated dynamics lead to inequities. The skill clustering of O-ring theory leads to uneven agglomerations of human capital in production, which, moreover, reinforce the agglomeration impacts of complementary social knowledge. Most production operates in teams. Within teams, one person's skill level influences the value created by others: human capital is complementary. Consequently, labor markets possess both supply- and demand-side incentives to match highly skilled workers with others of similar skill. Valuing quality, firms screen for such matches, and highly skilled workers earn more when so matched.

A simple equation illustrates. Ignoring capital and assuming only two workers:

(4.2) $a_j = q_1 q_2,$

where a_j is labor productivity in sector (or firm) j, and q signifies the skill level (quality of production) of workers 1 and 2; $0 < q \leq 1$. A worker with $q = 0.9$ produces more when matched with another 0.9 than with a 0.1 worker.[6] Consequently, less skilled workers, who would benefit from working with more highly skilled colleagues, often cannot do so because firms and highly skilled workers both place greater value on high-high matches. Equation (4.2) thus implies sectoral- and firm-specific skill clustering—agglomerations of human capital.

Furthermore, the combined influences of labor turnover and product quality complementarities that exist among firms from different sectors within the same location create incentives for similar agglomerations of human capital—again, at national, regional, and local levels. If firm A produces roads and firm B produces automobiles, firm B's local sales value may depend on the quality of firm A's local output (Basu 2000a, 38–39). A corresponding location-specific version of equation (4.2) states: $a_L = q_j q_k$, where j and k represent distinct sectors that draw labor from the same pool and/or sectors that experience product quality complementarities; q_j and q_k each reflect a sector quality. New York City attracts highly skilled financiers, lawyers, architects, and so on. Rural Kentucky does not and, consequently, experiences much lower per capita income.[7] The same applies to downtown Mexico City contrasted with the state of Morelos.

Assertion 3: Social Imitation, with a Model of Assertions 1–3
Social imitation theory (e.g., Durlauf 2006) implies that imitation processes reinforce localized knowledge and skill complementarities. Specifically, individual decisions to invest in acquiring new human capital respond in part to group-based social incentives that accompany role-model and peer effects, along with related incentives from various forms of coordination. These influences have three basic sources: reciprocal motivations, relevant social norms, and dependencies of individual payoffs on group attributes (as already implied by skill matching).

Another simple model can illustrate the combined influences of assertions 1–3. Standard economic logic implies that when individuals expect sufficient returns, they invest time and effort into acquiring human capital. From as-sertions 1–3, an individual's return to knowledge acquisition (r_{hi}) depends on her present human capital (h_i), the average human capital (skills) of locally available coworkers (H_L), the available stock of local social knowledge (A_L), which is a function of the local social network connections (Γ_L), and pertinent social norms related to reciprocal interactions (Ψ_{RL}).[8] Note that in addition to influencing social incentives, norms (as shared mental models), along with anticipated patterns of conformity, influence agents' understandings of re-lationships between their existing human capital and possible returns to ad-ditional investment.[9] In an environment dominated by conflict among rival warlords, for example, investments in learning mathematics most likely yield low returns. Such expected returns also depend on the available knowledge infrastructure K_{HL} (e.g., schools). In summary, investments in acquiring new human capital pay if

$$(4.3) \quad r_{hi}(h_i, H_L, \Psi_{RL}, A_L(\Gamma_L), K_{HL}) > r_{fl},$$

where r_{fl} is the return to no investment (e.g., working in the fields). Equa-tion (4.3) addresses individual (micro-level) decisions that, in sum, influence meso- and macro-level outcomes. Four implications follow: First, individu-als will not invest in knowledge acquisition unless their expected return, r_{hi}, is sufficiently high. This notion alone can explain a great deal of apparently irrational behavior, such as the failure of individuals in many localities and social contexts to invest in human capital acquisition that could pay off—were they situated elsewhere. Second, new human capital builds on existing human capital (the role of h_i). Third, the skill complementarities implied by H_L and group reciprocity effects implied by Ψ_{RL} signify that individual returns to knowledge investment depend on the attributes and expected investment decisions of potential colleagues, friends, and local role models.[10] Fourth, the surrounding knowledge context, represented by terms A_L and K_{HL}, condition these relationships: high levels of either term enhance r_{hi}, *ceteris paribus*. Ul-timately, (4.3) implies multiple possible investment equilibria, in particular both high and low human capital equilibria.

For given levels of A, K, and Γ, moving from a low to a high equilibrium requires resolving an, often substantial, coordination CAP among local ac-tors; it requires an expectation of simultaneous investment on the part of a critical mass of participants. Figure 4.1's simple multiplayer game of assur-ance illustrates the basic problem.

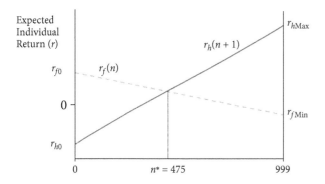

LEGEND: n = the number of *other* local individuals expected to invest; r_h and r_f, respectively, signify expected returns to investing in human capital and working in the fields.

FIGURE 4.1 Multiplayer Human Capital Investment Game

Each individual from a group of 1,000 decides between strategies h (invest in human capital) and f (work in the fields) to receive respective returns r_h and r_f. In linear form, holding other factors constant, we can write both returns as functions of the number of *other* group members (n) who a given individual expects to choose h:

(4.4) $r_h = rh_0 + \beta_h(n + 1)$ and

(4.5) $r_f = rf_0 + \beta_f(n)$,

where β_j shows the impact of a change in n on each r_j ($\beta_j = \partial r_j / \partial n$, which is assumed constant). Human capital return r_h increases in n, reflecting the joint influences of skill matching and conformity effects from reciprocity norms.[11] The negative payoff at r_{h0} represents an expected negative social sanction for nonconformity; likewise, r_{hMax} represents the maximum conformity payoff to investing. A mirror-image logic applies to r_f illustrated by its downward slope as the expected return moves from conformity payoff r_{f0} to nonconformity payoff r_{fMin}.

This model has three equilibria: one stable equilibrium at $n = 0$, with the individual choosing f; another stable equilibrium and at $n = 999$, with the individual choosing h; and an unstable internal equilibrium at n^*. The accompanying dynamics illustrate the gist of the coordination CAP. At both stable equilibria, the individual payoff to continuing the indicated strategy exceeds that from shifting, and small deviations create incentives to return to the initial equilibrium. Path dependence follows. Either stable equilibrium persists until a noticeable shift in underlying parameters or group expectations alters the incentives.[12]

The unstable third equilibrium ($n = n^*$) at which the individual is indifferent between h and f, illustrates the model's critical-mass property. A small deviation from n^* in either direction induces continued movement in that same direction—reflecting a positive-feedback (increasing returns) dynamic (the larger n, the greater r_h, and vice versa).[13] The coordination CAP logically follows: from an initial position at $n = 0$, individuals have no incentive to invest unless they expect a critical mass of others ($n > n^*$) to do so. The positive-feedback dynamic, moreover, suggests a self-fulfilling prophecy of shared expectations: initial expectations concerning n's relation to n^* influence subsequent equilibrium outcomes, and so become self-fulfilling.

Finally, the model's key parameters, r_{h0}, r_{f0}, β_h, and β_f, each depend on structural influences from the relevant social context, represented by equation (4.3)'s arguments H_L, Ψ_{RL}, $A_L(\Gamma_L)$, and K_{HL}. They may also reflect factors such as expected political stability (γ). For example, we can write

$$(4.6) \quad r_{h0} = r_{h0}(H_L, \Psi_L, A_L(\Gamma_L), K_L, \gamma_L).$$

If no one else invests, the return to investing in human capital in a specific area is low and well below the return from working in the fields, as shown in Figure 4.1. Nevertheless, an increase in H_L, A_L, Γ_L, K_L, and/or favorable changes in Ψ_L and/or γ_L shift the r_h function upward, moving n^* to the left, signifying a somewhat less difficult coordination CAP. These same changes could also increase β_h, augmenting this effect by rotating the r_h function upward. For example, in 1979 Bangladesh, investing in acquiring knowledge related to textile production would likely offer a very low return (low r_{h0}). That year, however, the Daewoo Corporation trained 130 Bangladeshi Desh Garment workers in South Korea. When the workers returned to Bangladesh, local textile-relevant human capital and knowledge (H_L and A_L) increased substantially, as did the relevant network for transferring textile knowledge (Γ_L). The entire r_h function for local textile production would correspondingly shift upward, arguably facilitating the achievement of a critical mass of local investors. As it turns out, by 1985, Bangladesh was a major producer of textiles.[14] More generally, sufficiently high values for the arguments of equation (4.6), as might be the case in areas with high levels of political and economic development, could eliminate the coordination CAP. Nevertheless, the uneven distribution of these underlying arguments, as implied by assertions 1–3 (and 4) once again suggests starkly uneven location- and sector-based investments in human capital and thus productivity growth.

Returning now to the rate of innovation, an augmented version of equation (4.1) incorporates sector-specific influences of these variables:

(4.7) $\partial A_j/\partial t = \varphi H_j(r_{hj}(\mu_j, \Psi_{RL}, A_L(\Gamma_L), K_L, \gamma_L) - r_{fj}(\cdot)) \times A_L(\Gamma_{LL})$.

The growth of technological know-how in a specific sector j depends on parameter φ and [resembling (4.1)] the product $H_j \times A_L$, where subscript j signifies *sector*. "Sector" may refer to a location, industry, field of knowledge, or any combination of these elements. Subscript L signifies the same possible entities at a somewhat more aggregated *local* level, where the relevant extent of aggregation may differ across variables. Here, the achieved amount of local human capital (H_j) depends on the return difference $r_{hj} - r_{fj}$, where both terms depend on sector skill matching from skill complementarity (μ_j) and local variables Ψ_{RL}, $A_L(\Gamma_L)$, K_L, and γ_L, as previously defined [$r_{fj}(\cdot)$ signifies this same dependence].[15] With low values of the arguments, $r_{hj} - r_{fj} < 0$. With a low H_j, the product $H_j \times A_L$ remains low, as does $\partial A_j/\partial t$.

CAPs of unequal development follow. Areas and sectors that possess substantial preexisting knowledge, high levels of human capital, strong network connections, supportive norms, substantial knowledge infrastructure, and strong institutions offer high incentives for investing in human capital and technological knowledge. Virtuous circles of innovation and growth follow. Absent these conditions, weak or nonexistent incentives for knowledge investment generate poverty traps.[16] Indeed, poverty traps can emerge from initial (self-fulfilling) expectations of noninvestment implied by phenomena such as established practices of children working in the fields after primary school. Second-order CAPs of coordinating a reversal of expectations across relevant groups follow. These CAPs—themselves outcomes of prior development processes—condition prospects for future development.

Section 2: How Production Externalities Enhance CAPs of Unequal Development

Production externalities, as the fourth source of locational complementarity, reinforce Section 1's outcomes at the macrolevel of national production, as well as for various meso-level production sectors and locations. Inter- and intrasectoral demand externalities jointly imply production complementarities that point to distinct developmental equilibria, again including poverty traps. Discussion begins with (largely macro-level) pecuniary externalities posited by big push development theory. It then addresses externalities that accompany within-sector production linkages, labor market thickness, training, capital market imperfections, and information discovery.

P. N. Rosenstein-Rodan's (1943) and Ragnar Nurske's (1953) big push concept offers an initial approach to developmental coordination that stresses pecuniary externalities associated with production decisions. A summary model (Murphy, Shleifer, and Vishny 1989) illustrates. Here, the presence of pecuniary demand externalities creates the possibility of two equilibria: one with and one without modernization. The basic model assumes a closed economy, but the argument also fits open-economy cases in which the modern sector benefits from domestic demand.[17] Assume the economy has two segments: traditional and modern. Both produce all products (i.e., operate in all sectors), though with different efficiencies. The traditional segment is competitive, has no fixed costs, and operates with constant returns to scale. Its wages, prices, and labor productivity are all normalized to 1. By contrast, modern production, which has an elastic labor supply, offers increasing returns to scale but faces fixed costs (F) to initiating production and must pay higher wages ($w_M > 1$).[18] For simplicity, assume one modern firm per (differentiated) product. Even so, competition from the traditional sector forces its product price to 1. Modern firms generate (small) positive demand externalities for each other because each payment of w_M contributes to domestic product demand.

At the outset, the entire economy operates in the traditional segment. If a single firm were to modernize, the demand for its product would not justify paying F and w_M.[19] But, if firms in all product markets modernize simultaneously, multiple payments of w_M would generate sufficient demand to support high wages—on account of pecuniary externalities. Two equilibria follow: either no firms modernize or they all do. At the outset, then, firms face a (second-order) coordination CAP like that represented by Figure 4.1 at its no-invest equilibrium. More specifically, a sector j firm modernizes only if

(4.8) $r_{Mj}(a_j(y_j(D_j(m))); F_j) > r_T$,

where r_{Mj} is a single-sector j firm's expected return to modernization, a function of sector productivity (a_j) and fixed costs (F_j). With increasing returns, a_j depends on sector output (y_j), a function of sector demand (D_j), which, in turn, depends on m, the expected number of modernizing firms in the economy; r_T represents the return on traditional production, assumed fixed. Market forces alone will not resolve this (second-order) coordination CAP of moving from $m = 0$ past a relevant m^* tipping point, but some type of big push policy intervention could do so.

This coordination logic applies more generally. Four additional factors influence relationships between fixed costs, increasing returns, and pecuniary externalities.

- Providing infrastructure can lower F_j and increase a_j at any given $y_j(D_j(m))$, reducing the m^* hurdle for modernization. Infrastructure investment (public or private), however, has many public good attributes and often cannot be justified unless a sufficient number of firms modernize. Why build a new highway for only one firm? An analogous coordination CAP follows—in addition to a first-order H1 CAP of funding infrastructure.

- Similarly, technological innovation can reduce F_j and increase a_j for a given $y_j(D(m))$; it can also augment the rate of increasing returns (i.e., increase $\partial a_j / \partial y_j(D(m))$). Consequently, the knowledge, skill, and conformity coordination CAPs of Section 1's assertions 1–3 and equations (4.3)–(4.7) influence production externalities, reinforcing the coordination and inequity CAPs that accompany distinct levels and rates of locational, sectoral, and economy-wide modernization.

- Imperfect capital markets generate credit constraints and collateral requirements that interfere with financing otherwise profitable endeavors, especially those with long-term payoff horizons (Stiglitz 1999), enhancing the severity of fixed-cost barriers to either unilateral or coordinated modernization.[20]

- Risk aversion can interfere. For example, farmers living close to subsistence maximize their probability of survival rather than expected income (Weitz 1971), providing another impediment to adopting new technologies. This logic also applies to urban informal-sector entrepreneurs. In either case, perceptions of risk often respond to the actions and perceptions of neighbors and colleagues, involving Section 1's conformity dynamics. Moreover, imperfect capital and insurance markets exacerbate the implied coordination CAPs. Since insurance has public good attributes, H1 CAPs also enter.

Jointly or separately, these production phenomena often lead to poverty-trap equilibria.[21]

Seven related dynamics reinforce both this macro-level coordination logic, as well as Section 1's three assertions, in a manner that informs meso-level sectoral and locational coordination CAPs. These dynamics, moreover, can induce middle-income traps.[22]

The first four dynamics relate directly to product sectors.

1. Specific industries face different production functions and wages. Within a particular industrial sector, firms may encounter sufficiently low fixed costs and immediate increasing returns to justify unilateral modernization—circumventing the big push coordination problem. In such cases, countries may experience partial, sector-specific moderni-zation with little or no coordinating policy. The vibrant textile industry in Bangladesh (with some external inducement and knowledge transfer from the South Korean firm Daewoo, along with protection from the Multifiber Arrangement [MFA] from 1974 to 2004, which limited tex-tile exports from competitors, such as South Korea) offers an example.[23]

2. If a single firm in a specific sector modernizes, it may achieve econo-mies of scale that create fixed-cost entry barriers for potential com-petitors. Technological advance may lag because a protected monopo-list has little incentive to adopt technological improvements achieved elsewhere, and potential entrants, who would adopt new methods, cannot overcome the barrier.

Conditions 1 and 2 imply potential for middle-income traps, reflecting partial modernization. Two additional conditions complicate matters.

3. Connections among modern firms involving backward and forward product linkages create pecuniary externalities among them.[24] A single modern firm may not generate sufficient input demand from upstream firms (backward linkages) to justify its modernization, but simulta-neous modernization among several firms from sectors with similar input requirements could prompt upstream investment. Sector-related coordination CAPs follow.

4. Single producers of new products in an area rarely have the capability of, themselves, addressing many downstream contingencies related to transportation, logistics, various standards, marketing, distribution,

and so forth. "So the firm is stuck with unattractive options—dealing with third-party brokers, poor transport links, ineffective marketing, and so on" (Hausmann and Rodrik 2005, 74). But if a sufficient number of firms engage in related forms of modern production, they could either coordinate on providing these services or, jointly operating at a larger scale, hire more qualified contractors.

Three additional points imply that pecuniary production externalities also have local dimensions that again engender coordination CAPs of attaining a critical mass.

5. Modernization often requires *thick labor markets*—that is, markets with a sophisticated division of labor with multiple gradations of skills that characterize complex production. As Adam Smith asserted, the degree of the division of labor depends on the extent of the market. Hence, firms operating in large markets generate additional positive externalities by supporting a sophisticated division of labor. Furthermore, the skill, knowledge, and conformity principles from Section 1 influence prospects for developing thick labor markets—additional coordination CAPs.

6. Much production-oriented training takes place on the job. Some such training is broadly applicable (general) and some is firm specific. Firms have large incentives to train workers in firm-specific skills and little incentive to offer general training that could facilitate workers finding alternative employment (Doeringer and Piore 1985). Yet, interfirm labor mobility conveys information about production techniques (Hausmann and Rodrik 2005). Because on-the-job general training confers positive externalities, firms underinvest from a social point of view. Coordination, however, could improve outcomes. Reflecting Section 1's principles, a clustering of firms can facilitate such information exchanges, enhancing prospects for general skill on-the-job training. The associated coordination CAPs, with critical-mass thresholds, thus apply to specific areas, specific sectors, as well as across sectors with similar technologies.

7. Considerable uncertainty, with multiple opportunities for failure, surrounds prospects of investing in new production techniques and products within locations and sectors. An investing entrepreneur

risks the costs of failure but, due to knowledge spillovers and competition, receives only a portion of any gain from success—another type of positive externality, with an associated H1 CAP. Furthermore, the various accompanying trial-and-error processes generate new information about how to apply technology within specific contexts— another social benefit that arises even in cases of failure. Without some assurance of coordination of experimentation across related types of production, entrepreneurs will hesitate to invest (Ibid.).

Noting location-based applications of this logic, Paul Krugman (1995) asserts that the big push model's assumptions are more plausible when combined with arguments from economic geography. For example, because one region can draw labor from another, regional labor supplies are often elastic even when a national labor supply is not. As Ritchie Lowry (1964; cited in Krugman 1995) suggests, firms locate where markets are large, and large markets exist where firms locate; pecuniary externalities operate within locations. Local investment and lack thereof are both self-reinforcing (positive-feedback) phenomena with corresponding high and low investment equilibria.

With related logic, Jacobs (1984) asserts that cities are the foundations of innovation and growth, both internally and for their regions. Cities develop as regional centers of production when local innovations generate opportunities for local production of items that the city had previously imported from elsewhere (regional import substitution). When such innovations occur, five types of growth ensue:

i. expanding city markets for rural goods and goods from other cities (pecuniary demand externalities);

ii. increasing numbers and kinds of jobs within the city (thicker labor markets);

iii. the transplanting of some city work to other locations with the crowding out of old methods of city production—beneficial for regional development (regional production externalities);

iv. increasing rural productivity from new uses of technology (knowledge spillovers); and

v. increasing city capital (investment response to innovation).

While not stated formally, this argument implies economies of scope, in addition to beneficial externalities from improved backward and forward linkages, thicker labor markets, and enhanced information exchange. Jacobs's argument also implies that urban innovation—when it occurs—generates a type of balance between urban and rural growth that can operate with backward and forward linkages.

Pulling together many of these principles, Krugman (1995) offers a model of modernization that incorporates a locational externality logic. Here is a brief summary. There are two sectors: an immobile agricultural sector and a manufacturing sector in which firms can move, but only over time. Manufacturing operates with scale economies under monopolistic competition (differentiated products; from Dixit and Stiglitz 1977); not all potential goods are produced.[25] Manufacturing firms base their locational decisions on expected market potential and transportation costs. Specifically, they weigh expected demand and scale economies against transportation costs. The model exhibits a cumulative causation that emerges from location-based pecuniary externalities. Firms move to attractive (demand-rich) areas, thereby increasing the attractiveness of such areas. Firms cast an agglomeration shadow that benefits adjacent regions (resembling Jacobs's innovative cities). In contrast, omitted areas become increasingly unattractive—that is, they become poverty traps.

Along similar lines, a model that augments equation (4.8) with elements from (4.3)–(4.7) can represent this combined sector-relevant externality and innovation logic of modern-sector investment. Two quite general equations—one for the return on sectoral investment and the other for a sectoral rate of innovation—point to the core idea. A modern firm's fixed costs, average productivity, and rate of increasing returns all depend on its accumulated human capital H_j, which reflects the skill matching of its labor force (μ_j); the local available knowledge (A_L), which, as in (4.3), depends on the local network (Γ_L); and on the knowledge infrastructure (K_L). In this formulation, Γ_L incorporates both backward and forward production linkages as well as location-specific connections (not shown as separate variables). Network connections of production, purchase, and local encounters not only influence demand-induced flows of output and revenue—with impacts on scale economies—they also influence multiple flows of knowledge via labor turnover and various other exchanges, possibly involving productive capital and technology. The creation, utilization, and maintenance of such linkages, moreover, depends (in part) on the expected demand for local and sectoral products, D_L. The pecuniary externalities of modernization thus not only influence incentives to invest in productive capital and knowledge, they also influence the very development of network connections. Ensuing transmissions of knowledge, product demand, and input supplies thus flow along backward and forward linkages as well as within and across locational networks—be they local, regional, national, or international.[26]

An expanded version of equation (4.8) may then represent a single-sector j firm's incentives to invest in modern production. The firm invests if

$$(4.9) \quad r_{Mj}\big(a_j\big(y_j\big(D_j(m_L, m)\big)\big), H_j(\mu_j, \Psi_{RL}, r_j), A_L(H_L, \Gamma_L(\cdot)); F_j; K_L; \gamma_L; \Phi_L; \Omega_L(D_L(m_L, m))\big) > r_T.$$

Here, r_{Mj}, r_T, D_j, F_j, and m remain defined as in (4.8); subscript L signifies combined local and sectoral influences, reflecting backward and forward linkages as well geographic location; $H_j(\mu_j, \Psi_{RL}, r_j)$ shows sector human capital as a function of sector skill matching, norms, and r_j. Locally available knowledge, A_L, depends on H_L (which depends on r_L, not shown) and on $\Gamma_L(\cdot)$, where $(\cdot)$ signifies that Γ_L's depends on $D_L(m_L, m)$ and on H_L. As in (4.3), K_L is local infrastructure (knowledge, communication, transportation, etc.). γ_L is local political stability; Φ_L and Ω_L, respectively, represent capital market imperfections and the thickness of the local labor market, which also depends on D_L. As in the big push model, the dependence of terms r_{Mj}, A_L, Γ_L, and Ω_L on D_L (which depends on m and m_L) reflects the across-firm coordination problem, which now incorporates backward and forward linkages, as well as location-specific demand externalities. Overall, (4.9) implies more substantial and persistent potential for multiple equilibria, including both poverty and middle-income traps—both of which reflect associated multilevel coordination CAPs.

Returning to the rate of innovation, we may now augment equation (4.7) by adding a term for local modern investment (I_{ML}), which, as already implied, depends on local modern returns r_{ML}, $[I_{ML} = I_{ML}(r_{ML})]$. Incorporating the logic of production externalities, both H_L and A_L depend on I_{ML}. Adding I_{ML} and (4.9)'s r_{Mj} function to (4.7), we have

$$(4.10) \quad \partial A_j/\partial t = \varphi H_j\big(I_{ML}(r_{ML}(\cdot))\big) \times A_L\big(\Gamma_L(D_L(m_L, m))\big); I_{ML}(r_{ML}(\cdot)); K_L\big),$$

where $(\cdot)$ represents the arguments from (4.9) applied to local area L. As in (4.7), $\partial A_j/\partial t$ depends on the product $\varphi H_j \times A_L$ and on K_L, reflecting assertions 1–3. As before, A_L depends on local network Γ_L, which now depends on $D_L(m_L, m)$; A_L also depends on modern-sector investment, $I_{ML}(r_{ML})$, accounting for labor market thickness and capital market imperfections [as in (4.9)] . If (4.9) holds for the threshold number of firms (m^*), local firms have an incentive to modernize. Modern investment, in turn, involves some transfer of technology and, simultaneously, induces learning—increasing the often tacit knowledge of production and organizational processes. More generally, the terms I_M, D_L, K_L, Ω_L, and Φ_L incorporate sector- or location-specific and economy-wide production externalities that reinforce the coordination CAPs and inequality dynamics of nonrival knowledge, skill matching, and social imitation.[27]

This sectoral logic thus implies that the coordination logic of big push arguments—in addition to its economy-wide elements—has locational and sectoral dimensions that operate along backward and forward linkages, reinforcing the coordination CAPs associated with knowledge and skill complementarities.

At higher levels of aggregation, several international dynamics further augment tendencies toward poverty and middle-income traps. Theories of dynamic comparative advantage (Grossman and Helpman 1990; Krugman 1981) suggest a complementary logic. Developing countries that follow a static principle of comparative advantage often specialize in exporting traditional-sector primary products, such as sugar, coffee, and cacao, which usually lack economies of scale. This international dynamic reinforces the aforementioned H2 CAPs of modernization. For example, such countries typically do not invest in infrastructure that could support a more diversified base of production.

Three additional factors reinforce these disadvantages. First, developed country tariff policy usually assigns the highest tariffs to agricultural products, restricting the markets for (nonmineral) primary products. Second, because primary products have low income elasticities, their terms of trade decline over time, reducing export revenue. Third, countries that rely on a few primary product exports suffer from price volatility in relevant markets; low demand elasticities, moreover, enhance price volatility.

Returning to a core theme of this text, the simultaneous presence of innovation centers, poverty traps, and middle-income traps generates CAPs of unequal distribution and access at multiple levels. Germany is better off than Mexico, which is better off than Nigeria. Within South Africa, Cape Town is more dynamic than rural Limpopo, but Cape Town has both a modern downtown and informal settlements—often consisting of tiny wooden, cardboard, or tin shacks. New York City has both Wall Street and a large homeless population.

Section 3: Spatial Location, Urbanization, Internal Migration, and Unbalanced Growth

Jacobs's arguments point to the economic importance of urbanization with a potential for innovative, balanced urban-rural growth. Whereas the preceding discussion of innovation clusters could imply that urbanization and modernization go hand in hand, and many developed countries historically experienced a close association between relatively gradual urbanization and industrialization, such an outcome need not occur. Indeed, in many developing countries, rapid rural–urban migration induces rapid urban population growth, and such migration "worsens rural-urban structural imbalances" (Todaro and Smith 2015, 355)—that is, unbalanced growth. *Urbanization without modernization* occurs in much of the developing world. Cape Town's informal settlements offer an example. More broadly, in sub-Saharan Africa, the proportion of the urban population living in slums was 55% in 2014; for Southern Asia 31% (United Nations 2015). These outcomes are consistent with the locational logic of Sections 1 and 2. Certain urban areas (neighborhoods) lack a critical mass of existing technical knowledge, human capital, infrastructure, and productive capacity. Migration often exacerbates such problems.

Broadly speaking, three factors lead to high rates of urban population growth: rapid overall population growth, a push from rural poverty, and a pull from urban development. The Harris-Todaro (1970) model represents such migration as a dynamic that equilibrates the expected net benefits of rural as opposed to urban life. In rural areas, tenant farmers live close to the level of subsistence. Potential migrants move to urban areas when they expect higher net earnings. More precisely, they compare their expected present value of rural earnings (EPV_R) with that for urban earnings (EPV_U). A rate of migration equation represents this logic:[28]

$$(4.11) \quad \partial Mg/\partial t = Mg(EPV_U(\rho_M w_M + \rho_I w_I + (1 - \rho_M - \rho_I)\omega_U) - EPV_R(P_R, \omega_R, \Upsilon)).$$

The rate of rural–urban migration, $\partial Mg/\partial t$, depends on the expected value difference $EPV_U - EPV_R$. EPV_U depends on relatively high urban formal-sector (modern) wages (w_M) and lower informal-sector wages (w_I), accounting for the expected probabilities of gaining employment in these sectors (ρ_M and ρ_I), and on expected unemployment income, including assistance from family members (ω_U), occurring with probability $(1 - \rho_M - \rho_I)$. EPV_R depends on the rural population (P_R), rural earnings (ω_R), and other factors (Υ), such as agricultural commodity prices, patterns of land ownership, the state of rural labor markets, environmental influences including climate change, and rural political stability. Civil wars and extreme droughts, for example, induce considerable push migration.

Three conclusions follow. First, wage differentials lead to rural–urban migration even in the presence of significant urban unemployment and the absence of urban innovation. Urbanization without modernization ensues. Second, the model provides additional rationale for Section 1's assertion that poverty pockets exist within urban areas. Third, many conditions and policies that, in the absence of migration, could reduce overall urban poverty may not do so. For example, increases in urban education may push up EPV_U (via w_M), leading to more migration and more unemployment.[29]

The unbalanced development implied by this model exacerbates the CAPs of unequal innovation and development discussed in Sections 1 and 2. Forms of development that would benefit urban populations in the absence of migration—such as technological advances or improved public services— often fail to do so for metropolitan areas because rising wages (or other benefits of urban living) induce more migration and higher unemployment.

To sum up this chapter's arguments, the coordination CAPs that emerge from transmissions of knowledge, skill complementarities, social influence, and a host of, often sectoral and locational, production externalities—along with rapid rural–urban migration—generate starkly unequal locational and sectoral patterns of development. These include unequal rates of innovation and growth, unequal distributions of wealth, income, education, health care and other services, along with unequal rates of population growth and limited capabilities for accommodating new migrants. In addition to economic deprivation across broad segments of populations, these factors also generate unequal distributions of power and myriad social conflicts that foster yet another large set of developmental CAPs—with significant political dimensions. Chapter 5 discusses a version of social conflict theory that addresses such conflicts and political constraints on development.

5 Power, Social Conflict, Institutional Formation, and Credible Commitment

Society is a game with rules, people are players in this game, and politics is the arena in which we affirm and change these rules.
—*Herbert Gintis*, Individuality and Entanglement: The Moral and Material Bases of Social Life *(2017)*

THE ENGLISH CIVIL WAR and the Glorious Revolution of 1688 shifted the balance of power between the monarch and Parliament in favor of the latter. In 1689, Parliament passed the Declaration of Rights, which limited the monarch's power by, for example, forbidding a standing army without the consent of Parliament. It also altered and created economic institutions. Parliament abolished the Royal African Company monopoly and ended a tax on fireplaces—the hearth tax that disproportionately affected manufacturing. In 1694, Parliament established the Bank of England, an action that facilitated banking and credit expansion. Nearly three centuries later, after achieving independence from Great Britain in 1961, the socialist government of Tanganyika (named Tanzania after 1964), led by Julius Nyerere, established the Tanganyika African National Union (TANU) as the sole political party, nationalized the banks and certain industries, instituted free universal public education, and implemented import-substitution policies. In both of these cases, shifts in political power led to the creation of new political and economic institutions.

Political economy addresses how distributions and exercises of power, by both private and public parties, affect economic and political interactions and, ultimately, development. Traditionally, the disciplines of economics and political science have conceptualized power in informative but limited fashions, emphasizing government exercises of power, union-employer bargaining, and monopoly power. Recent works, however, point to deeper and more pervasive roles for power—exercises related to acquiring assets, defining and enforcing property rights, and seeking various forms of distributional advantage, even within exchange processes (e.g., Bowles 2004; Bardhan 2005; Acemoglu and Robinson 2008). Indeed, economic and political institutions are both outcomes of and foundations for exercises of power.

This chapter develops our two social conflict hypotheses: H3 and H4. Jointly, these hypotheses concern how distributions of power—key axes of social conflict—affect political economic outcomes by influencing institutional evolution and the credibility of related commitments. H3 addresses institutional impacts: Unequal distributions of power shape the creation, evolution, and demise of economic and political institutions. H4 points to implications: Powerful parties, left to themselves, cannot credibly commit to refrain from using their power for their own future benefit. Jointly, these hypotheses imply significant CAPs related to unequal political and economic influence combined with problems of creating (and maintaining) a set of provisions that credibly limit both the ability and desire of powerful parties—private and public—to seize the gains from others' efforts and investments, economic and political.

This chapter's discussion proceeds as follows. Section 1 introduces H3, with background on power: its sources, manifestations, instruments, and domains. Section 2 illustrates H3's core logic with a dynamic flowchart, a slightly modified version of one that appears in Daron Acemoglu, Simon Johnson, and James Robinson (2004). The diagram traces paths of influence from sources and manifestations of power to political and economic institutions and subsequent outcomes that feed back into sources of power. These interactions confer a punctuated equilibrium dynamic to institutional evolution. In so doing, they generate formidable sets of CAPs that accompany creating, reforming, and dismantling political and economic institutions that, in turn, condition developmental trajectories and outcomes. On this foundation, Section 3 addresses H4's CAPs of commitment, using a model of an economic hold-up problem to illustrate. Finally, Section 4 develops two additional implications: (1) Elites may use their disproportionate access to de facto power to undermine reforms that threaten their interests, sometimes capturing democratic institutions; and (2) Creating social order requires establishing some form of political settlement that entails mutual understandings among powerful parties that establish politics, rather than violence, as the principal method for settling disputes. Additional developmental CAPs, such as how to reduce corruption without unduly undermining political stability, follow.

Section 1: Power—Sources, Manifestations, Dyads, and Triads

As the examples at the opening of this chapter illustrate, distributions of power condition institutional evolution. More precisely:

> **H3**: Unequal distributions of power shape the creation, evolution, and demise of economic and political institutions.

Five basic assertions underlie this hypothesis. First, recall that *economic institutions* are mutually understood and expected informal and formal behavioral prescriptions that address allocating (scarce) resources. As such, they specify procedures for coordinating exchange. They assign property rights (either selective or universal), rights of economic access, mechanisms of contract enforcement, and procedures for addressing market failures related to public goods, common resources, externalities, incomplete information, and macroeconomic stability. Economic institutions structure material incentives, shape flows of information, influence expectations, and—as shared mental models— shape participants' understandings of core economic activities, including the following: how to attain employment and acquire capital; the returns to labor and to investing in physical, financial, and human capital; distributions of output; procedures for applying land, labor, and capital to production; and prospects for technological change. For example, under the institutions of Western European feudalism, most wealth holders lacked a contemporary understanding of investment: they did not conceive of investing a portion of their inherited wealth for the purpose of making money (Heilbroner 1992).

Economic institutions thus structure processes of exchange, production, growth, and distribution. Institutional arrangements for managing H2 and H1 CAPs related to coordinating production and providing public goods, including defining and enforcing economic rights, facilitate growth by allowing specified parties to reap returns from their efforts and investments in skills, technology, and capital—albeit with distributional consequences and attendant externalities. Social arrangements to provide public goods and limit negative externalities confer benefits to segments of relevant populations, though private valuations of such benefits may differ across individuals or groups, and some nominally public goods operate as selective club goods. Moreover, property rights, when enforced—selectively or not—shape distributional outcomes by regulating, for the economic sphere, who gets what, when, and how.[1]

Second, because economic institutions shape distributional outcomes, conflicts of interest permeate their creation and evolution. Parties with political power tend to dominate such conflicts—because they can. Consequently, powerful parties—principally elites and organizations—shape the formation and modification of economic institutions in manners that fit their own understandings and goals, reflecting their material interests as well as concerns for reputation and power.

Third, because political institutions prescribe rules for allocating decision-making authority, powerful parties also have interests in their design. They use their power to shape the formation and evolution of political institutions as well. Fourth, by specifying positions of authority, political institutions are themselves a key source of power. Consequently, political institutions influence the creation, evolution, and demise of economic institutions. Fifth, the distributional outcomes arising from economic institutions feed back into the distribution of resources as a source of power.

Some background concepts of power will inform the subsequent discussion.

Concepts of Power

Combining ideas from Robert Dahl (1957), Michael Taylor (1982), and Steven Lukes (1974), I define power for this text as follows: party A's *power* is its ability to influence the incentives facing one or more other parties (B) and/or influence B's understanding of such incentives in a manner that affects B's activity in directions favorable to A's goals that B, if rational, would not have otherwise taken. Note that incentives may be either material or social (e.g., reciprocal response, conformity, status, revenge, etc.).[2] This definition is consistent with the following three properties (articulated by Bowles and Gintis 2008). First, power involves relationships between or among people; it is not a property of an individual in isolation. Second, exercises of power constitute equilibria of relevant strategic interactions—equilibria in appropriately specified games. Party A will not exercise power unless it expects that doing so will generate at least as good an outcome as not exercising power. Correspondingly, party B will not comply unless it believes it has no better alternatives.

Third, exercises of power are "normatively indeterminate" (Ibid., 566); they sometimes generate positive-sum gains. Parents often compel their children to eat well, even when children prefer ice cream. In efficiency wage models, a firm's exercise of power over employees enhances both effort and wages.[3]

There are three fundamental sources of power:

1. Access to resources, including information. Money can fund armies and political campaigns. Knowing an adversary's objectives and capabilities may facilitate impeding or redirecting their efforts.

2. Institutionally designated positions. Legislators, who attain their positions only after following a set of electoral rules, enact laws.

3. Capacities for resolving internal organizational CAPs. All else equal, coherent organizations or coalitions exert more power than disorganized ones. With given resources and positions, a unified political party stands a greater chance of winning an election than a factionalized one; an army with low morale is less likely to prevail.

These foundations of power interact and reinforce each other. Access to resources can facilitate attaining positions and resolving organizational CAPs. Positions can grant access to resources and facilitate resolving organizational CAPs. Resolving organizational CAPs can facilitate greater resource access and the creation or enhancement of institutional positions.

These three sources of power, in turn, influence its *manifestation*, of which there are two types: de facto and de jure power. *De facto power* is immediately operative (on-the-ground) power. It arises from the resolution of organizational CAPs and from investing resources into directly achieving influence via such means as acquiring weapons, paying armies, financing political campaigns, rewarding supporters, and lobbying officials. Distributions of income and wealth, obviously, affect such resource access. On the field, armies and political coalitions exercise de facto power as they adapt to rapidly changing circumstances. Mass protests express de facto power. Even when potent, de facto power, however, tends to be short-lived—unless institutionalized, in which case it becomes—more enduring—de jure power. *De jure* power emerges from positions designated by established formal political institutions—often with support from complementary norms—and from access to similarly designated resources (e.g., assigned budgets). De jure power reflects and grants access to various decision arenas and associated positions (e.g., legislatures, committee chairs, or for the public in democracies, the status of adult citizenship). These two manifestations of power interact. Institutions can designate relatively long-lived resource access, such as designated budgets and assigned staff. Exercises of de facto power can alter institutions and reconfigure designated positions.

Two assertions follow:

1. Elites (parties who possess direct influence on policy) invest resources in attaining de facto power, with attention to the costs and benefits of doing so in specific contexts (Acemoglu and Robinson 2008). Coherent organizations often do the same.

2. For given investments in de facto power, the relative importance of de jure versus de facto power depends on the strength of institutions. Strong institutions enhance de jure power.

Nevertheless, successful exercises of de facto power can disrupt institutional arrangements, sometimes dislodging de jure power—as in the case of revolution. Moreover, a gradual weakening of institutions—that is, institutional decay—increases opportunities for decisive exercises of de facto power.[4]

Exercises of power, be they de facto or de jure, utilize two basic *instruments*: sanctions and manipulative communication. Sanctions may be positive or negative, as in rewards and punishments. By altering incentives (i.e., expected payoffs), actual or threatened sanctions can induce various parties B to undertake actions they would otherwise avoid. Bribes, for example, can persuade officials to grant favors. Likewise, prospects of arrest, physical harm, or job loss can inhibit political protest. Regarding manipulative communication, misleading information, such as false accusations, can inhibit, induce, and alter action. Potential supporters may turn against maligned politicians.

Finally, power operates through three basic domains of influence (or faces; Lukes 1974). Exercises of power directly affect behavior, alter rules of engagement (including access), and manipulate preferences and beliefs concerning the nature or even the existence of conflicts. More precisely, power has three domains of influence:

- *Power1* refers to the direct application of force, bargaining strength, or voting power within a given and well-understood set of rules. In an election with fixed rules, garnering votes constitutes an exercise of power1. In union-management bargaining that operates within established rules (set in contracts, etc.), the proportion of employees belonging to a union influences its bargaining strength: its power1.

- *Power2* refers to altering rules (of the game) and associated expectations concerning others' actions in order to bias subsequent interactions. Exercises of power2 are strategic moves (Schelling 1960). They often deny opponents access to relevant resources or arenas (Bachrach and Baratz 1962). For example, altering rules of voter eligibility constitutes an exercise of power2. The institutionalization of the Jim Crow system of legal segregation effectively disenfranchised the African American population in the US South from circa 1885 until the passage and implementation of the 1965 Voting Rights Act.

- *Power3* refers to manipulating an opponent's preferences and beliefs about the nature of conflict itself—specifically regarding the possibility or appropriateness of opposition, or even the very existence of conflict. Male power holders or leaders of dominant ethnic groups, acting as normative entrepreneurs, may invoke and interpret prevalent social norms to convince potential opponents that challenge is inappropriate. Adept politicians may shift blame, and hence the axis of conflict, to others. Appeals to nationalism may induce citizens to act or vote against their economic interests—effectively eliminating the perception of an economic conflict of interest.[5]

Before addressing how distributions of power shape institutional creation and evolution, it is useful to distinguish two basic classifications of power relationships: dyadic and triadic.

Dyadic and Triadic Power

Georg Simmel (1902) asserts that triadic social relationships—interactions among three or more parties—differ fundamentally from dyadic relationships.[6] In dyads, each participant (be it a person or an organization) largely retains its individual characteristics: "Unions in pairs, as contrasted with those of larger numbers, favor a relatively higher individuality of the participants" (Ibid., 159). Each participant depends entirely on the other for any common action. No "majority which can override the individual" exists (Ibid., 158).

The addition of even one member reconfigures the social dynamic because triads permit majorities. Indeed, triads take on a superindividual character, meaning they exhibit characteristics that their individual constituents simply do not possess. Moreover, triads often facilitate unclear attribution of specific actions—by allowing agents to delegate responsibility to group structure. "It's the system; the way things are." Triads thus allow or encourage individuals to act in manners for which they would not care to assume responsibility (Wolff 1950). Furthermore, each party may act as an intermediary between the others. Consider agents B and C. B shares quality x with C, but not quality y, and C shares x but not z with B. Party A enters, sharing y with B and z with C. Each party could then utilize the reciprocal relationships between any pair (AB, BC, CA) to its own advantage. Because triadic relations offer such potential, whereas dyadic relations do not, triadic power relationships differ fundamentally from dyadic power relationships.

Most conventional discussions and models of power either explicitly or implicitly assume *dyadic power* relationships: ones in which the presence of power involves and influences only two parties (A and B). Such models abstract from any possible involvement of or influence on other parties.[7] This approach has many uses. It can often illustrate relationships between suppliers and purchasers, business partners, duopoly firms, unions and management, two legislative parties, two armies at war, and so on. Moreover, interactions between consumers or firms and the market implicitly involve only dyads because the market exhibits the characteristics of a unified whole or field of interaction. Individuals and firms interact dyadically with the entire field.

Dyadic conceptions of power, nonetheless, have serious limitations for political economy. Often, one cannot discern which party, in fact, exercises power. For example, if party A ends up paying B for a political favor, did A bribe B or did B extort payment from A? Knowledge of context can often resolve these kinds of questions, but dyadic models often fail to represent such asymmetries. More important, many exercises of power—some of which appear dyadic on the surface—do, in fact, involve or affect other parties. This last statement often applies to apparently voluntary exchanges and, more generally, to exercises of power2 and power3.

By incorporating elements of triadic social interactions, triadic models of power offer five key advantages over dyadic models: (i) they directly represent power asymmetry; (ii) they illustrate counterintuitive instances of coercion—specifically, how coercion may infuse apparently voluntary exchanges (Basu 2000b); (iii) they illustrate how power can infuse market exchanges (Bowles and Gintis 1992, 1993; Oleinik 2016); (iv) they illustrate important dynamics of power2 and power3; and (v) triadic models can relate exercises of power to deliberate institutional and policy change.

There are seven basic (somewhat overlapping) *formats* for triadic power relationships, some with a few variations. In formats 1–6, we assume three parties, A, B, and C, in which (for simplicity) party A exercises triadic power over party B or over both B and C. Initially for formats 1–4 and 6, we assume that A, B, and C are single entities (individuals or organizations).[8] In the first five formats, A has a direct interest in relations between B and C, whereas in the sixth, A is (at least relatively speaking) nonpartisan. In format 7, we have parties X, A, B, and sometimes C, where the latter three involve multiple individuals. Here are the basic formats; details follow.[9]

1. *Direct interference*: A can disrupt B's relationship with C and uses such potential to extract concessions from B.

2. *Denial of access*: A can deny B access to exchange with A unless B ceases to interact with C. A could intend to harm C, B, or both.

3. *Competition for favor*: A exploits efforts by B and C to gain A's attention or favor. A may then extract increasing concessions from one in response to concessions from the other, especially in cases where A's favor could tip the balance in any competition between B and C.[10]

4. *Divide and conquer*: There are three variations:
    i.   A prevents B and C from cooperating in cases where such cooperation might harm A;
    ii. A breaks up an existing collaboration between B and C against A; or
    iii. A incites a dispute between B and C—often by taking advantage of or exacerbating a potential source of friction or cleavage (pride, jealousy, ideology, ethnicity, etc.).

5. *A triadic environment*: The mere presence of one or more Cs influences the relationship between A and B to A's benefit;

6. *Nonpartisan actions*: A's nonpartisan position may arise from standing above the other two or from caring equally for both, but A may still use its position to secure some gain. Three variants arise:[11]
    i.   B and C are pursuing independent paths, and A initiates their contact;

ii. A mediates in some dispute between B and C, guiding their process of negotiation without taking sides. The parties themselves must construct the solution; or

iii. By mutual agreement, A arbitrates a dispute between B and C. The parties have handed responsibility for resolution to A. At the end of the process, A must take sides or strike some compromise.

7. *Gatekeeping* (Oleinik 2016): A powerful third party, X, influences the proportion of participants in what might otherwise appear to be a set of competitive and dyadic interactions between two types of parties, A and B, in which A might be considered the more powerful (as in an employer). Specifically, X influences the ratio of As to Bs by limiting the access of potential As to the field of interaction, such as a market or political arena. X's action grants some potential As privileged access to the field and reduces Bs' choice set by reducing the number of available As.

This section's remaining discussion begins with format 1 and then relates its logic to formats 2, 3, and 4 before addressing formats 5, 6, and then 7.[12] Based on an example from Kaushik Basu (2000b), discussion begins with a relatively simple version of format 1. Party A exerts power2 over B by credibly threatening to interfere with B's relationship with a single C. When credible, this threat represents a form of coercion that influences the outcome of an apparently voluntary exchange. Figure 5.1a illustrates.

The dashed line signifies that A can block B's interactions with C. Suppose that landowner A hires tenant laborer B, offering wage w. B's nonemployment fallback position, d_B, signifies the value of leisure or alternative work. In a pure competition model with a dyadic labor exchange, the equilibrium wage

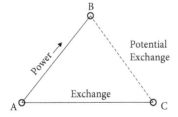

FIGURE 5.1A Format 1 Power Triad
Adapted from Basu (2000b, Figure 6.1, 149).

$w_e = d_B$. Now suppose that both A and B trade with merchant C, generating values V_{AC}, V_{BC}, V_{CA}, and V_{CB}—all greater than 0. If A can credibly threaten to cut off B's relationship with C, A can offer any w that meets the condition $d_B - V_{BC} \leq w < d_B$, and B will accept. For A's threat to be credible, however, C must value trade with A more than trade with B ($V_{CA} > V_{CB}$). (Figure 5A.1 in Appendix 5A shows a triadic power game model.) If so, party A's threat is an exercise of power2 that alters the rules of exchange, shifting the distribution of income in A's favor. Because A's threat has changed B's expected payoffs to refusing A's offer, the competitive outcome ($w_e = d_B$) does not apply. In fact, A *exploits* B in the sense of paying $w < d_B$ and, fearing loss of trade with C, B voluntarily accepts the offer. Thus, A's triadic power2 has coerced B into accepting a wage below its fallback position. Therefore, in triadic relationships, the mere presence of choice in exchange is not a sufficient condition for the absence of coercion or exploitation. Accordingly, in triadic market relationships (many of which may fit different formats), exercises of power2 influence distributional outcomes. Triadic market exchange incorporates its own political dynamic.

Formats 2, 3, and 4 reflect variations of this logic. In format 2, A can use B's desire for exchange with A in order to harm adversary C. The Helms-Burton Act of 1996 offers an example. This act strengthened the US (party A) trade embargo on Cuba (party C). It threatened non-US owned companies (B), whose trade with Cuba could involve any property formerly owned by US citizens or by Cuban nationals now living in the United States, with barring company representatives from entering the United States. This triadic relationship enabled the United States to extend its embargo of Cuba beyond US-owned companies—a dynamic that would not be possible in a dyadic relationship.

Turning to format 3, consider this example: in forming parliamentary coalitions, small parties (A) can often extract considerable benefits from a larger partner (B) by tipping its competition with another large party (C) to B's advantage. On September 9, 2018, Sweden's far-right Sweden Democrats won third place in the national election. On September 24, they sided with the center-right Moderates and Alliance to vote no confidence in Prime Minister Stefan Löfven, a Social Democrat.[13] In format 4, party A influences, blocks, or reduces the degree of cooperation between B and C, or A enhances conflict between them, in order to gain an advantage that would be unattainable in any purely dyadic relationship with either. European colonialists often utilized such triadic relationships to enhance their power by fostering or exacerbating divisions among ethnic groups in Africa and Asia.

Returning to format 1, now consider the possibility of many Cs. Here, A can exert greater power2 (cet. par.) if it can credibly threaten to affect B's relationship with more than one C, in many instances effectively ostracizing B with respect to certain types of interactions. Here, A can alter various parties' opinions of or reactions to B—perhaps those of merchants or potential employers, trade partners, financiers, political allies, friends, and so on. In so doing, A influences B's expectations about Cs' responses to B. This strategic move changes the rules of the game. For example, in the aftermath of the July 2016 failed coup in Turkey, the government of President Recep Tayyip Erdoğan fired and then blacklisted thousands of civil servants accused of harboring sympathies with the Gülen movement. This move effectively denied them employment in many other areas—blocking their access to relationships with multiple Cs.

The presence of many Cs can also facilitate exercises of power3. In such cases, party A can utilize either the presence of many Cs and/or B's potential relationships with them (in formats 1–4) to manipulate B's fundamental beliefs concerning the nature its conflict with A. For example, A may induce conformity with its desires by invoking, implying, or reinterpreting a norm: "None of them challenge me, how dare you?" In this regard, normative entrepreneurs (see Chapter 1) can utilize power3. In the early 1950s, Senator Joseph McCarthy combined triadic exercises of power2 and power3, ostracizing individuals from the media, entertainment industries, the State Department, labor unions, and the Democratic Party whom he had labeled communist sympathizers—effectively precluding objection from many others who dared not challenge his interpretation of prevalent social norms related to the concept of patriotism.

Alternatively, the potential for triadic ostracism sometimes promotes development. Lineage networks within rural Chinese villages illustrate this principle. Potential ostracism from one's lineage network deters defection from cooperative endeavors (He et al. 2018).

Now consider format 5. Here, we bring in many Cs and find a variant of power2 that operates within exchange processes. Particularly striking (and somewhat underappreciated) instances occur in relatively standard efficiency and fair wage models of labor markets and other market settings, a point stressed by Samuel Bowles and Herbert Gintis (1992). In a standard effort model in which monitoring workers' actions is both imperfect and costly, an employer (A) pays an above market-clearing wage ($w > d_B$) in market equilibrium. This wage, combined with monitoring and contingent renewal of the employment contract, with a credible threat of job loss for any observed effort that fails to meet a specified standard, induces workers (Bs) to enhance the diligence of the effort they provide within the space of an hour. Because $w > d_B$, job loss is costly. The firm pushes the wage up to the level where the marginal wage cost equals the marginal benefit from higher productivity gained via greater diligence. In a simple model, all firms in a labor market use this strategy. The equilibrium wage ($w_e > d_B$) thus generates an excess supply of labor (involuntary unemployment). Format 5 triadic power enters because the threat of dismissal induces the worker to increase effort in a manner he would not otherwise undertake, and the presence of many unemployed (Cs), who could replace an employee, renders this threat credible. Note, however, that this exchange is a positive-sum game: both effort and the wage increase; the employer is better off and the worker is compensated for higher diligence and is better off than if unemployed. A fair wage model (along the lines of Akerlof 1982, with explicit consideration of unemployed workers) can generate a similar result, typically with a larger positive-sum gain.[14]

As noted in Chapter 4, efficiency and fair wage models also provide a useful foundation for the presence of excess labor supply in a modern or urban sector for various models of developmental dualism, such as that incorporated in the Harris-Todaro (1970) migration model. In the urban formal sector, the exercise of format 5 triadic power, with many Cs who either have informal-sector jobs or are unemployed, leads to a formal-sector wage above the (fallback) agricultural wage ($w_M > w_R$). A dynamic (self-reinforcing) equilibrium arises because w_M attracts rural laborers to cities, especially when an urban location offers families a type of earnings insurance. Some migrants might attain formal-sector jobs, and their earnings can contribute to overall family income. Migration, moreover, assures an excess supply of urban formal-sector labor (Todaro and Smith 2015).

In related models of capital markets, financiers charge a below market-clearing rate of interest, which attracts multiple loan applicants (Cs). Lenders discipline borrowers—that is, reduce their propensities to take on undue risk—by requiring collateral and contingently renewing loans based on prior behavior. Following format 5 logic, the presence of multiple Cs (from the excess demand for loans) renders credible implicit threats of denying or not renewing loans to certain applicants.

More dramatically, combined formats 1 and 5 triadic power shape various sharecropping and debt-peonage arrangements that often characterize employment-land relationships in areas with highly unequal distributions of land ownership. For example, in the debt-peonage sharecropping system that dominated agriculture for black (and many poor white) farmers in the post-Reconstruction US South, local merchants acted as financiers, and they had first claim on the crop (collateral). As the sole suppliers of local finance, local merchants exercised a "territorial monopoly . . . [that was] the source of the merchant's ability to influence those political, economic and social affairs that interested him. . . . [T]he merchant forced the farmer into exclusive production of cotton by refusing credit to those who sought to diversify production" (Ransom and Sutch 2001, 127, 149). This arrangement established cotton, as opposed to other crops for which the farmer's return would have been greater, as the relevant collateral. The triadic arrangement reinforced merchant power. "Despite his desire to escape, the farmer was still locked into the production of cotton. His lack of self-sufficiency, of necessity, forced him to seek credit year after year, and the merchant's conditions for the loan insured that the farm could not become self-sufficient" (Ibid., 163).[15] Indeed, these arrangements were "the roots of Southern poverty" (Ibid., 171–99). Ransom and Sutch use the term "trap of debt peonage" (Ibid. 149–70). (Appendix 5B discusses debt-trap models.)

Regarding format 6, a potential mediator (party A) can have interests related to interactions between B and C that range from nonpartisan to fully interested. In the relatively nonpartisan region of a pertinent spectrum, A's mediation or arbitration can resolve various disputes between B and C, in many instances contributing to the welfare of some larger group by also resolving a CAP of potentially disruptive conflict—often a positive-sum outcome. Nevertheless, the greater A's stake in a B-versus-C competition, the more likely A tilts its mediation to its own advantage and the less likely (or lower) a positive-sum outcome. In Chapter 6, I assert that policy brokers—parties who mediate policy conflicts between competing coalitions—operate using these triadic principles.

Triadic format 7, the *gatekeeper*, comes from Anton Oleinik's (2016) work, *The Invisible Hand of Power: An Economic Theory of Gatekeeping*. Oleinik's concept of a gatekeeper provides a distinct but related perspective that includes elements of several triadic formats: format 1's interference, format 3's competition for favor, format 4's divide and conquer, and format 5's triadic environment. Here, a *gatekeeper* influences the proportions of the other parties who enter into a field of economic or political interaction. This approach involves multiple parties who can be grouped into the A, B, and sometimes C components of a triad. Here is the basic logic in terms of a product market, but the same principles can apply to other types of markets and to arenas for political exchange.

Consider market transactions between two types of actors: producers and consumers. In a neoclassical market with free entry and exit, both types could conduct exchanges with many of the other type. Within each type, then, competition among members limits the bargaining power of specific parties. Now consider a triad in which a third party, call it X, acts as a gatekeeper in the following sense: X can limit the entrance of producers (As) to the market, rendering the market a bounded field, but X does not limit consumer (B) access. By limiting their numbers, X has placed the subset of producers who gain entry (A_es) on the *short side* of the market, allowing them to earn monopoly rents. In return for granting them entry, X demands a portion of A's rent in the form of a tax or a bribe. Other potential producers (A_os) do not attain entry. In contrast, the Bs, who experience no limits on entry, now occupy the *long side* of the market, where they face a limited choice set. X's gatekeeping has restricted the number of A_es with whom Bs may conduct transactions. The A_es can thus charge a relatively high price to Bs, who have no power to respond. Regarding exercises of power, X exerts power directly over A and indirectly over B (by constraining B's choices). Additionally, A, who derives power from X, directly exerts power over B. Figure 5.1b adjusts Figure 5.1a's triad for this case.

Format 7 triadic power offers several important implications:

1. Oleinik asserts that power here is *invisible* because it does not emerge from specific commands. X does not tell either A or B to do anything;

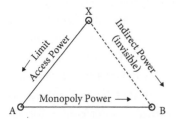

FIGURE 5.1B Format 7 Power Triad

X only shapes the market context. Power thus emerges from the constellation of interests among the three types. Specifically, X wants to receive a bribe; the As hope to attain market access and gain rents; and the Bs desire exchange with As. The Bs may not even be aware of X's existence. This notion of invisibility relates to Václav Havel's (2015) concept of a post-totalitarian system and related applications to institutional systems, discussed in the next subsection.

2. The basic story fits many instances of corruption and selective enforcement of property rights (more in Chapter 9) related to monopolies (or oligopolies) whose entry barriers involve regulation or enforcing limits on access to point-source resources.

3. Regarding production sectors, X limits access to the formal sector. Excluded producers (A_os) become informal-sector producers. Consumer Bs may then purchase either high-quality formal-sector goods or inferior informal-sector goods for a lower price.

4. Regarding labor markets, we consider the As to be employers and the Bs workers. Gatekeeping power operates at two levels. First, X limits the number of As in the market, placing them on the short side of a format 5 market, where each A_e then plays the role of a second gatekeeper (see next paragraph). At a macrolevel, X's gatekeeping might operate via fiscal and monetary policy on aggregate demand (Oleink suggests this option). At a meso level, X may restrict the number of producers in specific locations (e.g., cities, industries), as in the previous producer-consumer story, but now regarding producers as employers. Either way, X grants entry to some employers, who become A_es. The excluded A_os may then operate in the informal sector, where entry is not limited, or they may become workers (Bs).

Given this allocation, individual A_e employers operate as micro-level gatekeepers by limiting access to employment; they only hire so many. Those employed become Bs and the unemployed become format 5's Cs. The format 5 dynamic ensues. The main addition of Oleinik's approach to format 5 is to consider gatekeeping on the part of X as a strategic exercise of power that influences the degree to which As operate on the short side of the market, which in turn influences A_e's ability to exert power over Bs, noting their role as a secondary gatekeeper.

5. As in format 5, all parties can gain from the involved transactions—power is not a zero-sum game, but the gains are asymmetric. X and the A_es receive more than the Bs—the distribution between X and A_es depends on their bargaining power. The Bs still gain (minimally) from exchange with the As, but those excluded from exchanges, the Cs and possibly A_os (should they not become Bs) gain nothing.

6. Format 7, like format 5, links economic and political power. Here, we can consider X's gatekeeping role an exercise of political power and A_e's monopoly pricing, as well as any bargaining between X and A_es, as economic power. Again, the political and economic sides of political economy merge and coevolve.

More generally, we may link triadic exercises of power, of whichever format, to institutional creation, reform, and abolition. Since institutions are effectively the rules of large social games as well as foundations of cognition, deliberate institutional changes that shift distributions of de jure power constitute triadic exercises of both power2 and power3. Regarding power2, deliberate institutional change—as in reform—amounts to a strategic move that alters rules of interaction and corresponding expectations concerning possible actions and responses of other players (Cs). Extending or restricting the franchise alters the rules of the political game. More fundamentally, as shared mental models, institutions shape conceptions of social categories and causation. Who is a citizen? What can citizens do? Who can own property? What does ownership mean? Political and economic institutions shape the associated collective understandings. Consequently, institutional change can alter various parties Bs' or Cs' beliefs about the nature of possible conflicts with A, A's beliefs regarding conflicts with X, and the Bs' (or Cs') understanding about whether X even exists (invisible power). Parties who shape institutional change can thus exercise power3.

As noted previously, normative entrepreneurs can manipulate understandings of conflict implied by interpretations of normative prescriptions. Formal institutional reform can also shape understandings of conflict. For example, 15 years after the passage of the 1964 Civil Rights Act and 14 years after the 1965 Voting Rights Act, former Alabama governor George Wallace, who in 1963 personally stood at the door of the University of Alabama to block the entrance of two African American students, began in 1979 to apologize for his prior positions.[16] The dramatic institutional changes of the civil rights era, over time, had altered the former governor's perception of racial conflict.

Triadic Power, Ideology, and Institutions

Havel's concept of power (2015) offers additional insight into relationships between triadic power, institutions, and ideology. Here, I first quickly summarize Havel's concepts and then relate them directly to the sources and faces of power, shared mental models, and triadic power.

Havel discusses exercises of power within the post-totalitarian (hereafter, PT) system of communism that operated in the USSR and Eastern Europe roughly between 1948 and 1989. He contrasts a PT system with a classical dictatorship. In the latter, exercises of power are overt: the population adheres to a dictator's authority to avoid well-understood punishment from the security forces. Opponents confront a (usually unresolved) free-rider CAP: fearing punishment, individuals fail to challenge the regime. A PT system, by contrast, operates indirectly. Individuals follow rules largely because they expect everyone else to do so. The force of conformity plays a greater role than the fear of direct punishment. Moreover, even though disobedience can induce punishment, the security forces perform their duties largely out of a similar fear of nonconformity. Each individual act of conformity thus reinforces the system by enlarging the sphere of both actual and expected conformism, reinforcing a norm of obedience and corresponding barriers to disobedience. In this sense, members of the general population are both victims and perpetrators of the system.

Havel offers an example. A Czech grocer places a sign in a vegetable bin: "Workers of the world unite." The grocer does not believe in the slogan, and the customers barely notice it. Yet, this simple act illustrates PT conformity. It signals that the grocer follows society's precepts; it also protects the grocer from informants and officials. Simultaneously, this act reminds others (customers, passersby), however subtlety, of society's behavioral expectations. A woman who pays no attention to the greengrocer's sign, nevertheless, hangs a similar slogan in her office corridor: "By exhibiting their slogans, each compels the other to accept the rules of the game and to confirm thereby the power that requires the slogans in the first place" (Havel 2015, 36). Across society, such acts create a norm of obedience. Individuals "surrender their human identity in favor of the identity of the system" (Ibid.).

These responses fit Timur Kuran's (1995) concept of preference falsification. Here, Kuran distinguishes between an individual's private and public preferences. The former represent the intrinsic value (utility) that an action or expression offers a person, entirely independently of others' opinions or reactions. In contrast, *public preferences*, manifested via observable actions or words, reflect a trade-off between *reputational* and *expressive utility*. The former responds to various social pressures and a desire for conformity, whereas the latter reflects the utility gained from expressing one's own private values to others. Accounting for these trade-offs, *preference falsification* "is the act of misrepresenting one's genuine wants under perceived social pressure" (Ibid., 3). By engaging in falsification, an agent endeavors to manipulate others' perceptions of his motivations and dispositions—doing so by conducting public actions that deviate from his private preferences.[17] (Appendix 5C summarizes Kuran's model of preference falsification.) Havel's grocer, the woman office worker, and most other members of society, engage in such falsification.

Public opinion—the distribution of public preferences across a population—thus reflects an aggregation of public expressions that include preference falsification. PT systems mold public opinion with common expectations that reward preference falsification and punish nonconformity. Multiple acts of falsification reinforce the ensuing social pressure; as Havel says, victims act as perpetrators. A distribution of public opinion that incorporates a high degree of preference falsification becomes a self-enforcing equilibrium.[18] And maintenance of the system relies on significant preference falsification. Kuran, in fact, cites communist Czechoslovakia (and Havel's grocer) as examples.

Returning to Havel, at a deeper level, the signs reflect the role of ideology in the PT system. Recall that ideologies are shared mental models that combine social categories and stories of causality and into shared visions of society (or community), with ethical content. Ideologies frame shared understandings of social environments with a normative vision of how society should be structured, maintained, or changed. The ideology of a workers' state (communism), with its moral imperative of creating a classless society, rationalizes the grocer's obedience. By avoiding direct admission of subservience, by avoiding excessive or uncomfortable preference falsification, it excuses the grocer's conformity. It offers a veil. Furthermore, the idea of a worker-state offers coherence that coordinates understanding and activity (Brown 2009). It advances a vision of the world that—even though a fantasy—makes sense out of similar acts of subservience on the parts of society's multiple "grocers." This ideology offers the system "metaphysical order," an "inner coherence" that provides both legitimacy and direction. Individuals confuse reality with "ideological pseudo-reality," and so conform without directly confronting their own loss of autonomy (Havel 2015, 32).[19] Ideology thus claims its own power. The system serves the ideology. Power becomes anonymous; it resides in ritual, in *diktat*.[20]

Unlike the classical dictatorship, where the dictator's influence is direct, the PT system is "thoroughly permeated by a dense network of regulations, proclamations, norms, orders and rules . . . [that function as] direct instruments of the complex manipulation of life that is intrinsic to the post-totalitarian system" (Ibid., 73). Norms arise from and reinforce the ideology. Normative conformity pressure reinforces preference falsification. Conformity signals that one is a "good" citizen. For their part, formal legal rules not only reflect the ideology, they enhance the system's legitimacy and coherence. Like ideology, the legal code excuses action and belief: "It wraps the base exercise of power in the noble apparel of the letter of the law; it creates the pleasing illusion that justice is done . . . [hiding] arbitrary actions of the security forces . . . [and] the state's utter disregard for the positive sections of that code (the rights of citizens)" (Ibid., 73). Even in a PT system, the law can evoke an expressive power.[21] The legal code reinforces the norms, and vice versa. Furthermore, formal rules designate hierarchy; they assign positions that both reflect and signal degrees of involvement, degrees of responsibility.[22] Higher-level officials bear greater responsibility for the existing state of affairs. They more deliberately exercise power. Yet, position only distinguishes ruler from ruled in a general sense, along a spectrum, unlike a classical dictatorship wherein class divisions are clear.

Finally, PT power contains its own vulnerability. The immobilized population may still exert some power by "living within the truth" (Ibid., 64). Havel offers an example of a beer brewer who genuinely cares about the quality of the product. Many such prepolitical acts can provide the foundation on which a type of public dissent may emerge. Dissent, which operates within constraints of the system, can still expresses nonconfidence. Dissidents may even demand official compliance with the established legal code. Dissent can exert some power when it achieves recognition. Referring to Czech dissidents: "They have, by virtue of their attitudes, managed to win a certain esteem, both from the public and from their government. . . . [T]hey actually enjoy a very limited and very strange degree of indirect, actual power in their own milieu as well" (Ibid., 57).

Along similar lines, Simmel asserts that subordination still reflects a "considerable measure of personal freedom" (1971, 97) whereby dominated parties choose not to oppose—obviously avoiding its high price. Subordination thus has a dual nature that releases the subordinated (those low on the hierarchy) from direct responsibility, yet implies indirect (perhaps weak) responsibility, which also permits subtle opposition because patterns of subordination would fail without acquiescence. "Its condition is our desire to escape from the threatened punishment or from other consequences of our disobedience" (Ibid.). Havel's "living within the truth" opposition manifests itself subtly by eroding such acquiescence.

Havel's concept fits and illustrates our discussion of triadic power2 and power3 by explicitly addressing the prescriptive, expectational, and shared-mental-model properties of institutions and ideologies. Havel's approach is clearly triadic; third-party interactions underlie the entire argument. Efforts by officials to sanction violation and, more deeply, to create social expectations of grocer-like conformity—via the state media, propaganda, and demonstrative actions—all constitute exercises of power2. The corresponding expectations of conformity act as a "rule" of the PT game that alters expected payoffs.[23] Complementary efforts (usually by officials) to adjust the legal code and enforcement procedures also invoke power2. Exercises of power3 include deliberate efforts (via propaganda, etc.) to establish an ideology and associated norms that underlie the system. Here, certain leading officials act as normative entrepreneurs (Posner 2000; Sunstein 1996). Moreover, by masking appearances of subservience, the PT ideology obscures and diffuses conflict as it legitimizes both exercises of power and corresponding (subtle) acts of subservience—along with a configuration of institutions that allocates power to upper-level positions. In communist ideology, the party not only acts in the interests of workers, it possesses the unique vision to order society (Brown 2009). By providing veneers of conformity, fairness, and equal treatment—an image of the rule of law—ideology reduces and deflects perceptions of conflict, establishing a foundation for the ensuing conformity. Those who shape ideology, normative entrepreneurs among them, thus exercise triadic power3 by establishing boundaries for conflict and patterns of conformity that induce preference falsification.[24]

Because established positions confer degrees of responsibility (de jure power), the more important a position—the greater its rank in a hierarchy—the greater the potential for deliberate exercises of power2 and power3. Corresponding interactions fit several of the previously mentioned triadic formats, all with multiple Bs, Cs, and sometimes As and X. In format 1, party A is a designated official—perhaps in the security apparatus or a party leader—whose actions contribute to forging or maintaining a shared expectation that effectively threatens the general public (Bs) with ostracism by multiple Cs (other members of the public and sometimes officials) for any act of nonconformity. Yet as individuals, the Cs also occupy position B: both perpetrators and victims. This dynamic also fits the divide-and-conquer logic of triadic format 4. Fear of ostracism presents a considerable barrier to collaboration among various Bs and Cs. Format 2's denial of access and format 3's competition for favor (from A) play a complementary role that leads to format 7 gatekeeping. In search of career enhancement, citizens compete for recognition by the party, which an official (X) may withhold, thereby denying them access to production (As become A_os), employment (Bs become Cs), or other exchanges.

The impacts of such exercises of power extend beyond intended influences on individual actions and social trajectories. Unintended consequences abound. Whereas the PT system emerges from, and indeed relies on, deliberate individual and organizational actions for sustenance, it also creates its own momentum via the force of expectation and conformity. The whole is greater than the sum of its parts. The emergent institutional system shapes belief and behavior via complex dynamics that escape the control and intent of individuals: what Havel calls the *diktat*. Security officials are also victims.

This mix of extensive individual compliance, preference falsification, norms, ideology, and legally defined positions that both reflect and confer asymmetric responsibility underlie and constitute Havel's PT system. Yet, as Havel notes, similar principles operate in other systems, though often less dramatically and possibly in less veiled manners. As shared mental models, institutions—themselves outcomes of individual and organizational activity, often with unintended consequences—shape understandings of social contexts and causality via a web of behavioral prescriptions; and they do so in a manner that no individual exercise of power could. The system achieves its own momentum; it takes on a life of its own.

This broader approach fits Simmel's concept of the architecture of power, in which power gives society its coherence. "Each group performs the architectonic function of constituting a whole from the fragments factored out of human personalities; and the constituted whole acts according to the laws of its own being" (Walker 1959, 157). Society "claims the individual for itself . . . to make of him a form that it can incorporate into its own structure" (Wolff 1950, 61).[25] In Havel's system, the social expectations that emerge from prevalent ideologies and institutions "claim" individuals. Many other institutional systems do the same, albeit normally to a less extreme extent, with less repression and opacity. They claim individual understandings of their social environment via the cognitive power of shared mental models and the conformity pressure that such understandings engender. These dynamics underlie and reinforce the path dependency and resilience of institutional punctuated equilibria.

Powerful actors, including normative entrepreneurs and designated officials who—reflecting the constellation of their (often conflicting) interests, motivations, and understandings, as well as those of constituent groups—shape the evolution of institutions, set such processes in motion, and tilt their evolutionary trajectories, with both intended and unintended consequences. With this background, discussion returns to H3's influence of power on institutional evolution.

Section 2: Asymmetric Power and Institutional Evolution

Individuals, organizations, and coalitions exercise both de facto and de jure power. Powerful individuals may be called *elites*: individuals, operating in either the private or public sector, who directly affect policy decisions within specific realms of influence, including localities (cities, nations) and/or policy domains (foreign policy, health policy, etc.).[26] Elite motivation for action stems from concern for material interests, reputation, and power. A key motive involves maintaining and enhancing their position—that is, *political survival*.[27] Organizations, as structured groupings of individuals unified around a set of goals, and *coalitions*, less structured groupings of organizations and individuals who share material interests and/or policy goals, also exercise power in pursuit of—sometimes loosely defined—common goals. These various agents exercise power not only to influence immediate outcomes within given institutions or rules of the game, such as rates of profit or election outcomes (power1) but also to exert deeper and more enduring influence by altering political and economic institutions—that is, by changing the rules of the game, preferences, and beliefs (power2 and power3). Concurrently, however, institutions set parameters for such interactions. They designate position and shape available alternatives, information, and shared understandings—as they confer power and condition other sources of power that could be available to elites and organizations. Political and economic outcomes respond to both dynamics.

To continue with this chapter's opening example, beginning in the sixteenth century, the British monarchy utilized its political institutions to establish economic institutions that facilitated a significant expansion of the British Atlantic trade.[28] Over the next 150 years, trade enrichment increased the resource share of merchants (and allies) sufficiently to finance the army (de facto power) that overthrew King Charles II during the English Civil War. Forty years later (following considerable instability), the Glorious Revolution of 1688 laid the foundations of the British constitutional monarchy.[29] Parliament institutionalized its power, limiting the power of the monarch and consolidating its gains from de facto power. It then created new economic institutions, notably the Bank of England, which provided a reliable source of credit for merchants, with subsequent feedback effects that continued to enhance their wealth and resource access, and so maintain their power.[30]

Figure 5.2, derived from Acemoglu, Johnson, and Robinson (2004), illustrates these processes and feedbacks.

The three basic sources of power occupy the left-hand column. In initial period t, political institutions generate the first manifestation of power:

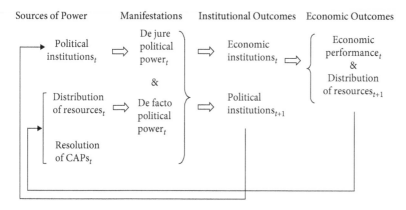

FIGURE 5.2 Power and Political and Economic Institutions
SOURCE: Adapted from Acemoglu, Johnson, and Robinson (2004).

de jure political power. Concurrently, the distribution of resources and an ability to resolve organizational CAPs jointly generate the second manifestation: de facto power. Together, de facto and de jure power shape institutional outcomes—namely, economic institutions in period t and political institutions for $t + 1$. Moving to the right-hand side, period t economic institutions affect economic outcomes: period t economic performance and the distribution of resources for period $t + 1$. Finally, the two $t + 1$ outcomes feed back into the respective sources of de jure and de facto power for subsequent periods. And so the process continues.

This logic of power generates a *political equilibrium*, an outcome wherein, for a given distribution of de jure power, elites have invested their desired proportion of resources into attaining de facto power—accounting for various associated costs and benefits (Acemoglu and Robinson 2008). Accordingly, elites and powerful organizations may utilize such investments to, within short time horizons, at least partially offset disadvantageous changes in de jure power, such as laws intended to expand democratization.

In the long run, this logic implies that power dynamics contribute to the punctuated equilibrium patterns of institutional evolution. When institutional prescriptions and outcomes sufficiently match the goals of relevant elites and organizations, institutional systems achieve stability that usually persists over medium-term time horizons. Powerful beneficiaries reinforce the stability of existing political equilibria by utilizing their de facto and de jure power to resist fundamental change. All three faces of power come into play. The security apparatus may intimidate dissidents. Gatekeepers may limit the opposition's access to decisive arenas. Normative entrepreneurs may broadcast interpretations of social norms that undermine the legitimacy of opponents. Dramatic change (punctuation) requires an unraveling of the system's mechanisms of coordination and enforcement, along with concurrent reevaluative social learning—alteration of shared mental models—on the part of a critical mass of affected individuals and groups.

The concept of a political settlement, introduced in Chapter 1, incorporates this logic, allowing for distinct variation among types of institutional systems, depending on configurations of power and included social groups (details appear in Part III). A stable political settlement arises when the (formal or informal) institutionally prescribed allocation of benefits, both political and economic, corresponds with the underlying distribution of de facto and de jure power held by relevant elites and powerful organizations. Such settlements underlie the stable phase of a system's dynamic evolution. Punctuation, however, follows from cumulative or sudden external and/or internal developments that undermine the associated social order—often doing so after one or more pertinent variables, such as the distribution of resources, crosses a critical-mass tipping point, shifting underlying distributions of power, along with complementary expectations.

In this process, certain variables, notably the distribution of resources, act as *quasi parameters*—variables that, over short to medium time horizons, operate as parameters for systemic interactions across a relatively broad range of values, but are endogenous to long-run political-economic processes (Greif 2006). During the stable phase of a cycle, changes in quasi parameters remain within boundaries; they do not cross pertinent critical-mass thresholds. When such crossings occur, however, they shift distributions of power so as to undermine mechanisms of coordination and enforcement, institutional legitimacy, and corresponding expectations. Punctuation follows. In the case of the English Civil War, the British Atlantic trade gradually redistributed resources, reaching a threshold circa 1648. Similarly, the economic success of the South Korean developmental state of 1960–87 distributed resources to unionized workers and the emerging middle class. Before 1987, this development did not significantly affect the regime, but starting in 1987, a series of large strikes and protests ushered in a transition to democratic institutions.

The key implication of H3 is straightforward: asymmetric access to the sources of power creates unequal influence over the evolution of both political and economic institutions. Powerful parties tilt institutional evolution in directions that favor their material and political interests—as they understand them. Corrupt, powerful elites, for example, can promote institutional evolution that reinforces their ability to extract rents. Substantial CAPs of inequitable political and economic access and influence follow. Furthermore, unequal distributions of power engender another set of CAPs that surround efforts to establish credible commitments for limiting exercises of power. Varying degrees of resolution condition developmental prospects. Section 3 elaborates.

Section 3: The Developmental Logic of Credible Commitment

H3's logic of power and social conflict creates additional, largely second-order developmental CAPs that permeate the politics of commitment.

H4: Powerful parties, left to themselves, cannot credibly commit to refrain from using their power for their own future benefit.

Prospects for development hinge on resolving such CAPs. Powerful parties (like others) have material and political interests and objectives. Because the possession of power facilitates attaining their objectives, in the absence of constraints or deterrent incentives, powerful parties cannot credibly promise to abstain from using power when exercising power could alter procedures and outcomes that affect their interests. In particular, they cannot credibly commit to resist attaining, often considerable, future gains attained by seizing various rewards from others' economic and political efforts and investments. There is no political Coase Theorem.

Accordingly, to develop, to achieve a broadly distributed steady enhancement of economic and political capabilities, a society must somehow create constraints and incentives—be they material or social—that induce powerful parties in both the private and public sectors to respect certain rights and avenues of political and economic access for less powerful parties. Societies must not only create implicit or explicit agreements—as in promises from power holders to extract only limited portions of economic returns or to not undercut political allies or unduly punish opponents—but make such agreements credible. Resolution of the ensuing, largely second-order CAPs requires establishing multiple understandings, arrangements, and mechanisms of restraint; it requires developing a set of functional and enforceable political and economic institutions—both informal and formal.[31] Absent such foundations of commitment, parties who might apply labor, knowledge, or capital to endeavors that could create future value should be wary.

Here is an example: Philip Roessler argues that political commitment problems underlie practices of ethnic exclusion and the prevalence of civil war in many states in sub-Saharan Africa:

> I provide evidence that ethnic exclusion and subsequent group rebellion are the outcome of strategic interactions between elites incorporated in the central government, especially co-conspirators, who collaborated to seize the state by force but find it difficult to sustain cooperation due to mutual fears that they may be ousted from power in the future. (2011, 302)

Roessler estimates that coconspirators (from previous anticolonial struggles) are four times as likely to be purged from government as other power holders,

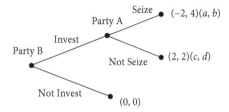

FIGURE 5.3 Simple Hold-up Game

and that this action increases the risk of civil war by a factor of 15 (Ibid., 302–3). Whereas these acts of exclusion were meant to circumvent a commitment problem—namely, that prior to their expulsion, the purged parties could not credibly commit to refrain from staging a coup—the act of exclusion often prompted a subsequent civil war. Commitment CAPs thus undermined political stability and development.

The Basic Holdup Problem
More generally, a two-player hold-up game model, such as the one in Figure 5.3, illustrates H4's basic logic.[32]

Party B moves first, choosing to invest (effort, finance, physical capital, human capital, or political capital) in producing some future economic or political value, or not invest. Party A, a powerful private or governmental individual or group, moves second. Should B choose Invest, A may then either seize the value produced or not. For Roessler's coup-related commitment problem, we may suppose that A and B are two anticolonial coalitions that jointly run the new postcolonial government for a period. B's Invest strategy signifies working with party A to create an effective government. For coalition A, the Seize strategy means staging a coup and seizing the political (and economic) gains from B's political investment.[33] Payoffs appear in both numerical and variable formats ($c > 0$; $a < 0$). Whenever $b > d$, seizing pays. Using backward induction, B anticipates seizure and chooses Not Invest.[34] Political development suffers. If a large number of society's potential producers or political partners have similar expectations regarding transactions that might permit an analogous type of seizure, economic and/or political development simply does not occur. A more sophisticated argument could involve expanding the model to make each variable a function of institutional and other contextual variables. For example, payoffs b and d can depend on the strength or cohesiveness of institutions (θ), such that $\partial b/\partial \theta < 0$ and $\partial d/\partial \theta > 0$. Coherent institutions enhance prospects for successful resolution of such enforcement CAPs; an increase in θ could reverse the inequality so that $b < d$, resolving the hold-up problem.

More specifically, hold-up issues imply three basic types of economic and political developmental CAPs. First, reflecting a direct application of Figure 5.3 to economic transactions, the prospect that one firm (or economic actor) could extract a bargaining advantage from another's sunk cost investment (follow Invest with Seize) can deter the latter from investing whenever the former cannot credibly commit to eschew such bargaining advantage. Note that "invest" could signify developing a new technology and "seize" could mean copying it (free ride on the sunk development costs). Alternatively, "invest" might signify entering an oligopolistic market and "seize" might connote temporarily cutting prices to drive the entrant out of business (predatory pricing).

Second, a variety of commitment CAPs pose substantial barriers to political participation by less powerful parties. Powerful authorities, interest groups, or private militias often cannot credibly promise to either refrain from punishing political expression that challenges their interests or promise to protect civil rights from public and private incursion—especially rights of minority populations. In terms of Figure 5.3, party B "invests" in political expression or exercises its rights only if A's promise to honor or protect such rights (not seize) is credible. For example, Mao Zedong's 1960–61 Let a Thousand Flowers Bloom campaign encouraged various expressions of diverse political opinions. Some regime critics apparently believed Mao's implicit promise to refrain from punishment, but Mao used this brief period of openness to identify opponents whom he then eliminated or silenced (Brown 2009). In such cases, a wary citizen would avoid political expression, hiding (i.e., falsifying) her or his preferences. From the opposite perspective, dictators who might resign if a revolutionary coalition could credibly offer them good terms, cling to power, fearing reprisals.

Applying this same principle to social cleavages, minority or disadvantaged ethnic, racial, religious, ideological, or lower-class groups may refrain from forming or joining a coalition, protesting, or even voting because they anticipate a hostile reaction from majorities or powerful parties. To protect themselves, they remain silent, effectively engaging in preference falsification. Political representation and capability building suffer. In addition to directly blocking avenues for accountability, preference falsification—a rational action under the circumstances—inhibits transmissions of information regarding the private preferences of individuals and groups (Kuran 1995). Governance cannot even account for, much less respond to, unexpressed preferences. Stated guarantees of political and civil rights, whether conveyed in written constitutions or mere pronouncements, often face such credibility CAPs. Political development depends on their resolution.

Third, political and economic credibility problems interact. As Acemoglu and Robinson (2000) point out, powerful parties endeavor to block technological advance and other forms of economic development, such as industrialization, when such activity threatens their power. To illustrate, consider an alternative version of Figure 5.3 that reverses elements of the previous example. Suppose that party B (instead of A) holds power and that for B "invest" signifies fortifying political or economic entry barriers as it seeks to maintain its power. In this case, the weaker party, A, would respond to Invest with Not Seize, either because B's power eliminates the Seize option, or it shifts A's payoffs to Seize and Not Seize, so that $b < d$. Anticipating Not Seize, as long as $c > 0$, B invests in maintaining power and A follows with Not Seize. Hence, B retains power. Now suppose that technological advance could undermine B's power; a new technology could increase b so that $b > d$. If so, A would choose Seize. Suppose that in this context, the Seize strategy involves entering an economic or political arena, so that competing firms or coalitions may "seize" some of B's monopoly profits or political power. As the initial powerful party, B hopes to prevent this outcome. Now, add a pregame in which B could choose to Block or Not Block the technological advance. Anticipating the demise of its barriers, B chooses Block (a strategic move). Following that action, B chooses Invest and A chooses Not Seize. Again, B maintains its power.[35]

Society, however, could benefit from the technology that would undermine B's power. For example, Acemoglu and Robinson contrast the response of powerful landed classes to possible industrialization in Great Britain with similar responses in Russia and Austria-Hungary. British landed aristocrats, who held dominant political power until circa 1850, did not resist industrialization. They did not feel threatened because the political institution of the House of Lords sufficiently protected their interests; they anticipated maintaining sufficient payoffs.[36] The House of Lords, inequitable as it was, resolved an H2 commitment problem: it rendered credible an implicit promise that industrialization would not unduly undermine landholder interests. By contrast, in Russia and Austria-Hungary, monarchs and aristocrats blocked industrialization because they (probably accurately) believed it would undercut their political power.[37] They continued to "invest" their efforts in maintaining inefficient technologies and various barriers to economic and political participation. A political credibility problem thus impeded economic and political development.[38]

Holdup, Strategic Moves, and Triadic Power

These credibility problems relate directly to Section 1's discussion of power. There are two basic considerations: (i) how powerful parties might create a set of conditions under which they could exercise hold-up actions to their advantage; and, (ii) given such conditions, how they subsequently exercise power to attain advantageous hold-up outcomes.

Creating favorable conditions for hold-up activity constitutes a strategic move, an exercise of power2, usually manifested at an institutional level. Mao's Let a Thousand Flowers Bloom campaign was such a move. His pronouncement, effectively a new rule of the Chinese political game at the time, facilitated his subsequent silencing of political opponents.

Once established, conditions for holdup permit triadic exercises of power2 and/or power3 that can either apply such conditions to exercises (or credible threats) of holdup or possibly unravel the requisite conditions for holdup. Three variations apply. First, direct applications of Figure 5.3's hold-up logic often involve triadic exercises of power. For example, potential opponent B might consider "investing" in challenging incumbent A. Using triadic power (format 1), A could threaten to end B's commercial and political relationships: an exercise of power2. Additionally, A might use appeals to nationalism, race, or ethnicity (often reflections of power3) to further isolate B. Utilizing triadic format 4's divide-and-conquer technique, powerful A might persuade certain Cs that B (e.g., immigrants), rather than A, is responsible for their problems (such as low wages or poor employment prospects). As A diverts Cs' attention away from itself, A further isolates B. Anticipating such outcomes, B may not invest time and resources into political participation.

Second, from the opposite perspective, exercises of triadic power can (often dysfunctionally) resolve certain instances of holdup (undermine its conditions) in a coercive fashion that exploits B. Using format 1 triadic power, A could threaten to cut off B's customer base or access to finance unless B, who would otherwise choose Figure 5.3's Not Invest (and receive 0), chooses Invest in a manner that allows A to seize the subsequent benefit. This strategic move pushes B's payoff to Not Invest below 0, to $-x$. If $-x < a$, B chooses Invest even though it knows A will seize the gains. Although this use of triadic power2 circumvents an investment holdup, it does so in a manner that favors A and exploits B ($a < 0$); B ends up worse off than it would have in its prior fallback position. Section 1's brief discussion of debt peonage can reflect prior exercises of such power.

Along similar lines, landowners or financiers can apply format 2 triadic power. For example, owner-financier A denies tenant farmer B access to credit unless B stops interacting with C, a merchant who might supply alternative seeds. Needing credit, B "invests" effort in growing crops even though she knows that the landlord-creditor will seize the benefits. In the post-Reconstruction South, merchant-financiers coerced tenant sharecroppers into using cotton, rather than more valuable crops, as loan collateral because cotton was easier to claim for debt repayment (Ransom and Sutch 2001).[39]

Third, anticipating the possibility of coerced investment, various parties B may exert minimal effort or investment in efforts to reduce A's incentives for seizure. Sharecroppers may, for example, refrain from acquiring human capital or improving agricultural productivity, anticipating that landlord A could force them into utilizing such acquisitions and then seize the benefits.[40] Triadic power relationships can thus help explain inefficiency and lack of dynamism in debt-peonage relations or, more generally, of excessively inequitable landholdings. (Appendix 5B presents a model of debt peonage.) More dramatically, during civil wars, civilians hide their wealth and talents and fail to pursue any form of economic enhancement. The able-bodied may even injure themselves to avoid forced recruitment by one side or the other. In all such cases, capabilities suffer.

All of these permutations of triadic power relationships and exercises of holdup also apply directly to political problems of institution building. Why should individuals or groups invest time, energy, and other resources in resolving a set of difficult CAPs related to constructing economic or political institutions if they expect some powerful party to subsequently seize the gains and deny them access?

Overall, these variations on holdup both reflect and imply CAPs that accompany initiating and sustaining methods and processes for creating social mechanisms that can deliver credible commitment. Consequently, prospects for both economic and political development—especially in the sense of long-run capacity building—hinge on resolving these, largely second-order commitment CAPs. These CAPs, moreover, directly link developmental prospects to distributions of power and resources. This section's arguments thus augment our understanding of Chapter 2's CAPs of inequality—as well as the magnitude of H1 and H2 CAPs from Chapters 3 and 4. Prospects for resolving such CAPs, moreover, arise and evolve in environments conditioned by H3's unequal political influence and H4's commitment problems. Discussion now turns to joint consideration of H3 and H4.

Section 4: Developmental Implications of Social Conflict Theory

H3's power-based asymmetric influences on institutional evolution interact with H4's CAPs of credibly limiting uses of power. This logic binds inequality and distributional conflict to institutional development, affecting the creation, composition, maintenance, trajectory, and endurance of institutional systems and social orders that, in turn, condition prospects for economic and political development. Distributional conflict and its mitigation thus underlie social stability and instability. Two corollaries point to related developmental CAPs. The first is implicit in the prior discussion of political equilibrium:

1. Elite power and adaptation (Acemoglu and Robinson 2008): Elites may use their superior de facto power to undermine reforms in formal institutions that threaten their interests; more dramatically, they may capture democratic institutions.

Economic and political elites not only have inherent advantages in acquiring de facto power (via access to resources and capacities for resolving organizational CAPs among small groups of well-positioned actors), they also have incentives to use this power to challenge or reverse unfavorable institutional changes initiated by others. Should democratic (or other) reforms threaten their de jure power, economic positions, or benefits, elites may invest resources in attaining de facto power in an effort to offset such political outcomes and, ultimately, unravel reforms (Acemoglu and Robinson 2008).[41] The post–Civil War South offers an example of elite capture of democratic institutions. The Fifteenth Amendment to the US Constitution, a formal institution adopted in 1865, specifies voting (and other) rights for all adult males, regardless of race. Yet, violent opposition, widespread intimidation, and political and legal maneuvering by wealthy landowners and political allies—largely less wealthy whites, ranging from merchants to field hands—transformed the political economy of the South. These exercises of de facto power fostered the development of the Jim Crow institutional system of legal segregation, which consolidated circa 1890. These actions effectively displaced the (de jure) Fifteenth Amendment; they effectively denied constitutionally prescribed voting rights to African Americans in the South until the passage and implementation of the 1965 Voting Rights Act (Foner 1998; Wright 2013).

The second corollary is as follows:

2. Creating social order requires establishing some form of political settlement that reflects a set of mutual understandings and complementary incentives that motivate powerful elites and organizations to rely primarily on politics, rather than violence, to settle disputes.

At the most elemental level, development requires that groups with a capacity to employ organized, systematic violence face incentives to refrain from its use and monitor other such groups (North, Wallis, and Weingast 2009). Even rudimentary development depends on the degree to which a society can resolve a series of arduous CAPs that surround establishing a peaceful social order, via some form of political settlement among parties that have the potential to exercise organized violence.[42] This statement, in fact, combines H3 and H4. Organizations with violence capacity possess de facto power that could obstruct the development of political and economic agreements—or that could disrupt existing social arrangements.[43] A failure to reach settlement, moreover, creates a mutual expectation that parties with violence capacity will use it to seize assets, the fruits of others' efforts, and territory. Furthermore, an ensuing lack of development reinforces the incentives for such parties to gain wealth via predation. Society enters or retains a conflict equilibrium. Escape involves negotiating, constructing, maintaining, and enforcing political settlements that offer organizations credible incentives to restrain their use of violence (Ibid.). Successful processes thus address a series of both first-order CAPs (violence is a form of defection) and second-order enforcement CAPs of honoring commitments, with at least rudimentary mechanisms and incentives for involved organizations or groups to conduct auxiliary transactions that would sanction uses of violence.

The credibility and sustainability of political settlements thus rely on the distribution of economic and political benefits to powerful participating parties. Contrary to some traditional economic reasoning, rent-sharing arrangements can, in fact, underlie political stability, removing critical barriers to growth and development. In many developmental contexts, the relevant counterfactual for the presence of rents is not a hypothetical competitive market but, rather, a society embroiled in disorder and violence (North et al. 2013). An expectation of future rents provides violence-capable organizations material incentives to avoid violence, monitor their own members, and monitor others. More generally, because rents influence the ability of groups to organize (a source of de facto power), they serve as a political medium of exchange—a currency of politics via discretionary conferral and withdrawal—that sometimes resolves second-order commitment CAPs.[44] Part III develops the logic of political settlements in detail.

Overall, H3's assertion that powerful parties disproportionately shape institutional development implies a series of CAPs of starkly unequal political and economic influence that condition prospects for creating and enhancing human economic and political capabilities. H4's issues of credible commitment and hold-up problems imply a related set of CAPs that accompany establishing social mechanisms for credibly limiting uses of power, so that less powerful parties face reasonable prospects for investing resources and time in economic and political activity. Development depends on such limits. Distribution and growth are thus inseparable—as are the political and economic sides of macropolitical economy.[45]

Social orders thus vary greatly according to the degree to which their configuration of institutions and motivations resolves or mitigates H3 and H4 CAPs. Varying degrees of resolution shape prospects for subsequent economic and political development. In other words, distributions of power that shape the creation, composition, maintenance, and endurance of institutional systems generate different motivations and capacities for resolving multiple developmental CAPs, including H1 public-good and externality CAPs, H2 coordination CAPs, H3 CAPs of unequal influence, and H4 commitment CAPs. Accordingly, the configuration of political settlements conditions both economic and political development. Part III elaborates.

Before turning to Part III, however, Chapter 6, somewhat more optimistically, addresses the potential for organizational and policy innovations to relax some political and economic constraints.

6   Policy Innovations Can Relax
Political Constraints

Ideas shape the course of history.

—*John Maynard Keynes (attrib.) in Laurence J. Peter,* The Peter Plan:
A Proposal for Survival *(1976)*

IN 1945, THE RICHEST 2.7% of South Korean rural households owned two-thirds of the land. In 1946, the US military government, which ruled South Korea from 1945–48, initiated land reform. It seized land previously held by the Japanese (11.7% of cultivated land) and distributed it to peasants, free of charge.[1] Starting in 1950, the regime of Syngman Rhee instituted a far more comprehensive land reform—a huge policy innovation in that society. The regime offered owners 150% of a year's crops in compensation and set an upper limit for land ownership of three hectares. It distributed 52% of cultivated land to former tenants (You 2013, 295–301). This reallocation offered former tenants—who, prior to the reform lacked protection from arbitrary predation by landholders and thus faced limited incentives to work hard—an owner's incentive to pay closer attention to their work effort and to invest in physical and human capital. By enhancing agricultural productivity, the new policy facilitated agricultural exports—earning needed foreign currency. More critically, it helped maintain low urban food prices, which proved important for maintaining political stability. Overall, the South Korean land reform created "an unusually equal distribution of income and wealth" (Ibid., 313). By redistributing land—a substantial resource—the reform also redistributed power. "The traditional *yangban* (aristocracy) landlord class was dissolved. . . . Land reform opened space for state autonomy from the dominant class, as there was no organized privileged class or special interest after land reform" (Ibid., 299). This reform thus facilitated resolving a large set of H2, H3, and H4 CAPs.

Development requires the creation, alteration, transformation, and abolition of institutions—both formal and informal—with complementary changes in the organizational elements of coordination and enforcement within institutional systems. Hereafter, I refer to combinations of both changes as *institutional change*.

This chapter addresses how policy and organizational innovations may sometimes promote institutional change that can relax political barriers and constraints on development. Specifically,

> **H5**: Policy innovations sometimes relax political and commitment constraints that follow from H3 and H4, as well as free-riding and coordination CAPs from H1 and H2.

Novel arrangements can enhance group capabilities for resolving various embedded CAPs. Such innovations, however, operate within the systems they might alter. Achieving innovation, therefore, involves addressing a set of context-specific CAPs.

Discussion proceeds as follows. Section 1 focuses on the concept of policy innovation, linking it to the concepts of technological change, social capital, and related CAPs. It sketches a few broad types of innovation and discusses key steps for successful innovation, with attention to adoption and implementation. Sections 2 and 3 consider the social contexts within which policy innovations occur, succeed, or fail. Specifically, Section 2 addresses institutional stability and change, using a punctuated equilibrium approach to institutional evolution. It considers specific types of incremental and dramatic change, deliberate and unintended change, internal and external causes, and relationships between reform and policy innovation. Section 3 focuses on the meso-level context within which policy innovation may or may not take hold. Drawing on the policy process literature, it discusses the terrain of interaction (the policy domain), structure (policy subsystems), and agency (policy communities, entrepreneurs, and advocacy coalitions). After defining these terms, discussion turns to the cognitive and institutional roots of meso-level punctuation dynamics and the role of competing advocacy coalitions within policy subsystems (hereafter, PSSs). These factors influence the scope and potential for successful policy innovation. Section 4 addresses dramatic policy change (punctuation), with reference to the concepts of focusing events, multiple streams, and information cascades. Section 5 concludes with a sketch of how policy innovations may resolve different types of CAPs.

Section 1: Innovation to Circumvent Political Constraints

Innovative ideas influence developmental outcomes through complex channels. H1's problems of free riding undermine motivations to invest time and energy into innovation. H2's coordination problems and corresponding inequities related to knowledge and skill transmission, social conformity, and production externalities jointly affect the inception, spread, and adoption of policy innovations. H3 and H4's distributions of power and issues of commitment within specific political contexts influence various degrees of access to and motivations for innovation, as well as potential impacts. Yet, well-targeted (or fortuitous) innovations can erode such constraints.

Policies are decisions made by public and private governing bodies about how to address—or sometimes ignore—some perceived problem or issue. Harold Lasswell and Abraham Kaplan offer a more dynamic definition that relates policy to belief: "a projected program of goal values and practices" (1950, 8). Policies usually specify conditions under which individuals or groups should, should not, may, or may not take certain actions. When observed and enforced over time, policies become a type of (usually mini) institution: they become institutionalized. For analytical purposes, however, it often makes sense to distinguish between implemented policies and institutions. Policies create context-specific decision rules that (usually) require less shared understanding and are more subject to change than institutions.

Policy innovations offer new approaches to resolving CAPs within specific social contexts. The underlying ideas need not be new, as for inventions, but their application should offer novel approaches within relevant contexts. Land reform is not a new idea, but in 1950s South Korea it was, indeed, innovative. Implementing innovations, such as land reform, moreover, requires idiosyncratic approaches that address a how policy idea can operate within the relevant political and economic environment.[2] The related term, *organizational innovation*, connotes adopting new methods for structuring procedures and relationships within specific organizations—often new ways of coordinating internal command, competition, cooperation, and compliance within particular organizational settings. For an organization, such innovations constitute or reflect new internal policies. Hence, I use the broad term *policy innovation* to include organizational innovation, noting that new policies can operate within both the private and public sectors.

The Role of Policy Innovation

Policy innovations play a role analogous to that of new productive technology. Whereas technological innovations improve the efficiency of converting inputs (land, labor, and capital) into outputs, successful policy innovations enhance the efficiency and effectiveness of social arrangements to mitigate CAPs. Equivalently, policy innovations augment social capital. A group's *social capital* refers to its set of social arrangements and shared understandings, including informal and formal institutions, that facilitate resolving CAPs. Social capital fosters mutual trust regarding individual and group commitments to abide by cooperative agreements (Poteete, Janssen, and Ostrom 2010). Within firms, for example, organization-specific social capital includes personnel policies and various mutually understood incentives, such as promotion procedures, salary formulas, and profit-sharing arrangements. Functional social capital builds loyalty to groups and organizations, diminishing or eliminating incentives to defect (Stiglitz 2000). It facilitates providing public goods, mediating conflicts, and achieving cooperation.[3]

Successful policy innovations thus create or enhance the efficiency of social arrangements for mitigating H1–H4 CAPs. Regarding H3 and H4, innovative ideas may alter distributions of power or related incentives; they may redirect flows of information, generate new expectations, create or enhance the efficacy of mechanisms of social mobilization, and establish credible restraints on the use of power. Alternatively, or concurrently, novel ideas may alter elite goals and strategic understandings in the direction of longer-term social benefit.

Accordingly, policy innovations constitute an important source of and impetus for political development, though of course some innovations (e.g., designing more efficient means of repression) may accomplish the opposite. Policy innovations can enhance the efficacy of each of the three key direct elements of political development. New ideas regarding bureaucratic organization, staff training, transmitting information, and generating internal accountability may enhance or mobilize state capacity. New ideas on crafting legislation, adjudicating disputes, and implementing and enforcing institutional prescriptions can enhance the rule of law. New ideas on structuring public input into political decision making (via elections and other mechanisms) and disciplining errant political actors may enhance accountability. Moreover, innovations can reduce (or exacerbate) conflicts among these three components of political development.

New policies also affect (and respond to) the less direct forms of political development—legitimacy and social mobilization. Innovations in state capacity can enhance public acceptance of government if, for example, improving delivery of basic public services reduces inconsistency and corruption. Legal innovations can enhance the predictability and hence legitimacy of economic contracts. Similarly, new approaches to achieving public accountability may lend legitimacy to political systems. Virtuous circle patterns sometimes arise when legitimacy fosters further policy innovations.[4]

Less direct, cognitive innovations may also facilitate building and strengthening legitimacy—though not necessarily with good outcomes. New policy images, narratives, and, more broadly, ideologies can reinforce (or undermine) public acceptance of various functional or dysfunctional governing arrangements. For example, communist ideology, with its professed long-term goal of a stateless and classless society, facilitated much public acceptance of (or acquiescence to) Soviet governance. Especially during the USSR's first few decades, this ideology rationalized the political monopoly of the Communist Party, the system of centralized planning, and the hardships that the general population had to endure. In this shared conception, the party had the vision and experience to "guide the less advanced citizens to this radiant future" (Brown 2009, 110). Indeed, as "an all-encompassing system of beliefs," communist ideology explained social development (Ibid., 109). Even in the post–Khrushchev period, when fewer and fewer officials and members of the public actually believed that the USSR was on such a path, the communist leadership could not renounce this ultimate goal because it underpinned the Communist Party's political legitimacy (Ibid., 110).

In an analogous fashion, policy visions and ideologies can motivate and channel social mobilization—easing the constraints of normally severe organizational CAPs. During its struggle against the apartheid regime in South Africa, the African National Congress's (ANC) Freedom Charter of 1955 articulated the following ideals[5]: a national vision of popular democratic governance; equal rights for all national groups; sharing of national wealth and land; equality before the law, with equal human rights; free trade unions; open doors to learning and culture; and universal rights to housing, security, peace, and friendship. This vision helped mobilize growing opposition to the apartheid regime, despite severe repression.

Although policy innovations can, in principle, promote various forms of political development, institutional systems resist change, and unintended consequences are not only possible, they are likely. Many policy innovations enhance the position of entrenched interests in entirely unintended fashions: the 1917 Bolsheviks, many of whom later suffered exile to Siberia, did not anticipate Joseph Stalin's rule; decades later, privatization in Russia engendered a wealthy oligarchy. While acknowledging such consequences, this chapter focuses on potential avenues for constructive innovation. Development policy should endeavor to create constructive and implementable policy innovations in a manner that fits the political-economic context of relevant societies. We now turn to functional innovations.

Achieving Functional Policy Innovations

Broadly speaking, there are five basic (interacting and not necessarily sequential) steps in achieving policy innovation:[6]

1. *Policy entrepreneurs*—individuals who devote resources to changing current policies—develop or import policy ideas that are new for their context.[7] Typically, such ideas must gain acceptance in the relevant policy community (not listed as a separate step, for simplicity).

2. A policy idea attracts the (necessarily) limited attention of relevant policymakers. It must reach their policy agendas—a scarce resource (Baumgartner, Jones, and Wilkerson 2011). Often, attention responds to activities of supporting coalitions and various media outlets.

3. Policymakers decide to enact a proposed policy.

4. Relevant civil servants and involved private parties implement the new policy.

5. The target audience (civil servants, specific outside groups, businesses, other organizations, or the public at large), who sometimes assist with implementation, must at least minimally accept the policy; they do not interfere with its implementation.

Step 2 merits brief elaboration. A *policy agenda* is a list of issues to which some participants pay attention. A hierarchy of concentric circles can illustrate distinct levels of agendas (Birkland 2011). An *agenda universe* (the largest circle) includes all possible policy ideas; a *systemic agenda* includes those

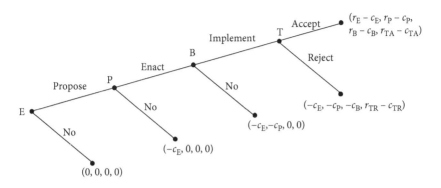

LEGEND: E = policy entrepreneur; P = policymaker; B = bureaucrat; T = target audience;

r = return; c = cost; subscripts A and R, respectively, signify acceptance and rejection.

FIGURE 6.1 Policy Innovation Game

regarded as appropriate for discussion in the relevant society; an *institutional agenda* includes ideas that policymakers actually consider; a *decision agenda* (the smallest circle) includes a short list of ideas that reach the table for policy decision. Step 2 then involves moving ideas from a systemic agenda to an institutional agenda and then a decision agenda. Step 3 implies a favorable decision outcome. In steps 4 and 5, success often depends on the perceived legitimacy of the relevant policy process, the policymakers, and the policy itself.

Figure 6.1's simple game illustrates basic trade-offs implicit in steps 1, 3, 4, and 5 (for simplicity, assume that step 2 automatically follows step 1). The game proceeds as follows: A policy entrepreneur (E) decides whether to propose a new idea; a policymaker (P) decides whether to enact; a bureaucrat (B) decides whether to implement; finally, the target audience (T) decides whether to accept or reject. Variable payoffs are shown. We assume positive returns (r) to policy adoption and that each player's costs (c) are independent of a specific source of policy rejection. For the new policy to be enacted, implemented, and accepted, four conditions must hold:

1. E's return must exceed the costs of proposing the policy ($r_E > c_E$);
2. P's return must exceed her decision costs ($r_P > c_P$);
3. B's return to implementation must exceed his implementation costs ($r_B > c_B$); and

4. T's net return from acceptance or acquiescence must exceed that from rejection ($r_{TA} - c_{TA} > r_{TR} - c_{TR}$).

In principle, the specific values for these various returns and costs depend on elements of the relevant context. For example, implemented (rejected) policies may enhance (diminish) E's or P's reputation, and the extent of impact depends on activities of the media or interested powerful parties. A more detailed model could incorporate the relevant functions. Now, using backward induction, if E and P anticipate either rejection by T (i.e., if condition 4 fails) or no implementation by B (condition 3 fails), they not should undertake the costs of proposing and enacting the policy. In a more complicated scenario, E and P might enhance their reputations by advancing ideas that B or T later reject.

From a broader perspective, achieving (or not achieving) these conditions follows principles of macro-level institutional change, discussed in Section 2, along with meso- and macro-level policy processes discussed in Sections 3 and 4.

Section 2: Macro-Level Institutional Change, Reform, and Policy Innovation

The trajectory of institutional change often follows a punctuated equilibrium dynamic: long periods of (relative) stability interrupted by bursts of change. Institutions, institutional systems, and social orders can, despite much internal contestation, persist over medium- to long-term time horizons. Large external shocks, such as wars or extreme droughts, occasionally lead to an unraveling of stable arrangements. Perhaps counterintuitively, dramatic change may also follow a slow accumulation of incremental developments. Punctuation ensues when such accumulations reconfigure social understandings and distributions of power—when they reach some critical-mass tipping point after which change becomes self-reinforcing. These dynamics operate at both a macrolevel of institutional systems and a mesolevel of single institutions or PSSs within policy domains. At either level, stability and change interact because institutions create ambiguities that invite contestation, and institutions require continuous reproduction by players who possess different interests and perceptions (Mahoney and Thelen 2009; Thelen 2003). Institutional trajectories thus reflect the combined influences of multiple (often conflicting) deliberate actions, as well as unintended or uncontrollable events and developments. Within such complex dynamics, successful policy innovation alters the trajectory of institutional change toward intended objectives.

These dynamics lend considerable *path dependency* to developmental processes: initial arrangements (outcomes of prior contestation) create durable patterns of cognition and interaction that persist over (and often beyond) the stable phase of a punctuation cycle. Such arrangements focus attention and limit input from new ideas and participants. Thus, despite continuous contestation among agents whose interests and perceptions differ, institutional stability and longevity arise from several sources:

1. Agents who derive power from existing arrangements (designated positions, allocations of authority, budgets, etc.) use their power to oppose change.

2. A broader constituency of system beneficiaries interprets benefits as entitlements, and likewise resists change.

3. A lack of time and attention to complex issues limits policy input from the (boundedly rational) public (Olson 1971).

4. At a deeper level, established institutions, as shared mental models, shape understandings of causal relationships and expected behavior—with ethical content in the case of norms. As people accommodate to manners of thinking and predictable social patterns, conceptualizing alternatives becomes difficult and exhibits its own free-riding CAPs. Many individuals lack the will to hazard the uncertainties of dramatic change. Indeed, some cognitive patterns persist long after punctuation.[8] British legal traditions still influence institutional development in many former colonies, including the United States.

5. Institutions generate network coordination that is difficult to unravel and hard to replace.

6. Complementarities among related institutions imply that prospects for changing a single institution often depend on simultaneous changes in others.[9] A coalition that could, in principle, alter one institution may fail without cooperation from other (not necessarily sympathetic) coalitions who focus on related institutions.

Institutions and their corresponding systems are thus inherently conservative. Once established, initial patterns reproduce themselves, resist fundamental change, and usually adapt slowly. Rough balances of contending forces tend to generate relatively small, incremental adjustments during the stable phase of the punctuation cycle. Accordingly, substantive reform usually requires overcoming substantial CAPs.

Over time, however, inadequate adaptations to myriad internal and external developments undermine stability. Confidence in institutional prescriptions and corresponding mechanisms of coordination and enforcement diminishes. Prior resolutions to CAPs erode. These developments weaken or distort political settlements, shift understandings, and reconfigure power relationships. Institutional systems become increasingly vulnerable to internal or external shocks. Ensuing punctuation can signify either significant institutional restructuring, as in radical reform, institutional dissolution, or some mix. After decades of resistance to apartheid, in 1994, Nelson Mandela became President of South Africa. After four centuries, the Roman Empire crumbled into the relative chaos of the European early medieval period.

Within such dynamics, institutional change—both gradual and punctuated—arises from a mix of inadvertent and deliberate actions and reactions. On the one hand, unintended change can emerge from myriad unforeseen internal reactions of policy implementers, targeted parties, opposing coalitions, or the public at large—often responding to new developments and inherent ambiguities in institutional prescriptions.[10] Concurrent developments, such as growth, migration, trade, or technological change, may alter distributions of power, often creating or compounding unintended consequences.

Reform, on the other hand, connotes deliberate institutional change as an outcome of policy decisions at some level of governance (Hall and Thelen 2009). Reform involves institutional and policy innovation. In established systems, it targets formal institutions, but success often involves altering or reinterpreting informal institutions and associated practices, as well as mobilizing implementation and support. Reform incorporates new or borrowed ideas that address at least several of the following: broad objectives, specific details or elements of change, methods for achieving change, methods for implementing new rules and procedures, and methods for sustaining new arrangements.

Reform itself, however, also generates unintended, unanticipated consequences—again from a mix of reactions, ambiguities, and concurrent external and internal developments. When Mikhail Gorbachev radically reformed the Soviet system by ending the political monopoly of the Communist

Party, via Perestroika, he (and colleagues) did not anticipate unleashing forces of Russian nationalism that would, in a few years, contribute decisively to his overthrow in the 1991 attempted military coup, followed by the breakup of the USSR under Boris Yeltsin (Brown 2009). Thus, while reform is deliberate, it may lack order and may utterly fail to achieve the intended objectives.

Mixing unintended and intended elements, Wolfgang Streeck and Kathleen Thelen (2005) and James Mahoney and Thelen (2009) offer a possibly contrasting vision of institutional change that emphasizes potential impacts of gradual institutional change. They identify four sources of institutional change:

1. *Drift*: Changes in social environments alter the impacts of existing rules, especially their implementation. Rule omissions and ambiguities permit abdication of responsibilities. Drift signifies the absence of deliberation, and often inadequate and unintended adaptation. Institutions, however, require maintenance. Drift can change the influence and effectiveness of institutions, without apparent change in their surface-level attributes.

2. *Layering*: Various parties supplement existing rules with new ones—usually too small to be labeled "reforms" (e.g., bureaucratic rules that interpret prior legislation). Involved parties often occupy lower-level policy positions. Such additions can generate significant change when they "alter the logic of the institution or compromise the stable reproduction of the original core" (Mahoney and Thelen 2009, 17). Layering can shift incentives, alter strategies, redirect information flows, and indirectly influence agents' understandings of processes and environments. It may induce differential growth of rules or practices, gradually enhancing the importance of initially nonthreatening alterations.

3. Institutional *conversion*: Various parties exploit ambiguous prescriptions by reinterpreting rules to suit their ends. Conversion has four basic sources: cognitive limitations of those who design (formal) institutions; compromises embedded in the initial rule design that were often needed to attain agreement (enactment) among coalitions whose interests and perceptions differ; deliberate efforts of interested parties to reinterpret rules; and the passing of time as institutions outlive initial purposes and supporting coalitions. Conversion can

reconfigure agents' understandings of processes, outcomes, and social environments. New interpretations and subsequent actions may defy initial purposes and undermine institutional legitimacy.

4. *Displacement*: New rules replace existing rules. Sometimes new institutions that compete with existing ones gradually gain prominence. If so, displacement need not signify punctuation. Alternatively, in cases of rapid institutional transformation, displacement implies punctuation. Meso-level punctuation eliminates and replaces the institutions that underlie PSSs. Sufficiently large-scale displacement that reconfigures or disrupts mechanisms of coordination and enforcement connotes punctuation of an institutional system or social order.[11]

Streeck and Thelen (2005) note a fifth source of institutional change:

5. *Exhaustion*: Gradual institutional breakdown arising from behaviors that existing rules allow or even induce.

Despite these authors' emphasis on how gradual changes create large impacts, much of this logic is consistent with a nuanced punctuation framework that allows a role for incremental roots of punctuation along with cases of significant change without obvious punctuation. Rather than regard gradual institutional change as antithetical to a punctuation approach, I choose to merge these approaches, with attention to five arguments. First, as suggested earlier, accumulated gradual changes that affect quasi parameters can induce punctuation by altering understandings and distributions of power past a critical-mass tipping point. The five sources of institutional change, separately or in combination, often induce such crossing. Second, Streeck and Thelen note that significant changes in outcomes can occur without much change in institutions. Nothing in punctuation theory precludes this possibility. Enduring institutions can still frame shared understandings, such as which types of players make which types of decisions, even if actual policy decisions and outcomes shift. In such cases, institutional punctuation has not (yet) occurred. Third, institutional displacement often involves punctuation, which can follow cumulative developments in points 1–3. Fourth, as Chapter 1's discussion of institutions as shared mental models implies, there are cognitive roots to punctuation dynamics that emerge when novel understandings of pertinent environments, processes, and outcomes spread rapidly. Fifth, as with many social scientific phenomena, the distinction between gradual change and punctuation can be a spectrum across gradations of stability, but dividing the spectrum into two categories has analytical value. Moreover, a nuanced punctuation framework facilitates examining variations in both stable-phase duration and degrees of punctuation intensity—operating at distinct levels of analysis (e.g., single institution vs. institutional system) and responding to elements within the underlying social context.[12] This text thus uses a comprehensive punctuation framework that incorporates these points, with some emphasis on how gradual changes might engender cumulative developments that induce subsequent punctuation.

The punctuation dynamic, with varying degrees of intensity and duration, thus operates at multiple, sometimes nested, levels ranging from macro-level social orders and institutional systems to meso-level institutions and location- or domain-specific PSSs, and even to micro-level group practices and individual cognition.[13] At the macrolevel, for example, a combination of increased international capital mobility and restricted labor mobility might shift distributions of resources, power, and shared understandings sufficiently to undermine a system's mechanisms of coordination and enforcement, weakening resolutions of second-order CAPs. For example, such processes may have weakened, at least the appeal of, Northern European social democracy. Within systems, meso- and micro-level economic arrangements may suffer as contract enforcement and credibility weaken. A self-undermining dynamic may then ensue, eroding the system's ability respond to external and internal changes, rendering it increasingly vulnerable to disruptive change. This notion fits Francis Fukuyama's (2014) concept of political decay. (Appendix 6A offers a simple model in which a (meso- or macro-level) system's ability to resist internal and external shocks diminishes at a rate that responds to the (given) initial strength of the institutional system, drift, layering, and conversion.

Alternatively, cumulative, largely unintended internal developments can induce rapid change. Between 1961 and 1987, the pro-growth industrial policies of the South Korean Park Chung-hee and Chun Doo-hwan dictatorships gradually disseminated resources to the middle and working classes, enhancing their de facto, and in some instances, de jure power. By the mid-1980s, Korean labor unions had the organizational capacity to significantly reduce national output, notably manufactured exports—a key source of regime access to foreign exchange. Simultaneously, growing incomes, rising levels of education, and the increasing complexity of exchange via the opening of new markets with previously unavailable products, shifted public aspirations and perceptions of the role of government. The regime's legitimacy declined. As unionized workers, students, and opposition parties demanded more representation, a series of successful strikes and demonstrations culminated in the June 1987 uprising—20 days of strikes and mass protests across many cities. This focusing event sparked a transition to a more democratic regime.

Now, to return to this chapter's hypothesis: How can policy innovations influence such complex developments? Reform requires policy innovations that fit local contexts. To achieve enactment by relevant policymakers, implementation by civil servants, and acceptance by constituencies, such innovations must overcome substantial hurdles posed by institutional inertia and potential opposition. The impetus for innovative reform must then somehow arise from multiple internal and/or external developments that cumulatively or rapidly generate dissatisfaction with existing distributions of resources, access, and power on the part of various private and public parties—individuals and organizations—who typically form coalitions to promote change.

Broadly speaking, successful reform involves two intricately related factors: political mobilization and changing understandings on the part of relevant participants. Sections 3 and 4 elaborate by addressing cognitive, informational, and institutional sources of meso-level stability and punctuation within PSSs, with macro-level implications.

Section 3: Meso-Level Stability, Policy Subsystems, and Advocacy Coalitions

These next two sections address meso-level policymaking, with attention to new ideas. This discussion merges Section 2's approach to institutional systems with three complementary approaches from the policy process literature. First, punctuated equilibrium theory (PET; Frank Baumgartner, Bryan Jones, and coauthors) considers how cognitive limits, information processing, and institutional frictions affect agenda setting so as to foster meso-level punctuated equilibrium policy dynamics within PSSs. Second, the advocacy coalition framework (ACF; Paul Sabatier, Hank Jenkins-Smith, and coauthors) addresses coalitions, core beliefs, policy visions, and policy learning within PSSs. Third, the multiple streams framework (MSF; John W. Kingdon, Nicole Herweg, Nikolaos Zahariadis, and coauthors) addresses relationships between conceptions of problems, political interactions, and policy ideas to explain the phenomenon of policy emergence—meaning significant reform.[14]

These three complementary frameworks supplement the social-conflict power orientation of H3 and H4 and Section 2's discussion of institutional change. PET tends to emphasize structural dynamics; the ACF tends to emphasize agency dynamics that can fit a punctuation framework; and the MSF focuses on sources of reform-oriented punctuation. This approach to merging these perspectives, moreover, is consistent with Jacob S. Hacker and Paul Pierson's (2014) policy-focused politics and E. E. Schattschneider's (1960) agenda competition and expansion of conflict.[15]

Although these conceptions of policy theory originate in studies of the United States and European democracies, their underlying concepts of bounded rationality, information processing, agenda setting, rival coalitions, and punctuation dynamics can apply to any developmental setting that has at least a rudimentary political settlement, with adjustments for institutional contexts—especially the relative importance of informal institutions and personal relationships.[16]

At the mesolevel, this approach to policy innovation and reform processes utilizes four basic units of analysis—respectively, one for the field of interaction, one for structure, and two for agency:

1. *Policy domains* are areas of meso-level policy focus, usually with both geographical and topical dimensions, such as housing policy in Cape Town, South Africa, or forest management in India.[17]

2. *Policy subsystems*, a unit of analysis common to both PET and ACF, are meso-level institutional systems that enact and implement policies. They are configurations of complementary institutions, organizations, and coalitions—both within and outside of government—that dominate policymaking within specific domains in semiautonomous but sometimes overlapping fashions.[18] PSSs are themselves outcomes of prior political contestation that reflect distributions of power (H3). Within such configurations, collective-choice rules (formal or informal) designate positions, assign responsibilities, allocate resources (budgets), and assign key players to positions—creating foundations of de jure agenda-setting power, which then reinforce underlying asymmetric distributions of power and policy input.

3. *Advocacy coalitions* are groupings or networks of individuals, interest groups, and relevant organizations who share policy core beliefs and often material or social interests, and/or common opponents.

These coalitions coordinate activity, and they project policy visions to advance their agendas. They treat policies as manifestations of these core beliefs. Members include coalition elites (*primary members*; Weible 2008) who belong to relevant policy communities, as well as auxiliary members, who lack direct influence.

4. *Policy communities* are groupings of civil servants; representatives of interests, including firms, lobbyists, NGOs, and sometimes foreign government officials; and various experts (researchers, consultants or knowledgeable practitioners) who, operating both inside and outside of governments, attain domain-specific policy expertise. Such expertise relates to issue characteristics, avenues for input, process, positions (who does what), connections (who knows who), and even personality (reliable or not). Members of policy communities may or may not affiliate with advocacy coalitions, or they may serve as brokers that operate between them. In many developmental contexts, policy communities are informal and fluid. Even without formal positions, participants exchange ideas about practices, relationships, and possible changes. Specialization can arise from experience.[19]

Within policy domains, policymaking follows a punctuated equilibrium dynamic (Baumgartner and Jones 1993; Baumgartner et al. 2009; Baumgartner, Jones, and Mortensen 2017). Within this dynamic, PSSs structure stable-phase interactions. They shape motivation (incentives), flows of information (who gets which reports), and cognition (predictions concerning how context interacts with policy rules) across multiple participants. They provide relatively stable contexts (arenas) within which agency operates. Competing advocacy coalitions then draw on policy communities—often a source of innovative ideas—as they seek to advance their policy programs, which may include reforming or abolishing a PSS. Punctuation substantially transforms, replaces, or abolishes a PSS.

For Baumgartner and coauthors, the *general punctuation hypothesis* of policymaking rests on two foundations:

1. The properties of information processing among cognitively limited, boundedly rational agents—involving both individuals and organizations at various levels of policymaking; and

2. Multiple institutional frictions, including Section 2's asymmetric influences and stability factors, along with certain dynamics of agenda

setting. In particular, the costs of decision making successively increase as items advance from lower- to higher-level policy agendas.

These factors generate a "stick-slip" dynamic that resembles the influence of plate tectonics on the incidence of earthquakes (Baumgartner et al. 2009). Limited individual cognition and institutional frictions generate a "status-quo bias," a "friction" that resists substantive change prior to a *cumulative* buildup of sufficient pressure.[20] Dramatic change (an earthquake) eventually follows. Because frictions succumb to cumulative rather than immediate pressure, large shifts in policy orientation lack a clear and direct (e.g., linear) relationship to measurable pressure for change at specific points in time. Indeed, dramatic policy changes often fail to respond to noticeable pressure and then, occasionally, overcompensate—that is, punctuate—sometimes following apparently small incidents (Ibid.).

Here is a macro-level example: Some argue that the assassination of Austro-Hungarian Archduke Ferdinand by a Serbian nationalist—arguably a rather small event from an international perspective—precipitated World War I; yet, the system of alliances and treaties that had generated relative international stability prior to the war's outbreak had suffered multiple stresses for years. Disentangling the causes of World War I is, therefore, problematic. At the mesolevel, such punctuation dynamics underlie the importance, the stability, and the ultimate demise of PSSs.[21] Power asymmetries that emerge from asymmetric information access reinforce these patterns. A few details follow.

Concerning punctuation hypothesis foundation 1, policy-relevant information processing fosters punctuation dynamics via limited and occasionally shifting individual attention and an intellectual division of labor within and across PSSs. These processes operate at three levels of aggregation. At the microlevel, boundedly rational citizens engage in *serial information processing*: with limited attention, they consider only one (or a very few) items at a time.[22] Individual attention to specific policy problems thus responds to flows of information and social influence, as in H2, and to compelling policy visons or images. By enabling boundedly rational actors to quickly envision problems and/or solutions, policy images (e.g., a bloated welfare state) reduce costs of cognition. In contrast, at the mesolevel, organizations and policy communities, as key elements of PSSs, employ *parallel information processing*: they concurrently investigate multiple issues by delegating specific topics to specific groups or committees. Governments, for example, create ministries that focus on distinct policy domains; analogously, firms create personnel and sales departments. Finally, at the macrolevel, top policymakers (e.g., prime ministers, dictators, top cabinet officials, and influential members of parliaments), whose portfolios span multiple domains, necessarily also engage in serial information processing, with concurrent reliance on information flows and policy images. The number of policy problems at hand vastly exceeds any reasonable number to which such officials can direct their limited attention.[23] The need to process information thus limits access to policy agendas.

Accordingly, agenda space is a scarce political resource—especially at the top. Limited top-level attention also underlies much of the relative autonomy of PSSs. Indeed, the association of distinct PSSs to different policy domains facilitates society-wide parallel information processing.

This contrast between serial and parallel information processing shapes the relatively stable workings of PSSs, along with occasional bursts of shifting attention among citizen and top-level officials. Within (and sometimes across) subsystems, organizations, and policy communities, parallel information processing achieves large economies of scale. PSSs parcel out the gathering and interpretation of information across relevant organizations, committees, or less formal groups, which thereby attain specialized knowledge. The associated division of intellectual labor resolves substantial second-order CAPs of coordinating and channeling information. In so doing, it lends structure and stability to PSSs. It also awards members of relevant policy communities, located within PSSs, enormous advantages (first-mover advantage, information access, etc.). These arrangements exclude or restrict input from less informed and experienced parties—serial information processers who, in any case, often lack the time to pay attention to policy details. On the one hand, this balkanization of expertise thus reinforces H2 CAPs of unequal distributions of knowledge—contributing to asymmetric power, stable-phase durability, and limited entry points for new ideas. On the other hand, the susceptibility of serial-processing individuals to shifting information flows and policy images—some of which may reflect new ideas—combined with the limited attention of serial-processing top officials, allows for occasional punctuation.

Regarding foundation 2, institutional frictions interact with and complement the punctuation logic of information processing. Section 2's various sources of institutional stability support the durability and domain-level influence of PSSs. Furthermore, as items advance through successively narrower and more focused agendas—moving from systemic to institutional and then to decision agendas—the costs of making policy decisions steadily increase, due to the combined influence of more complicated organizational CAPs, additional avenues for blocking action (veto points), and the compounding influence of more intricate layers of institutional rules. Access to policy agendas and to higher levels of official attention correspondingly declines. New ideas that may appear on systemic agendas usually encounter inattention or resistance that blocks their path to decision agendas. Limited agenda access thus enhances the exclusivity of subsystem information processing. Achieving reform requires gaining, and often shifting, the limited attention of policymakers as they strive to advance desired items along increasingly scarce and contested agendas.[24]

On these foundations, PSSs both structure and dominate stable-phase policymaking within their respective domains. Associated policy communities hammer out domain-specific policy details, exchanging ideas about policy design and implementation strategies. Their acquired expertise (of whatever type) serves as an entry barrier that limits substantive participation to small, frequently interacting groups who share understandings of intricate policy details, subsystem rules, procedures, and channels. Indeed, such communities usually resolve disputes internally in order to avoid attracting the attention of either the public or top-level officials. Policy communities normally hide many deliberations from the public (Kingdon 2003; Cairney 2012). Subsystem elites thus shape public opinion by withholding and selectively releasing information.[25] Macro-level officials, who play larger roles in setting broad directions for policy, rarely have time to involve themselves in such meso-level detail. Finally, more subtle subsystem stability flows from the cognitive influences of corresponding institutions that shape understandings of policy-relevant problems, actors, actions, and consequences. Pertinent social norms may, for example, incline people to respect the authority of subsystem elites.

Despite these limits on input, various internal and external activities afford some opening for participation and innovation, either of which may reinforce or undermine system stability. Agency enters.

Operating within and sometimes across subsystems, advocacy coalitions—key conduits of political contestation—promote new policy ideas and defend old ones. Coalitions advance their preferred policy programs (sets of ideas) by mixing contestation and cooperation.[26] Individual and organizational attachment can be informal and transitory—especially for auxiliary members, who may join coalitions more for material or social opportunity than from conviction. Coordination within coalitions can be more spontaneous than planned. Organized interest groups (e.g., manufacturers' associations) often, at least loosely, associate with coalitions—or operate between coalitions, as policy brokers. Members of policy communities and broader *issue networks* (informal and often fluid groupings who express interest in specific issues) may associate or sympathize with certain coalitions, act as brokers, or remain neutral.

Within such interactions, shared beliefs and interests among coalition members usually lend coalitions some durability. Beliefs are the "glue" that holds coalitions together (Sabatier and Weible 2007), offering interpretations of contexts, problems, and possible solutions. As such, coalition beliefs offer an entrée for policy ideas: new and old ideas affect coalition formation, dynamics, and success.

Beliefs operate at three levels (Sabatier and Jenkins-Smith 1993, 1999; Jenkins-Smith et al. 2018):

1. *Deep core beliefs* are normative and ontological, concerning core philosophy about human nature, society, natural systems, good versus evil, and freedom versus security. These beliefs are not policy specific; they span coalitions. For example, in the United States, many evangelical Christians supported the abolition of slavery, while others opposed it, many supported Franklin Roosevelt's New Deal, and currently many support Republican Tea party policies.

2. *Policy core beliefs* have normative and empirical content that applies to specific policy topics and locations (hence to specific PSSs). Values, such as which groups are most deserving of citizenship or state support, influence evaluations of policies and outcomes.

3. *Secondary beliefs* concern policy details, such as rules for allocating food stamps and strategies for implementation.[27]

Deep core beliefs reflect identities and respond to conformity pressure. Highly resistant to change, they are a source of social cleavage. Policy core beliefs respond to conformity and reflect identity to a lesser degree. Advocacy coalitions form around them, and over time, association tends to harden the ensuing positons.[28] Shifts in deep and policy core beliefs involve micro-level individual and group punctuation dynamics that accompany reevaluative learning (as in Kahneman 2003). Of these three types, secondary beliefs respond most readily to evidence (learning via hypothesis testing) and offer the most likely, albeit circumscribed, entry point for new ideas.

As advocacy coalitions advance their policy core beliefs and programs, they project and defend policy images and narratives that jointly constitute policy visions. *Policy visions* are meso-level policy ideologies; they establish conceptual frameworks (mental models), applicable to specific policy domains, that define problems and convey stories of causality, which convey ethical prescriptions for remedy. By justifying policy core beliefs, policy visions legitimize coalition agendas. Indeed, dominant coalition visions can rationalize basic PSS features, such as which types of players can make which types of decisions. Successful visions shape and indeed frame both public and policymaker understandings.[29] As such, they reinforce subsystem stability.

Now consider the following stylized description of a PSS. Coalitions A and B each possess distinct policy beliefs, resources, and strategies. Coalition A is dominant, though with possible variation in its degree of dominance, ranging from a policy monopoly to collaboration with B. Policy brokers, including government officials and representatives of organized interest groups, mediate A-B interactions, formulate relevant procedures, and often allocate resources and positions (Sabatier and Weible 2007). The boundaries (e.g., who is and is not a broker) can be somewhat fluid. In this environment, policy communities—including elite members from both coalitions (fewer from B) and upper-level brokers—process information, establish agendas, and enact policies.

Dominant players (primarily coalition A elites) defend a functioning subsystem that serves their political and economic interests and other policy goals. They exercise power toward achieving these ends by utilizing their advantages with respect to information processing, resource access, position, and their ability to resolve organizational CAPs. They utilize existing, mutually understood privileged access and available resources to shift a policy's net benefits in desired directions (power1).[30] They also adjust subsystem rules, set decision agendas, and (sometimes subtly) threaten to punish certain types of participation, such as questioning top officials (power2).

More fundamentally, coalition elites and allies utilize policy visions to frame public understandings of conflict and appropriate roles for public policy (power3).[31] Dominant visions can portray an issue in complex and inaccessible terms, represent it as a private matter, declare that it is not a problem, or shift blame to irrelevant targets or opposing coalitions. A libertarian vision, for example, may effectively blame poverty on the welfare-state policies of an opposing coalition. Additionally, by invoking applicable norms (e.g., responsible citizenship, patriotism), policy visions may diminish the will of opponents to resist. Complementary stories may discredit opposition with labels like *unfair, greedy, elitist, unpatriotic,* or *naïve.* Indeed, much political contestation within subsystems involves competing coalition visions that legitimize alternative agendas, discredit opponents, and mobilize support among their own constituencies. Powerful parties, moreover, sometimes placate potential opponents with symbolic gestures—such as narrow appeals to nationalism: "The most intensive dissemination of symbols commonly attends the enactment of legislation which is most meaningless in its effects on resource allocation" (Edelman 1964, 378).[32]

Furthermore, triadic power relationships infuse various interactions between brokers and coalitions. Coalition A, utilizing triadic formats 1 or 7 (see Chapter 5), may threaten to restrict B's access to brokers. Brokers, who may favor one coalition—more likely A—may refuse to deal with B unless it meets certain terms that tend to favor A (format 2). Alternatively, brokers may play A and B off against each other—to their own advantage (format 4). Consequently, opposition coalitions often operate on the sidelines. Furthermore, the cognition-economizing, serial-information-processing public usually allows dominant narratives to both influence beliefs and contribute to apathy. Policy visions and narratives lower the costs of exercising cognition; they simplify complex issues, and most people have many other claims on their time.

These interactions all imply a limited potential for the entry of new ideas, especially ideas related to substantive reform. Yet, several caveats apply. Coalition B (or C), or an internal faction within A, may have distinct programs with alternative ideas. A few possible entry points follow.

First, within any coalition, say B, the ability to resolve organizational CAPs of free riding and internal conflict affects its capacity to project its vision and mobilize support for its agenda. Innovative methods for lowering the costs of participation can reduce free-riding incentives. New approaches to managing internal disputes can foster unity. New conceptions of problems, stories of causality, or ethical narratives can facilitate crafting a coherent policy vision that, as an element of social capital, could enhance commitment and cooperation, attract recruits, and diminish external opposition.[33]

Second, external sources (other subsystems, NGOs, foreign firms, or governments) may contribute new ideas concerning visions, procedures, policies, implementation, and internal organization. Such ideas, however, most likely take hold when they complement coalition goals and beliefs. Alternatively, external ideas may enter during punctuation.

Third, coalition A's inclination to absorb and utilize ideas from coalition B depends on the PSS structure. Christopher Weible (2008) proposes three basic PSS structures, or types, each with distinct implications on intra- and intercoalition policy learning:

I. *Unitary* (policy monopoly): A single coalition (A) fully dominates subsystem policymaking with only weak opposition from B. Coalition A restricts key interaction to a few venues, with limited access. Its policy vision achieves a monopoly on political understanding that frames public and policymaker conceptions of problems and solutions to A's advantage. A's vision also legitimizes subsystem dynamics—including A's dominant position therein (Baumgartner and Jones 1993). Most members of policy communities either affiliate with or behave as if they belong to A. The PSS exhibits centralized authority, independent from other subsystems. Policy outcomes disproportionately distribute benefits to A's members and assign costs more broadly.[34] External ideas reach the attention of A's elites only if such ideas serve their interests. Policy learning focuses on maintaining power and delivering A's agenda.

II. *Collaborative* (policy oligopolies): Two or more coalitions cooperate and compete, with intermediate levels of conflict that reflect intermediate levels of belief compatibility, with distinct but largely complementary policy visions. Coalitions share access to authority, though not necessarily equally (A can be dominant). Brokers mediate, with opportunities to exercise triadic power that exceed those normally available in type I or III subsystems. Relatively decentralized authority implies links to other subsystems (environmental policy influences energy policy). Relatively open and collaborative venues allow for flexible policy instruments and offer relatively transparent procedures and decisions. Policy outcomes offer positive-sum gains. Both coalitions accept (some) ideas from the other and sometimes from external sources. Policy learning may extend beyond instrumental position maintenance to inform policy effectiveness.

III. Adversarial: Rival coalitions (usually more than two) with incompatible beliefs vie for dominance, projecting incompatible policy visions. Intense contestation yields fragmented, often incoherent, authority that is, nonetheless, centralized within specific realms. Coordination occurs within coalitions, rarely between them. Coalitions achieve resource access via affiliated interest groups and sympathetic (or affiliated) agencies. They contend over venues, seeking those that favor their ideas and input. Localized brokers, who rarely exhibit neutrality, use triadic power (e.g., divide and conquer) against disfavored coalitions. Typically, rigid and often coercive policy outcomes are zero-sum games. Disgruntled coalitions try to expand conflict, shift venues, and involve macropolitical actors, members of other subsystems, and the public. Successful conflict expansion induces punctuation. Often operating in settings with weak institutions, type III PSSs are usually the least stable. Yet, with a stable distribution of power, adversarial relationships can persist.[35]

For types I and III, traditional venues "are limited in resolving conflict" (Weible 2008, 624). Legislatures write vague policies; agencies respond with top-down decisions; courts resolve procedural issues, but not substantive disputes. Indeed, the emergence of type III (or less dramatically factional contestation within types I and II) follows from Sabatier's concept of *devil shift*, whereby political contestants tend to overestimate both the power and maliciousness of opponents. This dynamic reflects an application of prospect theory (Quattrone and Tversky 1988) in which negative memories (losses) hold greater salience than positive memories (gains), and core beliefs filter interpretations of observed phenomena.[36] Devil shift generates a dynamic of rising conflict and distrust that undermines policy solutions and implementation.

New policy ideas thus find the least traction in type I systems where A's core beliefs and dominant vision focus attention away from policy alternatives and toward methods for retaining power. By contrast, collaboration within type II fosters cross-coalition exchange of ideas, with some focus on policy success. Type III's fragmented authority also allows considerable scope for new ideas, but such ideas rarely take hold outside of limited constituencies and many innovations concern seeking advantage against rivals.

Utilizing related ideas, Kuhika Gupta (2014) applies the ACF framework to India. Forestry policy operates as a PSS with two main advocacy coalitions. The dominant coalition (A) consists of state and industry officials, unified by the policy core belief that, as national assets, India's forests should serve national interests. The opposition coalition (B) consists of representatives of local populations, villages, and tribes unified by the belief that forests are community assets that should support community livelihood. Beginning in the colonial era and extending into the 1970s, coalition A operated as a centralized policy monopoly that restricted policy input (a type I PSS). Subsequently, the 1990 Joint Forestry Management policy encouraged more state-level autonomy with input from local actors and NGOs acting as mediators (brokers). The PSSs became more collaborative, type II.[37]

To sum up this section, stable-phase dynamics arise from subsystem economies of information processing, institutional frictions—including steadily increasing decision costs as items advance to higher-level policy agendas—and asymmetric distributions of power. These factors jointly underlie the formation and persistence of PSSs, the importance of policy communities, and the relative dominance of specific coalitions within. Here, the motivational, informational, and cognitive influences of subsystem institutions reinforce asymmetric distributions of power that, in part, reflect subsystem allocations of resources and positions. Restricted access to participation and decision arenas follows, reinforced by organizational and coalition abilities to utilize parallel information processing, an ensuing balkanization of expertise, and the limited attention of the serial-information-processing public. Moreover, macro-level policymakers, who also possess limited attention, rarely intervene. Consequently, new ideas related to substantive reform face considerable barriers to adoption—a set of CAPs for reform coalitions.

These sources of stability and exclusion notwithstanding, persistent contestation among advocacy coalitions; internal factions; policy brokers; macro-level officials; members of policy communities; issue networks; the public at large; and external actors from other subsystems, regions, or nations fosters the entry, though not necessarily adoption, of new ideas. Moreover, coordinated shifts in the attention of both the serial-information-processing public and macro-level actors can disrupt subsystems, precipitating punctuation (Baumgartner and Jones 1993). Punctuation, which often follows a "stick-shift" cumulative buildup of pressure, removes entry barriers to contrasting ideas, but it also undermines system predictability. Section 4 elaborates.

Section 4: Policy Emergence and Punctuation

Punctuation reconfigures the structuring, operations, and prevalent understandings within PSSs and, more dramatically but less frequently, that of macro-level institutional systems and social orders. Punctuation arises from a mix of internal and external cumulative developments and/or shocks.

Table 6.1 illustrates four combinations of the timing and loci of punctuation. In cells A and B, evolving internal and/or external developments gradually weaken current arrangements. For example, accumulated changes in technology, trade, or migration can shift distributions of resources and power across elites, organizations, and coalitions. Some of these developments, such as macro-level intervention (a new executive abolishes the environmental ministry) and spillover effects from other PSSs (restructuring energy policy alters environmental policy) operate internally from a macro perspective, but externally from a PSS perspective. At both levels, internal developments include things like turnover of key personnel. Gorbachev's 1985 ascension to become General Secretary of the Communist Party of the USSR, for example, precipitated Perestroika (Brown 2009). Likewise, common external developments include shifts in global trade and actions of international actors. In all of these cases, successive gradual developments can shift interpretations of institutional prescriptions—such as their fairness—and so gradually undermine the legitimacy of existing arrangements in multiple complementary, though often disjointed, fashions. Corresponding institutional drift, layering, conversion, and the associated erosion of dominant coalition power and status quo legitimacy may approach a critical-mass threshold; an accumulation of pressure weakens the (meso or macro) system. Increasingly conflictual inter- or intracoalition, ethnic, religious, racial, national, and/or class relations may ensue. Contested sovereignty follows.

These disjunctures render a system, at either a meso- or macrolevel, increasingly vulnerable to internal and external shocks. Sudden events may now alter social understandings. Certain incidents can precipitate sudden shifts in public and policymaker attention and associated understandings of problems and solutions, and so become *focusing events*, rather than mere incidents.

Accordingly, in cells C and D, sudden focusing events rapidly alter agents' understandings of specific problems and system procedures—generating waves of criticism (Schattschneider 1960) or enthusiasm (Downs 1972) that undermine legitimacy and shift distributions of power.[38] New perceptions

TABLE 6.1 Possible Loci and Timing of Key Punctuation Developments

		Timing	
		Cumulative → TP	*Sudden FE*
Locus of Underlying Developments	*Internal endogenous*	**A** Internal outcomes e.g., changes in distribution, positions	**C** Primarily internal FE e.g., Tahrir Square protests
	External exogenous	**B** Foreign or nonhuman causes e.g., shifting trade patterns, sanctions, climate change	**D** Exogenous FE e.g., Fukushima tsunami

TP = tipping point; FE = focusing event

of relative deprivation and biased procedure, for example, may loom large. Multiple parties adjust their mental models; collectively, they engage in re-evaluative learning. Attention shifts. Previously compelling policy visions and prior understandings of coordination (everyone else will follow the procedures) and enforcement (violation induces sanction) unravel. Expectations about others' behavior may cross a tipping point, reversing the conformity pressure of social incentives. Once a prior balance starts unraveling, previously functioning procedures encounter hurdles; previously established limits on participation and policy implementation falter. Members of policy communities increasingly question procedures and outcomes; some may defect to opposition coalitions. Excluded groups and new ideas increasingly enter debates. New opportunities for mobilization disrupt prior system equilibria. Conflict increases. Opposition coalitions seek new venues for airing grievances. Previously successful social mechanisms fail. For example, Mohamed Bouazizi's self-immolation on December 17, 2010, an event involving just one person, precipitated widespread protests; President Zine El Abidine Ben Ali of Tunisia resigned 28 days later. Less dramatically and at a subsystem level, Japan reoriented its nuclear policy after the tsunami flooding of the Fukushima nuclear plant.

Within subsystems, punctuation creates opportunities for substantive reform. At a macrolevel, punctuation affords opportunity for radical systemic reform, though with no guarantee of success; many CAPs remain. For well-placed, alert, adaptive, and innovative activists and coalitions, punctuation can quickly resolve multiple, otherwise insurmountable second- and first-order CAPs—though the ultimate outcomes often defy prediction and intent.[39]

The concept of policy emergence offers additional insight.

Policy Emergence, the Multiple Streams Framework (MSF), and Policy Ideas

The MSF concepts of policy emergence and three distinct streams of activity, initially proposed by Kingdon (2003), offer a complementary logic that informs our concept of punctuation. The MSF mixes political dynamics with shared concepts of problems and solutions; it also stresses a particular form of agency: that of a policy entrepreneur. Although initially developed to portray the emergence of national issues on important policy agendas in the United States, the MSF logic can apply to multiple meso- or macro-level policy or institutional processes in both industrialized and developing nations.[40]

The MSF's somewhat less formal approach to policy theory rests on five assumptions, derived from Michael Cohen, James March, and Johan Olsen's (1972) "garbage can model."

1. As in PET, time-constrained individuals use serial information processing.

2. In complex environments, agents confront ambiguity: "a state of having many ways of thinking about the same circumstances or phenomena" (Feldman 1989, 5). Shifting definitions of problems permit many ideas about solutions and a role for compelling images or narratives.

3. Agents thus experience *problematic preferences*: time-constrained policymakers make decisions before working out their preferences over incompletely understood alternatives (Zahariadis 2007).

4. Working in environments with overlapping jurisdictions and turf disputes, agents lack clear understandings of relevant *organizational technologies*, meaning processes by which organizations transform largely informational inputs into decision outputs. Colloquially, the left hand does not know what the right hand is doing.

5. Policy participation is fluid: agents move into and out of agencies and organizations, adding and subtracting information, perceptions, and understandings.[41]

Given these assumptions, Kingdon's *policy emergence* connotes the rapid ascension of a previously unconsidered, substantive policy idea to the attention of relevant policymakers—analogous to Victor Hugo's "idea whose time has come." Interpreted broadly, emergence can refer to new policy ideas, substantial reforms, or new institutional systems. In the latter two senses, emergence disrupts policy equilibria, undermining prior procedures: a type of punctuation that ushers in significant reform rather than, say, civil war. Policy emergence, however, requires a rare conjunction of three basic, semi-autonomous streams of activity, each of which can respond to new ideas.

First, the *problem stream*, as part of the social context within which policy ideas either succeed or fail, represents the flow of perceptions and understandings about relationships between physical and social environments on one hand, and policy on the other. Influenced by institutions, ideologies, and policy visions, this stream reflects shared mental models—held by the public, the media, various coalitions, policy communities, and policymakers—that speak to the immediacy and seriousness of various undesirable situations that policy might address. Two conceptual distinctions affect whether specific undesirable situations enter the stream: (i) that between a condition (which humans cannot affect) and a problem (which humans can); and (ii) that between problems in the public sphere (policy might address) and the private sphere (policy should not address). For example, for a large segment of the US population, climate change is not a policy problem because it does not exist, is an unavoidable condition, and/or is none of the government's business.

Within this stream, conceptions of problems arise from three key sources: First, we have *indicators*—measurements of developments in the social and physical environment (e.g. megatons of carbon or sulfur dioxide emitted into the atmosphere) that are often transmitted and interpreted by various specialists and the media. Here, H2 CAPs and knowledge flows influence the construction of indicators and interpretations, as do policy visions. Second, we have *policy feedback*—namely, evaluations that point to problems with existing policies that comes from officials, experts, interests, coalitions, the media, and the public, conditioned by information, resources, incentives, and interpretations (Pierson 1993). Third, occasional focusing events, such as famines or general strikes, can shift shared understandings, directing public and official attention to specific issues. Problems that emerge from this stream achieve at least temporary attention, implying entry onto systemic and sometimes institutional agendas, with at least an implied demand for remedy. Actual impacts on policy decisions, however, depend on the other two streams.

The second stream, the *political stream*, represents flows of power relations and political contestation that ultimately affect policymaker attention to specific problems and policy ideas. This stream embodies interactions among competing advocacy coalitions, various special interests, officials, and (often nonneutral) brokers, with input from issue networks and, at times, the general public—all conditioned by evolving distributions of power.[42] Ideas that do not fit the criteria of powerful parties rarely emerge. Even so, innovative ideas about political causality can influence this stream's interactions (a goal of social science).

Reflecting expectations of success and underlying perceptions of legitimacy and support, political acceptance of policy ideas exhibits bandwagon effects. Interest groups and think tanks, who participate in coalitions or act as brokers, seek out sympathetic officials. To attract official support, they may, for example, offer *legislative subsidies*—relevant information and/or mobilization of related constituencies—that can advance policymakers' goals (Hall and Deardorff 2006; Mahoney and Baumgartner 2015).[43] Once an idea gains momentum, politically minded agents seeking recognition lend their support. Ideas that emerge from the political stream end up on institutional and decision agendas, although without guaranteed success.

Third, the *policy stream* filters the flow of ideas within and among policy communities. As a key arena for expert influence on policy (Weible 2008), this stream creates and transmits policy ideas and innovations among participants. Its internal operations reflect an evolutionary dynamic whereby specialists select proposals on the basis of their perceived technical feasibility, financial feasibility, and normative acceptability to themselves—with some attention to the same for constituencies and policymakers (Kingdon 2003). Accordingly, policy visions, ideologies, and specialist coalition affiliations influence idea selection.

As in the political stream, selection processes exhibit bandwagon effects— here arising primarily from specialist efforts to influence others with information, opinions, and concepts. H2 dynamics condition selection via knowledge flows, analytical compatibility, skill clustering, and social conformity pressure across the pertinent networks. Selected ideas secure placement on relatively short lists of proposals that participants hope to place onto decision agendas.

Policy entrepreneurs within the policy stream often seek problems to which they can attach their "pet" solutions; they act like surfers waiting for waves (Kingdon 2003, 165). Ideas that emerge from this stream (selected ideas) necessarily operate in the context of the other two streams. Proposals that fail to accord with social understandings of salient problems do not attain access to institutional agendas. Ideas that fail the political criteria of powerful actors do not reach decision agendas. In the United States, various climate policy ideas move onto and off these agendas, in response to political- and problem-stream activity.

These dynamics complement our discussion of the punctuation cycle. During the stable phase, the streams operate largely independently. Linkages occur within the confines of incremental change—including manifestations of drift, layering, and conversion—but rarely displacement or policy emergence. Within PSSs, dominant parties manipulate elements within the three streams to uphold their relative power. In the problem stream, dominant party visions project and define problems to suit their policy goals. In the political stream, such players exercise power, often barring the access of policy-stream ideas onto institutional or decision agendas—a type of gatekeeping. Moreover, because implementation requires credible commitments, policy ideas that challenge the interests of implementers or potential obstructers (civil servants, private interests) may, responding to anticipated outcomes, fail to achieve agenda access (an H4 dynamic). Thus, interactions within the problem and political streams typically confine applications of policy-stream ideas to relatively incremental policy or institutional adjustments—sometimes with new angles on implementation or evaluation. Regarding cognition, although new ideas can influence internal-stream dynamics, reigning mental models, as manifested in policy visions and ideologies, usually inhibit widespread reevaluative policy learning.

Stability, however, does not last as environments evolve. The MSF complements our prior discussion of punctuation, with implications for innovation. As in cell A of Table 6.1, cumulative internal developments related to drift, layering, and institutional conversions—now operating within each stream—can sow the seeds for punctuation. In the problem stream, drift can signify a failure to recognize new problems from changing environments. Layering can involve new conceptions of problems—often as amendments to existing interpretations. Conversion can imply reinterpreting a previously salient or not salient problem.

Within the political stream, opportunists may engage in layering by introducing amendments that favor their interests; they may promote institutional conversion with reinterpretations of procedures, norms, and rules.[44] Hidden opponents, in particular, may insert discrete, incremental innovations that could later facilitate greater change. For example, relatively small adjustments to policies and procedures in the USSR, introduced by increasingly disgruntled Communist Party officials during the early 1980s, eased the path for Gorbachev's radical reforms (Brown 2009). As cumulative effects undermine system legitimacy, some agents, including elites, may become disgruntled and defect to an opposition coalition, as in the case of Francisco Madero as a leader of the Mexican Revolution (see Chapter 8).

Likewise, within the policy stream, incidences of drift may induce specialists to discover deficiencies in existing policies. New data and methodologies—perhaps layers on prior techniques—may uncover poor implementation and other bad outcomes (increasing capital flight, tax evasion, poverty). Certain experts may covertly support opposing coalitions. For example, during the 1960s, disgruntled scientists within the US Atomic Energy Commission leaked information on nuclear safety to environmentalists (Baumgartner and Jones 1993).

Additionally, as in Table 6.1's cells B, C, and D, cumulative external developments and/or internal or external focusing events can push reactions across tipping points, redirecting activity within the streams. New conceptions of problems become compelling; opponents exploit divisions within the policy community, altering distributions of power and reconfiguring coalitions. New policy solutions pass selection to emerge on short lists. Such ideas may suddenly address previously unrecognized but now salient problems and, simultaneously, meet the political criteria of newly powerful parties. Within these dynamics, policy entrepreneurs seize opportunities to merge the streams. They attempt to attract public and macro-level attention to emergent policy ideas as solutions to increasingly salient problems.

Concurrently, patterns of information processing and social learning escape prior boundaries. Established mental models repeatedly produce flawed predictions. Disjunctures emerge between prior conceptions and new developments. Agents experience "double-sided" reevaluation; they reinterpret the meanings of events and existing beliefs in light of each other (Hall 2005, 136).[45] Participants find themselves torn between competing mental models. Reevaluative learning follows. Indeed, agents engage in disproportionate information processing; bursts of attention reflect hypersensitivity to new signals (Jones and Baumgartner 2005). Policymakers (and others) face uncommonly pervasive ambiguity. Previously stable patterns of coordination and enforcement unravel, weakening institutional prescriptions.[46]

Waves of criticism or enthusiasm may then spread rapidly across large social networks.

The streams converge on the precipice of policy emergence, opening a window of opportunity. Policy entrepreneurs seize opportunities to gather public and macro-level attention as they shove their ideas through the window onto institutional and decision agendas. More generally, reform coalitions can instigate substantial change—that is, if they can resolve remaining, often substantial, CAPs of coordinating activity and challenging opponents in deeply uncertain environments. If so, the political stream's resistance to change transforms as bandwagons shift. The induced punctuation may then foster meso-level policy emergence or macro-level radical reform.

Emergence as an Information Cascade

From a social network perspective, policy emergence is an *information cascade* (Lohmann 1994, 2000).[47] This dynamic signifies the rapid spread and adoption of a new or previously dormant idea, manner of thinking, or practice across a large social network.

Social network models (not reproduced here) can illustrate. These models specify links (communications, relationships, or exchanges) among multiple agents (nodes). Some agents are well connected, others less so. Some individuals, *innovators* (usually operating in the policy stream), create or import new ideas or practices. Others, *early adopters*, embrace innovation if a small number (or proportion) of colleagues, acquaintances, or friends do so first. *Late adopters* join in only if many others—a critical mass—do so first. Finally, *inert* players resist adoption.

Information cascades arise when a few well-placed innovators can readily transmit new ideas to a sufficient number of early adopters who, via their positions within network subregions, induce imitation among multiple connected late adopters. When rates of adoption within several regions simultaneously cross critical-mass thresholds, new ideas or practices spread rapidly.[48] Rapid adoption of "new" ideas, however, need not generate good outcomes. The collapse of Lehman Brothers when it filed for bankruptcy on September 15, 2008, initiated panic in global financial markets.

Susanne Lohmann's (1994, 2000) model of collective-action cascades can describe punctuation events that follow either meso- or macro-level merging of the three streams—or separate incidents of emergence from each. She envisions a multiperiod game among imperfectly informed heterogeneous individuals, arranged along a spectrum of attitudes toward the current regime (or practice), from negative to positive. At the beginning of each period, all players observe the last period's total participation in reform activity, and each receives a private signal concerning the state of the regime, good or bad. The probability of receiving "good" depends on a player's location on the spectrum. Each player then decides whether to participate in opposition activity (i.e., adopt a new idea or practice) during the period. If actual participation then exceeds expected participation, some agents reevaluate their understandings of the regime and the associated net benefits from opposition activity. In Timur Kuran's (1995) terms, each adjusts her balance between private preference and public expression. Participation increases. A sufficiently long sequence of such occurrences in appropriately connected network regions generates an information cascade of new thoughts and practice—ushering in reform.

Whether modeled as the unraveling of a PSS, the convergence of three streams, or as an information cascade, punctuation opens the floodgates for new ideas. Yet, it does so in a manner that confounds predicting which specific ideas receive acceptance and, more dramatically, anticipating subsequent political, economic, and polity impacts.

Section 5: Conclusion—How Innovative Ideas Can Relax Constraints

Policies embody efforts to resolve CAPs. Without CAPs, there would be no need for policy. Policy innovations apply new knowledge and techniques—from the point of view of local context—to resolution. H5 follows logically: policy innovations can sometimes relax political power and commitment constraints imposed by H3 and H4 CAPs, as well as free-riding and coordination CAPs from H1 and H2. Yet, innovations must achieve adoption within existing political contexts.[49]

A list of the possible types and applications of policy innovations would be endless. To quote Kingdon, "ideas come from anywhere" (2003, 71). Consequently, this section only sketches ideas on five topics: types of problems that innovations might address, types of innovation, intended targets, timing, and policy learning.

Types of Problems

Policy innovations should address how to achieve sustainable capability-oriented economic and political development, with particular attention to H1–H4 CAPs operating within specific social contexts. Indeed, these four categories of CAPs point to directions for innovation.

For H1 CAPs of free riding, fruitful innovations can address methods of generating contribution (new interpretations of norms of fairness; new, possibly more legitimate ideas on how to distribute tax burdens; collection techniques), methods for reducing negative production or consumption externalities (new conceptions of social responsibility, carbon markets, inside smoking regulations), or ways of managing conflict (mediation techniques). Since these endeavors require cooperation, building trust among and across relevant communities can engender voluntary contribution and reduce the need for threatened sanctions in areas such as tax collection and compliance with environmental regulations. Indeed, a well-functioning economy rests on policies that foster good citizenship (Bowles 2017). Innovative techniques for building an inclusive sense of community (neighborhood, village, city, region, nation), such as new types of reciprocal exchange and visions of common purpose, can enhance social capital and foster common trust.

For H2 CAPs, innovations might concern how to extend knowledge access (distribute cell phones in Africa), enhance skills (new techniques of training and education), create positive educational role models for underprivileged children (classroom visits by athletes with degrees), develop ways to facilitate and coordinate new production techniques across firms (sometimes an outcome of industrial policies), and extend credit to underserved areas (microfinance). Regarding H3, innovations might concern how to alter distributions of power (land reform, legalization of independent trade unions), mobilize previously marginal constituencies (organizational innovations of Mohandas Karamchand Gandhi, which were adopted and transformed by Martin Luther King Jr.), or shift elite goals away from short-term gain to long-term socially beneficial outcomes (appeals to inclusive patriotism). Policy innovations might address H4 CAPs by introducing new commitment mechanisms (microfinance uses small-group connections and reputation for enforcement) and new techniques for enhancing the legitimacy of existing forms of commitment (new ways to encourage viable reciprocity or observe defection).

Types of Innovations

Normative policy entrepreneurs might promote new interpretations or foci for existing social norms (e.g., fairness applies to all, regardless of gender, race, or ethnicity), which could enhance trust and build a sense of moral purpose for cooperation and exchange. New formal institutions (laws, regulations), when perceived as legitimate, can facilitate coordination (who is supposed to do what) and affect public expressions of preference (e.g., cooperation) by altering expectations about others' behavior. The passage of the 1965 Voting Rights Act fundamentally shifted African American access to voting in the US South, as well as society-wide expectations concerning political participation. At a more instrumental level, strategic innovations related to matters such as internal agency or coalition organization may facilitate membership participation and policy implementation. New ideas on venues for public or expert input can improve accountability. Novel measurement techniques can identify problems and contribute to evaluating existing policies. At a cognitive level, new ideologies and policy visions can, by fostering legitimacy, motivate contributions to public goods, mitigate conflict, and facilitate coordination and enforcement. Tanzania's founding president, Julius Nyerere, advanced his concept of African socialism from 1964 to 1985. Even though this project failed economically, it created a national identity around socialist ideology rather than ethnicity, reducing ethnic conflict—in contrast to Kenya. This ideology enabled nation building, which facilitated economic growth after 1999 (Fukuyama 2014, 329–33).

Intended Targets and Timing

Intended audiences include policymakers and communities, brokers, advocacy coalitions, civil servants, interests, specific communities, and the public at large. Successful innovations reflect understandings of relevant audiences. Unlike that of many other postcolonial African rulers, Nyerere's political organization (TANU) "penetrated the countryside" rather than solely focusing on cities (Ibid., 231). Attention to audience facilitated nation building.

For given innovations and audiences, the likelihood of successful adoption depends on timing. The punctuation cycle suggests a general prescription: during the stable phase, incremental ideas, often with elements of layering or conversion, have the best chance of adoption. Innovative layering might extend successful approaches or target adjustments toward identified shortcomings. Innovative conversion might stress cooperative elements of existing social norms or point to poorly enforced laws that are ostensibly aimed at protecting rights, as a way to create pressure for enforcement of such rights. Beginning with the 1977 formation of Charter 77, Czechoslovakian dissidents used the "principle of legality" to expose the state's legal façade to (slowly) undermine the legitimacy of the communist regime (Havel 2015).

Prior to punctuation, a policy entrepreneur's trick involves fostering stream convergence, with appropriate timing. Pertinent techniques may entail simple matters, like introducing players from different sections of policy communities (different streams or network regions) or, more generally, creating network connections to extend transmissions of ideas. New ideas may also address methods for communicating goals with reference to existing norms. Nyerere devoted considerable effort into making Swahili Tanzania's national language (Fukuyama 2014). As a result, network connections expanded exponentially.

Punctuation, in contrast, opens avenues for diverse and radical ideas, but it does so in unstable environments, with shifting receptivity, audiences, and outcomes. Fruitful innovations need to address methods for retaining audiences, coalitions, and focused attention on coalition goals: daunting CAPs, implied by the title of a civil rights folk song, "Keep Your Eyes on the Prize."

Policy Learning

During either phase of the cycle, the transmission of policy ideas depends on policy-oriented learning—a feature of information processing within and across policy communities and issue networks. *Policy-oriented learning* connotes "relatively enduring alternations of thought or behavioral intentions that result from experience and/or new information and that are concerned with the attainment or revision of policy objectives" (Sabatier and Jenkins-Smith 1993, 123).

By interpreting mistakes, altering strategies, and occasionally altering mental models, various participants may improve adaptations to changing environments and discover opportunities for promoting new ideas. Such learning naturally occurs at multiple levels. This brief treatment, however, focuses on learning within and between advocacy coalitions.

There are three overlapping categories of policy learning:[50] *instrumental learning* relates directly to policy design or implementation; *political learning* focuses on enhancing coalition (or individual) position vis-à-vis others; and *organizational learning* concerns techniques for building social capital and resolving internal CAPs. All three operate within and respond to subsystem dynamics.

In societies with at least marginally successful political settlements, relatively durable stable phases offer relatively predictable, albeit restrained, environments for introducing new ideas. Reflecting existing patterns of information processing, agents consider new ideas at a "casual driver's pace" (Weible 2008, 618). Learning involves testing hypotheses within established cognitive frameworks, as shaped by core beliefs and prevalent visions. As such, it principally affects secondary policy beliefs. The spread of new ideas within or across coalitions and policy communities depends on rates of membership turnover, political pressure for change, degrees of belief compatibility, and the persuasiveness of evidence—all via the cognitive filters of reigning policy visions.

Regarding streams, the policy stream is the chief locus of innovation. Many ideas enter (Kingdon refers to a "primeval soup" of possible ideas [2003, 116]), but few pass selection. Most often, incremental and instrumental ideas emerge. Such ideas may include new approaches to implementation or adjustments from institutional layering. By contrast, problem-stream innovations concern new understandings of existing problems or realizations that certain undesirable conditions are, indeed, policy problems. In the political stream, innovative ideas focus on strategy (political innovation)—within or between competing coalitions. In all three cases, most ideas remain within their streams.

PSSs shape the context within which policy learning and new ideas find or fail to find acceptance. A few general principles, such as stable-phase focus on secondary beliefs, apply to all three types of PSSs. Cross-coalition learning occurs when influential members expect political gains from using external ideas and/or when developments render such ideas impossible to ignore. All three PSS types engage in all three types of learning, but type I monopolies have the weakest incentives for organizational learning, and type III (adversarial) systems have the strongest incentives for political learning (Weible 2008).[51]

Regarding further distinctions, in type I PSSs, dominant coalition policy visions offer little incentive or room for outside input. External ideas that achieve acceptance tend to acknowledge problems without challenging core beliefs. By contrast, type II subsystems allow cross-coalition learning, particularly when coalitions have access to pertinent expertise. Relatively open forums offer conduits for expert advice, which has greater impact when experts agree.[52] Even so, acceptable ideas usually focus on secondary beliefs, such as how to adjust (layer) an existing policy or improve its implementation. In type III PSSs, coalitions use specialist opinion in political competition. For example, opposing sides in environmental disputes may recruit their own engineers or scientists to discredit the other side's arguments. Whereas competing and incompatible policy visions offer distinct approaches, a coalition's innovations usually take hold only within its area of influence. Succumbing to Sabatier's devil-shift dynamics, coalition A's evidence may only increase B's attachment to its own vision, and enhance its resolve to challenge A. The US gun debate appears to follow this dynamic.

Despite these limitations, new stable-phase ideas can sow the seeds for, sometimes constructive, policy emergence.[53] Clever policy entrepreneurs may incorporate permissible layering to subtly shift patterns of interaction. They may employ institutional conversion—a potentially powerful technique that can operate without reprisal—to shed new light on extant rules, norms, and procedures. Some such entrepreneurs may be system insiders, even elites, who hide private preferences for substantive reform. In the pre-Gorbachev Soviet Union, hidden reformers rationalized modest but meaningful proposals with their own interpretations of Vladimir Lenin's ideas (Brown 2009). In the aforementioned case of US nuclear scientists, insider release of information undermined the legitimacy of the nuclear energy PSS (Baumgartner and Jones 1993). Such maneuverings may also suggest new visions that could merge the streams. If discrete incremental innovations tip the balance of shared understandings, actors may overcompensate for their previous neglect of information by shifting their mental models (Weible 2008, 618). Innovative ideas may thus alter understandings, coalition activity, and distributions of power—and so link the streams to usher in policy emergence.

When new ideas offer implementable techniques for building trust, for enhancing access to the means of political and economic achievement or foreclosing barriers to such achievement; when ideas offer feasible methods for reducing inequities, coordinating activity, limiting the influence of powerful parties, and reorienting their goals toward long-term social benefit; and when new ideas enhance the credibility of implicit or explicit promises to respect others' rights and exercise power with attention to broad social benefits, then such ideas contribute to resolving H1–H4 CAPs. If so, such ideas facilitate political and economic development.

Social peace underlies development. Part III extends this analysis by categorizing political settlements in order to identify key features of alternative developmental contexts and associated CAPs.

III TYPOLOGIES AND A NEW FRAMEWORK FOR DEVELOPMENT THEORY

PART III ADDRESSES SEVERAL approaches to classifying political settlements (hereafter, PSs) and social orders as it constructs the central component of this text's conceptual framework for the political economy of development. Recall that social orders are macro-level equilibria of institutional systems that persist over the stable phase of a punctuated equilibrium cycle, and PSs are mutual understandings held among elites and powerful organizations that establish politics, rather than violence, as their primary social mechanism for handling disputes. PSs underlie institutional systems and corresponding social orders. Classification of PSs thus facilitates inquiry into relationships between distributions of power, the composition and motivation of political constituencies, configurations of institutions, distributions of benefits, CAPs, and, ultimately, developmental prospects. Chapter 7 sets the stage by addressing several approaches to categorizing social orders and PSs that appear in the literature. Building on these concepts, Chapter 8 develops my approach. It develops a typology of PSs that addresses distinct political foundations of social orders, where each element of the typology implies a distinct set of CAPs that shape a society's prospects for economic and political development. Chapter 9 extends this basic typology into business-state relations and potential feedback effects of economic returns on settlement stability. It pays particular attention to second-order CAPs associated with rendering exchange agreements credible, as well as associated impacts on allocations of benefits and power that, in turn, either reinforce or undermine configurations of institutions and PSs. Jointly, Chapters 8 and 9, with attention to H1–H5, offer a new conceptual framework for analyzing the political economy of development.

7 Alternative Typologies of Social Orders and Political Settlements

> Bangladesh was born out of two violent partitions, each caused by the elites' inability to agree about the distribution of rents.
>
> —*Mushtaq Khan, "Bangladesh: Economic Growth in a Vulnerable LAO" (2013)*

IN 1947, FOLLOWING INDEPENDENCE and the partition between India and Pakistan, the new Pakistani government faced not only humanitarian and economic crises related to violence and massive relocation of populations, but also a constitutional crisis. "A viable ruling coalition that included representative members of the elites from the two wings [East and West Pakistan] simply could not be constructed" (Khan 2013, 26). A weak settlement that lacked an accepted mechanism for allocating decision-making authority ensued. By 1960, however, the military asserted greater control. It created a bureaucratic ruling coalition (hereafter, RC) that established close ties to select business elites and distributed rents to affiliated businesses and rural political representatives who were not members of traditional political organizations. Relative political stability permitted *learning rents* (profitable returns from adaptation and innovation) that allowed for early industrialization. Nevertheless, powerful interests protected inefficient businesses and, more ominously, the narrow distribution of rents. The relative exclusion of East Pakistani elites fostered a revolt in the East and the establishment of Bangladesh in 1971 (Ibid.).

Between 1971 and 1975, the new nation suffered a chaotic period of rent capture and asset-stripping by multiple previously excluded parties. The government attempted to form a broad populist coalition within a one-party state, but "it was clear there were not enough rents to satisfy everyone" (Ibid., 28). Between 1975 and 1990, the military reasserted some control but permitted political parties to participate in elections. This arrangement included "enough political organizers in the dominant coalition to minimize the required threat of force to an anticipated level" (Ibid., 29): arguably a weak, though more inclusive, PS. Even so, in 1990, the autocratic rule of President Hussain Muhammad Ershad ended with violence and street protests, followed by a transition to competitive elections and a more open system.

Starting in 1991, Bangladesh moved toward a more competitive political arrangement, with rival parties distributing rents to supporters. That year, the Bangladesh National Party (BNP) won enough seats to lead a coalition government, naming Khaleda Zia prime minister. In 1996, the rival Awami League (AL) formed a coalition government naming Sheikh Hasina Wazed prime minister. The BNP and Zia returned to power after the 2001 election. In 2007, however, following street violence and several general strikes, a military-backed emergency government took control. In 2008, elections returned the AL to power. During this post-1990 period, political and economic organizations could emerge without prior approval of an RC, but such organizations required "purchased" support for sustainable operation. Bangladesh operated under a system based on *competitive clientelism*, which corresponds with a *semimature limited access order* (Ibid., 24–31).[1]

Recall from Chapter 1 that PSs include shared foundational or constitutional understandings of informal and formal rules that underlie institutional systems and social orders.[2] The Bangladesh example suggests fundamental shifts in such understandings occurring in (approximately) 1947, 1960, 1975, and 1991. On a smaller scale, within a tribal society, a PS may involve a common understanding that a council of elders resolves certain disputes. In contrast, for established democracies, constitutions, as components of PSs, set certain parameters for political engagement. More generally, by both reflecting and reproducing balances of power, PSs set boundaries for dynamic interactions among constituent groups, organizations, and coalitions. In so doing, they condition the emergence, viability, and longevity of institutional systems and social orders that then shape the trajectories of political and economic development.

This chapter summarizes several prior approaches to conceptualizing such interactions. Specifically, it reviews four distinct but related sets of typologies of social orders and PSs. Each approach denotes categories of settlements (or social orders) on the basis of elemental political and institutional characteristics. Each approach offers a method for analyzing how specific contexts condition developmental problems and prospects. As such, each typology, while necessarily abstracting from multifarious detail, offers a framework for social scientific inquiry; each offers a diagnostic tool for development policy (Booth 2015).

Discussion proceeds as follows. After brief consideration of the related concept of a political equilibrium, Section 1 summarizes Douglass North, John Joseph Wallis, and Barry Weingast's (2009) one-dimensional typology of social orders. Section 2 addresses Brian Levy's (2014) two-dimensional developmental typology of institutions and PSs. Section 3 reviews a few alternative approaches to defining PSs followed by a summary of Mushtaq Khan's (2010) three typologies of developmental contexts, PSs, and business-state relations. Continuing with the theme of business-state relations, Section 4 summarizes typologies of markets and deals from Lant Pritchett, Kunal Sen, and Eric Werker (2018).

Section 1: Antecedents to Political Settlement Typologies: Political Equilibria and a One-Dimensional Approach to Social Orders

Chapter 5's discussion of H3 and H4 has utilized the Acemoglu-Robinson (2008) concept of a political equilibrium. To reiterate, a *political equilibrium* occurs when the institutional distribution of de jure power offers elites no incentive to alter their investments in attaining de facto power. In other words, elites find institutional allocations of power and benefits sufficiently satisfactory that they perceive no net gain—given the costs of investing additional resources in de facto power and potential consequences—from undertaking such investment for the purpose of altering or undermining existing institutional arrangements. Such an equilibrium implies a form of PS, though because not all investments in de facto power would necessarily undermine a PS—at least in the short run—a political equilibrium is a more general concept: over time, a single PS could incorporate more than one political equilibrium, but persistent political disequilibrium will undermine a PS.

North, Wallis, and Weingast (2009) offer a typology (hereafter the NWW typology) that distinguishes types of social orders along a linear spectrum using two effectively combined criteria: institutional strength and the accessibility of political and economic organizations. This combination reflects their *double balance hypothesis*: sustainable open economic institutions require correspondingly open political institutions, and vice versa. The NWW logic suggests a spectrum with five regions, ranked by the strength and accessibility of economic and political institutions. On the left (implied but not discussed) is a chaos order: a Hobbesian state of nature with continuous violence and no institutions. The escape from chaos depends on society's ability to restrain violence via rent-sharing agreements among powerful parties. Though not stated explicitly, this transition implies some form of PS. Three types of limited-access orders (LAOs) follow: fragile, basic, and mature. Movement toward a mature LAO connotes increasingly viable institutions. The right-hand end of the spectrum denotes the open-access order (OAO).

In the *fragile* LAO, the distribution of violence capacity across groups determines a distribution of rents. A tenuous dominant coalition barely maintains power against internal and external rivals. In the *basic* LAO, a somewhat stable dominant coalition serves as the principal source of economic access and rents. Elites and organizations, seeking advancement, usually affiliate or accommodate. Fear of expropriation inhibits much private economic activity. Exchanges rely far more on informal and personalized relationships than on impersonal rules. In the *mature* LAO, by contrast, a stable dominant coalition permits nonaffiliated organizations to operate, but economic and especially political access usually requires dominant coalition approval. This order reflects some development of impersonal rules, notably economic institutions. Three *doorstep conditions*, which largely reflect political development, permit movement from a mature LAO to an OAO: a rule of law that applies to elites, a state monopoly over organized violence, and the relatively long-term persistence of NGOs. The OAO reflects a full Weberian state, with strong institutions and relatively open access to both political and economic participation. Finally, although one could interpret this typology as a stages-of-development sequence, societies move in both directions along the spectrum.

Despite some limitations, the NWW typology establishes several useful principles:

1. Categorizing social orders facilitates systematic developmental comparisons.
2. To create social order, a society needs to create social mechanisms for managing violence; it must achieve minimal resolution of CAPs posed by group capacities for exercising violence—that is, it must achieve some form of PS.

3. For many developing countries (LAOs), elite bargaining over workable distributions of rents underlies a, sometimes tenuous, ability to restrain organized violence.

4. Political and economic development involve strengthening institutions and broadening access. Notably, in the absence of the doorstep conditions, attempts to import OAO institutions into LAOs will most likely fail because powerful parties have strong incentives to limit access as they utilize and retain rent-seeking opportunities. Imported rules that mimic OAO arrangements remain largely unenforced (a second-order CAP).

5. Societies can move in either direction on the spectrum—achieving a particular level of institutional development does not preclude decay, dissolution, or complete destruction. This notion implies a punctuated equilibrium dynamic.

6. Inequality is both a cause and consequence of interactions within and between types of social orders. LAOs rely on and reproduce inequitable political and economic relations.

7. Each type of social order implies a series of basic developmental CAPs. In a chaos order, for example, the most pressing CAPs concern managing the distribution of violence capacity and controlling its exercise.

Three limitations of this approach stand out: First, it permits but does not substantially develop a concept of private-sector exercises of power. Second, it cannot explain periods of growth acceleration and deceleration, a common phenomenon in developing nations (Pritchett et al. 2018). Third, a one-dimensional approach overlooks important distinctions, especially among types of PSs. Different kinds of settlements exert distinct influence on institution building and developmental CAPs. The next typology moves in the direction of addressing this third concern.

Section 2: A Two-Dimensional Typology of Social Orders

Two-dimensional typologies permit more nuanced distinctions among categories of social orders. Levy's (2014) typology, resembling the NWW one, designates categories of institutional strength; it also distinguishes two types of PSs. This combination yields six kinds of developmental institutional systems (social orders). Each signifies a distinct (punctuated) social equilibrium.

Figure 7.1 illustrates. The horizontal spectrum designates four classifications of institutional strength. Beginning on the left, a *conflict order* (as in NWW) signifies no PS, as in Syria, Yemen, Somalia, and sections of Iraq in 2017–18. Four categories span the middle range: *dominant discretionary* and *personalized competitive* on the "Low" end of the middle spectrum, with *rule by law dominant* and *rule of law competitive* toward the "High" end. In the former two, monitoring and enforcement procedures "are built around the specific identities (and threat potential) of the parties involved" (Ibid., 20). Such arrangements depend on personalities and personal networks; they shift or collapse with the replacement or death of key individuals. In contrast, for the latter two, impersonal institutions signify codified rules (formal institutions) with monitoring and enforcement activities assigned to third-party (relatively impartial) organizations. Specific procedures thus depend less fundamentally on personalities and personal networks. Certain social prescriptions (e.g., protection of property rights, assignments of political positions) become impersonal (at least relatively speaking). These arrangements reflect either a *rule-by-law* order, whereby impersonal rules apply broadly, but not to elites (upper right), or a *rule-of-law* order (bottom right), whereby elites must also follow rules. Impersonal systems achieve degrees of stability and impartiality that personalized rule orders cannot provide. Finally, at the far end of the horizontal spectrum, *sustainable democracy* resembles NWW's OAO.

Figure 7.1's vertical spectrum depicts two types of PS, two ways to escape a conflict equilibrium. *Dominant* settlements, as the name suggests, connote rule by a single dominant coalition (or person)—whether a dictator, a one-party state, or a military junta. With personalized institutions, a dominant settlement becomes discretionary; with impersonal institutions, it creates or adheres to a rule by law. By contrast, *competitive* settlements rely on informal (personalized) and formal (impersonal) rules and understandings that delineate procedures for transferring power between two or more coalitions (usually via elections). The competitive-dominant distinction depends on the difference in violence capacity between ruling and opposition coalitions—specifically on how such difference influences the level of commitment an opposition coalition would need to attain among its members to displace an incumbent set of rulers (Ibid., 26). In either dominant settlement, the

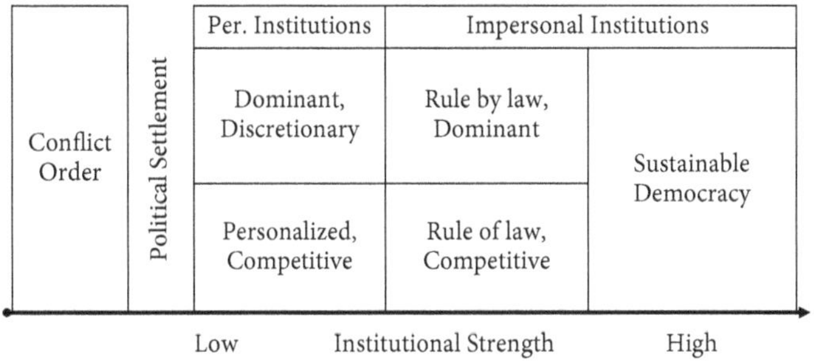

Conflict Order	Political Settlement	Per. Institutions	Impersonal Institutions	
		Dominant, Discretionary	Rule by law, Dominant	Sustainable Democracy
		Personalized, Competitive	Rule of law, Competitive	

Low   Institutional Strength   High

Per. = personal.

FIGURE 7.1 Levy's Typology of Social Orders
SOURCE: Adapted from Levy (2014, Figure 2.1, 16), adjusted slightly.

RC possesses far greater violence capacity. Successful opposition would thus require large commitments, implying a complex organizational CAP with a low probability of success. By contrast, a small disparity in violence capacity implies a far less substantial organizational CAP for regime opponents. If so, competing coalitions would face strong incentives to negotiate a set of informal or formal rules for transferring power—that is, incentives for creating a competitive PS.

Each type of social order implies a distinct set of developmental CAPs. For near conflict orders (similar to fragile LAOs), informal agreements among powerful warlords, who often possess more arms than the central government, can reduce violence. Consequently, well-meaning attempts to build participation in governance (elections), reduce corruption, or provide security—often at the behest of various external agents (the United States, the UN, NGOs; possibly China)—can undermine fragile arrangements to restrain violence. Warlords may feel threatened by extensions of local community power, such as efforts at democratic reform attempted in Somalia in the early 1990s, or by a central government's attempts to provide security.[3] In contrast, a rule-by-law–dominant social order, such as contemporary China, poses a different set of CAPs. Although established impersonal rules can facilitate efficient state functioning, contract enforcement, and economic development, important CAPs involve placing durable limits on the power of the dominant coalition (the Chinese Communist Party) so that it does not excessively hoard resources or exclude potentially productive actors from participating in economic activity. Alternatively, in a personalized, competitive social order—such as

Bangladesh between 1980 and 2006—major CAPs include reducing corruption by establishing legal and bureaucratic procedures and providing adequate infrastructure, and doing so without augmenting violence.

As punctuated equilibria, social orders eventually succumb to external and/or internal shocks that usher in a different social order (moving in any direction within the typology). The institutional strength of a society (its position on the horizontal axis) influences the ability of its social order to withstand such shocks (in mathematical terms, institutional strength influences the size of the basin of attraction surrounding the relevant punctuated equilibrium). Societies at the personalized end of the horizontal spectrum often move back and forth between dominant and competitive social orders.

Overall, Levy's typology builds on the NWW spectrum, adding a second dimension with two types of PSs. This adjustment explicitly recognizes that transition out of a conflict order requires some form of settlement. Moreover, Levy distinguishes between two types of settlements on the basis of disparities in violence capacity and ensuing oppositional commitment CAPs, with surmountable CAPs permitting competitive settlements. This distinction, somewhat comparable to the Acemoglu-Robinson distinction between extractive and inclusive institutions, offers an important first step for analyzing PSs. Nevertheless, additional distinctions between settlement characteristics imply additional CAPs that affect the development of economic and political institutions. Khan's approach more fully develops the concept of PSs and traces their relations to institutions in more detail. It also addresses power relationships between the private and public sectors.

Section 3: The Concept of Political Settlements and Three Overlapping Typologies

PSs underlie the creation of institutional systems and social orders and shape their evolution with mutually understood, yet evolving, arrangements for addressing CAPs related to managing organized violence. The systematic categorization of settlements, in terms of their key foundational characteristics, facilitates analyzing how types of settlements reflect and generate specific sets of CAPs that constrain development in specific social contexts. In this regard, Khan (2010) develops three relevant typologies that offer insight into how configurations of institutions, growth, balances of power, and business interests interact.

Before addressing Khan's typologies, however, various approaches to PSs from the literature merit discussion. These approaches all refer to power, at least indirectly. Key distinctions among them concern a focus on agreements versus a balance of power, a static versus dynamic conception, and a focus on elites versus organizations as key agents.

With emphasis on contentious bargaining, Jonathan Di John and James Putzel define a PS as "the balance of power among contending social groups and social classes on which any state is based" (2009, 4). This balance could be interpreted statically—as an outcome of contention at a point in time—or dynamically—as an evolving set of relationships.

Two additional definitions offer the more static concept of an outcome of interaction that takes the form of an elite agreement or understanding. From the (British) Department for International Development (DFID): "the forging of a common understanding, usually between elites, that their best interests or beliefs are served by a particular way of organising political power" (2010b, 12; citing Whaites 2008). Such understanding includes informal and formal institutions. Similarly, the Australian Agency for International Development (AusAID) suggests a bargaining outcome: "an agreement between elites on the processes by which power and resources are shared and decisions made" (2011, 13). These approaches imply that settlements incorporate a type of foundational political institution—at least at the informal level of shared understandings of procedures for addressing disputes.

Edward Laws and Adrian Leftwich address both agreement and process, though with an emphasis on outcome: "the informal and formal processes, agreements, and practices that help consolidate politics, rather than violence, as a means for dealing with disagreements about interests, ideas and the distribution and use of power" (2014, 1). Note that DFID retains the idea of bargains and notes distinct possible (dynamic) outcomes: "a political settlement describes the types of informal as well as formal political bargains that can end conflict and bring sustainable peace, promote reform, development and poverty reduction—or fail to achieve any such progress" (2010b, 11).

Laws's (2012) rather detailed approach combines outcomes and dynamic process, with attention to power relationships, institutions, and inclusivity. Settlements involve the following attributes:

- bargaining outcomes, reflecting compromises among elites;
- evolving process that affects elite power relations and bargaining;

- adaptive responses to changes in social environments;
- dynamics that both respond to and influence institutions;
- a two-level game with both horizontal (elite-elite) and vertical (elite-follower) elements; and
- varying degrees of inclusivity.

Khan (2010) develops a comprehensive concept that emphasizes interactions between power, institutions, and dynamic processes of reproduction: "A political settlement is an interdependent combination of a structure of power and institutions at the level of a society that is mutually 'compatible' and also 'sustainable' in terms of economic and political viability" (Ibid., 20). A workable settlement "emerges when the distribution of benefits supported by its institutions is consistent with the distribution of power in society" (Ibid., 25). In other words, to achieve stability, a settlement's distribution of benefits must accord with power relations among groups and their beliefs concerning distributions of power. A settlement's institutions and distribution of power reinforce each other when acceptable institutions generate acceptable economic performance and reproducible economic activities.

PSs, moreover, operate at both higher and deeper levels. The higher level connotes "a description of the 'social order' that describes how a society solves the problem of violence and achieves a minimum level of political stability and economic performance" (Ibid., 20). Here, social order is an outcome with institutional features—a notion compatible with the DFID-AusAID static definitions. In contrast, the deeper level "implies an institutional structure that creates benefits for different classes and groups in line with their relative power" (Ibid.). At this level, distributions of power affect the enforcement of institutions and their evolution—a dynamic concept that is somewhat closer to Di John and Putzel's version.[4]

The deeper level statement, moreover, creates two immediate implications: First, institutional change can be analyzed by considering gradations of resistance to a given distribution of power—notably, the degree to which inevitable conflict may be contained within the settlement—a notion compatible with Levy's between-coalition differences in violence capacity. Excessive resistance undermines enforcement provisions (i.e., the resolution of second-order CAPs). Second, relating directly to the politics of economic development, societies often face a growth-stability trade-off—the severity of which depends on elements of their underlying PSs. In other words, economic growth (or other elements of development) can destabilize certain arrangements by redistributing power. Anticipating such outcomes, RCs often resist growth-enhancing change.

In a later piece, Khan shifts focus, emphasizing organizations and power balance. A PS is a "description of the distribution of power across organizations that are relevant for analyzing specific institutional or policy problems. . . . A distribution of organizational power is a political settlement if it reproduces itself over time" (2017, 5–6). As in the 2010 definition, reproduction requires that expectations of economic and political benefits awarded by relevant institutional arrangements accord with distributions of power. More controversially, however, he posits that settlements need not eliminate (organized) violence, but rather establish "normal" levels of violence. For example, a settlement could exist in Afghanistan if the intergroup conflicts reproduce an organizational distribution of power—a broader definition of PS than that from other authors.

These contrasting approaches to the concept raise the following questions:

- Are PSs static one-time events, patterns of evolution, or both?
- Are PSs balances of power or are they agreements and shared understandings—that is, a type of foundational institution?
- Do PSs establish the primacy of politics as opposed to violence for dispute resolution? Or do they merely establish a reproducible normal level of violence that may sometimes override politics?
- Are the key agents of PSs elites or organizations?

My approach, developed in Chapter 8, allows for both possibilities in each of the first two questions, but with an emphasis on mutual understandings. Regarding the third question, I side with the primacy of politics, though only among parties that are actually included in a settlement—meaning that insider-outsider violence may persist. Regarding the fourth question, I address both types of agent, though with more emphasis on elites.

Now, a somewhat detailed discussion of Khan's typologies offers insight into relationships between social orders, balances of power, economic development, and business-state relations. As such, it offers additional background for Chapters 8 and 9.

Khan's Three Typologies

Khan (2017) asserts that PS analysis can address two questions: why the same set of institutions works in some places and not others, and why different sets of institutions can address the same problems in different locations. This approach sheds light on how power, institutions, and rent-seeking behavior interact within the context of distinct types of PSs. Institutions generate rents and powerful organizations require acceptable rents to lend their support to maintaining the institutional configurations that accompany a given settlement. Accordingly, Khan (2010) develops three related two-dimensional, four-quadrant typologies that delineate key characteristics of settlements with attention to configurations of institutions, power, growth, and businesses. Khan's first typology combines the degree to which formal institutions underlie power (vertical dimension) with the potential for formal institutions to support growth (horizontal dimension). The second typology expands one cell of the first (the clientelist PS cell) to focus on the distribution of power relations within the insider coalition (vertical dimension) and that between insiders and excluded groups (horizontal dimension). The third typology, which also applies to the clientelist cell of the first typology, relates the power of productive investors (vertical dimension) to their technological-entrepreneurial capabilities (horizontal dimension).

In the first typology (see Table 7.1), the vertical dimension contrasts cases in which holding power is "aligned with" formal institutions to those in which informal arrangements play a far greater role.[5] Here is Khan's reasoning. The institutional component of settlements differs fundamentally according to levels of development. In developed countries, formal institutions deliver sufficient benefits to power holders, which then motivate adequate enforcement of formal prescriptions. Accordingly, the bulk of social power flows from formal institutions. In contrast, for developing countries, formal institutions cannot support inherited distributions of power because few powerful groups have capabilities that allow them to benefit from a rule of law and protection of (universal) property rights (Ibid., 26).[6] Because formal institutions cannot deliver sufficient benefits to support enforcement of their provisions, informal institutions are the primary mechanism for distributing benefits. Informal institutions and personal relationships thus underlie enforcement. Note that Khan's vertical dimension resembles Levy's horizontal axis—both represent the strength of institutions, but Khan directly addresses the importance of power relationships for generating these distinctions.

Khan's horizontal dimension distinguishes between cases in which formal institutions (to the degree they exist) are or are not growth oriented. Could such institutions, in principle, address a society's chief market failures? In

TABLE 7.1   Khan's Typology I: A Typology of Political Settlements

	Formal institutions potentially support growth	Formal institutions are not growth-oriented or have collapsed
Holding power aligned with formal institutions	Capitalist political settlement	Precapitalist political settlement
Important sources of holding power not aligned with formal institutions	Clientelist political settlement	Political settlement in crisis

SOURCE: Adapted from Khan (2010, Figure 16A, 49).

developed countries, property rights manage many market failures; in other countries, they might do so—if sufficiently developed. By contrast, in precapitalist (feudal) societies, even established formal institutions cannot foster growth: "The emerging productive economy is initially structurally uncompetitive as a result of market failures that would not be sufficiently addressed simply by enforcing property rights and contracts a little better" (Ibid., 29).[7]

Table 7.1 illustrates. Its upper left quadrant depicts a *capitalist* PS. Formal institutions define and enforce property rights. The combination of property rights and income largely underlie the power of capitalists, workers, and other groups. Redistribution, when it occurs, operates through formal mechanisms. Indeed, challenging property rights is typically not possible. Distributional conflicts, especially with labor, occur within economic and political tolerance limits of the dominant capitalist economic interests. Economic growth generates sufficient output to sustain a distribution of benefits that supports the division of power. This quadrant exhibits a potential for developing a Weberian state (NWW's OAO), but that outcome also requires establishing a rule of law (one of NWW's doorstep conditions). Late-nineteenth-century Germany offers an example of a capitalist settlement that lacked a rule of law.

The upper right quadrant represents precapitalist social formations. Even though formal institutions prescribe distributions of land and armaments that underlie distributions of power, such arrangements cannot support growth because the foundations for effective exchanges of land, labor, and capital simply do not exist. Despite the absence of growth, however, this settlement is stable because the assigned rights accord with distributions of power. Examples include variants of feudalism. Contemporary North Korea (not mentioned by Khan) might also fit.

The lower right quadrant represents a PS in crisis: formal institutions do not confer power and any that have not collapsed cannot support growth.

Conflict consumes most resources; violence and threats of violence dominate informal economic activity.[8] This cell implies a very weak settlement, as in NWW's fragile LAO, or a chaos order.

The lower left quadrant depicts a clientelist PS—the one most relevant for developing countries. Even though formal institutions are not a principal source of power, they could support growth. More precisely, formal institutions exist, but do not "describe the operation of a significant enough productive sector such that incomes flowing from these rights constitute a dominant source of power" (Ibid., 54). Because many productive rights lack enforcement, organizations can gain rents by distorting the implementation of policies and formal institutions (Khan 2017). Moreover, powerful parties usually oppose the transparency that accompanies formal rules.[9] Parties that do benefit from formal institutions must strike compromises with other powerful groups. Ultimately, power relies on the income generated from the organizational capabilities of informal organizations and associated personalistic relationships, patron-client networks, and nonformal incomes, such as off-budget resources. This quadrant represents a transition phase: precapitalist institutions have broken down and formal institutions are not self-sustaining. Relevant societies may or may not transition to a capitalist order.[10] Examples include both developmental states and states on the verge of crisis, ranging from military rule to clientelist party competition.

Because this cell characterizes most contemporary developing countries; it cannot, by itself, explain divergent developmental outcomes. Specifying institutional strength matters but only takes the analysis so far. Khan's remaining two typologies depict relationships within the clientelist cell. His second typology addresses horizontal and vertical distributions of power across and within coalitions. Developmental outcomes depend critically on associated enforcement capabilities. Development also depends on the power and capabilities of capitalists in the productive sectors—the focus of the third typology.

Khan's Typology II

Khan's second typology, Patron-Client Factions and the Structure of the Ruling Coalition, is the one most often cited in the literature. It addresses structures of power within a clientelist settlement, wherein informal institutions, networks, and personal relationships underlie distributions of power. Given that context, Khan designates four additional developmental categories that depend on two sets of power relations: those within an RC, and those between

TABLE 7.2 Khan's Typology II: Patron-Client Factions and the Structure of the Ruling Coalition (RC)

Vertical Distribution of Power: → Lower-Level Factions are . . . ↓	Horizontal Distribution of Power: Excluded Factions are . . .	
	Weak (RC, long-term perspective)	*Strong* (RC, short-term focus)
Weak (RC can implement policy)	**A** Potential Developmental Coalition	**B** Vulnerable Author-itarian Coalition
Strong (Resistance blocks implementation)	**C** Weak Dominant Party	**D** Competitive Clientelism

SOURCE: Adapted from Khan (2010, Figure 17, 65).
RC = ruling coalition

the RC and excluded factions. Khan regards such relationships as a "lens through which to look at the interdependent evolution of institutions, politics and economics in clientelist political settlements" (2010, 69). He notes, for example, that configurations of patron-client relationships create substantial differences in the operation of military regimes whose formal structures may appear deceptively similar.

In Table 7.2, the vertical dimension depicts the power of lower-level factions within the RC: weak or strong. *Strong* signifies that lower-level factions can block policy initiatives, whereas *weak* allows RC elites to implement and enforce policies. The horizontal dimension represents the power of excluded factions—those not part of the settlement. *Weak* excluded factions implies that the RC can expect to retain power for a relatively long period. Their ensuing long-term perspective aligns their interests with growth and development. By contrast, the presence of *strong* excluded factions encourages a short-term RC orientation.

Before moving to typology III, here is more detail on II's four quadrants:

A. *Potential developmental coalition* (weak/weak): Because the RC operates with both a long-term time perspective and the capacity to implement and enforce policies, this quadrant implies the most favorable trade-off between stability and growth. It shows necessary, but not sufficient, conditions for a developmental state. Outcomes depend on the third typology. Examples include South Korea in the 1960s.

B. *Vulnerable authoritarian coalition* (weak/strong): The RC can im-plement and enforce policies, but powerful excluded groups render

it vulnerable to overthrow. It thus relies on legal restrictions and/
or threatened or actual force to control external groups; the weaker
the RC, the greater its reliance on force. Additionally, the RC may
struggle to maintain internal allegiance because some insiders might
enhance their positions by aligning with external groups. This type of
PS is usually not sustainable for long periods unless the RC has access
to resource rents or external military support.[11] Examples include
Pakistan in the 1960s and Bangladesh in the 1980s and 90s.

C. *Weak dominant party* (strong/weak): With a long-term perspective
but problematic implementation, the RC needs to distribute rents
to strong lower-level insiders, even if it consistently wins elections.
Moreover, the RC may face the prospect of disaffected insiders joining
excluded factions to increase their power.[12] The RC faces an inclusiveness trade-off: allowing certain groups insider access can weaken its
ability to enforce and implement policies, but maintaining exclusion
risks the prospect of them attaining power. Examples include India
under Congress in the 1950s and 1960s.

D. *Competitive clientelism* (strong/strong): This combination emerges
when steadily declining conditions undermine a dominant party or
authoritarian coalition. Facing strong internal factions and external
groups, the RC needs to distribute rents across inside factions, but
does so with limited ability to implement policies. This quadrant
faces the worst growth-stability trade-off. There are too many factions to include all in an RC but also too many to exclude by legal
or military means. Excluded groups might be able to organize rival
coalitions. Accordingly, the RC consists of political entrepreneurs
who bring factions together while minimizing short-term costs to
themselves. The ensuing PS can be stable if it creates credible mechanisms for rotating power among factions and if certain factions do
not believe they have the capability to coalesce into a dominant coalition. India, an unusual case with myriad groups scattered across a
huge landmass, has achieved political stability by successfully rotating
power via elections conducted by the states, with federal oversight.
The federal government has strong incentives to intervene to prevent
state electoral abuse. Bangladesh, by contrast, lacks credible third-
party electoral oversight. RCs have gotten away with manipulating

election rules, generating electoral crises and occasional military intervention.

Khan's Typology III

Khan's third typology, Patron-Client Structures and the Organizational Power of Emerging Capitalists, considers how economic capability and power affect an RC's choice of and ability to implement policies. Entrepreneurs and investors, like internal and external factions, can either accept or resist various policies, especially those related to market competition and industrial policy. Their ability to influence policy depends on their capabilities and power. Khan notes that successful industrial policy thus requires an embeddedness of government within the private sector.[13]

Table 7.3 illustrates. Its horizontal dimension distinguishes *High* from *Low* technological and entrepreneurial capabilities, which obviously affect productive potential. These slowly changing capabilities arise as outcomes of prior historical accumulation and learning. The vertical dimension distinguishes *High* from *Low* investor holding power. Such power need not arise solely or even primarily from enterprise profits. Given the primacy of informal institutions within clientelist settlements, an entrepreneur's informal network connections may generate power structures, "through which formal rights can be protected at an appropriate price" (2010, 70). Whereas in some cases patron-client networks and RC positions depend on enterprise revenue, in others, especially when an RC has independent access to resource rents, such dependence is low or nonexistent.

Here is more detail on quadrants E–H:

E. *High capability and powerfully networked*: Capitalists can drive accumulation, but they are hard to discipline. Counterintuitively, this quadrant may not foster growth, at least not broadly over long periods. Given a clientelist settlement, powerful investors strive to create and maintain rents. They resist policies that would encourage market competition or force higher investment or effort. They may oppose industrial policy, especially any attempt to move it beyond an early protective stage. Even so, they may use international connections, where present, to import new technology. For example, pockets of connected capable capitalists have driven growth, as in India after the 1980s and Thailand in the 1980s and 1990s.[14]

TABLE 7.3 Khan's Typology III: Patron-Client Structures and the
Organizational Power of Emerging Capitalists

Holding Power of Productive Investors	Technological-Entrepreneurial Capabilities	
	High	Low
High	E High capability and powerfully networked	F Moderate to low capability and powerfully networked
Low	G High capability but politically weak	H Moderate to low capability and politically weak

SOURCE: Adapted from Khan (2010, Figure 18, 71).

F. *Moderate to low capability and powerfully networked*: Low-capability
entrepreneurs attain power through network connections with
powerful factions. With a weak RC and strong lower-level and/or
excluded factions (Table 7.2's quadrants B, C, or D), entrepreneurs
can block policies that threaten their interests. Even though they may
favor early import-restricting industrial policy that fosters a favorable
short-term growth-stability trade-off, well-connected entrepreneurs
can undermine an RC's attempts to subsequently withdraw subsidies
and impose discipline. "Aligning institutions and policies with the
powerful is particularly problematic in contexts where powerful organizations have low productive capabilities and are more likely to distort formal rules to capture resources" (Khan 2017, 15). For example,
during the late 1950s and early 1960s, India and Pakistan (which then
included current-day Bangladesh) experienced growth accelerations
with early industrial policies, but growth subsequently slowed, in
part on account of "the political ability of the entrepreneurs receiving
support to block attempts to discipline them" (Khan 2010, 73).[15]

G. *High capability but politically weak*: A developmental RC that operates
in Table 7.2's quadrant A can generate industrial policy without significant resistance from business. From the 1960s to the 1980s, South
Korean industrialists, who—as a legacy of the Japanese occupation—
faced low public acceptance (low legitimacy), encountered a limited
ability to align with or form powerful coalitions. Consequently, the
regime could institute an export-oriented industrial policy with
enforced discipline related to private-sector effort and learning. By
contrast, in Thaksin Shinawatra's Thailand (2000s), which also had

capable but weak investors, the (weak/authoritarian) RC sought to maximize its own rents and maintain power with populist redistributive policies. Productive structural- industrial transformation did not occur. Somewhat analogously, in West Bengal, the ruling CPM (Communist Party [Marxist]) sidelined capable but weak industrialists as it responded primarily to its agrarian base.[16]

H. *Moderate to low capability and politically weak*: Entrepreneurs face the greatest constraints; outcomes depend on the RC. In Tanzania, entrepreneurs, many of whom have Asian or European origins, have little power or engagement with the RC, which has access to resource rents and foreign aid, with correspondingly low incentives to engage with them. Nonetheless, an RC with a longer-term vision could promote capital accumulation and learning. Ethiopia's efforts at learning policy in the late 2000s offer a tentative example (Ibid., 75).

Comparing typologies II and III, institutions that foster growth in one context may lead to stagnation or decline in another. Several such combinations appear in the preceding discussion. Notably, Table 7.2's potential developmental state most likely succeeds when combined with capable but weak investors (as in South Korea), though there is a danger that the RC will subsequently utilize power in less constructive manners. By contrast, if powerful capitalists collude with government to restrict competition and maintain subsidies long after a potentially useful (infant industry) period, structural transformation most likely fails. Alternatively, with relatively stable competitive clientelism, capable and locally powerful entrepreneurs can achieve local success, as they have in India.

The next set of typologies, which probes more deeply into micro-level business-state transactions, generates additional insight into conditions that affect the likelihood of economic success.

Section 4: Rents Spaces and Ordering Deals

Pritchett, Sen, and Werker (2018) and Pritchett and Werker (2012) offer an alternative approach (hereafter, the PSW approach) to business-state relations, again operating within Khan's clientelist PS. To motivate their approach, these authors assert that much of the growth literature cannot explain episodes of growth acceleration, collapse, stagnation, and booms experienced

TABLE 7.4 Pritchett, Sen, and Werker's Rents Space

Orientation/Structure	Regulatory Rents	Market Competition
Export	(1) Rentiers	(3) Magicians
Domestic	(2) Powerbrokers	(4) Workhorses

SOURCE: Pritchett, Sen, and Werker (2018, Figure 11.1, 21).

by many developing countries—and, in particular, conditions that underlie maintaining stable rates of growth.[17] To proceed, they use four typologies. The first is Khan's typology II (Table 7.2). The second (see Table 7.4) depicts the *rents space*—market configurations that influence the demands that businesses place on the state. The third addresses policy climates for growth and business arrangements, distinguishing between impersonal rules and selective deals. The fourth, the *deals environment*, categorizes less-than-formal agreements between business and state actors.

Like Khan, Pritchett et al. assert that the outcomes from each of Table 7.2's quadrants depend on the activities of economic elites (Khan's investors). Whereas Khan focuses on the blocking power of capitalists, the PSW approach focuses on the demands that economic elites place on the state that, in turn, depend on how configurations of markets influence their material interests.[18] Accordingly, Table 7.4's rents space focuses on market orientation and sources of profits. The vertical dimension specifies the orientation of targeted markets: export or domestic. Developing country business investments typically focus on one or the other (Musacchio and Werker 2016). The horizontal dimension specifies market structure: whether most profits come from regulatory rents or market competition. *Regulatory rents* reflect policy decisions, either discretionary government action—such as licenses for resource access, firm-specific (as opposed to industry-specific) tax advantages—or deliberate inaction, such as ignoring monopoly pricing or a lack of antitrust regulation. Some rents, such as those that firms can earn via brand differentiation, innovation, increasing returns from capital investments, and locational advantages, do not count as *regulatory*.[19]

The four named quadrants are as follows:

1. *Rentiers* have agreements with the state that confer access to natural resources or rights over land (not attained on the market) in return for fees or taxes. These firms are usually foreign owned (Pritchett and Werker 2012).

2. *Powerbrokers* include state-owned enterprises, legislative monopolies, and natural monopolies in regulated environments that limit competition. Examples include utilities, ports, petroleum refining, and some resources for domestic markets, such as timber.[20] Firms in this quadrant tend to form close relations with government regulators.

3. *Magicians* create markets for export. Relevant sectors include garments, manufacturing, processing, service exporters including tourism, and export-oriented agriculture (e.g., coffee).

4. *Workhorses* are small firms that often operate in the informal sector. Examples include subsistence farmers, restauranteurs, petty traders, local manufacturers, builders, village lenders, and some importers. This sector produces most consumer goods.

Firms within each quadrant place different demands on the state. Rentiers demand specialized infrastructure, contract enforcement, subsidies, and exclusivity. Magicians demand the first three items, along with transparent rules and common infrastructure. Workhorses demand transparency, common infrastructure, and contract enforcement. Powerbrokers demand exclusion. Ensuing interactions with the state influence the business environment, the development of state capabilities, overall institution building, and, ultimately, the stability of PSs.

To motivate their remaining two typologies, Pritchett et al. note a common lack of correspondence between measures of de jure regulation (e.g., officially announced days to get a construction permit) and survey data on entrepreneurs' actual experiences—typically much longer delays. The third typology (not reproduced here) distinguishes among environments for business transactions. Its vertical dimension (resembling Levy's strength of institutions) distinguishes *impersonally enforced rules* from *selectively enforced deals* (personalized arrangements). The horizontal dimension (echoing Khan's first typology) specifies whether the official legal and regulatory climate is *conducive* or *not conducive* to inclusive growth. Given the present focus on clientelist settlements, the most relevant quadrants are two *selectively enforced deals* quadrants, in which informal deals are either predominant (formal rules are not conducive to growth) or mixed with formal arrangements, when formal arrangements are at least somewhat conducive to growth.[21]

Finally, in clientelist PSs, interactions between business demands and state actors (usually) operate within the *deals environment*: the fourth PSW typology (a close approximation appears in Figure 9.2). They define a *deal* as "a *specific* action between two (or more) entities (or individuals) that is not the result of the impersonal application of a rule, but rather of *characteristics* or *actions* of specific entities which do not spill over with any precedential value to any other future transaction between other entities" (Pritchett et al. 2018, 24). Deals rely on personal relationships, networks, and informal institutions. This typology's vertical dimension distinguishes *ordered deals*, ones that will be honored, from *disordered deals*—honored only if doing so fits the short-term interests of political elites. Such unreliable commitment creates uncertainty (unresolved H4 hold-up CAPs). The horizontal dimension distinguishes *closed deals*, for which achieving a deal depends on an agent's identity, from *open deals*, for which actions rather than identities determine eligibility. For example, the ordered/closed deal combination implies credible delivery of terms available only to select clients—cronyism, as in Vladimir Putin's Russia. The ordered/open combination fits "retail corruption," as in attaining a driver's license in Delhi (Pritchett and Werkler 2012, 28).

Returning to the larger picture, PSs, rents spaces, and deals environments interact. They jointly create overlapping political and economic feedback loops that may enhance or impede development. For example, in addition to directly affecting growth, exogenous transnational developments, such as commodity price shocks or unsettling technological change, often shift coalition alignments and power distributions that then alter economic returns, perhaps favoring rentiers. If so, rentiers can augment their demands for closed deals to increase their revenue share, creating economic feedback that can enhance their bargaining power. They may then offer revenue to political coalitions with whom they affiliate, creating political feedback that can reinforce distributions of power and, ultimately, PSs. Indeed, this logic offers insight into institutional dimensions of a resource curse: a curse typically empowers the rentier and powerbroker sectors.

Now, returning to the more focused question of growth acceleration, a move from disordered to ordered deals accelerates growth because credible commitments to honor agreements foster investment (resolving some H4 hold-up CAPs). A transition from disordered to ordered deals can arise in two fashions, but only one favors development. The favorable route resembles NWW's doorstep conditions: stronger rule-bound institutions benefit the competitive rent-space sectors, whose enterprises then devote resources to achieving greater openness, common infrastructure, and contract enforcement. Alternatively, strong dominant coalitions can award credible deals to selective constituents who predominantly inhabit Table 7.4's regulatory rent quadrants. The relevant elites devote resources (de facto power) to enhance both rents and exclusion, rendering long-term growth maintenance unlikely. For example, in post-1986 Ghana, growth revenue flowed to rentier and powerbroker sectors, which then funneled revenue to political elites whose policies and connections tended to uphold exclusion and support the clientelist PS (Bukenya and Hickey 2018).

This last point raises the question of how to achieve growth maintenance. Two paths apply. Long-term sustainable growth arises from the first feedback loop: key economic constituencies demand good institutions that facilitate structural transformation and continued growth. Alternatively, medium-term growth sometimes follows a succession of sheer luck. A commodity price boom, discovery of a natural resource, availability of cheap finance, and substantial foreign aid, can support medium-term growth without structural transformation. In the long run, however, such growth usually does not persist.

In conclusion, the PSW approach complements prior studies with several improvements. First, it addresses head-on the questions of growth acceleration, maintenance, and decline. Second, it suggests a method for analyzing distinctions within each type of PS that considers how PSs interact with both market structures and the most relevant micro-level transactional arrangements for developing countries: deals. Here, the rents space addresses the kinds of demands that businesses place on the state, and the deals typology provides a context for considering economic agency, as well as a platform for analyzing business-state interactions within distinct institutional environments. Third, associated feedback loops address broader dynamic questions of institutional development and the sustainability of PSs.

Even so, there is room for additional analysis. Chapter 8 develops an approach to PSs with its own typology. Discussion focuses on specific sets of developmental CAPs operating within each type of PS, yielding implications on potential for capability-enhancing political and economic development. Chapter 9 integrates that approach with a slightly modified concept of the rents and deals spaces, combining those concepts with attention to the principles of H1–H5, along with specific components of political development, elements of economic development and structural transformation, associated inequities, and a host of associated CAPs that condition developmental potential. These final two chapters in Part III offer a conceptual foundation for systematic inquiry into the political economy of development.

8   How Context Influences Development

A New Typology of Political Settlements

How do you reform a country where gunmen torch Ebola clinics?
—The Economist *(August 3, 2019)*

THE DISCOVERY OF DIAMONDS in South Africa altered relations between the British colonies, the native populations, and the Dutch Boer settlements in a manner that induced both repression and conflict. The British colonists set the precedent for future political economic relations by establishing a segregated labor system that required black people to carry passes, banned them from certain desirable occupations, and prohibited them from mining diamonds. In 1871, the British took the Transvaal diamond fields—an area settled by Dutch farmers, the Boers. The British defeated the Zulu Kingdom in 1879, and then conquered the inland Boer Republics during the Boer War of 1899–1902. In 1910, they formed the Union of South Africa as a dominion of the British Empire. The 1913 Land Act imposed a system of territorial segregation across South Africa. The act set aside territorial reserves for blacks, which included the least fertile lands, and required that black workers leaving the reserves have proof of employment by Europeans. These developments laid foundations for the post-1948 apartheid system, which achieved some economic growth—enjoyed mostly by the white minority—and excluded the black majority from political participation until 1994.

In Bangladesh, between 1975 and 1990, leaders of various coalitions negotiated separately for inclusion in the military-led dominant coalition. The leadership wanted to maximize the number of important group leaders at the lowest possible price in terms of rents demanded. The price a leader could reasonably demand depended on "proven organizational capabilities and the significance of their departure for undermining their erstwhile partners" (Khan 2009, 48). In other words, for a given set of organizational capabilities, the dominant coalition considered whether a leader's entry into the coalition was worth the rent price. Moreover, even the possibility of future negotiated entry bought some acquiescence from excluded elites. Yet, because the top military position was not open to negotiation, rivalry within the military and among resentful political parties gradually undermined the regime. It succumbed to mass protests in 1990.

Consider these two questions:

- How can we characterize a set of underlying political conditions that influence prospects for political and economic development?
- How do such conditions relate to a series of CAPs that permeate developmental processes?

Chapter 7 reviews various definitions of political settlements (PSs) and approaches to typologies of social orders that appear in the literature. Drawing on that literature, this chapter addresses my approach.

PSs establish foundations for development. They underlie distinct configurations of institutional systems (social orders) that arise from and shape key developmental processes. This chapter develops a two-dimensional, four-quadrant typology of PSs, with an additional distinction between paths within two of the quadrants. Utilizing divisions across two spectra that characterize fundamental social context—specifically, social foundations and configurations of authority—this typology points to critical quadrant-specific tensions and sets of CAPs that condition, complicate, and impede political and economic development. Section 1 presents my approach to the PS concept, with attention to related concepts in the literature. Section 2 develops the typology, with implications. Section 3 concludes by noting the power of PS analysis.

Section 1: The Concept of Political Settlements

A *political settlement* is a mutual understanding, held among elites and powerful organizations, to use politics, rather than violence, as the primary means for settling disputes. Such understandings underlie the creation of institutions, institutional systems, and social orders and shape their evolution—in the process both resolving and creating specific types of CAPs. Accordingly, identifying basic categories of PS, with attention to implied political tensions and corresponding sets of CAPs, informs developmental political economy.

Based on, modifying, and extending a typology from Tim Kelsall and Matthias vom Hau (2019), I propose a two-dimensional typology of PS. This approach offers a parsimonious method for classifying PSs according to their social foundations and configurations of authority, both of which affect corresponding sets of developmental CAPs. Before discussing the typology, drawing on Chapter 7's literature and elaborating on Chapter 1's introduction to PSs, here is more detail on the basic concept.

Attributes of Political Settlements
Recall that Chapter 1 introduces the complex relationship between institutions and PSs by stating that institutions are antecedents, components, and outcomes of PSs. The following list of PS features elaborates:

1. A PS reflects outcomes of prior historical processes; it emerges from disruptive political contestation and concurrent and subsequent implicit or explicit bargaining among powerful parties (elites) from distinct social groups in a society. Acting as antecedents that specify key elements of pertinent social contexts, preexisting institutions shape these interactions and condition multiple associated understandings. For example, after decades of struggle, when Nelson Mandela became the first president of nonapartheid South Africa, the new regime retained many preexisting economic institutions, such as contract law and property rights over land.

2. A PS need not be formally negotiated or written, although portions of it may be. But even for written provisions, such as key elements of enforced national constitutions, informal understandings—often embodied within political norms—shape pertinent interpretations shared among contesting parties, such as specific actions that nobody would even think about using.

3. As a common understanding of a broad behavioral prescription (use politics, not violence), a PS constitutes a type of institution. Even when many associated understandings have not been explicitly negotiated and remain contested, a PS establishes a type of, often informal, *constitutional-choice rule* (Ostrom 2005, 58) that specifies members of a community (those included in the PS) and at least rough bound-

aries for political contestation—specifically regarding exercises of violence. Furthermore, a PS establishes either the distribution of broad avenues of decision-making authority that affect dispute resolution and rough allocations of political and economic benefits—or at least an implicit understanding concerning how such allocation can be achieved via political contestation rather than violence.

4. The configuration of a PS reflects the distribution of bargaining power, principally among insider elites and powerful organizations, though with some attention to their respective constituencies. Relevant distributions of power thus have both a horizontal dimension across insider groups and a vertical, within-group dimension between elites and followers.

5. The basic parameters of PSs exhibit punctuation dynamics. Settlements typically persist over medium-term time horizons, yielding path dependence in the sense that initial outcomes influence (but do not determine) subsequent developments.

6. To become a sustainable medium-term equilibrium, a settlement's corresponding institutional system must deliver policies and (net) political and economic benefits in a manner that reflects and reproduces underlying distributions of power and, for given distributions, at least minimally meets important goals of powerful parties. Concurrently, PSs must foster—usually via a far more detailed set of prescriptions and procedures generated by corresponding institutional systems— the organizational and group dynamics that deliver necessary coordination and enforcement.

7. A PS includes some socially salient groups (insiders) and excludes others (outsiders). Sufficiently powerful groups become insiders because they could overturn a settlement that excludes them. Insiders either accept or acquiesce to a PS; they find its distributions at least minimally sufficient to ward off disruptive contestation.

8. Outsider groups typically do not accept a PS but (at least initially) do not disrupt it because they lack the will, resources, and/or organizational capability for doing so. Three possible relationships ensue: (i) during the stable phase of a punctuation cycle, outsiders remain excluded because they fail to attain the resources or resolve pertinent CAPs that would generate sufficient de facto power; (ii) an

accumulation of power brings them into the PS—they become insiders; or (iii) they eventually attain and use sufficient power to undermine the settlement. Fearing the latter, insiders often devote resources to achieving acquiescence among excluded groups via some mix of overt repression, divide-and-conquer technique (applications of triadic power), and/or symbolic repression and cooptation (applications of power3; see Chapter 5).

9. Ultimately, PSs underlie institutional systems and social orders. The basic configuration of a PS, reflecting the distribution of power (as implied by H3) and the composition of included and excluded groups, fundamentally shapes, circumscribes, and conditions—but does not determine—the creation, reform, maintenance, and demise of political and economic institutions that arise within its parameters. PSs are the foundations of social order.

10. The precise configuration of influence between institutions, institutional systems, and PSs depends on the level of analysis. As a foundation of social order, established PSs operate at a macrolevel. As in point 6, however, their durability depends on the degree to which such arrangements fit the goals of powerful parties on whose support they rely. Hence, at a macrolevel, PSs are endogenous to (usually long-term) political developments within the social environment. In contrast, at a microlevel, a PS—as well as key institutions within a social order—is effectively exogenous. A PS establishes (quasi) parameters that set boundaries for interaction, within which less foundational institutions evolve, in the process of establishing arenas for dynamic social interactions.

I add two final comments: First, although the notion of a shared understanding to eschew organized violence may appear static—indeed, during the stable phase, a PS (as an equilibrium) retains some structural uniformity—PSs are continuously reaffirmed, adjusted, and implicitly renegotiated outcomes. Over the cycle, interactions among insiders and between insiders, excluded groups, and external parties or events, affect a host of institutional and policy details. These, in turn, influence the degree to which a PS is either self-reinforcing or self-undermining—hence, its duration.

Second, again on the surface, the PS concept may appear entirely structural, but agency enters via actions of elites, their interactions with respective constituencies, and by the actions of (functional) organizations.[1] Elaborating on point 6, with a focus on agency, relevant elites must at least minimally accept the contours and outcomes of a given PS. They do not care about PSs per se (PSs are public goods among affected parties), but elites do care about power and benefits. They continue to support (or not resist) a given PS, so long as its distribution of benefits (often in the form of rents) and allocations of power accords with their basic interests, given their ability to influence outcomes—as reflected in the existing distribution of power. Constituent powerful organizations must likewise find minimal acceptance of—that is, not (strongly) resist—a settlement's allocations of benefits and power. Moreover, organizations must encounter some incentive for bearing the costs of adherence to a PS—especially costs of disciplining their own members. Militias, for example, may disarm their members; unions may censure wildcat strikes; a political party may expel a member who physically attacks a member of another party. Likewise, organizations must encounter incentives to undertake their share of enforcement costs or activities. Such potential for organizational discipline, in turn, depends in part on vertical relationships within insider groups.[2] Internal elites must maintain at least minimal legitimacy among their own constituencies.

Overall, PSs establish the foundations of governance and, by extension, developmental trajectories. They limit the extent of social conflict, establishing politics, rather than violence, as the principal mechanism for resolving insider disputes. In so doing, by reflecting and reproducing balances of power among contending social groups and classes, they condition the emergence, viability, and longevity of institutional systems and social orders that shape the subsequent trajectories of political and economic development.

Distinctions from Somewhat Related Concepts in the Literature

It is important to distinguish PSs from several related concepts in the literature. As should be clear from point 9, a PS is not the same as a social order (or macro-institutional system)—rather, PSs underlie social orders. Likewise, there is no one-to-one correspondence between PSs and regimes. A *regime* is "the ensemble of patterns, explicit or not, that determines the forms and channels of access to principal government positions, the characteristics of the actors who are admitted and excluded from such access, and the resources [and] strategies that they can use to gain access" (O'Donnell and Schmitter 1986, 73). A regime could be a one-party state, a parliamentary democracy, or a charismatic dictatorship. As the following discussion shows, the same type of PS can support either democracy or autocracy.

A PS is not a treaty. Whereas a treaty could be a component of a PS, treaties need not imply any specific distribution of power among constituent groups, and settlements need not rest on peace treaties. Finally, insider groups need not be members of a governing coalition—rather, the broader concept of insider groups includes all to whom policymakers must pay some attention (Section 2 elaborates).

The concept of a PS, however, does bear some resemblance to Robert Keohane's (1982) idea of an international regime. For Keohane, international regimes are not quasi governments; they "are more like contracts" among actors "with long-term objectives who seek to structure their relationships in stable and mutually beneficial ways" (Ibid., 330). They resemble quasi agreements among oligopolistic firms. Like PSs, international regimes operate in environments with no third-party enforcers and in which uncertainty—especially regarding others' behavior—abounds. Norms and reciprocal behavior facilitate many transactions. International regimes, such as the World Trade Organization (WTO), establish negotiating frameworks and stabilize expectations about others' behavior. In so doing, they address various types of market failure (CAPs) that impede the success of ad hoc agreements (Keohane 1982). Thus, international regimes both reduce transactions costs and provide information. PSs share these characteristics, but they operate within nations or regions rather than internationally. Even so, we could interpret some international regimes as a type of transnational PS. The WTO has restrained the magnitude of trade disputes—at least until 2018.

With this background, we turn to categorizing PSs.

Section 2: Categorizing Political Settlements, with Corresponding Tensions and CAPs

A PS's social foundation (hereafter SF) and its configuration of authority (hereafter COA) set parameters for its internal dynamics, including institutional development, with a corresponding set of CAPs and developmental prospects. A typology that utilizes these two elements can then inform developmental political economy theory. Specifically, the typology that follows incorporates these two features as foundational dimensions—as two spectra that delineate four basic categories of PS and, within two of them, a pair of distinct developmental paths. Each specified category of PS has its own set of developmental prospects and constraints, reflected in a corresponding set of CAPs.

First Dimension: The Social Foundation
The SF of a PS designates the included socially salient groups (insiders) and the excluded groups (outsiders). The breadth of an SF can be represented by a spectrum that extends from broad—nearly all socially salient groups belong—to narrow—most are excluded. For simplicity, this discussion focuses on broad and narrow as discrete categories. Salient groups may be defined on the basis of ethnicity, race, religion, social class, ideology, organization (e.g., unions), and other criteria. *Social salience* requires either the presence of substantial numbers (say, greater than 5% of the population) or, for smaller groups, the possession of notable disruptive power. For example, certain foreign diplomats or officials from powerful NGOs or foreign corporations, though not representative of domestic populations, may operate as insiders. More precisely, *insiders* are groups to which policy must somehow respond, whether or not they actually participate in negotiations or governing. For example, Chinese government policy responds to needs of the rural population, even though this group has little official national representation. Insiders thus extend beyond a governing party or coalition. As such, insiders may either accept or merely acquiesce to a PS. In either case, insider groups receive some type of side payment (or other benefit) within the settlement—enough to warrant their not actively disrupting it. Note, however, that disrupting a settlement could require resolving substantial organizational CAPs. Even so, the precise combination of insider groups can change within the parameters of a single settlement, but only if such adjustment alters the distributions of benefits and power in a manner that is at least minimally acceptable to incumbent insider elites and powerful organizations.

Excluded groups, by contrast, do not receive side benefits. They can be ignored, as in the case of many indigenous peoples in parts of Latin America, or repressed: directly with force (power1); less directly with threats of violence (power2); with divide-and-conquer techniques (triadic power2 or power3); and/or indirectly via symbolic manipulation, such as appeals to patriotism (power3). Note that divide-and-conquer techniques and symbolic manipulation can silence excluded groups at relatively low cost. Moreover, these manifestations of power could operate within a broad interpretation of Václav

Havel's post-totalitarian system within which people "behave" because they expect others to do so (see Chapter 5).

The distinction between insider and excluded groups depends on one or both of two criteria. First, does a group possess (actual or anticipated) disruptive power? Second, is a powerful group coopted or repressed? Insiders can exclude and ignore groups that lack disruptive power. In contrast, groups that might significantly disrupt a settlement—say, by withholding critical production or investment or by staging mass demonstrations, a general strike, or armed insurrection—are either coopted via policy that pays attention to some of their needs—or excluded via repression. Otherwise, a PS would not form or would not last.[3] Lacking institutions that facilitate broad cooptation, weak states often resort to repression.

There are four principal reasons for designating the SF as one of two underlying dimensions for this typology. First, as the name suggests, the SF characterizes a settlement's basis of support. Second, other things equal, exclusion can undermine long-run viability because excluded groups may attain power in the future. Third, the breadth of an SF influences the leadership's incentives to distribute benefits to groups across the general population: the broader the SF, the greater the incentive for distributing across groups. Fourth, the insider-outsider distinction informs the relationship between a PS and the use of violence. A settlement's mutual understanding to avoid violence for politics applies only to insiders. In fact, insiders often utilize violence to repress outsiders. Likewise, outsiders may use violence to dismantle political arrangements. If the settlement holds, however, such violence is not sufficient to disrupt the social order. Thus, in a society like Colombia between 1990 and 2015, one could argue that the nation as a whole had a PS, despite violent and unsuccessful efforts of the *Fuerzas Armadas Revolucionarias de Colombia* (FARC)—an excluded group—to overthrow the regime. A more detailed analysis might reveal that specific regions within Colombia lacked a PS, but the PS was relatively strong in urban areas.[4]

Second Dimension: The Configuration of Authority
This typology's second dimension, the insider COA, focuses on those who most directly influence policy: insider elites. At one end of the spectrum, *functional unipolarity* signifies a coherent allocation of decision-making procedures and authority among such elites. Functional unipolarity thus reflects some prior resolution of insider CAPs related to bridging social cleavages, re-

solving disputes, delegating broad authority, and achieving certain basic coordination. At the opposite end of this spectrum, *multipolarity* signifies no such coherence, often reflecting active social cleavages that foment conflicts among insider factions. With such unresolved insider CAPs, *multipolarity* implies scattered and uncoordinated authority dispersed across various elites, coalitions, and other centers of power, such as regional governments, powerful firms, and local patronage networks. All else equal, societies with multipolar COAs exhibit more subnational diversity in political arrangements than do those with unipolar COAs.[5]

Before proceeding, two key distinctions between the SF and the COA merit comment. First, the unit of focus includes all social groups for the SF but only insider elites for the COA. Second, although both spectra involve power relationships, the SF implies an asymmetric distribution of power between insider and excluded groups, whereas the COA reflects a power distribution only among insider elites. Note further that insider elites need not directly represent every insider group, but they must devote some attention to any insider group.[6]

There are four reasons for designating the COA as a foundation of this typology. First, the extent of functional unipolarity influences a society's prospects for establishing a minimal consensus on broad national purpose. Can the relevant elites roughly agree, for example, on the contours of state-market relations or those between the state and religion? Second, unipolarity implies that elites can issue broad policy objectives without resorting to continuous renegotiation, whereas multipolarity implies the opposite. Accordingly, and third, the degree of unipolarity influences prospects for resolving existing and future CAPs of policymaking and implementation. In multipolar configurations, one or more groups can veto provisions or obstruct the implementation of policies they dislike. Fourth, the prior three points jointly imply that a society's position on this spectrum influences its prospects for building state capacity—a key domain of political development. Functional unipolarity facilitates state building (and often reflects prior state building).[7]

I have two additional comments: First, functional unipolarity can exist in vastly different political regimes ranging from a well-functioning parliamentary system with a rough consensus on national goals—like that in the Netherlands—to a functional one-party state, such as China. Likewise, multipolarity can apply to incoherent democracies as well as disorganized autocracies.

Second, building on the idea that PSs emerge from prior political contestation—notably that across fault lines of social cleavages—Dan Slater's (2010; admittedly Hobbesian) discussion of the ability of an authoritarian regime to order power illustrates the unipolar-multipolar distinction specifically for authoritarian cases (though he does not mention unipolarity or multipolarity). *Ordered power* means that elites have resolved a set of CAPs so that their key members (state officials, economic elites, merchants, middle class and communal elites) unify behind an authoritarian state, and do so because they share the perception that the state will protect them from an existential threat. In particular, they are willing to sacrifice resources (taxes) in return for state provision of security—an arrangement Slater (2010, 5) calls a *protection pact*. For example, during the 1960s elites in both Malaysia and Singapore formed effective coalitions to counter a mutually understood threat of social revolution from large, organized mass-based communist insurgencies, which in both cases included large urban contingents that manifested both class and ethnic characteristics. Singapore, for example, faced huge communist-led strike waves in 1946 and 1955. The latter wave had an ethnic Chinese element that threatened predominantly Malay elites. For Slater, a protection pact (a core element of the respective PS) emerges from prior political contestation that threatens elites from key social groups.[8]

In contrast, after World War II and extending into the 1960s, Thailand, with no significant mass insurgency, achieved no such elite unity. Instead, rival factions confronted each other, sometimes violently, with assassinations. An unstable dictatorship—interrupted by a few periods with elections—ensued. Likewise, in the Philippines under Ferdinand Marcos, elites failed to unify behind the authoritarian regime, leaving it unable to secure revenue from elites, who largely pursued separate interests (Ibid.). Despite its authoritarian features and pretensions, such a regime reflects a multipolar PS. Analogously, a multipolar electoral system operates without elite cohesion, just with a different set of (typically weak) formal political institutions.

This concept of multipolarity also fits Guillermo O'Donnell's (1993) idea of weak states. O'Donnell refers to two dimensions of state capacity: (i) the functional presence of the state in terms of bureaucratic functionality and legality; and (ii) the ability of the state to extend its influence over territory. Countries such as Norway are strong in both dimensions, whereas Peru is weak in both. Multipolarity implies weakness in at least one of these dimensions, often both. In many developing countries, such as India and Colombia,

TABLE 8.1 A Basic Typology of Political Settlements

Social Foundation	Configuration of Authority (Insider Elites)	
	Multipolar	*Unipolar*
Broad	Quadrant 1	Quadrant 2
Narrow	Quadrant 3	Quadrant 4

various forms of patronage infuse much (though not all) of the bureaucracy, and there is a strong geographic dispersion of centers of authority with corresponding differences in the extent of a rule by law; the strongest institutions typically operate in urban centers.

Now, putting the SF and COA together, Table 8.1 illustrates the typology. The reader may notice that this typology bears some resemblance to Khan's (2010) typology II (see Table 7.2). The COA collapses Khan's two dimensions of power into one. Unipolarity could fit *weak* on both of Khan's dimensions, with multipolarity fitting *strong* along at least one of them. Nevertheless, Khan's vertical dimension contrasts (relatively) weak versus strong lower-level factions. Although low-level weakness could imply unipolarity, there are two notable caveats. First, Khan focuses on vertical within-group relations, rather than on horizontal relations across elites. Second, functional unipolarity could exist with strong low-level insider groups—if insiders have successfully resolved CAPs of allocating basic authority across the levels. The SF concept is somewhat less analogous to Khan's horizontal distribution of power. Whereas a broad SF usually implies that the few excluded salient groups have little power, for a narrow SF, either excluded groups lack (de facto) disruptive power, or repression holds them in check (for the duration of the PS). A change in circumstances could alter this distribution, rendering the PS vulnerable to disruption. Hence, as the subsequent description shows, the combination of narrow/multipolar (quadrant 3) is compatible with Khan's vulnerable authoritarian coalition (weak/strong), with the stipulation that legal, informal, and/or repressive exclusion have, for the time being, prevented excluded factions from attaining sufficient de facto power to unsettle the PS, but they could do so in the future. We now turn to specifics.

The Quadrants and Their Properties

Table 8.1's four quadrants designate specific categories of PSs. Each implies a distinct set of tensions and CAPs that constrain economic and/or political development—similar to binding constraints in Ricardo Hausmann, Dani Rodrik, and Andrés Velasco's (2005) approach.[9] Simply identifying key CAPs, even without specifying the likelihood of resolution, facilitates policy analysis because CAPs constitute a core element of a given social context that influences probabilities of developmental success. Indeed, each quadrant in this typology implies specific trade-offs between political stability—notably, restraining widespread violence—and various forms of economic and political development that, desirability notwithstanding, could undermine such stability.

To proceed, recall the core goals of elites: (i) political survival and advancement, (ii) attaining private wealth, (iii) distributing goods to specific individuals or factions, and (iv) ideological goals with respect to the uses of power, which may then influence policy preferences. Of these, political survival (i) usually outweighs the others because inattention to it diminishes a party's influence. Political power is an instrument for attaining goals (ii) and (iii) and is always an instrument for (iv). Elite support for various elements of political and economic development thus depends on how they believe it will affect their political survivability and other goals.[10] Many CAPs that emerge from specific PSs follow disjunctures between elite goals, responses of relevant organizations and coalitions, and various desiderata of economic and political development.[11]

Turning to the quadrants, we consider the following five topics for each: (i) specific implications of the SF and the COA; (ii) implications of a quadrant's specific combination of both features; (iii) the quadrant's likely initially achieved political development regarding state capacity, rule by law, and public accountability; (iv) inherent tensions within each PS; and (v) implied developmental CAPs. This discussion addresses (i) and (ii) in order, with some examples and commentary on (iii), before proceeding to (iv) and (v).

First Quadrant (Q1): Broad SF and Multipolar COA

Societies operating within the first quadrant achieve limited political and economic development. In terms of Chapter 3's discussion of state capacity, Q1 represents a redistributive state (S2), exhibiting relatively weak state capacity with little economic or political rule by law. Yet these arrangements achieve some *substantive* public accountability, related to distributing benefits across insider groups, but little *procedural* accountability.[12] Regarding economic development, such societies typically fall into a middle-income trap. Here is the logic.

Concerning specific attributes, the broad SF signifies that a large proportion of the salient groups possess disruptive potential. Even though the few excluded groups usually pose no immediate threat to the PS, divisions among insider groups could undermine its duration. Consequently, maintaining the settlement requires a form of substantive accountability. Elites need to arrange distributions of rents and other benefits to insider-group elites and organizations, with some pass-through to constituent members. Q1 societies achieve that element of political development. Yet, with a multipolar COA, unresolved internal decision-making CAPs and the attendant need for renegotiation imply a general lack of direction on broad national goals, with regional and/or sectoral variation.

The combination of a broad SF with a multipolar COA focuses elite attention on delivering short-term benefits rather than longer-term economic capacity building, which would involve education, health care, and viable infrastructure. Provision of such public goods suffers from typical CAPs of free riding among insiders: Which groups sacrifice how much? If they could forge an agreement, could they enforce it? Instead, populist policies with extensive clientelism follow. Insiders thus have limited potential to develop fiscal or legal state capacity. Patron-client relationships condition economic and political exchanges more than impersonal rules can. Patron-client networks, often local, selectively enforce property rights held among their constituents—reflecting exercises of format 7's *gatekeeping* triadic power (see Chapter 5). Corruption abounds. Officials, responding to demands from powerful clients, violate formal rules to benefit themselves and their clients, and such behavior is widely expected. A weak or nonexistent rule of or by law on both political and economic dimensions augments problems of low state capacity. Still, the broad distribution of patronage reflects some degree of substantive accountability.

Country examples of Q1 include post-1990 India, Ghana, and Kenya. For India, political factionalization increased substantially during the 1990s, creating, in Khan's terms, a competitive clientelist PS (Sen, Kar, and Sahu 2018) that also fits a multipolar COA with a broad SF. The two current major parties, the Indian National Congress (INC) and the Bharatiya Janata Party (BJP), represent distinct coalitions whose national aspirations, particularly with respect to the role of religion, differ sharply. Moreover, especially after 2000, regional parties, with their own sets of demands, have played an increasing role. Reflecting the broad SF, the central government must pay considerable attention to regional interests in addition to basic Hindu, Muslim, and Sikh social groups (though to different degrees). "The regional parties became important components of the ruling coalition in the 2000s, and exerted a significant influence on what the main ruling party (whether INC or BJP) could or could not do" (Ibid., 273). Since the mid-1990s (at least until 2014), India fits Q1.[13]

Ghana also fits Khan's competitive clientelist category (Yanguas 2017; Abdulai and Hickey 2016) and Q1. Since 1992, Ghana has been a democracy with two competing large parties (National Democratic Congress and New Patriotic Party) representing distinct factions based on political tradition. There have been three alterations of power. The unstable power balance between these factions has engendered within-faction patronage politics. The party that wins an election enjoys nearly absolute power and access to considerable political and economic resources. Party elites, especially the president, award key positions to supporters. The winning party allocates jobs to its foot soldiers. These are lower-level groups, such as unions in mining and civil services, who extract benefits in return for loyalty. Elections have thus become a zero-sum game; each party maximizes turnout via divisive constituent appeals. Reflecting multipolarity, the parties find it nearly impossible to achieve consensus on national goals (Gyimah-Boadi and Prempeh 2012). "Short time horizons and suspicions of politicisation have undermined institutional continuity across administrations" (Yanguas 2017, 10). This description also fits Pranab Bardhan and Dilip Mookherjee's (2017) description of clientelism, whereby the delivery of public services to a group or area depends on demonstrated political support for the relevant official or party.

Q1 settlements thus exhibit internal tensions that arise from various conflicting perceptions and interests of insider elites and groups, who often occupy different sides of social cleavages. Sufficient divergence could undermine the PS at some future point.

Philip Roessler's (2011, 2017) discussion of the internal security dilemma or civil war—coup trap faced by multiethnic coalitions in postcolonial Sub-Saharan governments implies this very tension for countries whose initial postcolonial PS fit Q1. Immediately after independence, many new African countries forged arrangements called *elite accommodations* (inclusion of elites from different ethnic groups in a governing coalition) as the "dominant institution for managing competition for state resources among rival groups"

(2011, 306). Elites distributed patronage benefits across multiple constituents, as in Q1. In many cases, unfortunately, elites from different ethnic groups experienced steadily increasing mutual distrust. A commitment problem (an H4 CAP) ensued: Would powerful elites from the "other" group, typically with military or police influence, defect and try to seize power? As distrust grew, one or both sides adopted a strategy of eliminating potential opponents by, when in power, purging members of a distrusted group from government and persecuting its members. This strategy reduced the probability of a coup, but did so at the risk of a future civil war—a less decisive and less immediate outcome; hence preferable—that is, worth the risk. Appendix 8A and Figure A.1 illustrate these principles in detail.

Roessler notes many cases of successful coups, failed coups, and preemptive strikes to avoid coups and civil wars. For example, the 1963 coup and assassination of Sylvanus Olympio (an independence leader) reversed Togo's ethnic balance of power. In 1965, after a coup attempt by Hutu officers, Burundi's ruling Tutsi elite purged Hutu leaders, who had been in the ruling coalition (RC) since independence in 1962, locking them out of power for the next 28 years. In 1982 in Zimbabwe, a simmering power struggle between former revolutionary comrades Robert Mugabe of the Zimbabwe African National Union (ZANU) and Dr. Joshua Nkomo of the Zimbabwe African People's Union (ZAPU) led to the latter's expulsion and escape from the country, along with repression of ZAPU members and civilians from their Ndebele ethnic base. Mugabe ruled until 2017.[14] In the present typology, such exclusion converts a broad SF into a narrow one, moving the relevant societies from Q1 to Q3.

Finally, Q1 implies five developmental CAPs for the affected societies:

1. maintaining the broad SF, especially in cases with deep social cleavages;
2. reducing reliance on patron-client relationships without undermining stability by antagonizing one or more potentially disruptive groups;
3. (and closely related) extending accountability beyond short-term benefits and patronage to longer-term capacity building, with some form of procedural accountability;
4. enhancing insider unity (moving toward functional unipolarity to circumvent continuous renegotiation) by institutionalizing collective-choice rules for allocating authority, yet doing so in a manner that does not exclude current insider groups; and

5. enhancing state capacity, often via a unified vision of national purpose, without loss of accountability.

Second Quadrant (Q2): Broad SF and Unipolar COA

Unlike Q1, Q2 offers considerable potential for building state capacity—albeit
in two distinct manners: paths A and B. Path A, on the one hand, involves
constructing foundational institutions for a developmental state that exhibits
sufficient state capacity and rule by law to support and coordinate capacity
building, growth-oriented economic development. Path B, on the other hand,
exhibits substantial politicization of public services. Which path a society follows depends on how specific contexts influence elite motivations to resolve
CAPs, especially H4 CAPs of credible commitment. The ensuing discussion
first addresses implications of Q2's SF and COA, followed by consideration of
how Q2's mix of SF and COA could, in fact, arise; it then provides some detail
concerning factors that distinguish path A from B, before addressing implied
tensions and CAPs.

As in Q1, Q2's broad SF creates incentives for providing widespread benefits: a form of substantive accountability. Here, however, functional unipolarity facilitates rough agreements and understandings regarding national goals,
such as state-market relations. A potential to build state capacity follows. The
extent of capacity building and the degree to which rule of or by law follows,
however, depends on the applicable path: A or B.

The combination of a broad SF with a unipolar COA may appear counterintuitive. Unifying decision authority across multiple insider groups with
differing interests and perceptions should itself present a formidable set of
CAPs, notably those related to bridging social cleavages. The establishment
of a Q2 PS, therefore, reflects some resolution—a prospect that arises in the
presence of at least one of two conditions:

i. substantial previous institutional development; and
ii. a compelling, shared sense of urgency held among insider elites that
encourages setting aside short-term interests in favor of functional
unity.[15]

Here are two brief examples (more detail appears later): First, between 1960
and 1987, South Korea had both characteristics (i) and (ii). During the 1910–45
occupation, Japanese colonialists built a substantial merit-based bureaucracy
in Korea (Kohli 1994), and after 1948, the North provided a well-understood

existential threat to the South. Second, post-1994 Rwanda faced condition (ii). Since the end of the civil war in 1994, the Tutsi-led Rwandan Patriotic Front (RPF) has governed Rwanda. The RPF proposed a unified vision of national development, expressed in Rwanda's "Vision 2020 Progress and Way Forward" (Ministry of Finance and Economic Planning 2011), which signifies a significant resolution of RC CAPs—implying a unipolar power configuration: "the RPF and its allies are gambling on the 'expensive' option of building support on a broad base by demonstrating an ability to provide more and better public goods" (Booth and Golooba-Mutebi 2012, 391). To prevent the reemergence of civil war and genocide, the Rwandan SF includes Hutus (80% of the population), who have received substantial benefits. For their part, the Hutus have—perhaps grudgingly—accepted this arrangement. In return for benefits, they have acquiesced to living under RPF direction.[16]

Even so, Q2 yields two distinct developmental paths.[17] Path A connotes a developmental state that reflects substantial capability for resolving second-order CAPs, whereas path B connotes a patronage state. Path A usually follows cases with prior development of political institutions. Path A fosters establishing functional economic and bureaucratic institutions—basic state capacity and a type of rule by law—that could later facilitate a transition to rule of law and public accountability. Path A, however, emerges only under stringent preconditions. Elites from the various social groups (economic, military, religious, and ethnic) must somehow find motivation to resolve the difficult first-order CAPs of allocating short-term sacrifice, along with second-order CAPs of coordination and enforcement that permit institution building over medium-term time horizons.

There are three prerequisites for path A:

I.   As for any broad SF, governing elites need to maintain at least minimal loyalty across a large population by delivering benefits—a type of accountability. Since the broad SF applies to both paths, this condition does not distinguish path A from B, though A offers longer-term and more capability-oriented benefits.

II. The RC must face a resource constraint, meaning no easily available point-source resources or readily exportable agricultural commodities and no credible long-term commitments of substantial external aid.

III. The RC must face a shared and mutually understood external or internal threat to the existence of the (unipolar) RC, and especially the positions of elites within it: a threat to their political survival. Such prospects encourage the development of a nationalist (or other) ideology that can unify elites and followers.[18]

These prerequisites, when mutually understood, motivate RC elites to establish institutions capable of generating substantial revenue over medium-term time horizons. To survive politically, they must maintain the allegiance (or acquiescence) of their broad SF and, simultaneously, address the compelling threat. They must somehow create or induce conditions for sustainable growth, including defining and enforcing (sometimes selective) property rights and building a relatively independent merit-based bureaucracy that can collect taxes, regulate activities that generate substantive negative externalities, enforce contracts (at least selectively), and provide key public goods and services. An RC must also coordinate complementary forms of economic activity (as implied by H2) that foster structural transformation. Path A thus implies some resolution of H1–H4 CAPs, along with H5 innovations that confer legitimacy, spread motivation to organizational and group constituencies, and establish needed policies.

Note that a shared understanding of an existential threat helps resolve particularly difficult H4 second-order CAPs—because, under these conditions, elites jointly understand that their political survival depends on honoring a set of mutual commitments. Even so, resolution of second-order CAPs need not follow, particularly in cases that lack much prior institutional development, such as Rwanda in 1994. In such cases, the combination of mutual understanding and reciprocity can instantiate a set of political norms that prescribe honoring announced commitments. Longer-term sustainability, however, demands establishing more formalized enforceable agreements. Rwanda may or may not achieve path A.

The East Asian developmental states of South Korea between 1960 and 1987 and Taiwan, over roughly the same period, offer examples of path A development.[19] In both cases, elites faced serious external threats (North Korea and China, respectively). The respective RCs needed to secure broad-based support to address the threat (a broad SF), while they lacked easy access to revenue from commodities, resources, or substantial credible long-term external aid.[20] In the early stages of their development (1950s to early 1960s), as they struggled to retain power, the RCs needed to generate substantial revenue from economic activity without draining the treasury, along with sufficient legitimacy across a broad SF. They faced three basic tasks: (1) create the capacity to collect taxes and deliver public goods, rather than provide mere side payments; (2) establish certain universal property rights, especially over land and workers' own labor time, along with at least selective property rights over industrial production; and (3) coordinate forms of complementary and export-oriented economic activity, primarily in the industrial sector.

To initiate structural transformation, both countries implemented substantial land reform during the 1950s (a policy innovation). Land reform offered these regimes a way to distribute significant benefits to the rural masses without subsidies that would drain the treasury. It also altered the distribution of power, diminishing that of large landholders, who would have likely blocked further reforms.[21] Additionally, these regimes invested scarce government resources into primary education—a substantial and relatively inexpensive benefit for the broad population. These two policies delivered enduring, capability-building benefits to the rural masses—doing so without significant budget impact. These measures also engendered sufficient legitimacy to establish support and acquiescence from the public—needed for political survival, given the presence of external threats. Additionally, land reform and (with some delay) primary education improved agricultural productivity, which then facilitated some agricultural exports and, more critically, stable urban food prices. This last outcome eased maintaining at least minimal allegiance from the urban workforce, who might have otherwise expressed communist sympathies. The joint impacts of these policies thus rendered the PSs in both countries economically and politically sustainable.[22] On such foundation, the respective RCs began, in the 1960s, to establish developmental states that supported sufficient economic activity to achieve a broader distribution of benefits to the population (more education, more health care) via export-oriented industrial policy.[23]

Rwanda offers an example of less established, more tentative development that might achieve path A. After the 1994 civil war, which destroyed prior state capacity, Rwanda established a relatively uncorrupt and capable bureaucracy that has initiated successful development policies (Chemouni 2017; Reyntjens 2013). Since 1994, GDP per capita has grown at an average annual rate of 6%.

Considered a Tutsi-dominated organisation ruling over a Hutu-dominated population previously marred in genocidal ideology, the RPF aimed at basing its strategy of legitimation on rapid socio-economic progress and impartial rules. This required an effective state, both able to implement the RPF ambitious developmental objectives and to project an image of impartial governance, thus making PSR [public sector reforms] a necessity. (Chemouni 2017, 6)

These measures established at least tentative foundations for political and economic development.

In contrast, path B patronage states lack path A's prerequisites II and III. They have relatively easy access to revenue through commodity exports, point-source resources, and/or substantial and reliable external aid; additionally, elites do not encounter mutually understood internal or external threats to their political survival. Given these conditions, distributing benefits does not require significant revenue collection. Consequently, elites lack strong incentives to undertake the costly, complicated, and slow processes of developing substantial economic and bureaucratic institutions that would facilitate broad taxation, growth, and structural transformation. Instead, to maintain sufficient allegiance across the broad SF, they focus available state resources on delivering side payments to multiple groups in return for political support. These arrangements resemble Q1's clientelism, with three differences. First, unipolar coalitions can focus the distribution of benefits and more closely monitor quid pro quos. An RC can use a portion of existing state capacity to generate and maintain group support for the regime. Second, benefit distribution is less politically competitive; it does not reflect and support significant factional conflict along lines of social cleavage. Third, there is less regional and sectoral variation than in Q1. Uganda between 1986 and 2001 (discussed later in this section) offers a likely example of Q2's path B.

Both paths A and B face two core tensions, but to distinctly different degrees: (i) maintaining unity within the unipolar RC, given the diverse interests among the many groups with disruptive power—more difficult for path B's relatively unmotivated patronage approach; and (ii) maintaining a broad SF, given the combination of diverse interests and a unipolar RC, which could exclude one or more groups—as in cases of a feared coup.

Similarly, both paths face three developmental CAPs:

1. broadening input into RC decision making without undermining functional unipolarity;

2. enhancing accountability without creating divisions that undermine functional unipolarity and excessively weaken state capacity; and

3. ending the neglect and repression of (the relatively few) excluded minorities, which requires further broadening of the SF, without undermining functionality or stability.

Turning to path-specific CAPs, note that the two path A examples represent authoritarian regimes—arguably a necessary condition for initial political development in Q2. In some circumstances, however, a transition to democracy can achieve further political development, transforming a rule by law into a rule of law and enhancing accountability. If path A elites possess a shared understanding that various occurrences could shift the composition of an RC, they encounter incentives to develop institutions for transferring power (a form of political insurance). In South Korea and Taiwan, successful industrialization disseminated sufficient resources to industrial workers and the middle classes, shifting the balance of power. In South Korea, a general strike in 1987 by then powerful unions in the exporting industries, combined with substantial student protest that earned the support of the middle classes, forced the hand of the political regime. A transition to democracy followed.[24]

More generally, significant public pressure for accountability, arising from the de facto power of a sufficiently encompassing coalition, can foster elite interest in creating impersonal mechanisms of political succession as a form of political insurance. A more balanced distribution of governing power, wherein functional unipolarity involves coordinated rule-based policymaking input from a variety of groups, may then follow.

Accordingly, path A societies also face two distinctive developmental CAPs:

4. transforming a rule by law into a rule of law by establishing workable institutions that regulate transfers of power and apply credible sanctions to powerful economic and political elites who violate laws and established procedures; and

5. creating procedural public accountability without undermining stability.

Path B countries, despite often achieving impressive rates of short- to medium-term economic growth, can fall into a middle-income trap. Unipolarity, some state capacity, and a need to widely distribute benefits notwithstanding, the absence of path A's prerequisites II and III allows elites to survive comfortably without addressing many formidable CAPs of institution building. These societies fail to achieve the levels of H2 coordination and H4 enforcement that would permit substantial structural transformation.

Uganda's successes and failures largely fit path B. Since 1986, the National Resistance Movement (NRM) has ruled Uganda. Because the previous decade's conflict had reduced the capacities of competing groups, the NRM faced few obstacles to its reform program (Hickey and Izama 2016). Nevertheless, the PS included most groups (except those in the North), fitting Q2. With no compelling external or internal threats, Uganda lacked path A's prerequisite III. Since the early 2000s, however, increased political competition, growing power among lower-level groups, and defections from the NRM weakened the RC's hold on power. The PS moved toward Q1 multipolarity. Economically, Uganda achieved stable growth from 1988 to 2001 (3.5% annual GDP per capita) and rapid growth from 2001 to 2010 (7% annually), along with a considerable reduction in poverty, from 56% to 19.7%. Yet, since 2000, the NRM has increasingly relied on populist policies to retain the loyalty of rural and other less powerful constituencies (Yanguas 2017, 11; Hickey and Izama 2016). These measures limited Uganda's potential for structural transformation.

Path B societies encounter the following specific developmental CAPs—largely related to moving to path A:

6. motivating elites and key organizations to undertake the short-term sacrifices needed for establishing basic state fiscal and legal capacity;

7. motivating elites and organizations to undertake sacrifices for building economic institutions and means of coordination that can deliver longer-term capabilities and benefits; and

8. reducing patronage without undermining functional unipolarity or antagonizing potentially disruptive groups.

Third Quadrant (Q3): Narrow SF and Multipolar COA

Q3 countries encounter substantial barriers to achieving either political or economic development. The three direct forms of political development face dim prospects: low state capacity, little or no rule by law, and little or no accountability. Without abundant resources, a poverty trap is likely; with resources, a middle-income trap is possible.

Unlike Q1 and Q2, Q3 rests on a narrow SF: a few insider groups possess disruptive power, and any RC has little incentive to distribute benefits broadly. Furthermore, the narrow SF renders the settlement vulnerable to disruption if excluded groups can attain resources and sufficiently resolve organizational CAPs to form viable coalitions with de facto power. Consequently, not only does an RC lack incentives for broad distribution, its fear that excluded groups might attain de facto power motivates symbolic manipulation, division, and repression of excluded groups. Multipolarity in Q3 signifies the presence of a few rival factions formed around active social cleavages. As in Q1, elites face unresolved CAPs of designating decision-making authority over basic policy; they have few shared understandings of national policy goals; and they encounter the prospect of renegotiation before undertaking key policy directives—usually a barrier to such endeavors.

This mix of a narrow SF with multipolarity yields the following implications: Because insider factions compete over both rents and political support, nonelite economic and political entrepreneurs seek affiliation with a faction in order to receive political or economic benefits—that is, patronage—with a premium on protection from rival factions and possibly resentful outsiders. Additionally, insider factions hope to maintain exclusion (the narrow SF), but lack effective coordination. Whereas they fear the possibility that excluded groups may attain power, a single faction may also stand to gain from recruiting excluded groups to challenge rivals. Consequently, all three components of direct political development falter.

Maintaining the PS involves several tensions. Factional conflict over rents and resources can undermine understandings and agreements. As they strive to gain relative power, factions may competitively recruit (i.e., coopt) outsiders. Here, they face a prisoners' dilemma scenario: each faction can benefit from such recruitment, but competitive recruitment enhances overall conflict, exacerbating multipolarity with potentially unstable extension of the SF and undermining PS stability.

In such instances, Q3 confronts a variation of Roessler's civil war–coup trap that begins with exclusion and considers inclusion, with several avenues for civil war. If an RC recruits an excluded group, a coup may follow if the new insiders translate their position into sufficient power—especially if they develop links to the army. Yet, maintaining exclusion can lead to civil war or allow a rival faction to recruit excluded groups. If rival recruitment enhances conflicts among insiders, it can also foster civil war. Moreover, excluded groups exacerbate such conflict if they play inside factions off against each other (triadic power format 5). Finally, certain insider elites (or groups) may defect, allying themselves with excluded groups in a manner that threatens the PS with another conduit to civil war. For example, in 1910, Francisco Madero, a scion of the Mexican elite with a lineage dating back to early colonial times, defected from the (by then factionalized) Díaz regime to become a leader of the Mexican Revolution—*la Guerra Civil Mexicana*—which lasted from 1910 to 1920.

Q3 settlements thus rest on unstable foundations; specific regimes tend to be short lived. Prospects for building state capacity, rule of law, and public accountability remain distant, as do prospects for economic development. Q3 usually implies weak states that face poverty traps.[25] Examples include the pre-Marcos Philippines, Ecuador in the early 1970s, Nigeria in the 1980s and 1990s, and contemporary South Sudan.

Large stability–development trade-offs ensue. More specifically, Q3 societies encounter these four basic developmental CAPs:

1. creating functional unipolarity in the presence of rival insider factions;
2. broadening the SF, without exacerbating existing divisions;
3. reducing reliance on rents, without enhancing factionalism and undermining stability; and
4. creating some accountability, probably initially via inclusive clientelism (a move toward Q1), without exacerbating multipolarity that would threaten stability.

Fourth Quadrant (Q4): Narrow SF and Unipolar COA

Like Q2, this quadrant fosters two distinct developmental paths: here, C and D. As in Q3, the narrow SF offers the RC little incentive to distribute benefits, and the prospect that excluded groups might attain de facto power creates incentives to repress, divide, and symbolically manipulate excluded groups. Unlike Q3, however, functional unipolarity facilitates resolution of insider CAPs related to national purpose, offering some potential to build state capacity. But for what purpose? The two paths differ.

Along path C, a protodevelopmental state (or limited dictatorship), ruling elites attain some long-term vision. They use their growing state capacity to gradually build and strengthen certain economic and bureaucratic institutions. They selectively provide public goods and services (club goods for inside cliques). They establish selective property rights—a type of rule by law that can facilitate economic development. Given the narrow SF, however, they do so with similarly narrow accountability, applied only to their own clients, not the general public—and they repress excluded groups.

In contrast, path D signifies a predatory state. Fearing that excluded groups could attain de facto power, the narrow unipolar RC focuses its limited state capacity on repression and extraction—rather than institution building. Insider elites coerce, divide, and symbolically manipulate excluded groups, extract rents, and when it suits their purposes, seize property. There is no accountability, no rule by law, and little state capacity beyond a repressive apparatus.

The distinction between paths C and D, like that between A and B, rests on how elements of the social context affect elite motivation to resolve a host of CAPs related to forging institutions—especially H4 commitment problems. Sufficient previously established institutions and/or a functioning network of regime supporters who can limit a dictator's ability to prey on select groups of potential investors inclines a society toward path C. As Chapter 9 illustrates, the ability of network supporters to limit an autocrat also depends on path A prerequisites II and III (the narrow SF rules out prerequisite I).

The 1870–1910 Díaz dictatorship in Mexico offers an example of path C supported by network enforcement. Porfirio Díaz issued promises to enforce the property rights of specific asset holders who had connections to his regime. The implied promises (not to seize new assets and returns) attained credibility because a network of Díaz's supporters had both motivation and position to punish him should he renege. This arrangement effectively limited the dictator's power and simultaneously resolved second-order CAPs of commitment. So constrained, the Díaz regime initiated Mexico's early industrialization (Razo 2008).

Augusto Pinochet's Chile offers another path C example, one with substantial prior institutional development. In the case of Chile, existing institutions, including a well-developed judicial system, limited Pinochet's power; the 1973 military coup could only overturn so much.

Path D examples include the Central African Republic under Jean-Bédel Bokassa, Equatorial Guinea under Francisco Macías Nguema, and—the worst-case scenario—Cambodia under Pol Pot.[26]

Despite their differences, paths C and D both exhibit a set of tensions related to maintaining the narrow SF's exclusion, and both face significant trade-offs between stability and development—more severe for path D. There are two common developmental CAPs:

1. broadening the SF without undermining stability and existing state capacity. Outsider resentment may enhance the difficulties, especially for path D; and

2. reducing the repression of excluded groups without destroying the PS. A two-sided (H4) commitment problem emerges: (i) Would the dictator honor a promise to reduce repression or cede power? (ii) If so, could repressed groups credibly commit to refrain from (unduly) punishing perpetrators? Consider Chile's transition from Pinochet's dictatorship to democracy and Mugabe's 2018 resignation in Zimbabwe, which occurred without violence, as opposed to the reaction to initially peaceful attempts at regime change in Syria before the civil war.

These CAPs suggest that path D societies face a postexclusion version of the civil war–coup trap. On the one hand, if the inside clique continues to exclude most social groups, it risks civil war. On the other hand, if it broadens the SF, allowing excluded groups inside, the end of repression could foster their attainment of de facto power and a possible coup.

Societies operating along each path also face their own sets of CAPs. For C:

3. developing accountability without excessive reduction in state capacity;

4. strengthening the bureaucracy and rule by law in economic institutions so as to reduce the selectivity of public good provision and property right enforcement, while maintaining functional unipolarity without sacrificing stability; and

5. in the longer term, moving toward establishing a rule of law, notably by addressing regime succession and creating credible means for sanctioning violations by powerful economic and political parties.

Path D societies thus face more daunting developmental CAPs:

6. achieving a more stable PS;

7. converting repression to cooptation or some other mechanism for addressing deep outsider grievances, without a coup;

8. alternatively, for outsiders and disgruntled insiders, organizing a revolution (or coup) that does not erupt into civil war or replace one predatory state with another;

9. assuming at least minimal resolution of CAPs 6–8, moving to early institution building, establishing rudimentary rule by law with some

selectively enforceable economic institutions and selective provision of public goods and services; and

10. developing rudimentary accountability, at least to selective groups, without undermining stability.

Addressing CAPs 9 and 10 imply moving to path C.

Section 3: Conclusion

The concept of PSs offers a foundation for analyzing relationships between distributions of power, institutions, and ultimately institutional systems and social orders. Classification of PSs, using the criteria of SFs and COAs, facilitates systematic inquiry into settlement-specific tensions and CAPs. These are key elements of the political-economic context that shape prospects for development; they point to context-specific constraints and possibilities. Within unipolar quadrants Q2 and Q4, after accounting for previous institutional development, further distinctions that depend on the presence or absence of mutually understood threats and resource constraints, facilitate differentiating paths A from path B (developmental vs. patronage states), as well as path C from path D (protodevelopmental vs. predatory states). Table 8B.1 (in Appendix 8B) summarizes relationships between the four PS quadrants, the paths that operate in Q2 and Q4, and, for each quadrant or path, key attributes, tensions, and associated CAPs.

Ultimately, this framework offers a foundation for designing more elaborate models that can spawn multiple testable hypotheses. Appendixes 8A and 8B, for example, develops a game-theoretic model of the civil war–coup trap. More generally, effective policy approaches need to account for the foundations of specific PSs, as represented in their SF and COA and, within the unipolar quadrants (Q2 and Q4), the applicable path (C or D). Policy analysts should then consider underlying tensions within each type of PS and the specific CAPs that accompany it as a lens for examining the prospects and pitfalls of potential remedies.

Chapter 9 continues this analysis by directly considering relationships between businesses and governments, with attention to the credibility of contracts and feedbacks of ensuing economic outcomes on the stability of political settlements.

9 Business-State Interactions

> The immediate central political issue in capitalism . . . is the relationship
> between business and government, or from our more distant perspective,
> between the economy and the state.
>
> —*Robert Heilbroner*, 21st Century Capitalism *(1993)*

LANT PRITCHETT, KUNAL SEN, and Eric Werker (2018) observe
four distinct patterns of long-run growth across multiple countries. First, for
over a century, developed economies (long-standing OECD members) have
exhibited low and stable overall rates of growth in GDP per capita: about 2%
per year, with small fluctuations. Second, many developing countries, such as
Kenya, Ghana, Uganda, and Thailand, have displayed far more growth variance, marked by periods of dramatic acceleration and sharp decline.[1] "There
is almost zero predictive value for a country's growth in the next decade from
this decade's growth" (Pritchett and Werker 2012, 7). Third, many countries,
such as the Central African Republic, appear to be stuck in poverty traps with
long periods of virtually no growth. Fourth, a few countries, such as South
Korea, Taiwan, and China, have exhibited extended periods of rapid growth.
Why such difference?

To explain these patterns, Pritchett et al. (Ibid.) consider how distinct political settlements (PSs) and configurations of markets (see Table 7.4), influence prospects for establishing accessible and credible agreements—the ordered versus open deals of their fourth typology. They note in particular that
a transition from disordered to ordered deals generates growth accelerations;
yet, maintaining growth over long time horizons and achieving structural
transformation requires more fundamental institutional development.

In the present framework, achieving substantial economic development,
including sustainable growth and structural transformation, requires con-

fronting a series of fundamental CAPs specified by this book's first four hypotheses: from H4, establishing credible commitments that powerful parties—both private and public—will not seize the benefits from others' investments in effort, knowledge, and physical capital; from H3, preventing or ameliorating undue influence of powerful parties on the construction and operation of economic institutions; from H2, coordinating the production of knowledge, matching skills, and harnessing production externalities; and from H1, mitigating large negative externalities and providing basic public goods and services.

Chapter 8's typology of PSs (see Table 8.1) takes us partway toward analyzing sets of conditions that influence prospects for resolving these CAPs. Additional progress requires closer examination of state-business relations. Mushtaq Khan (2010) addresses this issue in his third typology (see Table 7.3), noting that powerful private interests influence both the structure and sustainability of PSs. Indeed, the durability of a given settlement—its propensity to be either self-reinforcing or self-undermining—depends on the degree to which its distribution of benefits to powerful parties accords with their goals, given their understandings of feasible alternatives. Such distribution, in turn, depends on economic institutions and business-state interactions.

This chapter extends Chapter 8's PS analysis by merging Khan's concern over economic distribution, investor power, and settlement durability with Pritchett et al.'s take on market configuration and credible (ordered) deals. This approach involves interactions within and across three levels of analysis. First, at the macrolevel, a PS establishes the basic political context within which institutions evolve. The breadth of a settlement's social foundation (SF) and the degree of unipolarity of its configuration of authority (COA) underlie the motivation and ability of a ruling coalition (RC) to broadly distribute benefits, repress excluded groups, and build state capacity. Especially in the multipolar quadrants (Table 8.1's Q1 and Q3), these parameters may also exhibit regional (meso-level) variation that responds to and influences regional economic development. Second, at the mesolevel, economic and political realms of influence interact. The configuration of markets provides sector-specific economic context that both conditions and responds to macro-level PS influences. Third, at a microlevel, political-economic transactions operate within a *deals environment* that—reflecting degrees of resolution of H3 and H4 CAPs—determines the credibility and accessibility of

TABLE 9.1 Market Configurations (Market Matrix)

Orientation/Structure	Monopolistic (M)	Competitive (C)
Domestic (D)	DM	DC
Export (X)	XM	XC

Adapted from Pritchett and Werker (2012, 21).

informally arranged economic and political transactions (deals). This chapter addresses these meso- and microlevels.

The meso-level configuration of sector-specific markets—their domestic or export orientation and their monopolistic or competitive structure—shapes the transactions conducted by key economic actors, affecting their interests and the demands they place on the state. Ruling elites, in turn, consider the capabilities and economic importance of domestic capitalists, including their influence on state revenues and foreign exchange—their structural power (Whitfield and Therkildsen 2011, 28). Ensuing business-state interactions condition public and private elite support for the institutional arrangements of the relevant PS—a key underpinning of its durability. Market configurations also influence the micro-level credibility of deals arranged within specific sectors, with significant impacts on prospects for growth.

Table 9.1 (a slight variation of Table 7.4) represents this meso-level economic context.[2] The vertical dimension specifies domestic (D) as opposed to export (X) orientation of the specific sector, and the horizontal dimension distinguishes between monopolistic (M) and competitive (C) sectors. The four possible combinations, DM, DC, XM, and XC, shape micro-level deals transactions and the ensuing economic revenue influences (i.e., feeds back into) private and public interests. Sections 1 and 2 elaborate.

At the microlevel, Pritchett et al.'s deals environment (noted in Chapter 7) draws two distinctions: (i) that between ordered (predictable/credible) and disordered (not predictable) deals; and (ii) that between selective (closed) and open deals. Table 9.2 illustrates the deals environment, divided into four quadrants:[3]

1. *Ordered/Closed*: available only to those with connections—officials will honor (cronyism, Vladimir Putin's Russia);

2. *Ordered/Open*: available to all who take appropriate actions—officials will honor (retail corruption, bribes for small permissions or favors; in Tajikistan, one might trade a sheep for a driver's license);[4]

TABLE 9.2 The Deals Environment

	Closed Deals	*Open Deals*
Ordered Deals	1 Ordered & Closed	2 Ordered & Open
Disordered Deals	3 Disordered & Closed	4 Disordered & Open

SOURCE: Adapted from figure 1.14 of Pritchett, Sen, and Werker (2018, 28).

3. *Disordered/Closed*: available only to the connected—honoring is uncertain (unreliable cronyism); and

4. *Disordered/Open*: available to all who take appropriate actions— honoring is uncertain (many informal-sector transactions).[5]

Table 9.2's implications are profound. A (vertical) transition from disordered to ordered deals establishes credibility, reflecting at least partial resolution of H4 commitment CAPs. Such a transition facilitates escaping poverty traps via growth accelerations.[6] The degree of success, moreover, reflects participants' abilities to resolve H1 CAPs within a given PS and market configuration. Additionally, the distinction between selective and open deals reflects the accessibility of economic exchange—itself a dimension of economic and political inequality that responds to prior resolution of H3 CAPs, or lack thereof.

Within these dynamics, the motivations of political and economic elites influence the prospects for resolving pertinent CAPs. Game-theoretic logic provides an avenue for analyzing how such motivation responds to macro- and meso-level contexts and to the specific micro-level terrains within which exchange agreements appear and operate.

This chapter's discussion proceeds as follows. Section 1 develops a relatively simple game representing the somewhat stringent conditions under which ordered deals can emerge. It applies the game's logic to the unipolar settlements (Table 8.1's Q2 and Q4), under the (somewhat) simplifying assumption that exchanges in these quadrants operate in Table 9.1's two monopolistic sectors (DM and XM). The game's key parameters reflect macro influences from a settlement's SF and its degree of unipolarity, as well as pre-existing and external conditions related to compelling threats and resource constraints. Indeed, these factors influence Q4's distinction between paths C and D (protodevelopmental vs. predatory state). Moreover, on path C (D), ordered (disordered) deals prevail. A briefer discussion then applies the same principles to Q2's distinction between paths A and B (developmental vs.

patronage state). Attaining path A also requires significant resolution of H2 coordination CAPs that can facilitate structural transformation via complex production and exchange.

Section 2 applies a similar logic to Table 8.1's multipolar configurations (Q1 and Q3). After a brief discussion of Q3, it develops Q1 (arguably the most interesting case), with specific attention to both macro- and meso-level implications of Q1's broad SF and multipolar configuration of authority (COA). Both parameters affect and interact with sector-specific market configurations and with the deals environment. Section 2 closes with commentary on how ensuing flows of revenue either reinforce or undermine the relevant PS.

Section 3 summarizes outcomes from Sections 1 and 2, shown in Appendix 9A's Table 9A.1, and applies Section 2's meso-level discussion of PSs and revenue feedback to the other quadrants.

Section 1: Economic Development and Commitment—Achieving Credible Deals in Political Settlements with Unipolar Configurations of Authority

This section's model offers five developmental implications. The first two may appear counterintuitive. First, in certain political contexts, rent sharing, often a form of corruption, may underlie the creation of (admittedly selective) credible agreements that can foster some economic development. Second, higher taxes may also facilitate development by reducing the incentives for potentially predatory dictators to seize returns from others' production.[7] Third, the model reinforces Chapter 4's assertion that more complex production requires greater coordination and thus stronger institutional mechanisms for resolving H2 CAPs. Fourth, the model implies a resource curse that interferes with establishing credible agreements. Fifth, the model details underlying logic for the assertion that movement from disordered to ordered deals can foster escaping from poverty traps.

Consider the game shown in Figure 9.1. It portrays the rather stringent conditions under which ordering deals offers involved parties higher expected payoffs than taking no action. In the latter case, disordered deals may ensue.[8] The game's basic political economy implication is clear: meeting its stringent conditions constitutes an elemental form of development, signifying at least partial resolution of H4 CAPs of establishing credible exchange commitments that can, in turn, foster escaping poverty traps.

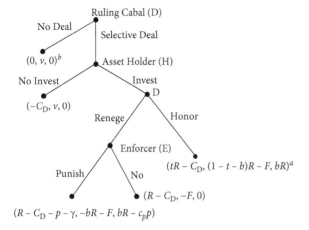

LEGEND: v = H's fallback income; C_D = D's cost of initiating a deal; t = tax rate; b = bribe rate; R = H's revenue; F = H's fixed costs to investing; p = amount of punishment; c_p = unit cost of punishing; γ = D's reputation cost for reneging. Superscripts ^{a} and ^{b} respectively = the *Honor* and *No Deal* subgame perfect equilibria.

FIGURE 9.1 Selective Ordered Deals Game
SOURCE: Adapted from Razo (2008 fig. 2.5, 46) and Ferguson (2013,fig. 13.3, 342), which was adapted from Razo).

In applying this game to Q4, we assume that a dictator or ruling cabal (hereafter D) operates within a unipolar COA. Because there is no independent judiciary (regardless of formal legal or constitutional statements), D cannot credibly promise to enforce universal property rights. The relevant H4 CAPs remain unresolved. Even so, D relies on powerful supporters who, when sufficiently connected, could administer punishment if D threatens their interests. This possibility, moreover, allows D to offer deals that specify property rights over specific types of production to selected individuals or firms—in return for some tax revenue. An asset holder (H) may then consider investing in costly modern (e.g., nonagricultural) production in the hope of attaining future returns. As a member of the economic elite, H also has ties to powerful members of the RC, such as army generals and large financiers, who, jointly, could impose sanctions on D. Collectively, they can act as a deal enforcer (E). Enforcement, however, is costly because challenging D carries some risk of losing a conflict. To offset this cost and motivate interest, H can offer E a bribe (b, a rent share) in return for an implicitly understood (unofficial) agreement to punish D if D reneges on a deal.[9]

The game unfolds as follows: D chooses whether or not to issue a selective deal to H, at cost C_D, in return for tax revenue tR, where $t < 1$ is a fixed percentage of R. The deal specifies that D will honor and protect H's property rights, including some form of rent-generating market entry barrier—whose enforcement costs constitute an important component of C_D. For mineral resources, this cost may be quite low. H then decides whether to invest by comparing her net earnings, $(1 - t - b)R$, to the sum of fixed costs (F) plus noninvestment (fallback) earnings (v)—the return to traditional production. Next, D decides whether to honor the contract or renege, where reneging implies seizing the earnings, for a payoff of $R - C_D$ minus the costs of being punished (p) and any (nonpunishment) reputation or legitimacy losses (γ). If D reneges, E decides whether or not to punish D (an auxiliary transaction), at a cost per unit (c_p) of administered punishment (p), doing so in return for a bribe (bR), where rent share b is a fixed percentage of R.[10]

Ordered deals and investment arise only under four conditions. Using backward induction (i.e., starting with step 4), we have (1) an enforcement condition, (2) an honor condition, (3) an investment condition, and (4) an initiation condition. Here is the intuition; details follow. If (1) fails, E will not punish D for reneging, so D will not honor a contract; anticipating this outcome, H will not invest. If (1) holds but (2) fails, D prefers reneging and receiving punishment to honoring; again, H will not invest. If (1) and (2) hold but (3) fails, H prefers fallback income v to net return $R(1 - t - b) - F$, and so will not invest. Finally, if (1), (2), and (3) hold but (4) fails, D will not initiate a deal to begin with. Ordered deals require all four conditions.

Turning to details, with backward induction, we start with enforcement. The *enforcement condition* relates the expected value of a bribe (bR) to E's cost of administering punishment $(c_p p)$, implying that rent shares can facilitate ordering deals. E punishes D only when

(9.1) $bR > c_p p.$

The key terms here depend on CAPs and power relations. Production revenue, R, reflects the presence of workable conditions fostered by resolving H1 and H2 CAPs: $R = R(H1, H2) = R(g_t, \theta_{t-1})$, where $g_t \geq 0$ signifies the amount of public goods provided (e.g., infrastructure) in period t; and $\theta_{t-1} \in [0, 1]$ signifies the strength of preexisting institutions for resolving H2 coordination CAPs.[11] The costs of enforcement increase in D's relative power: $c_p = c_p(BP_D/BP_E)$, where BP signifies bargaining power. Attaining condition (9.1) becomes easier the greater the expected earnings (R) and rent share (b), and the lower

BP_D/BP_E, c_p, and p. Hence, counterintuitively, eliminating corruption-related rents can undermine growth by rendering condition (9.1) infeasible.

Next, the *honor condition* relates D's expected net gains from reneging (seizing R) to the cost of being punished (p) and reputation costs of breaking deals (γ). If enforcement condition (9.1) holds, D honors only when $tR - C_D > R - C_D - p - \gamma$; or

(9.2) $p + \gamma > R(1 - t)$.

Here, t depends on resolving H1 CAPs that underlie the development of state fiscal capacity (see Chapter 3): $t = t(H1)$. Note that higher taxes can promote growth by reducing D's incentive to renege. D's reputation cost γ responds to preexisting institutional strength, the breadth of the SF, and the presence of a mutually understood threat T: $\gamma = \gamma(\theta_{t-1}, B_{SF}, T)$.[12] Whereas condition (9.1) implies minimum values for R and t, by specifying a maximum tR, given $p + \gamma$, condition (9.2) sets a limit on R, given p, γ, and t. Jointly, conditions (9.1) and (9.2) may then prescribe a narrow or nonexistent range for R that permits ordering deals.

The *investment condition*, operable if both (9.1) and (9.2) hold, relates H's expected after-tax-and-bribe return on investment to traditional production fallback income v. H invests if

(9.3) $R(1 - t - b) - F > v$ or $R > (F + v)/(1 - t - b)$.

Here, fixed costs (F) decrease in degrees of resolution of H1 and H2 CAPs and increase in the complexity of production (ζ): $F = F(H1, H2; \zeta) = F(g_p, \theta_{t-1}; \zeta_t)$.[13] Fallback earnings v increase in resource rents (rr), the average size of top-decile landholdings (η), and agriculture's share of GDP (y_a/y): $v = v(rr, \eta, y_a/y)$.[14] Condition (9.3) sets another minimum level for R (cet. par.), along with maximum levels for t, b, F, and v, with corresponding maxima or minima for θ, ζ, rr, η, and y_a/y, *ceteris paribus*. Not surprisingly, business and state tax incentives push in opposite directions, as do H's and E's (conflicting) rent-sharing incentives. The minimum R threshold again points to H1 and H2 CAPs. Here, the relative importance of H2 (and θ), which reflects pecuniary externalities (Rosenstein-Rodan 1943), increases in production complexity (ζ): the greater the complexity of production, the more important are strong institutions (θ) for resolving H2 coordination CAPs. Additionally, high fixed costs (F)—more likely with complex production—can also inhibit investment. Furthermore, *rr* again implies a resource curse, this time by augmenting H's fallback alternative *v*. Concentrated landholdings (a high η) imply a corresponding antigrowth effect from highly inequitable land distributions, and a large agricultural share of output (y_a/y) implies a self-reinforcing inhibition on structural transformation.

Now, combining (9.1), (9.2), and (9.3), and for simplicity assuming $\gamma = 0$, ordered deals arise only if $v + F < R(1 - t - b) < R(1 - t) < p < bR/c_p$. Ordered deals arise only within a possibly narrow range for R.[15]

Finally, the *initiation condition*, only relevant when (9.1), (9.2), and (9.3) hold, specifies the minimum revenue D must expect to justify the costs of offering a selective deal to begin with. D offers if

(9.4) $tR > C_D$.

Here, C_D depends on product complexity ζ and on the RC's degree of unipolarity, which depends on the strength of its coordinating institutions (θ_{RC}). Specifically, $C_D = C_D(\zeta, \theta_{RCt-1})$. Because a high ζ implies a high information content of production (and related processes), a high ζ enhances the difficulty of enforcing property rights and entry barriers, increasing C_D. In contrast, a high θ_{RCt-1} facilitates RC agreement on issues related to offering selective contracts, reducing C_D. Relation (9.4) also implies minimum levels for t and R, or a maximum C_D.

If all four conditions hold, a subgame perfect equilibrium (SPE) exists in which D offers, H invests if offered, D honors if H invests, and E punishes if D reneges. The ordered deals outcome (superscript *a* on Figure 9.1) follows. The failure of any single condition (9.1)–(9.4) leads to the alternative SPE outcome, with no offer (superscript *b*), for any $C_D > 0$.

For any outcome in which D does not offer an ordered deal, two possibilities arise: no deals or disordered deals. "Honoring" disordered deals implies no protection from private predation. It implies only that D will not seize output, occurring only when such restraint suits D's short-term interests—for example, when the costs of discovering or measuring R exceed its value or when seizing might risk a costly confrontation with a gang. With no protection, it costs D nothing to "offer" disordered deals ($C_D = 0$), and D's supporters have nothing to enforce. Hence conditions (9.1), (9.2), and (9.4) become irrelevant and (9.3) simplifies to $R(g_t, \theta_{t-1}) > F(g_t, \theta_{t-1}, \zeta) + v$. This condition typically holds only for simple (though not necessarily low-value) production with low fixed costs and minimal need for public goods or coordination with either the state or private producers; it requires only correspondingly low levels of H1 and H2 CAP resolution.

To proceed, let $\rho_h < 1$ signify the probability that D honors a disordered deal. For simplicity, let $\rho_h = 0.5$.[16] Assume no risk aversion and constant returns to scale (diminishing marginal returns to all factors) along with no pecuniary externalities; these assumptions fit simple production. If so, disordered deals offer at most half of the development potential of ordered deals for equivalently simple commodities. In poverty traps, disordered deals facilitate some noncomplex, usually informal-sector, production. Again, escaping poverty traps via growth accelerations occurs when prevalent deals move from disorder to order.

Quadrant 4: Narrow Social Foundation/Unipolar—Honoring
Deals and Distinguishing Between Paths C and D

With this background, we now apply Figure 9.1's logic to prospects for ordering deals within Q4. With a unipolar COA, the RC—having resolved many internal CAPs—can apply existing state capacity (at whatever level, reflecting prior resolution of H1 and H2 CAPs) to achieve elite goals. With a narrow SF, elites face no incentive to distribute benefits broadly. This situation raises the specter that excluded groups, by resolving internal CAPs and attaining resources, could develop sufficient de facto power to undermine the settlement. Consequently, elites in this quadrant have some incentive to repress and divide excluded groups. How, then, will the RC employ its state capacity? Either path C (protodevelopmental state) or D (predatory state) may follow.

Along both paths, the narrow SF offers no incentive to define and enforce universal property rights. Regarding production, the monopolistic quadrants dominate the meso-level market matrices. Selective deals, as opposed to open deals, dominate the deals environment—with some exceptions in the informal sector (ignored here for simplicity but addressed in Sections 2 and 3). Here, Figure 9.1's D can offer selective deals to enforce selective rights that underlie and maintain the monopolistic sectors. With ordered deals, monopolistic firms could generate sufficient revenue to pay taxes and bribes, and enforcers could receive enough rent to have a stake in both restraining D and upholding the system. Along path C, these arrangements function well and ordered deals prevail. Path D, however, lacks the necessary prerequisites.

Examination of Figure 9.1's conditions (9.1)–(9.4) illustrates these distinctions. Along both paths, unipolarity implies little internal RC contestation over issuing deals. Accordingly, C_D is low and the offer condition (9.4) is attainable. But here the similarities end.

The distinction between paths C and D depends on elite ability and motivation to resolve H4 commitment and H1 provision CAPs. As noted in Chapter 8, the relevant elite incentives depend on the presence or absence of path A prerequisites II and III: respectively, a resource constraint and a compelling, mutually understood external or internal threat to the political survival of insider elites. These requisite conditions motivate elites to put aside their short-term interests in favor of the difficult and costly tasks of building capable institutions for resolving H4 and H1 CAPs—an especially difficult prospect in cases with little prior institutional development.[17]

To apply the model, first consider a case with a resource constraint (implying a low v) but no compelling threat and little prior institutional development. Given the narrow SF, the latter two conditions suggest a low reputation loss for reneging ($\gamma = 0$). Figure 9.1's enforcement condition (9.1) becomes problematic, but some potential for ordered deals remains. Figure 9.2 illustrates the narrow set of conditions that permit ordered deals. Its horizontal axis shows the level of punishment, p, that E may deliver to D. The vertical axis shows total revenues and costs associated with bribes and enforcement (bR and $c_p p$) for given values of b, c_p, and R. The diagonal line from the origin shows, for a given c_p, how increasing p affects enforcement cost $c_p p$. The horizontal line shows E's total rents, bR, for a fixed b, assuming that R is independent of p. Here, enforcement condition (9.1) holds only within the triangle bounded from below by $c_p p$ and from above by bR. The apex at $p^* = bR/c_p$ shows the maximum p that meets (9.1). For ordered deals, the relevant values for honor condition (9.2) must fall within this triangle. The figure shows the following artificial but illustrative values: $p^* = R = 100$; $b = c_p = 0.10$; $t = 0.05$; $F = 10$. Here, (9.2) holds only for $p > p_{Min} = R(1 - t) = 90$, a narrow range. The resource constraint (RESC), however, implies a low v, $v_{RESC} = 0.4R = 40$. With the low v_{RESC} and $F = 10$, the investment condition (9.3) is easily met. Even so, (9.1) and (9.2) restrict the relevant space for ordered deals to the small shaded triangle to the right of the segment $R(1 - t) = 90$. Note that increasing R would make meeting (9.1) easier but could preclude meeting (9.2). Increasing t would move the $R(1 - t)$ line left, relaxing (9.2) and increasing the triangle's area, but if $R(1 - t)$ were to fall below 50, (9.3) would fail. With these values, the resource constraint offers a fair amount of latitude. We conclude that in Q4, with a resource constraint and no external

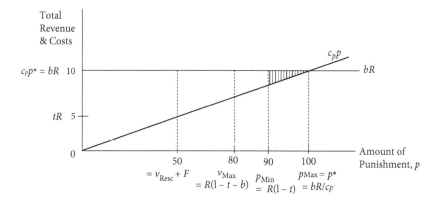

LEGEND: c_p = unit cost of punishing; p = amount of punishment; t = tax rate; b = bribe rate; R = H's revenue; v = H's fallback income; v_{Resc} = v with resource constraint = $0.4R$; shaded area: conditions (9.1) and (9.2) both met.

FIGURE 9.2 Ordered Deals Space

threat, attaining ordered deals characteristic of path C is difficult but not impossible.

As noted in Chapter 8, path C fits Mexico's early industrialization under Porfirio Díaz between 1870 and 1910 and Chile under Augusto Pinochet (a case with much higher prior institutional development). Chile later shifted its PSs toward a democratic version of Q2 after Pinochet lost a 1988 plebiscite on his continued rule. Figure 9.2's model also fits Ghana's 1980–99 growth experience, occurring without structural transformation—as one would expect along path C.

Now, taking these conditions but adding a mutually understood compelling threat to elite political survival pushes short-run interests aside, rendering path C likely. Elite motivations change in several fashions. First, D now faces a significant reputation loss for reneging ($\gamma > 0$), and D's own fears lower c_p. This combination relaxes the joint constraints from conditions (9.1) and (9.2), expanding the size of the feasible honored deal triangle. Indeed, a sufficiently high γ obviates any need for p. Second, with short-term interests set aside, coalition elites willingly contribute to public goods related to defense, productive infrastructure, and developing a skilled, merit-based bureaucracy (at least for defense). Resolving H1 CAPs becomes more feasible, facilitating higher R and relatively efficient tax collection (tR). Similarly, E—also setting aside its short-run interests—requires smaller bribes (b). Investment condition (9.3) becomes even easier to meet. Honored deals emerge, permitting development along path C.

Removing the resource constraint while maintaining a compelling threat, however, renders path D more likely. Here, γ remains high and c_p low, so condition (9.1) is still attainable. The RC also faces incentives to provide defense-related public goods, with state capacity in that area. But without a resource constraint, the RC need not resolve H1 CAPs of providing nondefense-related public goods and developing administrative capabilities that permit efficient tax collection. With a low t, D may still find seizing nondefense output profitable, rendering (9.2) problematic—especially for complex production in nondefense areas. Furthermore, with no resource constraint, investor H may have a large fallback income v (from point-source resources and/or agricultural exports from large landholdings), eliminating incentives for modern investment, perhaps increasing $v + F$ above 90 in Figure 9.2. Condition (9.3) then fails, especially for complex production. Finally, the simultaneous presence of a large defense sector and weak nondefense sector reduces the costs of repressing excluded groups, encouraging state predation. The society may develop defense sectors with only simple nondefense production. Path D dominates C. The Soviet Union under Joseph Stalin offers an example of a predatory state with resource access that, in the face of an enormous external threat from Adolf Hitler, achieved substantial development in its military sector.

With similar logic, cases with no resource constraint and no external threat motivate few, if any, ordered deals, again implying path D. Note that in these latter two cases, this model implies a resource curse in which readily accessible rents impede investment because they undermine the credibility of exchange and production agreements.

Overall, for Q4, the highest motivation for path C arises in the presence of path A prerequisites II and III: a resource constraint and a compelling internal or external threat, though a resource constraint alone can be sufficient. Absent these conditions, however, a unified RC operating with a narrow SF will likely find path D predation more profitable.

Quadrant 2: Broad Social Foundation/Unipolar

In Q2, as in Q4, unipolarity implies that RC resolution of internal organizational CAPs has fostered some state capacity, but here the broad SF creates a need to widely distribute benefits. Two distinct paths, A and B, developmental and patronage states, follow.[18] Path B, though inefficient and corrupt, resolves some H1 CAPs. It operates with largely ordered deals and is (generally) not predatory because the broad SF demands some accountability. Path A fosters more development by addressing H2 coordination CAPs. Discussion begins with path A.

Recall from Chapter 8, that path A emerges only in the presence of three prerequisites: prerequisite I, a compelling need to distribute benefits broadly—already implied by Q2's broad SF, which applies to both A and B—in addition to prerequisites II and III. Given these three requirements, Section 1's logic implies ordered deals, as on path C. Here, however, the broad SF increases reputation costs (γ), enabling more complete resolutions of H1 and H4 CAPs and thus more substantial provision of public goods. As noted in Chapter 8, path A elites also possess sufficient motivation to resolve H2 coordination CAPs, fostering a developmental state with high steady growth and structural transformation, like that in South Korea between 1960 and 1987.

Developments in post-1994 Rwanda illustrate relationships between ordered deals, market configuration, and a preliminary (tentative) path A trajectory operating in a setting with little previous institutional development. The 1994 civil war destroyed the economy. Yet, facing prerequisites I–III, elites within the new governing RPF understood that, with no easily exploitable resources, their political survival depended on generating economic activity and distributing enough revenue to maintain loyalty across the broad SF—so as to hold off the compelling internal threat of a return to civil war. They understood the necessity of building institutions that could promote sufficient growth and distribution.

Rwandan growth has thus involved a mix of open and closed ordered deals. The ruling RPF retained control over rents in selective-deal monopolistic sectors, but it also supported open deals (some disordered) in the competitive sectors. This combination has facilitated growth.[19] More specifically, in relatively monopolistic sectors, the government has offered some open deals, but it retains state control by selectively revoking and awarding contracts (Behuria and Goodfellow 2018). The RPF has used state-business relationships and ties with the military to manage rents, in a centralized fashion, with attention to long-term developmental goals. It encouraged the emergence of capitalist enterprises via measures such as providing basic infrastructure, supporting skill building, and acquiring technology. The RPF-owned Tri-Star Investments/CVL holding company, for example, financed 11 leading

Rwandan companies that now compete with regional (Kenyan) and international (Chinese) firms. This company has financed roads and housing, along with startup funding for firms in areas such as basic dairy products, private security, bottled water, building materials, printing, and mobile phone production. Spillover benefits, moreover, have enabled establishing new Rwandan information technology firms. Critically, the ensuing tax revenue and dividends from these and other ventures have freed the RPF from reliance on traditional clientelism to finance its operations (Booth and Golooba-Mutebi 2012), resolving key H3 CAPs that often impede resolution of H1, H2, and H4 CAPs. Path A remains possible.

In contrast, Path B emerges in cases without prerequisite II's resource constraint, III's compelling threat, or both. In Q4, these conditions would lead to path D. In Q2, however, the broad SF requires a wide distribution of at least short-term benefits: a type of substantive accountability that encourages some provision of public goods, which a unipolar RC can deliver. Consequently, levels of g and t exceed those for path D. By increasing R, the former may relax investment condition (9.3) somewhat. The broad SF also enhances the reputation and legitimacy costs to reneging ($\gamma > 0$), relaxing (9.1) and (9.2). Selective ordered deals thus predominate in the formal sector, and there is little predation. Even so, elites lack sufficient motivation to resolve the more substantial H2 CAPs of coordinating production. Path B countries often encounter a middle-income trap.

Malaysia provides an example of path B development. Between 1955 and 1997, Malaysia's PS fit Khan's potential developmental coalition (Table 7.2's weak horizontal and weak vertical opposition). Moreover, with access to revenue from oil and foreign investment (Sen and Tyce 2018), Malaysia did not face a (significant) resource constraint. In terms of Table 8.1, Malaysia's regime was unipolar. At least through the 1980s, the RC paid considerable attention to distributing benefits across all three large ethnic groups (Malay, Chinese, and Indian), signifying a broad SF—albeit with increasing emphasis on distributing benefits to Malays.[20] For example, the regime's New Economic Program, instituted in 1971, taxed Chinese enterprises, redistributing 30% of their assets to Malay interests, in order to benefit the largely rural Malay population. This program set quotas for Malay ownership and participation in urban labor, but it indirectly rewarded Chinese enterprises by encouraging (quite successful) export-oriented economic growth (Sen and Tyce 2018; Ritchie 2005).

In the early 1990s, Malaysia, like South Korea and Taiwan, appeared to be a growth success. Between 1955 and 1997, Malaysia achieved average annual growth of per capita GDP of 4.9% (Kar et al. 2013). It also achieved some structural transformation in terms of both product complexity and manufacturing's share of GDP. Unlike South Korea and Taiwan, however, Malaysia's rapid progress ended after the 1997–98 Asian financial crisis.[21] Malaysian elites failed to resolve difficult H2 coordination CAPs associated with more sophisticated technological development; the country did not experience path A development.

Regarding market configurations and deals, Kunal Sen and Matthew Tyce (2018) assert that Malaysia used a partially successful, yet ultimately self-undermining dual strategy that focused on two elements of the market matrix. First, as it strove to reduce poverty and distribute benefits across the key ethnic groups, Malaysia encouraged export-oriented industrialization by promoting electronics and textiles and encouraging open honored deals in competitive export sectors, with tax relief. The government created tariff-free export processing zones. By 1996, electronic goods comprised about half of their exports (an indication of some structural transformation). At the same time, Malaysia developed "pockets of effectiveness" in the Ministry of Finance, the Ministry of Trade and Industry, and the Malaysian Industrial Development Authority (Sen and Tyce 2018, 303). Feedback from export revenue reinforced pressure for various types of liberalization.

Second, beginning in the early 1970s, the government shielded Malay-owned low-technology industries from competition—notably those in construction, logging, rubber dealing, trade, and transport. Especially after the mid-1980s, they offered "extremely closed deals" to high-rent domestic and export sectors (Ibid., 303). Revenue from oil and foreign investment facilitated subsidizing domestically owned firms in these sectors. Additionally, a sequence of privatization beginning in the late 1970s, which accelerated in the 1980s (initiated under pressure from international financial institutions to liberalize their policies), "became a political mechanism for fostering [Prime Minister] Mahathir's industrial elite" (Ibid., 303).[22] These policies encouraged rent seeking by large multinational corporations (MNCs), providing little incentive for domestically owned firms to pursue exports (Ritchie 2005). The revenue feedback from these closed deals created demands for greater patronage and more economic exclusion that, over time, shifted domestic policy emphasis in the direction of benefiting Malay elites—a development that ultimately undermined the broad SF.

Even the relatively successful export promotion, which facilitated a surge in foreign direct investment (FDI) that helped generate average annual per capita GDP growth of 6.4% between 1980 and 1992, failed to achieve needed technological upgrading characteristic of path A development. Malaysia fell into a "suffocating structural squeeze" (Ritchie 2005, 746) whereby it both lost competitiveness in low-wage manufacturing to China and Vietnam and failed to enhance productivity sufficiently to compete with Singapore, South Korea, and Taiwan (Sen and Tyce 2018).

Even though the government endeavored to relax labor supply constraints, enhance skills by promoting firm-level training, and augment local productive technology, political constraints (H3 and H4 CAPs) precluded sufficiently effective action. Five related factors intervened. First, an increasing need to satisfy and protect the dominant Malay group blocked effective relaxation of immigration limits that constrained the labor supply. Second, low investment in primary and secondary education "coupled with political loyalty to Malay as the language of instruction, hampered math, science, and English language education" (Ritchie 2005, 752). Moreover, ethnic quotas on higher education (demanded by coalition pressures) encouraged talented ethnic Chinese to leave Malaysia for university education. Many did not return—an H2 CAP. Third, pressure from MNCs precluded serious incorporation of labor representation into coordinating production. Fourth, political pressures from the large Malay constituency inhibited developing network connections that might have transferred information and technology between MNCs and local ethnic Chinese enterprises. Finally, "intimate patron-client relationships between wealthy Chinese entrepreneurs and Malay politicians minimize[d] the need for large local firms to rely on product innovation to support their bottom lines" (Ibid., 753). Ultimately, the combined presence of patron-client relationships and insufficiently connected firms with limited education and skills—all manifestations of how H3 CAPs interfered with resolving H2 CAPs—"exacerbated difficulties in technological development across numerous sectors, including semiconductors, automobiles, and telecommunications" (Ibid., 753).

When the 1997–98 Asian financial crisis hit, Malaysia had not developed strong enough coordinating institutions to effectively resist the shock. Politically, the government lacked sufficient accountability and decision rules.

Deputy Prime Minister Anwar Ibrahim, who opposed Mahathir's efforts to rescue favored clients, was beaten and imprisoned. The RC factionalized as Anwar's wife led an opposition coalition. The COA shifted toward multi-polarity.[23] In the years that followed, Malaysia displayed increasing reliance on lower-level patronage clientelism, as disputing factions sought to mobi-lize voting blocks in their favor. In Khan's terms, parties on the lower end of the vertical power axis were no longer weak. As the role for high-rent sectors increased, the importance of competitive exporting (XC) firms diminished. Revenue feedback from selective deals reinforced these tendencies.

Overall, even though Malaysia's 1980s dual strategy generated a long period of high growth with some structural transformation, those develop-ments did not last. The various RCs operated within the parameters of the 1955–96 Q2 PS without serious resource constraints or external threats. Re-sponding to powerful constituencies, elite efforts to maintain (or enhance) their political positions undermined prospects for resolving the difficult H2 CAPs of building institutions that could usher in structural transformation. Over time, increasing reliance on rent sharing and lower-level competitive patronage—reinforced by revenue feedback—not only blocked path A devel-opment, it undermined the Q2 (path B) PS, moving toward Q1 or Q3 multi-polarity. Deals became increasingly selective and disordered. Despite prior growth success, Malaysia fell into a middle-income trap. Insufficient reso-lution of H2 CAPs rendered it unable to compete with the East Asian newly industrialized countries.

Section 2: Open or Closed Deals?
Political Settlements with Multipolar
Configurations of Authority

Multipolar power configurations underlie Q1 and Q3 PSs. Factional-ized insider elites, with unresolved CAPs of delegating basic macro-level decision-making authority, lack consensus on broad goals, such as church-state relations. They possess limited ability to resolve H1 CAPs of developing (macro-level) state capacity, as well as H3 and H4 CAPs related to creating a rule of law. At the macrolevel, these conditions suggest interpreting Figure 9.1's player D as a fractured insider leadership that must negotiate internally before taking decisive action—pointing to high transactions costs of decision making—rendering nation-level ordered deals problematic. Yet, such relative lack of coherent national policy, with correspondingly weak enforcement, fosters substantial regional and sectoral variation in power alignments and economic outcomes. Under these conditions, the configuration of markets and a potential for open deals in specific areas play more prominent roles than that which appeared in Section 1's (admittedly simplified) analysis. Before proceeding, a brief discussion of open deals is in order.

Open Deals and the Rents Space

Now consider the distinction between open and selective deals. *RC elites may offer open deals to entrepreneurs, selective deals to monopolists, or no deals.* To model the strategic interactions, we assume, for simplicity, that they offer open deals to n identical entrepreneurs and selective deals to a single monopolist. Figure 9A.1 (see Appendix 9A) illustrates. Here, we merge Figure 9.1's players D and E into a single player, RC_e (RC elites). With no separate enforcers (E), Figure 9.1's punishment strategy and enforcement condition both vanish, but a reputation cost to reneging (γ) still applies. For investment revenue, we replace monopolistic revenue R with single-entrepreneur competitive revenue Γ; $R > \Gamma$. Likewise, we replace $t + b$ with τ, the sum of competitive-sector taxes plus bribes, both of which flow to RC_e. For open-deal initiation costs, replace C_D with $C_d(n)$, where n is the number of small firms covered by the deal.

Resembling Figure 9.1's logic, there are four conditions for creating ordered open deals: an honor condition, $\gamma > \Gamma(1 - \tau)$; an investment condition, $(1 - \tau)\Gamma > F + \upsilon$; an initiation condition, $\tau\Gamma > C_d(n)$; and an open versus selective condition. The logic of the first three closely resembles that for Figure 9.1 (see Appendix 9A for details on these conditions). The open/selective condition is

(9.5) $n\tau\Gamma - C_d(n) > (t + b)R - C_D$, or $n\tau\Gamma - (t + b)R > C_d(n) - C_D$.

For RC_e to prefer initiating open to selective deals, the corresponding difference in its tax plus bribe revenue must exceed the difference in initiation costs. As before, the resolution of H1 CAPs affects public goods, revenues, and taxes (g, τ, t, Γ, and R). Additionally, we now distinguish between universal and selective public goods, where the latter are club goods provided to specific elites, firms, and/or constituencies.[24] Providing universal public goods requires resolution of more substantial H1 CAPs—due to the larger number of beneficiaries.

Now consider the difference $C_d(n) - C_D$. Both terms include the (marginal) costs of enforcing investors' property rights with respect to rival factions and non-RC_e parties (e.g., gangs). *Ceteris paribus*, the larger n, the greater this difference. Because protecting many small firms from private predation usually costs more than enforcing rights and entry barriers for monopolistic firms, we assume that $C_d(n) - C_D > 0$ in the formal sector but is indeterminate in the informal sector, where little state enforcement occurs in any case.

Because the monopolistic sectors operate with selective deals, condition (9.5) offers insight into the political economy of allocating certain forms of production between the high- and low-rent sectors. The size of the difference $R - \Gamma$ depends on monopoly rents, which reflect economies of scale, possession of unique resources, and relevant government-induced entry barriers, such as licenses. For point-source resources, $R - \Gamma$ is likely high enough to dwarf the influence of the other terms—effectively ruling out open deals. The same applies to domestic monopolies in sectors such as utilities; it also applies to large landholdings—relevant to both primary product exports and domestic agriculture. Accordingly, RC_e often affords large firms (and owners) substantially greater protection of property rights than that for smaller operators and, likewise, provides them localized or sector-specific infrastructure—effectively club goods, which tend to increase monopoly rents and entry barriers, *ceteris paribus*.

The competitive sectors, by contrast, rely on open deals. Yet, whenever condition (9.5) fails for a particular type of production, the relevant firms either operate informally—often with a mix of ordered and disordered deals—or they achieve some formal recognition at subnational levels of governance, where the actual manifestation of PSs may vary. Q1's discussion elaborates, but first we discuss Q3.

Quadrant 3: Narrow Social Foundation/Multipolar
As stated in Chapter 8, a Q3 PS offers bleak developmental prospects. Multipolarity implies limited state capacity, with little rule by law, and the narrow SF affords little incentive for distributing benefits—that is, low accountability. Attention to market configurations and deals reinforces this conclusion. As in Q4, the narrow SF implies that high-rent sectors dominate the market configuration for formal-sector production—and for portions of the informal sector that affiliate with RC factions. Remaining informal production operates with open deals, often disordered. Neither affords much prospect for economic development.

Applying Section 1's logic to Q3's selective deals, we again find that low state capacity implies low levels of g, t, and R, and internal factional conflict implies a high C_D. Additionally, potential deal enforcers (powerful RC factions) may anticipate interference from resentful excluded groups (e.g., petty theft or gang predation); accordingly, they require large bribes to offset costly deal enforcement (a high c_p). Moreover, as rival factions compete for power, or as they fear the future attainment of power by excluded groups, such factions may seize returns from productive efforts of the unaffiliated. For these reasons, conditions (9.1)–(9.4) should fail. The presence of a resource curse, often an attribute of societies in this quadrant, renders ordered deals even less likely.[25] Disordered deals prevail, though localized enforcement rings may attain some ordered deals within specific regions for simple production or resource extraction.

A Q3 PS can survive because rival insider factions use their own patronage networks and resource rents to bolster their position within the RC, reinforcing the multipolar allocation of selective deals. By applying some revenue to repressing excluded groups, they reinforce the narrow SF. Yet, as noted in Chapter 8, Q3 settlements are relatively fragile and often exhibit a civil war–coup trap: to avoid a coup, they exclude and repress groups (often former allies in the struggle against colonialism), and in so doing they risk civil war (Roessler 2011). These factors jointly tend to foster poverty traps.

Quadrant 1: Broad Social Foundation/Multipolar

As noted in Chapter 8, countries in this sector often face a middle-income trap. An examination of the market configuration and deals matrices reinforces this assertion—and offers additional insight into often substantial Q1 meso-level variation. Here, the distinction between macro- and mesolevels applies to both the workings of PSs and the market matrix. We first consider macro-level implications.

Like Q3, Q1 exhibits multipolarity, but here the broad SF requires distributing benefits across many groups. This condition, as in Q4, motivates some resolution of H1provision CAPs, improving prospects for development. Yet, as noted in Chapter 8, Q1 distribution focuses on immediate benefits rather than long-term investments—limiting resolution. Some bureaucracy and weak tax capacity may follow, but state capacity remains low compared to that developed along both Q2 paths and along Q4's path C.[26] Applying Figure 9.1

to Q1 suggests weak prospects for creating ordered selective formal-sector deals. In addition to relatively low levels for g, t, and R, factional disputes should generate a large C_D and high c_p along with a low γ (low reputation with other factions regardless). As in Q3, enforcers may require unattainably high bribes. Conditions (9.1)–(9.4) thus appear unlikely.[27] Yet these societies often achieve middle-income economic development—largely due to meso-level factors.

Multipolar configurations, especially in large countries such as India, create considerable regional and sectoral variations in political transactions and developmental potential. In terms of Figure 9.1, a meso-level agent D can represent the leader of a faction, region, or gang, who may offer selective deals to constituents or supporters, with no need to consult other factions. In such cases, distinct meso-level settlements may operate in different regions, some with unipolarity.[28] An informal, clientelistic quid pro quo deal in return for political support allows for a low C_D and a high γ. Furthermore, the need for patronage creates location or sector-specific networks of enforcers who have the capacity to punish relevant meso-level leaders for reneging on pledges to deliver benefits (i.e., high p and low c_p)—though not necessarily for complex (high F) production. Moreover, within specific regions, sectors, or patronage networks, resolution of localized CAPs permits intermediate levels of g (here club goods), t (possibly racketeering extraction), and R. Meeting conditions (9.1)–(9.4) within certain factions and localities becomes feasible. Q1's distribution of immediate benefits, however, creates high fallback income (v), which lowers prospects for meeting (9.3)—especially for complex production. Furthermore, macro-level factional conflict impedes resolving a series of H2 coordination CAPs that could facilitate structural transformation. Hence, we expect Q1 to exhibit a mix of selective ordered and disordered deals in noncomplex meso-level formal sectors, along with much open, often disordered, informal production. More on this point follows.

Turning to the market matrix and considering informal production, we find roles for both high-rent and competitive firms. A need for patronage implies that in monopolistic sectors, political links to specific factions foster selective deals, which can be either ordered or disordered. Yet, the combination of weak formal institutions, prevalent informal institutions, and a broad SF encourages informal-sector competition, with both ordered and disordered open deals. In the export-oriented sectors, Q1's weak institutions allow substantial latitude for high-rent resource extraction, which can operate alongside both high- and low-rent agricultural products; the relative shares depend on the distribution of land. Additionally, a potential for pockets of competitive exports can emerge in areas that require little government support, regulation, or coordination. Open-order condition (9.5) most likely holds for simple production, with low initiation costs (C_d). The garment industry in Bangladesh offers an example. In Q1 then, growth accelerations and substantial medium-term growth can follow, but broad sectoral transformation is unlikely because H2 CAPs remain insufficiently resolved.

I offer two examples of Q1 market-state interaction. In India during the 1990s and 2000s, contested elections and a need for short-term finance shortened elite time horizons, focusing their attention on extracting immediate rents. Deals became less formal and more selective, with factions arranging deals among their own constituents. Political parties raised campaign funds from businesses in return for informal allocation of discretionary contracts (Gowda and Sridharan 2012). During the post-2000 period, a small monopolistic natural resource export sector emerged. Comparing the periods 1993–2001 to 2002–7, the share of (capital-intensive) petroleum products in gross manufacturing value added increased from 5.6% to 13.03%, whereas that of (labor-intensive) textiles and apparel declined from 13.8% to 11.09% (Sen, Kar, and Sahu 2018, 256; also see Kar and Sen 2016). Similarly, the share of high-rent domestic telecommunications and construction increased, whereas relatively competitive manufacturing sectors—food, beverages, tobacco, textiles, apparel, and machinery—declined. Overall, between 2002 and 2010, the economy exhibited some movement away from complex products. Structural transformation did not continue.

Like India, Ghana appears to face a middle-income trap. From 1983 to 1999, annual per capita GDP growth averaged 4.4%; 6.5% between 1999 and 2014. With ample resources, post-2001 Ghana developed a large high-rent export sector, including point-source gold, diamonds, and, more recently, oil, along with large domestic firms that benefited from foreign aid. The high-rent sectors jointly produced 60% of GDP (Osei et al. 2018). Because competitive sectors lacked substantial organization, demands placed on the state favored closed deals, arranged through patronage connections. The 2007 discovery and 2010 initiation of oil production will likely increase political pressure for clientelism (Gyimah-Boadi and Prempeh 2012). Despite its substantial growth, Ghana's clientelist PS has impeded structural transformation (Osei et al. 2018, 162).

Section 3: Concluding Remarks

Table 9A.1 (see Appendix 9A) summarizes outcomes from Figure 9.1 across the four PS quadrants and, within Q2 and Q4, for paths A, B, C, and D. The first column lists the types of PSs, and the next four columns depict ordered deals conditions (9.1)–(9.4) and, for each type, the degree to which the condition is met. The final column shows, for each type, the likely formal-sector outcome with respect to ordering and selectivity.

This chapter completes this book's framework for conceptualizing the political economy of development. It augments Chapter 8's typology of PSs with direct consideration of how meso-level market configurations (Table 9.1) and micro-level deals environments (Table 9.2) influence the following dynamics: the nature of competition, demands that economic actors place on government, the potential for forging credible agreements (ordered or disordered deals), and the accessibility to such agreements (open or selected). Ensuing revenue flows, which affect power relations, ultimately support or undermine specific arrangements within a PS. The core analysis, which can apply at either the macro- or mesolevel, revolves around applying Figure 9.1's selective ordered deals game to each of the PS quadrants Q1–Q4 and, within Q2 and Q4, to paths A, B, C, and D. Specifically, this analysis considers how a settlement's underlying SF and COA, along with the presence or absence of preconditions related to resource constraints and compelling threats (prerequisites II and III) influence the feasibility and likelihood of resolving underlying H1–H4 CAPs that facilitate establishing ordered deals. When achieved, ordered deals facilitate growth accelerations, which, in turn, permit escaping from various poverty traps that often accompany Q3 and Q4 path D settlements. Growth accelerations, however, are not sufficient for structural transformation. Escaping middle-income traps requires more substantial institutional development—more substantive resolution of H1–H4 CAPs, especially those of H2 coordination—a condition most likely attained under the restrictive conditions that appear conducive to Q2's path A. Nevertheless, Q1's broad SF and somewhat disorganized RC may offer some opportunity for a mix of selective and open-ordered and disordered deals—with the relative influence of each depending on interactions between sectoral market configurations and regional variations in the PS. Q1 conditions may also foster local and/or sectoral capacity-building economic development, sometimes referred to as "islands of effectiveness" (see, for example, Bukenya and Hickey 2018, 212).

Conclusion

A Conceptual Framework for Development Theory

DEVELOPMENT ENTAILS CREATING HUMAN capabilities across a society's members and groups. It not only means providing and broadly distributing basic material foundations of human functioning—including income, wealth, productive implements, health care, and skill sets that follow from education and training—it also requires creating and sustaining social mechanisms of cooperation, constructive competition, credible agreement, and accessible participation in production, consumption, exchange, and decision making.

At its foundation, development relies on mutual understandings that establish politics, rather than violence, as a society's primary method for resolving disputes. Accordingly, development requires resolving myriad collective-action problems (CAPs). Moreover, because establishing credibility for potential agreements to resolve first-order CAPs of free riding requires prior attention to second-order CAPs of coordination and enforcement, development involves exercising and channeling power. It relies on creating functional economic and political institutions, with a corresponding set of complementary organizations capable of signaling desirable activity, coordinating myriad activities, and enforcing impersonal rules. Economic development entails steady augmentation of living standards, with particular attention to the poor and those in the lower regions of income and wealth distributions, in addition to providing sustainable foundations of productive and consumption capabilities via health care, education, and infrastructure.

It both requires and entails creating functional institutional systems that provide critical public goods, limit negative externalities, manage conflict, enforce universal—as opposed to selective—property rights, and, concurrently, remove barriers to and create avenues for economic participation. Political development entails not only limiting private and state predation by establishing a rule of law and multiple mechanisms for public accountability, it also entails creating and motivating state capacity that facilitates the provision of public goods; contract enforcement; and protection of economic, political, and civil rights, as well as legitimizing governance arrangements and mobilizing broad participation. All such endeavors involve addressing CAPs.

Inequality permeates these processes—as both cause and effect. Inequitable access to income, wealth, employment, productive resources, education, health care, rule enforcement, and political participation, combined with a host of associated entry barriers, constrain economic, political, and ultimately human development. Many ensuing unequal economic and political outcomes reproduce and reinforce initial inequities. Consequently, developmental CAPs not only include balancing the often contradictory goals of achieving political stability and restraining private and public abuse; they also include motivating production and yet broadly distributing both access and benefits; and they include limiting power without undermining political stability or various motivations to produce output, innovate, and resolve organizational and society-wide CAPs.

My approach in this text is to merge five core developmental hypotheses with a typology of political settlements (PSs) and corresponding social orders. H1: Development requires establishing social arrangements that deliver key public goods and services and that concurrently mitigate important negative externalities. H2: Inherent complementarities that emerge from the nonrival properties of knowledge, skill matching, social imitation, and production externalities generate uneven locational and sectoral agglomerations of production, knowledge acquisition, innovation, and growth. H3: Unequal distributions of power shape the creation, evolution, and demise of economic and political institutions. H4: Powerful parties, left to themselves, cannot credibly commit to refrain from using their power for their own future benefit. H5: Policy innovations sometimes relax political and commitment constraints that follow from H3 and H4, as well as free-riding and coordination CAPs from H1 and H2.

The dynamics implied by these hypotheses interact. When powerful parties shape institutional construction (H3), they not only condition capabilities for resolving H1 CAPs related to public goods and externalities, they condition the distribution of production capabilities that require or respond to such public goods and externalities. Powerful parties also influence, but do not control, H2 flows of knowledge, the utilization of skill complementarities, processes of social imitation, and various productive complementarities and externalities—all of which condition the (unequal) spread and distribution of technology and innovation across sectors and locations. The attendant economic and political exchange processes, moreover, cannot adequately function in the absence of social mechanisms of credible commitment (as in H4): mechanisms that generate credible motivations and restraints that deter powerful private and public parties from seizing the gains from others' investments of time, effort, human capital, and physical capital into economic and political activities. Inequities abound and multifarious CAPs ensue. Yet, as in H5, policy and organizational innovations—new methods for constructing rules, procedures, and interactions within a social context, whether invented or imported into compatible local contexts can, with adjustment, sometimes resolve, mitigate, or circumvent at least some of the pertinent CAPs. Innovation can permit and enhance the efficiency of resolving CAPs. It can generate social capital that fosters a balance between functional competition and requisite cooperation, along with underlying enforcement, coordination, legitimacy, and trust. And yet, underlying political-economic contexts, already existing public goods, mechanisms of coordination, distributions of power, interests of powerful parties, and associated mechanisms of commitment—or lack thereof—shape the potential adoption and spread of such innovations within societies, regions, or sectors. Policy success requires systematic analysis of and adjustment for relevant contexts.

Achieving any measure of economic and political development requires establishing adequate social peace. It requires creating and maintaining some form of PS that, in turn, permits the evolution and construction of functional informal and formal institutions, with associated organizational mechanisms and patterns of coordination and enforcement. Analysts can categorize PSs. Their basic types depend on the combination of their social foundations (SFs) and configurations of authority (COAs). SFs specify the groups included in a given settlement: groups to which policy must devote some attention, even if they do not participate in governance. COAs rely on the degree to which insider elites can resolve various internal organizational CAPs related to delegating broad avenues of decision-making authority and achieving some unity regarding the basic contours of governmental purpose.

Consequently, in this text, I develop a typology of PSs. I utilize a two-dimensional, four-quadrant matrix that denotes discrete categories (along relevant spectra) of broad versus narrow SFs on the vertical dimension and functionally unipolar versus multipolar COAs on the horizontal dimension. The breadth of SF influences a ruling coalition's incentives to distribute benefits across populations, and the unipolar/multipolar distinction influences the capacity of states to provide public goods and establish a rule of law. For each of the two unipolar configurations, I further designate two distinct developmental paths: A and B for the unipolar/broad combination; C and D for unipolar/narrow. The A-B and C-D distinctions, in turn, depend on the presence or absence of resource constraints and mutually understood internal or external threats to the political survival of insider elites. The absence of a resource constraint implies a political resource curse, whereby resource access undermines elite motivation to address many formidable CAPs of public good provision and institution building. A mutually understood threat to political survival, or absence thereof, influences the degree to which functional unipolarity can motivate elites' sacrifice of short-term private interest for long-term social benefit—namely, their motivation to provide key public goods, including institution building, which could foster sufficient innovation and coordination of production to enable structural transformation. This typology, therefore, relates categorizing specific foundations of PSs to critical developmental CAPs that shape the functionality of ensuing institutional systems and social orders and their developmental prospects.

Finally, because economic outcomes—notably the production and distribution of output, physical and human capital, and productive and organizational technology—influence the distribution of power, Chapter 9 addresses business-state relations. Here, meso-level market configurations reflect degrees of competition and export orientation within production sectors. Specific configurations, delineated with a four-quadrant typology, influence the demands that—potentially powerful—businesses place on the state, as well as the environments within which exchange agreements (deals) operate in the respective sectors. Macro-level PSs set the contours for such interactions by, for example, influencing the proportion of monopolistic firms in key sectors. The ensuing dynamics shape micro-level access to exchange agreements—open versus selective deals—and their credibility, ordered or not. In societies in which narrow SFs of PSs foster weak institutions, a move from predominantly disordered to ordered deals—possible when unipolar ruling coalitions can limit the power of autocrats—can accelerate growth enough to permit escaping poverty traps. Moving beyond middle-income status, however, requires sophisticated resolution of H2 coordination CAPs, a prospect that appears most likely with broad SFs and functional (path A) unipolarity. Nevertheless, broad/multipolar PSs permit localized variation in regional manifestations of PS, market configurations, and the extent of open and ordered deals. Certain locations may become islands of effectiveness that could foster more substantive future development. In all such configurations, the revenue earned in various sectors and the associated demands that businesses place on the state influence distributions of power and the degree to which powerful parties accept distributional outcomes implied by economic and political institutions. These outcomes, in turn, affect the sustainability of institutional systems, social orders, and underlying PSs.

Ultimately, this reasoning presents a conceptual framework for analyzing the political economy of development. It addresses the social scientist's dilemma, posed in the Introduction, concerning how to frame and orient systematic inquiry into the myriad complexities of political-economic development. It does so by following an approach analogous to that of biology. It establishes a set of categories embodied in the typology of PSs, along with a set of quite general causal propositions concerning the political economy of development. These propositions arise from this text's five developmental hypotheses as well as its discussion of how PSs and market configurations shape a society's capabilities for resolving multiple developmental CAPs that condition the creation, maintenance, destruction, and replacement of institutional systems and social orders.

This argument, moreover, has merged concepts from important components of the political economy, development, and policy literature including, but not limited to, a capability approach to development, bounded rationality, institutional economics, rational-choice institutionalism, historical institutionalism, theories of the policy process, punctuated equilibrium dynamics, social conflict theory, and the concept of PSs. And it does so with attention to game-theoretic reasoning that incorporates economic, political, and social incentives.

As a scholarly product, this framework can underlie a research program that could incorporate many more detailed theoretical models and a wide variety of corresponding empirical hypotheses. Several, still quite general, modeling examples appear in the appendixes. In each case, one could augment specific relations and functions by adding or more fully specifying variables and relationships among them. Additionally, as already implied by the examples at the opening of each chapter, this framework provides a method for interpreting a wide variety of developmental conditions and histories. It also facilitates interpreting case studies and considering their broader implications.[1]

In last this regard, Nancy Cartwright and Jeremy Hardie (2012, 36) assert that the increasingly popular method of conducting randomized control trials (RCTs)—a technique they say is "supposed to be the gold standard" for assessing policy outcomes within specific contexts—fails to sufficiently establish that a policy that works in one social context will, indeed, work elsewhere.[2] They pose this question: It works here, but will it work there? Establishing the latter, they continue, involves two steps. The first step requires assessing what causal role a specific policy could play in achieving the desired outcome, an assessment that can establish whether a policy works "here." The second step concerns identifying the supporting conditions that operate within the pertinent social context of "here." Causes operate in teams. Using the analogy of making (American) pancakes, they say that mixing flour, eggs, and sugar can indeed produce pancakes, but only under the condition that one adds baking soda to the mix. To illustrate their broader argument, the authors note the relative success of the Tamil Nadu Integrated Nutrition Project (TINP), which provided nutritional education to pregnant mothers in the Tamil Nadu State of India, compared to the unsuccessful Bangladesh Integrated Nutrition Program, which was modeled on the TINP.

My developmental framework offers a systematic approach to analyzing whether a set of supporting conditions that accompany certain institutional configurations or policies that work somewhere, say Chile or Botswana, would work elsewhere, say Kenya. This typology of PSs, the market configurations, these five hypotheses, this discussion of power relations, and this consideration of first- and second-order developmental CAPs operating in the context of a capability approach to political and economic development, permits identifying combinations of conditions that may either support or undermine the adoption and implementation of desirable policy prescriptions or institutional configurations. This approach should thus facilitate interpreting the applicability of outcomes from various case studies, including RCT studies. It should facilitate systematic inquiry relating empirical findings of effective policies in one social context to the presence or absence of supporting conditions. One might ask, for example, if a society with clientelistic political and economic relations would allow the successful implementation of institutional prescriptions that specify Western private property rights. What CAPs might interfere? How might underlying power dynamics that emerge from specific SFs and COAs influence any prospects for resolution?

A related question concerns whether a program that appears to work well in one setting will continue to do so over time. For instance, Anthony Hall (2008) discusses both the successes of and problems with Brazil's *Bolsa Família* program. The program offers conditional cash transfers (CCTs) to poor families based on their children's school attendance and the mother's use of health-care facilities. Impressively, the program reached the target audience and contributed to poverty reduction. Yet Hall, writing in 2008, fears that the program's popularity can generate political incentives related to clientelism that may undermine its success. He contrasts the positive impacts of the politicization of social welfare policies in industrialized nations with pitfalls that emerge in less developed countries: "a key question in the context of developing countries concerns the nature of this process and in what ways the politicization of social policy, CCTs in this case, might serve to actually undermine longer-term policy formulation and planning" (Ibid., 814).

Again, this text's conceptual framework offers avenues for interpretation and further inquiry. Arguably, Brazil has been operating under a PS characterized by a multipolar COA combined with a relatively broad SF. As Chapters 8 and 9 imply, a correspondingly dispersed distribution of powerful actors creates incentives for clientelistic politics, considerable regional variation, and selective and often problematic enforcement of property rights, with regional mixes of relatively closed-ordered deals and more accessible (open) disordered informal-sector deals. Establishing selective-ordered deals can indeed achieve impressive short- to medium-term growth, as Brazil has experienced. Moreover, a governing coalition, such as Luiz Inácio Lula da Silva's Workers' Party (*Partido dos Trabalhadores*), should pay attention, as it did, to a broad SF—by broadly distributing benefits. Yet, opportunities and political-economic incentives for corruption abound. Recent developments, notably the arrest of Lula under charges of corruption, appear to confirm Hall's fears. Furthermore, the ensuing political conflict may unravel Brazil's now somewhat fragile PS, exacerbating a host of CAPs, and so undermine Brazil's developmental prospects.

My approach to such developmental dynamics opens multiple avenues for future inquiry. As noted in the Introduction, numerous related theoretical models can more precisely specify causal mechanisms operating within certain types of PSs. For example, one might specify mechanisms that affect how resource availability alters important political and/or economic incentives facing unipolar as opposed to multipolar COAs. One might consider the degree to which the multipolar configurations might experience distinct developmental paths, analogous to the unipolar A-B and C-D paths. Each such inquiry may generate a series of testable empirical hypotheses. In this regard, the Effective States and Inclusive Development Research Centre (ESID), located at the University of Manchester, with multiple connections to scholars located elsewhere, is formulating a comprehensive empirical research program based on a closely related conception of PSs.

To close, I mention a few broad areas for extending this framework. Even though Chapters 4, 6, 8, and especially 9 pay some attention to regional and local distinctions in the geographic dispersion of innovation, distinct production sectors, specific policy domains, and regional variation within multipolar PSs, one could extend this framework to more fully address subnational interactions. Pertinent topics for additional inquiry include meso-level institutional configurations that rely on meso-level PSs operating within and responding to various configurations of larger PSs. For example, in recent history, Colombia experienced a functional PS in Bogota and other urban areas, even as rural areas experienced guerilla warfare. Analogously, one could extend and adapt elements of this framework by adding detail concerning specific economic sectors and policy domains that operate within regions or within and across nations. One might also address vertical distributions of coalition power operating within distinct types of PSs. At a broader level, the same principles can apply to international cooperation, or lack thereof, related to the WTO, UN, EU, and the reach of multinational corporations. Even though Chapter 8's SFs of PSs allows for including international actors (representatives of NGOs, MNCs, diplomats, etc.), additional inquiry could focus more directly on how international influences affect PSs, institutional systems, corresponding CAPs, and prospects for development within nations and/or regions.

This book's conceptual framework—its five core hypotheses; its typologies of PSs and market configurations; and its consideration of institutions, asymmetric power relations, unequal resource distributions, and corresponding CAPs—establishes foundations for many such extensions. More generally, this approach offers multiple avenues for systematic context-specific social scientific inquiry into processes of building and widely distributing combinations of human capabilities that both enable and constitute economic and political development.

APPENDIXES

Chapter 3 Appendixes: Appendix 3A

Fiscal Capacity Game: The Base Case Model

There are two coalitions (A and B) and two time periods (t_1 and t_2). Both coalitions are unified; each acts as a single player. Both have equal membership and power. Both coalitions fully utilize tax capacity τ. Both have the same utility functions: agents gain utility from consumption and from public goods, where consumption depends on disposable income plus transfers. We have:

$$u_t = (1 - \tau_t)\omega_t + v_{jt} + \alpha_t g_t,$$

where subscript t signifies period 1 or 2; τ is a fixed percentage of income per person (wage ω); v_j = the average transfer to a member of coalition J (A or B); g = public goods provided; $\alpha \in [\alpha_L, \alpha_H]$ is the marginal productivity of public goods; $u(g) = \alpha g$; and the utility of income and transfers = the dollar (currency) value.

During each period, the ruling coalition (hereafter RC) faces the following budget constraint:

$$(3A.1) \quad R + \tau_t \omega = g_t + I_{Ft} + (v_{At} + v_{Bt}),$$

where R = government resource rents (plus revenue from foreign sources), which are constant; $R_1 = R_2 = R$; I_F = investment expenditure on fiscal capacity, where the amount of investment $\iota_F = \tau_2 - (1 - \delta)\tau_1$; and δ signifies depreciation. Any invested amount reflects steadily increasing (convex) cost of investing in administrative capacity (C_F); $C_F' > 0$ and $C_F'' > 0$; hence, $I_F = C_F \times \iota_F = C_F \times [\tau_2 - (1 - \delta)\tau_1]$. Regarding transfers: $\upsilon_J = \sigma(\theta)\upsilon$ whenever J is in power, and $(1 - \sigma)\upsilon$ whenever the other coalition is in power; $\sigma \in [0.5, 1]$ is J's share of transfers (υ), a function of the cohesiveness of political institutions $\theta \in [0, 1]$; as $\theta \to 1$, $\sigma \to 0.5$. High-value public goods, α_H, occur with probability φ; low-value public goods, α_L, occur with probability $(1 - \varphi)$.

The game unfolds in four steps (two for each period):

1. Past history and nature determine the following variable and parameter values: initial fiscal capacity τ_1, α $(= \alpha_H$ with probability φ), resource rents R, institutional coherence θ; the initial coalition in power (A), and the probability that B will assume power in the next period as determined by the political instability parameter (γ).

2. At the beginning of t_1, coalition A fully utilizes τ, $\tau = \tau_1$. Coalition A chooses the expenditure levels I_F, g, and υ, allocating υ between the two coalitions according to $\sigma(\theta)$.

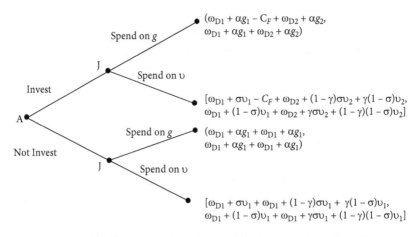

LEGEND: ω_D = disposable income; $\alpha = \varphi\alpha_H + (1 - \varphi)\alpha_L$, the expected value of public goods (g); subscripts H and L respectively = high and low; φ = the probability that $\alpha = \alpha_H$; C_F = the cost of investing in fiscal capacity I_F; υ = value of transfers; γ = probability that B becomes the ruling coalition in period t_2; σ = incumbent's share of υ; subscript 1 indicates payoffs for period t_1 and payoff for t_2 when the payoff has not changed; subscript 2 indicates payoffs for period t_2 in cases when t_2 payoffs differ from those for t_1; A = the t_1 incumbent; J = the t_2 incumbent (A or B).

FIGURE 3A.1 Fiscal Capacity Game

NOTE: Following Not Invest ($I_F = 0$), payoffs g, υ, and ω_D remain at their t_1 values. If $I_F > 0$, $g_2 > g_1$ and $\upsilon_2 > \upsilon_1$.

3. At the beginning of t_2, A retains power with probability $1 - \gamma$; and $\tau_2 = \tau_1(1 - \delta) + I_F$; $I_F \geq 0$, as determined by A's choice in t_1.

4. The new RC (J = A or B) taxes at τ_2 and chooses policy expenditure variables g and v.

Figure 3A.1 illustrates a simplified version of this game. Having inherited items under point 1, incumbent coalition A decides whether or not to spend on I_F. If I_F (minus depreciation) > 0, $\tau_2 > \tau_1$. In t_2, the new RC [J = B with probability γ and A with probability $(1 - \gamma)$] chooses whether to spend government revenue $R + \tau_2\omega$ on g or v. For simplicity, this is an either/or decision that depends solely on whether $\alpha \geq \sigma_j v$. Let disposable income $\omega_D = \omega(1 - \tau)$.

For simplicity, we assume each coalition spends all noninvestment revenue on either g or on v and that A's t_1 choice of g versus v matches that of coalition J in period 2 (in this simplified model, the relevant parameters do not change). For simplicity, if $C_F = 0$, $g_2 = g_1$ and $v_2 = v_1$, and $\omega_{D2} = \omega_{D1}$.

Using backward induction, we start with period 2:

- In t_2, coalition J (either A or B) chooses g whenever $\alpha g_2 \geq \sigma v_2$. If so, both receive value αg_2. If not, J chooses v, so that it receives σv_2 and the other coalition receives $(1 - \sigma)v_2$.

- Coalition B becomes the t_2 RC with probability γ.

- Coalition A anticipates these outcomes.

- In t_1, if A invests, $\tau_2 > \tau_1$; hence $g_2 > g_1$ and $v_2 > v_1$; otherwise, these variables retain their t_1 values.

As discussed in Chapter 3, there are three possible outcomes: a common-interest state, a redistributive state, and a weak state.

1. The *common-interest state* (S1). As in the text, this outcome arises when:

(3.5) $\alpha_L > \sigma(\theta)v$; or $\varphi = 1$.

The value of public goods always exceeds that of an incumbent's share of transfers. Using backward induction, in t_2, J spends on g. Anticipating this outcome, A chooses I_F in order to receive more highly valued g in t_2. The actual amount of investment will depend on C_F.

2. The *redistributive state* (S2). This state arises when $\alpha_L < \sigma_j(\theta)v$—that is, when condition (3.5) fails, and

(3.6) $\varphi\alpha_{H} + (1 - \varphi)\{(1 - \gamma)\sigma(\theta)v + \gamma[1 - \sigma(\theta)]v\} > 1.$

With the simplifying assumption that all noninvestment expenditure goes either toward g or v (never a mix of both), we ignore the first term of condition (3.6). With backward induction, in t_2, J will always choose v. Anticipating this, with sufficiently low values for γ and θ, A will spend on I_F because it expects to receive high transfer share $\sigma(\theta)v$ with a fairly high probability in t_2.

3. The *weak state* (S3). This state arises when both (3.5) and (3.6) fail.

Since (3.5) fails, J will only spend on v in t_2. Anticipating this outcome and knowing that γ is sufficiently high so that it cannot expect a large share of transfers, (3.6) fails, coalition A chooses Not Invest in t_1.

Appendix 3B

Fiscal and Legal Capacity Outcome Tables

TABLE 3B.1 Fiscal Capacity Conditions and Outcomes*

State	Conditions	Outcome	Logic	CAPs	Fixed Costs	Polarization (different values on α)	Inequality $\omega_j/\omega_K > 1$	One Elite Coalition
S1	(3.5): $\alpha_L > \sigma(\theta)\upsilon$, or $\varphi = 1$	$I_F > 0$ $g > 0$	High α means valuable g; hence A invests	H1 from prior limits on τ and g	Lower I_F ↑ H1 CAPs in t_2	Same as in the basic case	Rich coalition: sets $t_x < \tau$; lower I_F; $> \upsilon$ (high σ); ↓ prob. of S1 (3.5) is no longer sufficient for S1;	↓ prob. S1; (3.5) no longer sufficient (per capita benefit of υ to elites exceeds $\sigma\upsilon$)
S2	(3.5) fails; (3.6): $\varphi\alpha_H + (1-\varphi)\{(1-\gamma)\sigma(\theta)\upsilon + \gamma[1-\sigma(\theta)]\upsilon\} > 1$	$I_F > 0$ $\upsilon > 0$	Low γ and high σ; A invests to gain $\sigma(\theta)\upsilon$ with high prob.	H1 + unequal coalitions; conflict	Lower I_F ↑ H1 CAPs in t_2	Lower I_F since next incumbent's g may be less valuable	↓ impact of θ (high marg. tax to rich) Poor coalition: tax $= \tau$; S1, S2 as in basic case, but if γ high, $I_F = 0$	Narrow clientelism & enhanced H1 CAPs
S3	Neither (3.5) nor (3.6)	$I_F = g = 0$ $\upsilon > 0$	No incentive for I_F or g	↑ H1 CAPs esp. from inequality & conflict	↑ prob. of S3	↑ prob. of S3	↑ prob. of S3	↑ prob. of S3

*See the discussion in Chapter 3, Section 2, for explanation of conditions.

Symbols: α = the expected unit value of public goods (g); subscripts H and L respectively signify high and low values; φ = the probability that $\alpha = \alpha_H$; υ = value of transfers; σ = incumbent's share of υ; θ = the cohesiveness of political institutions; I_F = investment in future fiscal capacity τ; τ = administrative tax-collection infrastructure; t_x = actual utilization of τ ($t_x \le \tau$); γ = political instability, i.e., the probability that B becomes the ruling coalition in the second time period (t_2); S1 = common-interest state; S2 = redistributive state; S3 = weak state; subscript 1 indicates payoffs for period t_1, and for t_2 when the payoff has not changed; subscript 2 indicates payoffs for period t_2 in cases when t_2 payoffs differ from those for t_1; Prob. = probability; marg. = margin.

TABLE 3B.2 Legal Capacity Outcomes*

Model	Basic Outcomes	Logic
One Sector: Full utilization of legal capacity (π)	1. *Taxes and growth:* τ increases growth.	Fiscal-legal complementarity role of α, γ, and σ as in basic fiscal model
	2. *States and legal investment:* fiscal model investment results for S1, S2, & S3 apply to I_L.	
	3. *Endogenous growth:* $Y \rightarrow I_L$, which increases π and Y.	Institutional endogenous growth
	4. *Locational inequality:* areas with high π grow faster.	
Two-Sector: Modern & traditional; Equal members; $\rho_M > \rho_T$; All members have the same chance of becoming coalition leader (an elite); Imperfect capital markets	5. *Rising inequality:* selective use of π; $L_{It} = \pi > L_{Ot} \geq 0$; unequal income growth.	Rent seeking; $\neq$ growth
	6. *Class-based policy:* rich prefer building legal capacity (π); poor prefer enhancing τ.	$\neq$ per capita tax; property to protect
	7. *"Genius of taxation":* S1 crosses $\tau^* \rightarrow$ full use of π.	Fiscal-legal complement & S1 value of g; π and growth
	8. *Class-based threshold* τ^*: poor coalition might cross in S2.	Rich: low tax & $\neq \pi$ Poor: low $\gamma \rightarrow I_F \rightarrow \tau$
	9. *State capacity trap:* low or zero I_F and I_L reinforce each other.	When $\tau < \tau^*$, low incentives for $I_F \rightarrow$ low I_L, and vice versa. Selective application of π reinforces. Likelihood of S3 increases.
Two-Sector with Elites & Followers: Add EROL (ψ); two thresholds yield: a. high ψ b. intermediate ψ c. low ψ	10. *Greater inequality:* reinforce 4, 7, 8; τ^* in 6; within coalition classes.	High per capita benefit from σv focused on elites
	11. *EROL (ψ) outcomes:*	
	a. high ψ: $L_{It} = \pi$,	High $\psi \rightarrow L_{It} = \pi$,
	b. intermediate ψ (oligarchic): $L_{It} = \pi, > L_{Ot} \geq 0$	Intermediate $\psi \rightarrow$ selective enforcement
	c. low ψ (predatory state): $L_{It} \rightarrow 0$; extract rent from nonelites in both coalitions	Low $\psi \rightarrow$ max. extraction

*See the discussion in Chapter 3, Section 3, for details.

Symbols (not already defined for Table 3B.1): π = legal capacity; I_L = investment in future legal capacity; Y = GDP; ρ_M and ρ_T respectively = returns to modern and traditional sectors; L_{It} and L_{Ot} ($\leq \pi$) respectively = amount of π actually utilized for enforcement of incumbent and opposition rights; τ^* = fiscal capacity threshold (see discussion in Chapter 3, Section 3); ψ = EROL parameter; EROL = economic rule of law; max. = maximum.

Chapter 5 Appendixes: Appendix 5A

Triadic Power Game

In this triadic power game (see Chapter 5, Section 1, for explanation of terms and variables), Party A moves first. With no offer, A and B both receive their fallback income and the value they receive from trade with C; C receives the value of its trade with A and B. If A Offers and B Accepts, A receives its labor profits, $x - w + V_{AC}$; B receives $w + V_{BC}$ and C receives the benefits of trade with both A and B ($V_{CA} + V_{CB}$; assumed to occur automatically in this case). If B rejects A's offer, however, A's possession of triadic power allows it to (implicitly or explicitly) threaten to cut off B's trade with C. At this point, C must decide whether to trade with B. If C trades with B, A cancels its trade relationship with C. Accordingly, A receives d_A; B receives $d_B + V_{BC}$, and C receives only V_{CB}. Alternatively, if C chooses No, A and C retain their trade values and B receives only its fallback (d_B).

Using backward induction, as long as $V_{CA} > V_{CB}$, C follows Reject with No. Anticipating this outcome, as long as $w + V_{BC} > d_B$, B will Accept A's offer. Knowing this, A chooses Offer as long as $x - w > d_A$, and A pays $w = d_B - V_{BC} < d_B$. Because A has triadic power, it pays B a wage below B's fallback income. Triadic power allows A to exploit B in this sense.

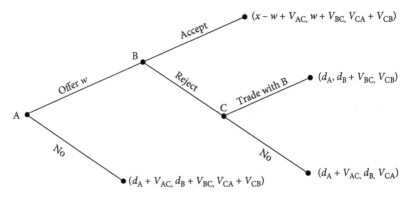

$(x - w + V_{AC}, w + V_{BC}, V_{CA} + V_{CB})$

$(d_A, d_B + V_{BC}, V_{CB})$

$(d_A + V_{AC}, d_B + V_{BC}, V_{CA} + V_{CB})$

$(d_A + V_{AC}, d_B, V_{CA})$

LEGEND: d_A = A's fallback income; d_B = B's fallback income; V_{ij}, (where i and j can be A, B, or C), = value to party i of trade with party j; x = A's revenue if B accepts; w = the wage paid to B.

FIGURE 5A.1 Triadic Power Game

Appendix 5B

Interlinked Markets and a Debt-Trap Equilibrium

This appendix sketches Amit Bhaduri's debt-trap model in sharecropping arrangements (1973), with some commentary on his usury model (1977) and a short verbal summary of Avashay Braverman and Joseph Stiglitz's (1982) interlinked agrarian markets model. Both models incorporate the notion that landowners operate in more than one market. Accordingly, both imply, but do not explicitly address, triadic exercises of power. Even though these models rely on somewhat different logic, the concept of triadic power renders them compatible.

Bhaduri (1973) presents a simplified model of semifeudal production, characteristic of West Bengal in 1970, in which sharecroppers are indebted tenant laborers working small plots. The tenants lack access to the capital market and to markets for selling their produce. Landlords are also the source of tenant borrowing for consumption. Before planting, tenants borrow from landowners, and they receive a crop share after the harvest. Lacking market access, tenants are victims of price fluctuations. Tenants end up borrowing when prices are high and pay back (in output), after the harvest, when prices are low. Effective interest rates are thus very high. In this setting, landowners practice "two modes of exploitation" arising from land ownership and extending consumption loans (Ibid., 121).

A quick sketch of the model's key relationship follows.[1] In a sharecropping arrangement, the tenant receives share αx of crop output x and gives $(1 - \alpha) x$ to the landlord. At the beginning of each time period t, the tenant borrows $b_t = c_t - [\alpha x - (1 + i)b_{t-1}]$, where i is the rate of interest. In a stationary state, none of the variables change, so that, assuming consumption c is at subsistence level $\bar{c}$ and annual output is fixed at $\bar{x}$, we have

$$(5A.1) \quad \hat{b} = \frac{\alpha}{i}\bar{x} - \frac{\bar{c}}{i}, ,$$

where $\hat{b}$ represents the steady-state value of b.

Without explaining the origins of debt, the model represents a debt trap. To illustrate with simple numbers, let $\bar{x} = 100$; $\alpha = 0.5$; $\bar{c} = 30$; and $i = 100\%$. Solving, we find $\hat{b} = 20$. Each period, the tenant keeps 50, owes 40, and thus must borrow 20 to attain subsistence-level consumption 30. More generally, any value of c between 30 and 50 could be an equilibrium.

This model, however, does not consider the possibility that the tenant could escape by slightly reducing consumption for one year to reduce debt (Basu 2000a; although, if $\bar{c}$ is really minimal subsistence, the tenant would need some alternative way to achieve consumption, possibly by begging). A more direct consideration of power can address this problem. Specifically, if we add surplus labor to the model, the landlord could exercise triadic power over the tenant (as in format 5; see Chapter 5), eliminating this escape route: the landlord could replace any tenant who refuses to take out a sufficiently large loan. Moreover, in terms of format 1, the landlord has the ability to deny the tenant credit. In format 1, the owner simultaneously occupies positions A and C. Moreover, if the landowner can deny the tenant access to a merchant (or other desirable parties, other Cs), the owner could also exercise additional format 1 triadic power. If, as in many cases, a merchant also owns land, the landlord-merchant could threaten to refuse merchant services to the tenant (again occupying positons A and C in format 1).

Bhaduri (1977), focusing on usurious interest rates, adds a few relevant points. In addition to unequal access to markets, many rural credit interactions involve personal relationships between lender and borrower, affording lenders knowledge of borrower valuation of assets.[2] If borrowers value the assets that are used as loan collateral more than do landlords, the landlord's credit market power can exceed traditional monopoly power—which by itself allows them to undervalue collateral. They can appraise collateral at below-market value in cases of foreclosure. For example, a large peasant family may value the small parcel of land it uses for subsistence more highly than either the market or the landholder would. Knowing that, the owner can push the interest rate on loans higher than pure monopoly power would allow. Moreover, landowners may deliberately induce foreclosure in cases when they value the asset more than the market would.

Braverman and Stiglitz (1982) find Bhaduri's (1973, 1977) arguments insufficient for the following reason: If the landlord can exploit the tenant by charging high interest, why not just do so by offering a lower share of the product (i.e., $\alpha < 0.5$)? They answer this question with a different logic, using a model that directly addresses moral hazard issues. They assert that the prevalence of sharecropping arrangements (rather than fixed rents or wage contracts) in developing countries arises because such contracts can address both risk and moral hazard. Regarding the former, sharecropping distributes risks of low harvests to both parties.

Regarding moral hazard, landowners cannot observe worker effort fully or without cost, and the worker has discretion over "the choice of production technique" (Braverman and Stiglitz 1982, 695). By offering workers a share of the residual, sharecropping provides an incentive to work hard, even though workers do not receive the full marginal product of their efforts (a lower incentive than full ownership would provide). Furthermore, landowners can increase incentives for effort or better production techniques, enhancing their profits, by linking markets. In addition to providing land for tenant labor, they also provide credit, marketing, and/or merchandise, such as fertilizer or food. They can "induce workers to behave" as desired (Ibid., 696).

Provision of credit, common to both models, merits more discussion. Borrowing facilitates tenant consumption. At near-subsistence levels, common in poor rural areas, consumption has a very high marginal utility. Thus, landowners can motivate effort with loans that finance consumption—providing them ample reason to link the land and credit markets. Owners can offer two types of loan contracts: a bonded labor clause, whereby tenants who fail to meet loan payments must provide a specified amount of labor; or a bankruptcy clause, whereby tenants can default with a guaranteed (at least) subsistence level of consumption. Braverman and Stiglitz note that bankruptcy contracts offer lower incentives for effort but greater incentives for choosing high-productivity techniques. Hence, a landholder's choice depends on which moral hazard problem (effort or technique) has greater impact on her profits.

Bonded clauses bear the closest resemblance to the Bhaduri model. Lending becomes a means of extracting labor. Bonded labor often leads to debt peonage. From a capability perspective, bonded contracts signify the more serious form of underdevelopment.

Even with bankruptcy clauses, however, market linkages can increase both effort and landowner profits. Owners can offer merchandise, such as fertilizer, and provide marketing services at above-market prices, even though some commodities might be available at market prices. The owners' market linkages increase tenant dependence on them.[3] Owner ability to withhold (or at least limit) tenant access to certain exchanges can hold tenants to their subsistence (or alternative reservation) utility and yet still induce effort or adjustments to production technique.[4] Accordingly, landowners can claim (virtually) all of the surplus from the labor exchange even when they cannot adjust crop shares; even when they cannot change α due to either social norms or laws that could specify, say, 50%. Although the authors do not make this claim, the availability of such provisions can help explain the prevalence and persistence of 50/50 sharecropping norms.

The concept of triadic power can bridge the gap between the Bhaduri and Braverman-Stiglitz approaches. The two models share the feature of interlinked labor and credit markets (though Bhaduri does not name it as such), with an ensuing potential for exploitation by tying tenants to needed borrowing (or other exchanges). Both arguments imply (but do not develop) triadic power. As mentioned in the prior discussion, the Bhaduri model's landowner, as the sole source of credit, combines elements of triadic parties A (employer) and C (banker) into one agent. Although one could infer a dyadic landlord-tenant relationship, the actual transactions, involve a triad that fits format 2: because the landowner can deny the tenant access to credit (or important merchandise), the owner can push the tenant below his reservation utility. Hence, the exploitation logic of format 1 applies. Here, we can interpret *reservation utility* as subsistence with low effort, but the credit (merchandise) arrangement generates subsistence with high effort, lowering tenant utility below a reservation level that would apply in a purely dyadic transaction. Moreover, the personal link between owner and tenant implies a potential for triadic threats to deny access to local merchants or other exchange partners (various Cs). The Braverman-Stiglitz argument implies a related triadic arrangement. Instead of a threat of loan denial, however, the owner's provision of credit induces additional effort via the utility of slightly higher consumption from borrowing and/or attempts to avoid the additional labor stipulated by a bondage contract. Limited access to merchandise, such as fertilizer, can reinforce the tenant's dependence. Again, the triadic nature of the transactions allows the owner to extract greater surplus than mere dyadic labor transactions would allow. In both models, the triadic power can push the tenant below the reservation utility.

Appendix 5C

Private and Public Preferences

A simple model (derived from Kuran 1995) illustrates how preference falsification interacts with different levels of expressed public support for or opposition to, say, a ruling coalition. Suppose that the private preferences of a population of size 100 ($N = 100$) are distributed across a spectrum ranging from 0, indicating full opposition to the regime, to 100, full support. Additionally, each individual chooses to express—via action and/or words (or perhaps lack of action)—a specific *public preference* (z_i). The choice of z_i reflects a trade-off between two values: the disutility associated with not expressing one's true preferences (e.g., expressing support when privately one would rather oppose) and any disutility associated with choosing a public expression that differs from the average publicly expressed across the population ($\bar{y}$). This second disutility may arise from sanctions (social, material, or physical) and/or internal discomfort from nonconformity.

Now assume a ruling coalition (A) and an opposition (B). For simplicity, individuals may only express full support for the regime, $z_A = 100$, or full opposition, $z_B = 0$. *Public opinion* at a point in time connotes the distribution of public preferences across the heterogeneous population at that time. At the beginning of each period, each individual observes the previous $\bar{y}$, forms an expected current value ($\bar{z}^e$), and then decides on her public expression z_i.

Now consider factors that shape the distribution of public support for coalition A. There are two key questions: First, how do individuals, whose private preferences range from 0 to 100, choose either z_A or z_B as they trade off preferences for self-expression versus conformity in response to different possible levels of $\bar{z}^e$? Second, given these individual responses, how does the cumulative distribution of z_A across the population respond to possible values for $\bar{z}^e$?

We define n as the number or percentage (base is 100) of the population who choose z_A. As n increases, the conformity pressure for z_A increases. For each individual, consider the level n_i^* at which that person becomes indifferent between z_A and z_B. To illustrate, consider an individual whose private preference reflects moderate displeasure with the regime: this person's $x_i = 30$. Now posit a simple utility function for this individual's choice between z_A or z_B. In the absence of social pressure, this individual would choose z_B (since $x_i < 50$), but the expected social pressure from a sufficiently high level of n could reverse this decision. Here n_i^* signifies this individual's critical-mass tipping point; below (above) n_i^*, the individual chooses z_B (z_A). At n_i^*, $U_{30}(z_A) = U_{30}(z_B)$.

More precisely, in a simple formulation, let

(5A.2) $U_{30}(z_A) = -\alpha(70)^a - \beta(50 - n)^b.$

Subscript 30 signifies $x_i = 30$, and exponents a and b reflect possible nonlinearities; α represents the marginal disutility from hiding one's true preference, given the absolute value of each unit of public minus private difference, $|z_i - x_i|$. Here, $100 - 30 = 70$. β signifies the marginal disutility of the sanction arising from each unit difference between the chosen z_i and n (the portion choosing z_A). For any n below (above) 50, this sanction is negative (positive), but decreasing (increasing) in n. Using the same logic,

(5A.3) $U_{30}(z_B) = -\alpha(30)^a + \beta(50 - n)^b.$

Assuming that $a = b = 1$, $n_{i=30}^*$ occurs at the n for which $-\alpha30 + \beta(50 - n)$ $= -\alpha70 - \beta(50 - n)$, or when

(5A.4) $n_{i=30}^* = 20(\alpha/\beta) + 50.$

In the simplest case, where $\alpha = \beta = 1$, $n^* = 70$, this individual chooses z_B whenever she expects $n < 70$—that is, whenever $\bar{z}^e < 70$—and she chooses z_A for all expected values of n above 70. Other individuals with different x_i have a different n_i^*. In a more complicated case, individuals could also differ with respect to their disutility for lack of self-expression (α) and sensitivity to social pressure (β); exponents a and b could be either greater or less than 1.

Now consider how the cumulative population distribution of public preferences $F(z_i)$ responds to steadily increasing values of $\bar{z}^e$, as shown in

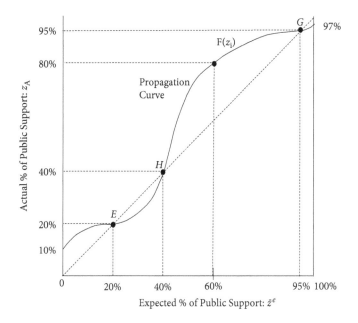

FIGURE 5C.1 Public Opinion Dynamics

Figure 5C.1's nonlinear propagation curve.[5] Each expression of average public opinion acts as a signal. Individuals within the population, employing Bayesian updating, observe the average public support for each period and revise their $\bar{z}^e$ for the next period. In the figure, the left-hand intercept shows the percent who choose z_A if $\bar{z}^e = 0$ (here 10%), and the right-hand intercept shows the same for $\bar{z}^e = 100$ (here 97%). In these two extreme cases, the individuals are strident supporters of A and B, respectively, who ignore social pressure. Intermediate levels of $\bar{z}^e$ yield intermediate amounts of public support. For example, at $\bar{z}^e = 20\%$, public support z_A is 20%; at $\bar{z}^e = 60\%$, 80% would choose z_A.

The figure illustrates three possible equilibria at points: E ($\bar{z}^e = 20\%$), H ($\bar{z}^e = 40\%$), and G ($\bar{z}^e = 95\%$). At each, the S-curve cuts the dashed line (45-degree angle at the origin), which traces the set of all possible points where $\bar{z}^e$ = the actual percent of z_A. The E and G Nash equilibria are stable, but H designates an unstable critical-mass tipping point. At G, for example, a slight downward deviation would signify $z_A > \bar{z}^e$; in the next few periods, $\bar{z}^e$ increases until the two become equal at G. By contrast, at tipping point H, if z_A falls below (above) 40%, $\bar{z}^e$ decreases (increases) to 20% at E (95% at G). The model exhibits path dependency. Starting at point G, expected regime support would need to fall below 40% to induce dramatic support for the opposition.

The model's comparative statics allow examination of how changes in external factors, such as the political environment, would affect parameters α and β, or in more complicated cases, a and b and the ensuing equilibria. In applying this model to the collapse of communism in Eastern Europe, for example, the initial equilibrium occurs at G, signifying 95% public support for the regime. A few dissidents, such as artists and writers, have private preferences that outweigh their concern for appearing nonconformist (and, reflecting Václav Havel's "living within the truth" [2015], their subtle acts of dissent may fall below the radar of authorities). This description could fit most Eastern European countries between 1948 and 1989, with temporary exceptions occurring in Poland in 1956 and again in 1981 (Brown 2009), Hungary in 1956, and Czechoslovakia in 1968. In 1989, the institution of Perestroika in the USSR (initiated in 1985), public statements by General Secretary Mikhail Gorbachev that the Soviet Army would not intervene to defend the Eastern European regimes from public opposition (reversing prior policy), along with Hungary's decision to open its border to Austria—with an ensuing exodus—shifted the political calculus. The general population began to expect more opposition.

The model can represent this development in a variety of fashions. The simplest is to say that these developments dramatically shifted expected public support from the prior equilibrium at 95% to some level below 40%. Once that happened, rising dissent precipitated greater dissent. A slightly more complicated rendition might incorporate a shift in the distribution of x_i—the private preference independent of social pressure. Retaining some simplicity, one might assume that the values x_i include the prospect of government sanction, which normally would not depend on $\bar{z}^e$ (at least not above some pertinent $\bar{z}^{e*}$). Gorbachev's announcement eliminated expectations of sanction from the USSR, which, between the 1968 (largely Soviet) overthrow of Czechoslovakian reformer Alexander Dubček and 1989, may have exerted considerable influence on private preference for dissent because most individuals expected dissent to fail in any case. A simultaneous reduction in x_i across the population would increase the y-intercept to some number greater than 10% (more will oppose regardless) and rotate the curve downward to the right, shifting the tipping point H to the right, permitting a dramatic drop in regime support once $\bar{z}^e$ falls below, say, 70% rather than 40%.[6] The Hungarian exodus may then have been sufficient to push $\bar{z}^e$ below the new threshold of 70%.

Chapter 6 Appendix: Appendix 6A

A Model of Punctuation

A simple two-equation model can illustrate the susceptibility of meso- or macro-level institutional systems to punctuation. Let χ represent the size of a threshold event (hereafter shock) needed to induce punctuation:

(6A.1) $\quad \chi_t = Z - \alpha(\theta_t)t,$

where Z is a constant; t is a discrete, sequentially advancing time period $t \in \{0, 1, 2, 3, \ldots\}$; and $\alpha > 0$ shows the marginal impact of a one-period change in time on χ, where α is a function of current institutional cohesion, θ_t. In this simple model, the threshold size of a disruptive shock decreases steadily with time, $\Delta\chi_t / \Delta t < 0$, but the rate of such decrease depends on α as determined by θ_t.[1] Naturally, θ can depend on several factors, such as the type of political settlement (see Chapter 8). To complete the model, add an equation that specifies the size of largest shock (X_t) that occurs during period t:

(6A.2) $\quad X_t = \beta_t(d_t, l_t, \gamma_t; \phi_t) + \varepsilon_t,$

where β_t, the nonrandom portion of X_t, is a function of d, l, and γ—respectively, drift, layering, and conversion; and ϕ, the stability of the distribution of power; ε_t is a random variable that reflects unpredictable influences.

Furthermore, $0 \leq \beta_t < Z - \alpha(\theta_{t-x})(t - x)$ for all t, signifying that a punctuation incident is not predictable more than x periods in advance, but its likelihood over certain time periods can be. Finally, at initial period $t = 0$, $X_t < \chi$; punctuation is not immanent.[2] Sufficient vulnerability and sufficient shock $(X_t > \chi_t)$ induces punctuation.

Chapter 8 Appendixes: Appendix 8A

Social Foundations of a Political Settlement and the Civil War–Coup Trap

This appendix develops a game-theoretic model of the civil war–coup trap by applying logic from Timothy Besley and Torsten Persson's (2011) fiscal and legal capacity models (summarized in Chapter 3 and Appendixes 3A and 3B) to Philip Roessler's (2017) civil war–coup trap—a condition that often applies to countries with weak institutions and abundant point-source resources. In terms of Table 8.1's typology, versions of this trap apply to Q1, Q3, and Q4, especially along path D.

Recall that the social foundation (SF) of a political settlement implies that a ruling coalition (RC) must pay attention to the insider groups. In this model, inclusion implies cooptation via a combination of public good provision (available to all included factions) and targeted transfers. Exclusion implies repression, with some potential to initiate civil war.

This model has two coalitions (A and B). They face a two-stage strategic interaction during a single period ($t = t_1$), with A as the RC, but they anticipate the next period ($t = t_2$) when, depending on the t_1 outcome, either A retains power or coalition B becomes the new RC. At the beginning of t_1, A chooses between Coopt (include B in the SF) and Repress (exclude). If A chooses Coopt, B responds with Accept or stage a Coup. If A chooses Repress, B chooses Acquiesce or initiate a Civil War. This interaction leads to

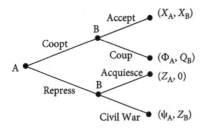

LEGEND: Subscripts A and B indicate the coalition receiving each payoff; each variable X, Φ, Q, ψ, and Z = payoff to the designated combination of strategies for the designated party. For example, X_A = A's payoff following combination Coopt/Accept.

FIGURE 8A.1 Civil War–Coup Trap Game

four possible outcomes: (i) peaceful inclusion of B in the SF, (ii) inclusion followed by a coup, (iii) exclusion followed by acquiescence, or (iv) exclusion followed by civil war. Figure 8A.1 illustrates a simple version of the game, with the payoffs as single variables.[1] These payoffs show each player's expected t_2 returns, accounting for expectations that follow each t_1 outcome concerning whether A or B will be the t_2 RC. Subsequent discussion will make each payoff a function of several other variables, such as available point-source resources.

This game incorporates the following three assumptions:

I.   Coalition A always does better if B does not resist: $X_A > \Phi_A$, and $Z_A > \psi_A$; moreover,

$X_A > 0; Z_A > 0; \Phi_A < 0;$ and $\psi_A < 0;$

where variables X_A, Φ_A, Z_A and ψ_A respectively signify coalition A's payoffs to combinations Coopt/Accept, Coopt/Coup, Repress/Acquiesce, and Repress/Civil War.

II. A coup costs A more than a civil war because it is more immediate and more predictable (Roessler 2011):

$\Phi_A < \psi_A$

III. Each coalition operates as a single unit, and all of its members are equal—meaning that all individuals have equal chances of becoming an elite member.[2]

This game has three possible subgame perfect equilibria. The following three underlying conditions determine which applies. We start with B's responses.

First, the *accept cooptation condition* (B prefers receiving transfers to staging a coup):

(8A.1) $X_B \geq Q_B$,

where X_B is coalition B's payoff to combination Coopt/Accept, and Q_B is B's payoff to Coopt/Coup.

Second, the *acquiesce condition* (B prefers enduring repression to staging a civil war):

(8A.2) $Z_B < 0$,

where Z_B is B's payoff to Repress/Civil War, and the payoff to Repress/Acquiesce is zero.

Third, the *prefer cooptation* condition (A prefers coopting B to repression in cases when B does not resist):

(8A.3) $X_A \geq Z_A$.

Note that assumption II establishes A's preference for risking a civil war over facing a coup.

Even without addressing the payoffs as functions of other variables, Figure 8A.1 offers some insight. Given assumptions I–III, the game has three possible subgame perfect equilibria.

1. *Inclusion*: A Coopts and B Accepts, which occurs when conditions (8A.1) and (8A.3) hold. If either fails, A chooses Repress.[3]
2. *Repression with Acquiescence*: A Represses and B Acquiesces, which occurs when (8A.2) holds and (8A.3) fails. Here, even though excluded, B does not choose Civil War.
3. *Civil War*: A Represses and B initiates a Civil War, which occurs when both (8A.1) and (8A.2) fail. If so, A knows it faces either a civil war or a coup. From assumption II, A prefers civil war and so chooses Repress.

Note that in the second and third equilibria, A excludes B from the SF.

Further analysis requires specifying variables X_A, Z_A, Z_B, Φ_A, ψ_A, Q_B and coalition transfer share, σ, as functions. These outcomes depend on the t_2 RC's policy decision regarding public goods and transfers—not shown on Figure 8A.1, but which can be inferred from the following logic. The t_2 RC's policy choice depends on the availability of point-source resources, as well as the preexisting strength of institutions and levels of state fiscal and legal capacity.

More specifically, consider the following functions, beginning with each coalition's payoffs at the inclusion outcome. The term X_A depends on A's expected t_2 return to retaining power. Any t_2 RC (here A) receives resource rent (R) and allocates this period's tax revenue τy (τ reflects existing fiscal capacity, an outcome of previous development) between to two government actions: providing public goods and funding transfers.

    i. Party A (the t_2 incumbent) provides public goods (g) with value αg (α specifies the unit value of g). Whenever B belongs to the SF, both coalitions consume αg. (Later, if A excludes B, A consumes αg alone, but the value αg does not change, since g is nonrival.)

   ii. Party A also allocates remaining revenue to transfers (v). In this inclusion outcome, A retains transfer share $\sigma(\theta)v$, leaving $[1 - \sigma(\theta)]v$ to coalition B.[4] Parameter θ ($\theta \in [0,1]$) represents the cohesiveness of political institutions, reflecting underlying political norms and formal rules that affect formulas for allocating transfers. Thus, θ determines the degree to which the RC (A in this case) skews the transfer distribution (σv) in its favor. Specifically, $\sigma = \sigma(\theta) \in [0.5, 1]$; as $\theta \to 1$, an RC must offer equal shares of transfers ($\sigma \to 0.5$).

This allocation operates within the government budget constraint $g + v = R + \tau y(\pi)$, where $\tau y(\pi)$ is total tax revenue, y depends on preexisting state legal capacity π, and R is the RC's rent from point-source resources. We assume that fiscal capacity τ, an exogenous outcome of prior development, is fully utilized, and that any RC provides at least some g and v.[5] Transfers are the residual expenditure: $v = R + \tau y(\pi) - g$.

    Accordingly,

(8A.4) $X_A = \alpha g + \sigma(\theta)v = \alpha g + \sigma(\theta)[R + \tau y(\pi) - g]$

With similar logic:

(8A.5) $X_B = \alpha g + [1 - \sigma(\theta)][R + \tau y(\pi) - g]$.

    Next, consider each coalition's payoffs in the event of a coup whereby B succeeds in displacing A with probability ρ. The winner (the t_2 RC) must pay all supporting troops combat pay w, an amount it must consider in the t_2 budget constraint: $g + v + L_j w(\pi) = R + \tau y(\pi)$, where $j \in [A, B]$, and w also depends on π. The winner denies transfers to the loser [$\sigma(\theta) = 1$; $\theta = 0$] because prior political institutions of cohesion have collapsed. For simplicity, assume that w is paid only during t_2 and that the loser's troops receive no combat pay.

Here is the basic equation for B's coup payoff:

$$Q_B = \rho(L^B)[\alpha g + (R + \tau y(\pi) - g - L_B w(\pi))] + [1 - \rho(L^B)]x_b,$$

where ρ depends on the share of the army that defects to B ($L^B = L_B/L$), and where L and L_B are, respectively, the size of the army and the size of the group that B successfully recruits ($L_B \leq L$); $x_b < X_B$ is B's payoff if the coup fails.

For simplicity, assume that $x_b = 0$ (benefits from any public goods B can still consume plus any bribes for surrendering equal the costs of imprisoned leaders, etc.). With these assumptions, we have

(8A.6) $Q_B = \rho(L^B)[\alpha g + (R + \tau y(\pi) - g - L_B w(\pi))].$

With probability ρ, coalition B wins, granting it access to R, g, and v, but combat pay w reduces the residual revenue left for v.

With similar logic, A's return to facing a coup is $\Phi_A = \rho(L^B)(\alpha g - \kappa) + [1 - \rho(L^B)][\alpha g + R + \tau y(\pi) - g - (L - L_B)w(\pi)]$, where κ is the direct cost to A of losing a coup (arrested leaders, etc.). For simplicity, assume $\alpha g = \kappa$, so the first term drops; hence:

(8A.7) $\Phi_A = [1 - \rho(L^B)][\alpha g + R + \tau y(\pi) - g - (L - L_B)w(\pi)].$

With probability $1 - \rho$, A retains power and so retains αg and all of v, which is reduced by the combat pay to the loyal portion of the army. A slightly more complicated version of this model could adjust the post-coup values of g, τ, and y, and possibly α.

Next, consider Z_A, A's expected return from repressing B in the absence of civil war.

(8A.8) $Z_A = \Omega_A(\Theta) + \alpha g + (R + \tau y(\pi) - g - Lw(\pi)),$

where $\Omega_A(\Theta)$ represents A's social payoff to repressing B, a function of social cleavage Θ; the greater the social distance between the coalitions (e.g., the greater racial or ethnic resentment), the greater Θ.

In this formulation (no civil war or coup), the entire army remains loyal to coalition A, but repression still requires combat pay (for simplicity assumed equal to coup combat pay).

Coalition B's payoff to acquiescence is normalized to 0 (as shown in Figure 8A.1).

Now consider B's expected payoffs if it chooses Civil War. Assume that the loser is excluded from the SF in t_2 and so receives no public goods or transfers ($\theta = 0$; $\sigma = 1$). If B loses, it receives its repression payoff (0) minus additional costs of losing the conflict. We have

$$(8A.9) \quad Z_B = \Omega_B(\Theta) + \rho_c[\alpha g_c + R + \tau_c y_c - g_c - L_{Bc} w_c] + (1 - \rho_c)\Psi_B(\Theta),$$

where Ω_B is B's social payoff related to attempting revenge for mistreatment, which is a function of social cleavage (Θ), which itself responds to prior mistreatment; ρ_c is the probability that B prevails; subscript c applied to g, τ, and y signifies their post–civil war amounts (always lower than pre–civil war amounts). $L_{Bc} > 0$ is the size of B's civil war army, which is no longer constrained by L (e.g., B may recruit peasant guerillas); $w_c < w(\pi)$ is the wage for B's recruited rebels. In addition, $\Psi_B < 0$ is B's payoff to losing the civil war, also a function of Θ; higher social cleavage induces more post–civil war repression.

In many cases, Ψ_B's material component (combatant and civilian deaths, seized property, etc.) exceeds its social component (greater exclusion). If so, Ψ_B, unlike Ω_B, signifies a primarily material (negative) payoff.

Before proceeding, we need to specify the ρ_c function. Whereas the probability of a successful coup (ρ) is treated as a function of L^B, ρ_c depends on the broader concept of relative access to sources of power: access to (not just point-source) resources, institutionally designated positions (A's initial advantage), and each coalition's ability to resolve internal organizational CAPs. In this simple formulation, ρ_c depends on the ratio

$$(8A.10) \quad \rho_c = \rho_c[(r + \eta_B + \mu_B)/(R + \tau y(\pi) + \eta_A + \mu_A)],$$

where r signifies resources available to B; η_A and η_B respectively signify positions of coalition A or B members that are not formal political positions, such as economic positions and/or positions in relevant social networks; and μ_A and μ_B signifiy each coalition's ability to resolve organizational CAPs. These terms may respond to a variety of social variables, such as resentment arising from prior repression and/or existing social cleavages; they may also reflect the legitimacy of A's incumbency from each coalition's point of view.

Now, for A's civil war payoff, we have

$$(8A.11) \quad \psi_A = \rho_c \Psi_A(\Theta) + (1 - \rho_c)[\alpha g_c + R + \tau_c y_c - g_c - (L - L_B)w(\pi)] < 0.$$

With probability ρ_c, A loses and receives $\Psi_A < 0$, which, like Ψ_B, most likely has a high negative material content and which also depends on Θ; with probability $1 - \rho_c$, A retains power and receives the designated payoff.

Returning to equilibrium conditions (8A.1)–(8A.3), first consider what happens when the accept cooptation condition (8.A1) fails. Here, B prefers staging a coup whenever $Q_B > X_B$ or when $\rho(L^B)[\alpha g + R + \tau y(\pi) - g - L_B w(\pi)]$ $> \alpha g + (1 - \sigma)[R + \tau y(\pi) - g]$.

With manipulation, we have

$$(8A.1')\quad \rho(L^B)\{\sigma(\theta)[R + \tau y(\pi) - g]\} > [1 - \rho(L^B)]\alpha g + \rho(L^B)L_B w(\pi).$$

The probability of a successful coup times the expected difference in transfer distribution (accounting for resource rents, tax revenue, and g) must exceed the expected loss of public good value from a failed coup plus the cost of paying the defecting troops if the coup succeeds. B's incentive to stage a coup increases in R and L^B and decreases in θ, αg, w, and L (for a given L_B, a large L implies a relatively small L^B).

This relation alone generates several implications:

i. Greater prior institutional development reduces B's coup incentive by increasing θ and lowering σ.

ii. An increase in R increases B's incentive to stage a coup—a political violence dimension of a resource curse [duplicated in (8A.3') later].

iii. The greater the previously established τ, the greater B's incentive to stage a coup.

iv. As intuition suggests, the more easily B can recruit army defectors, the more likely a coup will occur. Here, L_B could be a function of several variables. There are two that merit mention.

   a. The first variable is the degree to which incumbent A distributes political and economic resources to the army as opposed to other endeavors (a potential for more targeted υ and the possibility that some portion of g is effectively a club good for the army).

   b. The second is A's legitimacy from the point of view of the army or a relevant faction therein, which can depend on social cleavages. If A and B represent different ethnic groups, then L_B can respond to the depth of cleavage between the two ethnic groups.

Understanding this dynamic, A may hesitate to include B in the SF (as suggested by Roessler 2011).

Now, continuing with the implications, we have:

v. The greater the value of public goods (α)—an outcome of previous development (not modeled here; see Chapter 3)—the lower B's coup incentive.[6]

vi. A greater amount of previously developed legal capacity (π) increases y and w, and thus lowers B's incentive to stage a coup (assuming $\partial w / \partial \pi > \sigma \tau (\partial y / \partial \pi)$—likely for reasonable values of τ).

vii. The greater prior economic development, in particular the degree of structural transformation (e.g., the ratio of manufacturing to agricultural employment), the higher w and the lower B's incentive to stage a coup.[7]

viii. The greater the overall size of the army, and specifically the size loyal to A (L_A) the lower B's incentive to stage a coup.

Note further that A's perception of the importance of these factors affects its initial move: A's fear of a coup can induce it to repress B (an H4 commitment CAP).

Turning now to the question of a civil war, condition (8A.2) fails (i.e., B prefers civil war to accepting repression) whenever $Z_B > 0$; equivalently, if

$$(8A.2') \quad \Omega_B(\Theta) + \rho_c[\alpha g + (R + \tau y_c - g_c) - L_{Bc}w_c] + (1 - \rho_c)\Psi_B(\Theta) > 0.$$

The sum of the social payoff to revenge, Ω_B (itself a function of social cleavage, which offers B an incentive for civil war), plus the probability of winning times the value of public good plus transfers (with $\sigma = 1$, $\upsilon = R + \tau y_c - g_c$) minus the cost of paying troops must exceed the expected cost of losing the civil war (the third term). Here, Θ offers B a social incentive for engaging in civil war, contrasting with a primarily material incentive to refrain (adjusted by probability $1 - \rho_c$). Assuming that Ψ_B is not prohibitively large, this analysis implies a large role for the relative access to power shown in (8A.10). Moreover, Chapter 5's discussion of triadic power could yield a more complicated model.

Finally, if condition (8A.3) fails, A prefers repression to cooptation whenever $Z_A > X_A$, or $\Omega_A(\Theta) + \alpha g + (R + \tau y(\pi) - g - Lw(\pi)) > \alpha g + \sigma(\theta)[R + \tau y(\pi) - g]$; or

(8A.3') $\Omega_A(\Theta) + [1 - \sigma(\theta)][R + \tau y(\pi) - g] > Lw(\pi)$.

The sum of A's social payoff to repressing B (again a function of Θ) plus A's expected gain in transfers (from excluding B), accounting for σ and θ, must exceed the army's combat pay.[8]

Again, several implications follow. Implications (i), (ii), (iii), (vi), and (vii) hold if applied to A's incentives for repression rather than B's incentives to stage a coup. Implications (iv) and (v) drop; (viii) holds in reverse. Finally, and not surprisingly,

ix. Greater social cleavage enhances A's returns to repression.

Overall, this model illustrates, at a quite general level, a variety of trade-offs associated with Roessler's civil war–coup trap, augmented with principles from Besley and Persson's discussion of fiscal and legal capacity; concepts of prior institutional development and structural transformation; social payoffs associated with achieving revenge; the concept of social cleavages; and power relationships derived from the three principle sources of power. This model, with slightly different interpretations of the first move, can apply directly to RCs operating in the multipolar and/or narrow SF quadrants of Table 8.1. In Q1, A's first move involves a choice between continuing cooptation and repressing. For Q4, especially for path D, A's move involves initiating coop-tation versus continuing exclusion. The same applies to Q3, but with more likely avenues for civil war. A full representation of these other Q3 possibili-ties would require a more complicated model, but this model still illustrates the core logic if we interpret coalition B as representing many coalitions that could initiate a civil war.

Additional insight may follow merging this model's implications with the prevalent developmental CAPs for each quadrant—an entrée into more spe-cific modeling and hypothesis testing.

Appendix 8B

Political Settlement Types, Attributes, Tensions,
and Associated Collective-Action Problems

TABLE 8B.1 Political Settlement Types, Attributes, Tensions, and CAPs

Quadrant/Path	Attributes	Tensions to Maintain	CAPs for Development
Q1	Broad SF & Multipolar	• Conflicting interests, perceptions, & social cleavages among insiders • Potential civil war–coup trap	1. Maintain broad SF, bridge social cleavages 2. Reduce reliance on patron–client relationships without undermining stability by antagonizing potentially disruptive groups 3. Extend accountability beyond short-term patronage to capacity building, with procedural accountability 4. Enhance insider unity; institutionalize rules for allocating authority without excluding insider groups 5. Enhance state capacity without loss of accountability
Q2 Overall	Broad SF & Unipolar	• Maintain RC unity (unipolarity) with a broad SF • Maintain broad SF with diverse interests, cleavages, & unipolar power	1. Broaden input into RC decision making without undermining unipolarity 2. Enhance accountability without undermining unipolarity or state capacity 3. End neglect & repression of excluded minorities (i.e., broaden the SF without undermining unipolarity or stability) 4. Transform rule by law into rule of law, via institutions that regulate transfers of power & sanction violations by powerful elites 5. Create procedural accountability without undermining stability
Q2 Path A Developmental State	Prerequisite II, resource constraint; & Prerequisite III, internal or external existential threat		6. Motivate elite and organizational sacrifice for state fiscal and legal capacity 7. Motivate elite and organizational sacrifice for building economic institutions, coordination, long-term capabilities and benefits 8. Reduce patronage without undermining functional unipolarity or antagonizing potentially disruptive groups
Q2 Path B Patronage State	Lacks Prerequisites II and/or III		
Q3	Narrow SF & Multipolar	• Factional disputes over rents & resources • Factions recruit excluded groups • Excluded groups play off insiders • Post-exclusion civil war–coup trap • Elites may defect	1. Create functional unipolarity among rival insider factions 2. Broaden SF without more divisions 3. Reduce reliance on rents without enhancing factionalism and undermining stability 4. Create some accountability without increasing multipolarity & threatening stability

Q4 Overall	Narrow SF & Unipolar	• Maintain narrow SF exclusion
		• Post-exclusion civil war–coup trap
			1. Broaden SF without undermining stability & state capacity, given outsider group resentment, especially for path D
			2. Reduce repression of excluded groups without destroying the PS; 2-sided H4 CAP:
			  i. Will the powerful honor a promise to reduce repression or cede power?
			  ii. If they do, can the repressed credibly commit to not punish RC elites?

Q4 Path C Protodevelopmental State	Institutional or network limits on dictator/cabal's discretion		3. Develop accountability without losing state capacity 4. Strengthen bureaucracy & economic rule by law (reduce selectivity) while maintaining unipolarity, without loss of stability 5. Move toward the rule of law, address political succession, & create sanctions for violations by the powerful
Q4 Path D Predatory State	No limits on dictator's discretion other than those implied by power		6. Increase stability of the PS 7. Convert repression to cooptation & address grievances of excluded groups without a coup 8. For outsiders & disgruntled insiders, organize revolution (or coup) without civil war or replacing one predatory state with another 9. With minimal resolution of CAPs 6–8, early institution building, rudimentary rule by law, some selective economic institutions, & selective provision of public goods 10. Develop rudimentary accountability, at least for selective groups without undermining stability (Resolving CAPS 9 and 10 implies moving to path C.)

SF = social foundation; RC = ruling coalition; PS = political settlement.

Chapter 9 Appendix: Appendix 9A

An Open Deals Game for Multipolar Q1 and Q3

To represent multipolar settlements, this game replaces Figure 9.1's ruling cabal (D) with the elite of the ruling coalition (RC_e) and, for simplicity, merges enforcer (E) into RC_e. Consequently, there is no separate punishment move, and the single variable τ represents the sum of taxes and bribes ($\tau = t + b$). RC_e moves first, choosing among three options: No Deal, offer an Open Deal to n identical entrepreneurs, or offer a Selective Deal to a (monopolist) asset holder (H). The trade-offs between No and Selective Deal remain as in Figure 9.1 with adjusted notation: Figure 9.1's two equilibrium outcome payoffs (denoted by superscripts a and b) appear in Figure 9A.1, adjusted by combining relevant payoffs to D and E into a single payoff for RC_e. We retain the notion of reputation costs (γ) for reneging.

In the first move, if RC_e chooses Selective Deal, asset holder H decides whether or not to invest. Figure 9.1's two subgame perfect equilibrium payoffs apply, with payoffs adjusted to fit RC_e.

Alternatively, if RC_e chooses Open Deal, a representative entrepreneur (ENT) chooses between Invest and No, after which RC_e chooses Honor or No. Payoffs are shown in the figure. Four conditions follow:

First, the *honor condition* for open deals applies when

(9A.1) $\gamma > \Gamma(1 - \tau)$.

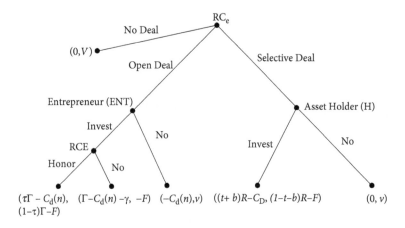

LEGEND: RC_e = ruling coalition elite; τ = tax + bribe for open deal; Γ = revenue from open deal; R = revenue from selective deal; C_d and C_D = cost of initiating open and selective deals, respectively; n = number of competitive firms; γ = RC_e loss of legitimacy from reneging; F = fixed costs of investing; v = H's fallback income; V = ENT's fallback income.

FIGURE 9A.1 Open Deals Game

As in Figure 9.1, γ is the RC_e's loss of legitimacy from reneging; Γ is total open-deal revenue; τ (combined taxes and bribery rate) is a percentage of Γ. This condition resembles Figure 9.1's condition (9.2). For RC_E to honor an open deal, its reputation loss from reneging must exceed the net revenue gain from seizing.

Second, assuming (9A.1) holds, the open-deal *investment condition* applies when

(9A.2) $(1 - \tau)\Gamma - F > v.$

Again, as in Figure 9.1, F is fixed costs of investment. ENT's net revenue gain must exceed the fallback value from traditional production v.

Third, assuming that (9A.1) and (9A.2) hold, the *initiation condition* specifies that RC_e will initiate an open deal if its expected revenue exceeds initiation costs—that is, if

(9A.3) $\tau\Gamma > C_d(n),$

where $C_d(n) \geq 0$ is the cost of initiating an open deal; $\partial C_d/\partial n > 0$.

Fourth, assuming that (9A.1)–(9A.3) hold, the *prefer open to selective deals* condition is

(9A.4) $n\tau\Gamma - (t + b)R > C_d(n) - C_D.$

RC_e prefers Open Deals whenever the difference in revenue exceeds the difference in initiation costs. Equation 9A.4 appears as equation 9.5 in Chapter 9.

This logic of (9A.1)–(9A.4) applies to deals in the formal sector. For the informal sector, assume that the government has no formal role in arranging deals, though specific members of the ruling coalition may or may not be involved at a personal level. For this case, consider RC_e as an informal grouping of local elites (as in a patronage network or gang). Variable τ may signify bribes or protection money. For open deals, RC_e is willing to offer the same terms to any interested entrepreneur.

Table 9A.1 summarizes the relationships between types of political settlements, as shown by quadrants Q1–Q4 and paths A, B, C, and D of the typology and the potential, within each type, to generate ordered deals.

TABLE 9A.1 Political Settlement Types and Deals

	Conditions for Ordered Deals from Figure 9.1				Ordered/Disordered, Selective/Open from Figures 9.1 and 9A.1
PS Quadrant	Initiate: (9.4) $tR > C_D$	Invest: (9.3) $R(1-t-b) - F > v$	Honor: (9.2) $p + \gamma > R(1-t)$	Enforce: (9.1) $bR > c_p p$	
Q1 Broad SF/Multipolar					
Low state capacity, with some regional variation; H1 slightly resolved; H2 not resolved	Macro: C_D high; need high tR to justify; *unlikely* / Meso: C_D varies; *can meet in some regions*	Macro: t low; b int.; F high for complex goods; R & v int.; *unlikely* / Meso: *variation; can meet in sectors/regions, especially for simple goods*	Macro: high c_p restricts p; $\gamma = 0$; t low; *unlikely* / Meso: *variation; low c_p and $\gamma > 0$ within some networks; can meet in some regions*	Macro: c_p high; p & R low; need high b, but ruled out by (9.3); *unlikely* / Meso: *within faction low c_p and lower p; → feasible in some regions*	Macro: mostly disordered; selective & open / Meso: mix of all types
Q2 Broad SF/Unipolar	C_D low; *can meet*			Low c_p	
Path A: Devt. State Prerequisites I–III met High state capacity, H1 & H2 resolved	R high; t int. *can meet*	R high; t int.; b int. or low; v low; *can meet for complex goods (with high F)*	High γ and t; *can meet with low p, even for high R goods*	R high; c_p low; *can meet*	Ordered with some movement to open deals over time
Path B: Patronage State Prerequisites II and/or III fail Int. state capacity H1 resolved, H2 not	tR int. *probably can meet*	R, t, b, & v int. *can meet for simple & int. goods (low enough F)*	γ low; t int.; *can meet for simple goods & for int. goods if enforcment network is strong*	R int.; c_p int.; *can meet with int. b*	Mostly selective; mostly ordered for relatively simple goods

Q3 Narrow SF/Multipolar

Low state capacity H1 & H2 not resolved	C_D high; t low; need high tR to justify; *unlikely*	t low; R low for complex; need high b to meet; v high for resources and land; *unlikely*	γ & R low; high c_p leads to low p; *unlikely*	c_p high; R low; needs high b, which (9.3) can rule out; *unlikely*	Selective within factions; mostly disordered; simple production

Q4 Narrow SF/Unipolar

				Retain exclusion	
Path C: Proto-devt. State Prerequisites II and III met Int. state capacity H1 resolved, H2 not	C_D low; t & tR int.; *probably can meet*	t int.; R int.; v low; *can meet for int. but not complex goods*	γ high; t int.; p high with enforcement network; *can meet for int. goods;*	c_p low; R int.; b int.; *can meet for int. goods;*	Mostly selective; Ordered up to int. complexity
Path D: Predatory State Prerequisites I–III fail Low state capacity H1 & H2 not resolved	C_D high; tR low; *unlikely*	t low; v high; *unlikely*	High c_p leads to low p; & t low; *unlikely*	c_p high; needs high b, which (9.3) can rule out; *unlikely*	Selective disordered predominate

exch. = exchange; int. = intermediate; devt. = developmental; italics show outcomes; Prerequisites I–III are explained in Chapter 8; C_D = ruling cabal's (D's) cost of initiating a deal; t = tax rate; b = bribe rate; R = H's revenue; v = H's fallback income; F = H's fixed costs to investing; p = amount of punishment; c_p = unit cost of punishing; γ = D's reputation cost for reneging.

Notes

Introduction

1. Chapter 1 elaborates on first- and second-order CAPs.

2. A framework is analogous to an Imre Lakatos (1978) research program that provides core untestable fundamental propositions (e.g., substantive rationality) that foster multiple testable propositions. The program offers a *positive heuristic* that specifies a set of related avenues for research: a research agenda that can guide more precise theory and hypothesis testing. Here, a *negative heuristic* incorporates empirical analysis and leads to rejecting paths that fail relevant criteria. A progressive research program leads to discovering novel facts. Brian Snowdon, Howard Vane, and Peter Wynarczyk (1994, 20–25) summarize this concept and apply it to distinct traditions in macroeconomic theory. Hank Jenkins-Smith et al. (2018, 136), noting that a Lakatos program offers "hardcore" axiomatic propositions with a "protective belt" of auxiliary hypotheses, call such a program an "ancestor" to their advocacy coalition framework, a topic addressed in Chapter 6.

3. For a comparison of rational choice and historical institutionalism, with commentary on the compatibility of these approaches, see Hall 2010. For a review of PET, see True, Baumgartner, and Jones 2007.

4. Many of these principles also appear in Acemoglu, Johnson, and Robinson 2002, 2004.

5. De facto power is immediately available, on-the-ground power; de jure power arises from institutionally designated positions, such as that of prime minister (Chapter 5 elaborates).

6. This statement also takes exception to Douglass North, John Joseph Wallis, and Barry Weingast's (2009) *double balance hypothesis*; more in Chapter 7. My approach

addresses critiques of Acemoglu and Robinson mentioned by Mushtaq Khan (2017), without rejecting much of their core logic.

Chapter 1

1. Author's calculation is from *World Development Indicators* (World Bank 2018).

2. Self-interest can reflect material preferences; it may also incorporate social preferences (e.g., status).

3. Ronald Coase (1937) (who did not coin the term "Coase Theorem," his colleague George Stigler [1989] did) used a simple two-party example to illustrate but then proceeded to assert that because transaction costs exist, institutions matter.

4. See Ostrom 1990 on institutional design as a second-order CAP. See Ferguson 2013, chap. 2 and 3, respectively, on first- and second-order CAPs. The overview of *World Development Report 2017: Governance and the Law* (World Bank 2017, 2–37) lists three key issues of development: attaining credible commitment, coordination of activity across multiple agents, and achieving cooperation among and across individuals and groups specifically with respect to free riding. All three are variations of CAPs. Cooperation to eschew free riding is a first-order CAP. Attaining commitment (via enforcement) and attaining coordination are the two basic variants of second-order CAPs.

5. Noting that Coase said little about the nature of transaction costs, Douglass North (1990) asserts that contract-enforcement costs are the chief component.

6. Information economics (e.g., Stiglitz 1987 develops these principles, though without referring to second-order CAPs.

7. There is a large literature on moral hazard and principal-agent problems. For a review with attention to nonclearing markets, see Stiglitz 1987.

8. Elinor Ostrom (2000) refers to this statement as Olson's zero-contribution hypothesis.

9. See Sobel 2005; Bowles 1998, 2004; Fehr and Gächter 1998, 2000, 2002; Fehr, Gächter, and Kirchsteiger 1996; and Fehr and Fischbacher 2002. Ferguson 2013, chap. 5, develops a game-theoretic approach to small-group resolution of CAPs via intrinsic reciprocity.

10. Chapters 6 and 7 of Ferguson 2013 present the microelements of this section in more detail.

11. For example, politician A does not know whether politician B prefers policy x or policy y, has reason to believe that a direct question will not produce an honest answer, and thus estimates that politician B prefers y with a 60% probability.

12. This question has inspired a huge economic literature including Knight 1965, Hayek 1945, and Keynes (1936) 1964.

13. Elinor Ostrom (1998) and Herbert Gintis (2009) refer to minimal conditions for rationality. John Conlisk (1996) reviews the literature on bounded rationality. Karla Hoff and Joseph Stiglitz (2016) refer to enculturated actors, meaning that culture shapes preferences (obvious but difficult to model).

14. W. Brian Arthur's (1994) concept of a problem-complexity boundary illustrates: within the boundary, problems are sufficiently simple that substantive rationality can apply—as in the case of deciding whether to buy an apple based on its price. Outside of this boundary, such as figuring how to coordinate activity across coalitions, deep uncertainty and multiple contingencies render full reliance on S2 impossible. Judgments require some intuition.

15. Ferguson 2013 summarizes social preference theory and bounded rationality in more detail, incorporating classical, evolutionary, and epistemic game-theoretic reasoning. On epistemic game theory, see Gintis 2009.

16. On the social dimension of cognition, see Gintis 2017.

17. For a far more detailed discussion of social influence on individual cognition, see Gintis 2017.

18. Political and economic institutions overlap in all of these regards—again, political economy.

19. For more on roles of institutions, organizations, and institutional systems, see Ferguson 2013, chap. 7. On cultural determinates of decision making and the influence of cultural mental models, see Hoff and Stiglitz 2016. On endogenous preferences, see Bowles 1998. Additionally, internalized norms shape conceptions of identity (another type of mental model). On identity economics, see Akerlof and Kranton (2000, 2005, 2010). For a discussion of norms that includes the Crawford-Ostrom (Ostrom 2005, chap. 5; Crawford and Ostrom 1995) ADICO institutional syntax, identity economics, and relationships to CAPs, see Ferguson 2013, chap. 8.

20. Informal organizations, such as gangs, use informal rules.

21 The state is a key component of a social order that embodies its political side.

22. Chapter 6 elaborates on this topic.

23. As the name implies, meso-level activity operates between micro- (individual or single organization) and macro- (society-wide) levels, with regional or sectoral dimensions.

24. World Bank 2017 offers a complete and intuitive discussion of these three functions.

25. Social roles, such as employee, doctor, waiter, wife, and colleague are "accompanied by a remarkably complex network of appropriate norms" (Sunstein 1996, 921).

26. "Norms establish conventions about the meanings of actions" (Sunstein 1996, 917).

27. Again, norms are themselves outcomes of complex prior social interactions (games; Aoki 2010), with historical and cultural roots.

28. See Posner 2000 for an in-depth discussion of relationships between laws and norms. Eric Posner, however, defines norms in a somewhat general fashion as equilibrium behavioral patterns that emerge from signaling. Like Masahiko Aoki (2010, 2011), I consider institutions (including norms) to be both outcomes of prior social processes (in this sense similar to Posner) as well as social parameters for future interactions (departing from Posner). Moreover, my conception of norms includes internalization of ethical content, which can motivate adherence independent of social

signaling (a characteristic that sometimes, though not necessarily always, distinguishes norms from laws and other formal institutions) and which often motivates sanctioning norm violators.

29. Avner Greif (2006) includes organizations in his definition of institutions for precisely this reason: because organizations deliver auxiliary transactions, their presence underlies institutional functions of coordinating expectation and activity. I incorporate Greif's key role for organizations within institutional systems but retain the somewhat more prevalent distinction between institutions (rules) and organizations (players) found in Bowles, North, Ostrom, and others. On nested interactions within and between institutional systems, see Ostrom 2010 on polycentric governance.

30. Referring to the post–World War I treaties that carved up the former Ottoman Empire, Eugene Rogan notes, "The borders of the post-war settlement have proven remarkably resilient—as have the conflicts the post-war boundaries have engendered" (2015, 405).

31. Acemoglu, Johnson, and Robinson (2004, 2005) and Acemoglu and Robinson (2006, 2008, 2012, 2013) discuss both hypotheses (though not always distinguishing between them).

32. Dani Rodrik (2014) makes this assertion, referring specifically to Acemoglu Johnson and Robinson's (2004) statements of social conflict theory (basically, H3 and H4). Kathleen Thelen (2003) notes the importance of conceptually separating mechanisms of reproduction of institutional relationships from sources of innovation. H3 and H4 speak to the former, whereas H5 speaks to the latter. Peter Hall and Thelen (2009) stress the importance of reinterpretation of institutions as a source of change.

Chapter 2

1. Daron Acemoglu and James Robinson (2006), citing Rock 2000, summarize these events.

2. Sen defines freedom as the capability to achieve functionings (1999, 39).

3. In contrast to much traditional economics, Sen does not define well-being in terms of utility, which reflects a current state of mind. If we represent a specific human functioning as a single vector, capability sets are collections of available vectors. They are sets of feasible alternatives for the achievement of human functionings that reflect degrees of effective or substantive freedom.

4. Sen (1999) points out that humans exercise agency related to their own well-being as well as broader goals, such as the well-being of family or society.

5. Sen (1999) notes that these items fit John Rawls's (1999) concept of primary goods.

6. Neglected tropical diseases (NTDs) "affect more than a billion people, most of them poor, with blindness, immobility, disfigurement and often great pain. The resulting disabilities keep sufferers mired in poverty; that poverty is what allows the diseases to thrive" ("Winning the Endgame," 2017, 51).

7. Francis Fukuyama offers a more restricted definition that equates governance with state capacity: "a government's ability to make and enforce rules, and to deliver services, regardless of whether that government is democratic or not" (2013, 350). Note that implementation implies both delivery and enforcement.

8. The narrower term "public policy" typically applies only to decisions made at some level of government.

9. For Elinor Ostrom (2005), cognitive development is a key advantage of self-governance. For Albert Hirschman (1970), the exercise of voice is an art that improves with practice.

10. In game theory, the rules of a game specify the following: who plays, all available actions for each player, the sequence of action (order of play), and all possible outcomes—meaning all possible combinations of actions—the net material and/or social benefits (payoffs) for each player at each possible outcome, and what the players do and do not know at every point where they can move (take action).

11. See Chapter 7 for a summary of relevant literature. Chapters 8 and 9 develop this text's approach to political settlements.

12. Timothy Besley and Torsten Persson (2011) define state capacity as an institutionalized capability to carry out policies and deliver services and benefits to citizens and firms. They note two complementary elements: First, fiscal capacity connotes the ability to tax broadly, which depends on infrastructure for administration, monitoring, and enforcement. Second, legal capacity is the ability to provide regulation and legal services such as protection of property rights and enforcement of contracts—via legal infrastructure of courts and educated legal officials. These items relate to the rule of law. The authors note high correlations between effective state institutions, an absence of political violence, and high per capita income.

13. This is analogous to the Marxian concept of class consciousness (Marx and Engels [1848] 1998; Lukas [1920] 1967), but here it is not restricted to classes defined by relations to production.

14. If we think of an institutional system as a dynamic equilibrium, enhancing legitimacy increases the size of the basin of attraction around the equilibrium.

15. "Legitimacy involves the capacity of a political system to engender and maintain the belief that existing political institutions are the most appropriate or proper ones for the society" (Lipset 1959, 86). I adopt Seymour Martin Lipset's concept with two modifications: extending the concept to institutional systems and striking the modifier "most appropriate."

16. A closely related statement is that economic dynamics involves production and reproduction. The latter involves replacing individuals who die or move on (via procreation and development of talent) and reproducing and altering economic institutions (Jayadev and Bowles 2006, 333).

17. GDP measures value of all production that occurs within a nation's borders, regardless of who produces it, whereas GNI measures that produced by national citizens, regardless of their location (inside or outside the country).

18. Alternative measures of aggregate living standards include median household or individual income.

19. Pritchett and Werkler (2012) further assert that shifts between growth episodes (accelerations, collapses, etc.) are analogous to phase transitions in physics—and respond to political dynamics between business and state actors. For example, autocracies have significantly higher growth variance than democracies.

20. As a factor endowment, land is fixed and thus largely not augmentable (Lin 2012). Infrastructure is both hard (e.g., roads) and soft (institutions); the latter does not directly appear in neoclassical growth models. Daron Acemoglu, Simon Johnson, and James Robinson (2004), who stress institutions, refer to labor, capital, human capital, and technology as proximate causes of growth. Rodrik (2013) combines ideas on structural transformation derived from the dual economy literature of W. Arthur Lewis (1957) and Gustav Ranis and John Fei (1961) and concepts of growth fundamentals derived from the neoclassical growth model of Robert Solow (1957).

21. Rodrik (2013) develops a two-dimensional growth typology with low/high investments in fundamentals on one axis and slow/rapid structural transformation on the other. The low/slow combination generates no growth; high/slow leads to slow growth; low/rapid leads to episodic growth; and high/rapid leads to rapid, sustained growth.

22. Even though technological knowledge can spread rapidly, a society's available technology may face a number of constraints that prevent absorbing technology developed elsewhere. Chapter 4 models a locally relevant rate of technological advance with attention to previously accumulated local knowledge, network connections, levels of human capital, and infrastructure.

23. For Justin Yifu Lin (2012), the economic structure of an economy is thus endogenous to its factor endowment structure. Upgrading endowment structures requires increasing the capital/labor ratio, and development relies on changing factor endowments and continuous technological innovation.

24. Berthold Herrendorf, Richard Rogerson, and Ákos Valentinyi (2013), for example, define structural transformation as shifts in the shares of employment, value added, and/or consumption out of agriculture and into manufacturing and services.

25. Hseih and Klenow 2009, cited in McMillan et al. 2014.

26. Rodrik (2013) cites McCaig and Pavcnik 2013 on these points.

27. McMillan et al. (2014) note that Latin America's productivity decline may be surprising, given the predominant view that the late-1980s and early-1990s reforms in many Latin American countries improved policies (e.g., inflation fell) and institutions (became more market oriented). Weighing countries by population, the within-sector component of productivity growth across all countries increases (mostly due to China's large population). Using this technique, the impact of Latin American structural change appears to be slightly positive.

28. Accordingly, Asian countries experienced a drop in the relative prices of manufacturing; African countries experienced much smaller declines. Botswana and

Ghana, nevertheless, unlike Malawi, Senegal, and South Africa, have experienced productivity growth for three or more decades, and Mauritius's export-oriented manufacturing has followed the Asian pattern (Diao et al. 2017).

29. "One of the few things that the Korean, Taiwanese, and Chilean states all shared was a high degree of discretion in their capacity to design, implement, and modify policy interventions and an almost absolute protection from public criticism" (José Miguel Benavente, quoted in Hausmann and Rodrik 2005, 97).

30. Sen (1992, 26) adds that there should be a correspondence between policy purpose and the information based upon which equity is evaluated.

31. On the impact of the distribution of wealth on human capital investment, see Galor and Zeira 1993.

32. Cutoffs at less extreme poverty are also possible. Related measures include the normalized poverty gap, which creates a 0–1 index by dividing the APG by the relevant poverty line cutoff (Yp), and the average income shortfall, which shows the amount by which income of a poor person falls below the poverty line. See Todaro and Smith 2015 for more details.

33. The Foster-Greer-Thorbecke index: $P_\alpha = \dfrac{1}{N} \sum_{i=1}^{H} \left(\dfrac{Y_p - Y_i}{Y_p} \right)^\alpha$, where N = population; H = poverty head count; Y_p = poverty line, and Y_i = individual income. With $\alpha = 1$, P_α shows the normalized poverty gap. With $\alpha = 2$, the impact of a poor person's income gain on P_α increases in proportion to the square of its distance from Y_p (Todaro and Smith 2015, 228–29).

34. The MPI index is based on Alkire and Foster 2011 and Alkire and Santos 2010. For a straightforward discussion of these and other measures of poverty and inequality, see Todaro and Smith 2015, 218–30, 242–47.

35. Heather Schofield (2014), reporting on a randomized control test (RCT) conducted among rickshaw drivers in India, finds that adding 700 calories to their diet increases their hours of labor supplied and earnings by 10%. Similarly, using the natural experiment of fasting during Ramadan, she finds a 20 to 40% reduction in productivity among Muslim participants.

36. The UNDP gives the GII's dimensions: "reproductive health, measured by maternal mortality ratio and adolescent birth rates; empowerment, measured by proportion of parliamentary seats occupied by females and proportion of adult females and males aged 25 years and older with at least some secondary education; and economic status, expressed as labour market participation and measured by labour force participation rate of female and male populations aged 15 years and older." UNDP Human Development Reports, "Gender Inequality Index (GII)," http://hdr.undp.org/en/content/gender-inequality-index-gii.

37. For a model of gender bargaining within households, see Basu 2006.

38. More precisely, Bhashkar Mazumder estimates an intergenerational earnings elasticity between fathers and sons of 0.6 and a similar magnitude for fathers and daughters, implying long-term intergenerational persistence of unequal family incomes: "existing inequalities may persist for many more decades than previously thought" (2005, 80).

39. Recall Harold Lasswell's (1936) definition: "Politics: Who Gets What, When, How."

40. Robert Fogel and Stanley Engerman (1974), for all their historical economic analysis of slavery, fail to mention this fundamental deprivation caused by slavery.

41. Chapter 5 elaborates on this topic.

42. Other inequality measures show the same pattern. The phenomenon of increasing within-country inequality in the late twentieth and early twenty-first centuries has been noted by many other authors, including Emmanuel Saez and Gabriel Zucman (2016), Anthony Atkinson and Thomas Piketty (2010), and Atkinson, Piketty, and Saez (2011). The World Inequality Lab (2018) offers comprehensive data.

43. Philippe Aghion, Eve Caroli, and Cecilia García-Peñalosa (1999) note that if the downward sloping portion of the Kuznets curve actually held, there could be a virtuous circle whereby growth increases equity, which then fosters greater growth, but developments since 1980 suggest no such pattern.

44. A "great leveling" occurred in Germany, the Netherlands, the United States, the United Kingdom, Japan, Italy, Chile, and (with delayed timing) Brazil. After World War II, inequality also fell in communist countries, though with little growth. Most countries experienced equalization during the third quarter of the twentieth century (Milanovic 2016, 70–86).

45. Milanovic notes that here he parts with Piketty (2014), who takes World War I as an exogenous event; their concepts of internal political mechanisms, however, are similar.

46. This point has been overlooked by some participants in the debate over the importance of technology as opposed to trade as a factor that had led to rising inequality.

47. Similar bargaining power arguments appear in Solow, "The Future of Work: Why Wages Aren't Keeping Up," *Pacific Standard*, June 14, 2017, https://psmag.com /economics/the-future-of-work-why-wages-arent-keeping-up, and Chau and Kanbur 2013. Related factors include the shift to service employment, a greater increase in within-sector inequality in services, and a reduction in union power. Citing Schiavone 2002 and Marx 1965, Milanovic (2016, 111) notes that the Roman Empire did not develop capital production because labor was so cheap. The Romans, in fact, invented a steam engine but used it as a toy.

48. Similarly, "The poorest half of the global population has seen its income grow significantly thanks to high growth in Asia (particularly in China and India). However, because of high and rising inequality within countries, the top 1% richest individuals in the world captured twice as much growth as the bottom 50% individuals since 1980. Income growth has been sluggish or even zero for individuals with incomes between the global bottom 50% and top 1% groups. This includes all North American and European lower- and middle-income groups" (Alveredo et al 2013, World Inequality Lab 2018).

49. Even if this estimate is off by a factor of 10, the richest 260 own as much as the poorest 50%. See also Larry Elliot, "World's 26 Richest People Own as Much as Poor-

est 50%, Says Oxfam," January 20, 2019, *The Guardian*, https://www.theguardian
.com/business/2019/jan/21/world-26-richest-people-own-as-much-as-poorest-50-per
-cent-oxfam-report?CMP=share_btn_link.

50. For a review, see Stiglitz 1987.

51. Oded Galor and Joseph Zeira (1993) develop a model in which imperfect capital markets generate higher interest rates for borrowers than for lenders. Wealthy
(poor) individuals thus face low (high) opportunity costs to investing in human capital. Kaushik Basu (2000a) offers an intuitive explanation of this model. At a macroeconomic level, Ostry and Bourguignon (2016), cite Raghuram Rajan's (2010) assertion
that the combined influence of pressure on rich individuals to save and poor individuals to retain consumption levels through borrowing contributed to the 2008 financial
crisis. Dean Karlan et al. (2014) focus on interactions between capital constraints and
risk. Using several RCTs conducted among farmers in Ghana, they find that attaining
insurance against rainfall risk acts as a stronger binding constraint than access to cash
finance, but they note that "the prospect of potentially binding liquidity constraints in
the future strengthens the responsiveness of investment to insurance (Ibid., 600n4).

52. Alfred Marshall ([1920] 1979) makes a similar argument for sharecropping
regarding tenant effort and incentives to invest. Reviewing this argument, and Amit
Bhaduri's (1973) counterargument that landholders can innovate, Basu (1999) points
to the possibility of a debt trap arising when landholders exert power over tenants.
Chapter 5, drawing on Basu 2000b, summarizes a related model.

53. For example, Stanley Engerman and Kenneth Sokoloff (2005, 2006) argue
that highly unequal early colonial distributions of land, mineral resources, and access
to labor led to delayed and restricted franchise in Latin America as elites strove to
maintain their political advantages.

54. Jayadev and Bowles (2006, 343) quote Nordhaus (2000, 259): Fisherian income is "the maximum amount a nation can consume while ensuring that members
of all current and future generations can have expected lifetime consumption or utility that is at least as great as current consumption or utility." Because institutional
deterioration would compromise future production, the costs of institutional maintenance constitute a form of depreciation.

55. These authors estimate growth spells by setting all variables at their median
level and then separately considering the impact of a 10-percentile increase in each
variable on growth.

56. "Health improves with income throughout the income distribution, and poverty has more than a 'threshold' effect on health" (Deaton 2002, 2). Even so, Deaton
does not regard redistributing income as an important way to improve adult health,
though it could affect childhood health, with effects later in life on both health and
income (2013).

57. James Heckman (2007) stresses dynamic complementarities between health
and education related to cognitive skills.

58. Specifically, Chattopadhyay and Duflo (2004) find increased provision of
water and roads in West Bengal—both goods favored more by women than men in

surveys. Likewise, in Rajasthan, where women prefer more water and fewer roads than men, they observed increased provision of water and reduced provision of roads in districts that followed the mandate.

59. For historical examples of excess inequality impeding development, see Engerman and Sokoloff 2005 and Easterly 2007.

Chapter 3

1. Following Mushtaq Khan's (2013) terminology, Brian Levy (2013) calls this arrangement a *competitive clientelist* limited-access order (LAO).

2. The variables (numbers) represent the net material payoffs to each player for each combination of strategies. Following convention, within each cell, the row player's (Maria's) payoffs appear first.

3. Whenever $a2 > a1 > a4 > a3$ and $b2 > b1 > b4 > b3$, the game has a prisoners' dilemma structure.

4. $G = \alpha \sum_{j=1}^{N} c_j$. For any given G, a larger N reduces an individual contribution αc.

5. As Douglass North (1990) points out, Ronald Coase failed to consider costs of enforcement as the single most important component of transactions costs.

6. Here, C connotes undertaking the costs of arranging coordination, and D signifies letting others do so.

7. Firms develop many of their own (private) policies, such as those governing hiring decisions.

8. This combination is not a Nash equilibrium, but a possible outcome, especially if the game is played only once.

9. More generally, any two-player normal-form game with two strategies and with two Nash equilibria that occur when the players choose different strategies constitutes a game of chicken. Table 3.4's variant is the most obviously relevant. Avinash Dixit, Susan Skeath, and David Reiley (2015) offer an intuitive discussion of three basic variants on chicken.

10. The Preamble to the US Constitution states: "We the people of the United States, in Order to form a more perfect union, establish Justice, insure domestic tranquility, provide for the common defence, . . . do ordain and establish this Constitution for the United States of America." Guillermo O'Donnell notes that states provide order, "the supreme collective good: it furnishes generalized social predictability backed by eventually decisive actions of pertinent public bureaucracies" (1993, 1357).

11. Martin Williams (2018) criticizes the metaphor implied by the term "state capacity" because it focuses on a potential rather than a set of complex and contingent political problems related to information, coordination, and commitment that surround actual implementation. My approach to state capacity, however, addresses this concern by incorporating power relations and second-order CAPs with informational, coordination, enforcement, and credibility elements.

12. Chapter 5 relates the credibility of agreements to the motivation of powerful actors.

13. Another dimension of state capacity, stressed by Fukuyama (2013), concerns the relative autonomy of bureaucratic agents within areas of their jurisdiction. Autonomy matters because it underlies bureaucratic adaptation and innovation, but excessive autonomy compromises accountability. Fukuyama poses an inverse U-shaped relationship between bureaucratic autonomy and government quality. Patronage systems typically bind bureaucrats to specific political interests. This chapter does not address bureaucratic autonomy, but Chapter 8's discussion of political settlements provides context for a more in-depth analysis.

14. Besley and Persson (2011) use slightly different notation and a related formula for transfer shares, but this distinction has no impact on the model's outcomes.

15. We could write $\varphi = \varphi(\theta_{t-1}, \Psi)$; Ψ signifies the perceived extent of external threat, with both $\partial\varphi/\partial\theta$ and $\partial\varphi/\partial\Psi < 0$.

16. Adding a fixed cost to Besley and Persson's (2011, 53) equation (2.8) illustrates this point.

17. We can write $\sigma = \sigma(\omega_j/\omega_K)$, where $\partial\sigma/\partial(\omega_j/\omega_K) > 0$ for incumbent J.

18. These statements fit the high correlation between high-income tax cuts and rising income inequality in the United States, noted by Thomas Piketty (2014). Economic inequality alone implies that a rich coalition fully utilizes existing tax capacity only if its marginal gain (in the form of public goods and transfers to its members) exceeds the ratio of its wage to the average wage. A very rich coalition A will not spend on I_P, since it bears most of the costs of taxation, whereas a poor A will fully utilize τ (Besley and Persson 2011, 73). Along these lines, Mauricio Cardenas (2010) finds that high inequality reduces incentives to invest in state capacity.

19. See Stiglitz 1987 and Bowles 1985. For a discussion of relations between third- and second-party enforcement, see Ferguson 2013, chap. 3 and 9.

20. The legitimacy and hence functionality of legal institutions (especially laws) typically requires some compatibility with prevalent social norms (Posner 2000; Basu 2000b).

21. "Impersonal exchange with third party enforcement . . . has been the critical underpinning of successful modern economic growth" (North 1990, 35).

22. This discussion abstracts from the fundamentally political decisions related to defining property rights (who gets what?)—a topic that Chapter 5's discussion of power touches on.

23. In this model, legal capacity (π) is a public good, although its application (L_j) may be selective.

24. Here is a related perspective: In a growth model in which taxes are used only for enforcing property rights, the first-order condition for maximizing growth with respect to the tax rate implies increasing taxes up to the point where "the deterrence-of-confiscation effect from governmental property rights enforcement activities" (the marginal benefit) equals the profit rate (the marginal cost of taxation) (Jayadev and Bowles 2006, 334).

25. "Thus investing in better legal capacity has a multiplier effect on income owing to the additional private capital that it generates" (Besley and Persson 2011,

143). The model offers a microfoundation for a key finding of new institutionalist economics and related literature (e.g., North 1990; Acemoglu, Johnson, and Robinson 2004). Greater utilization of legal capacity also increases the demand for modern-sector labor.

26. Besley and Persson (2011) apply this principle to a case in which the modern-sector wage exceeds that in the traditional sector, which then generates the equivalent of a one-sector model with all production in the modern sector. In a slightly more complicated labor market with efficiency wages, however, production occurs in both sectors, with a higher efficiency wage in the modern sector.

27. The difference $L_1 - L_0$ decreases in θ; coherent institutions foster equal application of legal capacity.

28. Along similar lines, Samuel Bowles (2006) shows an evolutionary model in which inefficient and inequitable institutions arise and persist from the superior collective-action capabilities of small groups of rich agents, compared to large groups of poor agents.

29. "An incumbent from the group with more entrepreneurs denies the opponent access to the legal system unless fiscal capacity is sufficiently high" (Besley and Persson 2011, 132). The complementarity between τ and π encourages equal utilization of π whenever such complementarity generates sufficiently high income to fund valuable g.

30. Besley and Persson (2011) allow an equal-members form of corruption, whereby the incumbent coalition (as a whole) extracts rents from the opposition. This possibility, which does not occur in S1, enhances the prior implications for unequal support of property rights and reduces incentives for investing in legal or state capacity.

31. Predatory states reflect incentives to deny legal protection and create ineffective legal protection (Besley and Persson 2011, 155). Production suffers.

32. A dynamic model could make γ a function of several variables, including R. Besley and Persson (2011, chap. 5) address endogenous political stability.

33. Here, $\partial I_F/\partial/\gamma$ and $\partial g/\partial\gamma$ both have higher absolute values.

34. Spending on guard labor is analogous to investment that only replaces depreciation (Jayadev and Bowles 2006).

35. Besley and Persson's (2011) chapters 4 and 5 make political instability endogenous, with attention to investments in violence capacity. Such investments fit the Acemoglu-Robinson 2008 concept of elite actions to maintain a political equilibrium.

36. Such claims often constitute exercises of power3. See Chapter 5 and Ferguson 2013, chap. 4.

Chapter 4

1. Karla Hoff and Joseph Stiglitz (2016) develop a sophisticated approach to patterns of social conformity that relates social contexts to cultural mental models that generate patterns of processing information.

2. The extent of sharing depends on the degree to which technology can be made exclusive—usually via institutional arrangements, such as patents. Such arrangements are typically imperfect, especially over time. Knowledge leaks.

3. Richard Nelson and Paul Romer (1996) distinguish between pure science (e.g., the theory of relativity), applied science (concepts of genetic engineering), and innovation—that is, the actual application of knowledge to production processes in specific (often somewhat idiosyncratic) productive units, such as factories. Innovation involves reconfiguring and extending ideas to fit real-world production.

4. Technical change "can be ascribed to experience" (Arrow 1962, 156).

5. Social network analysis can contribute decisively to the study of knowledge transmission. For an overview of social network theory, see Jackson 2008. On network transmission of knowledge about pineapple growing in Ghana, see Conley and Udry 2010.

6. More formally, $\partial w / \partial q > 0$ and $\partial^2 w / \partial q^2 > 0$, where w is the wage: each incremental increase in q increases labor productivity (and hence wages) at an increasing rate (Basu 2000a, 37).

7. Conventional marginal productivity theory without production complementarities predicts that low average human capital in rural Kentucky should yield a high marginal product and attract skilled workers to that location. Frank Neffke (2017), using Swedish data on 491 educational tracts, finds that skill complementarity increases wages, whereas skill substitutability lowers wages.

8. Chapters 5 and 8 of Ferguson 2013 discuss reciprocity and social norms in detail.

9. Chapter 6 relates this notion to the influence of ideas on development.

10. The magnitude and sign of derivative $\partial r_{hi} / \partial h_i$ depend on the other variables.

11. All individuals possess the same two options and the same expected return functions. The term $(n + 1)$ signifies that if (and only if) the individual chooses h_i, then there are $n + 1$ participants. A (significantly) more complicated model could introduce heterogeneous individuals.

12. *Sheepskin effects*, which occur when the attainment of specific levels of education (e.g., finishing primary or secondary school) enhances marketability, imply an analogous logic. Specific signals of accomplishment associated with attaining specific graduation points generate increasing returns to investing in human capital in regions close to relevant thresholds. If most of the children in an area finish primary, but not secondary, school, additional hurdles may inhibit further educational pursuits (McGavock 2017).

13. Though unstable, n^* is a Nash equilibrium: given expectations, no player has a unilateral incentive to change strategies. Note that "positive" and "negative" feedback are not normative terms. Positive feedback implies that motion in one direction induces subsequent motion in that same direction (good or bad). With negative feedback (as in a supply-demand model), motion in one direction prompts a counteracting response. Positive (negative) feedback dynamics generate unstable (stable) equilibria.

14. William Easterly (2002) offers a succinct summary of the relevant developments.

15. Stefano Breschi and Francesco Lissoni (2001) criticize the knowledge spill-over literature for failing to account adequately for pools of skilled workers and trans-action relationships conducted across networks. The present formulation addresses both concerns. Additionally, as Section 2 indicates, capital market imperfections can affect both H_L and r_{hj}.

16. For an overview on approaches to poverty traps, see Bowles, Durlauf, and Hoff 2006. Aart Kraay and David McKenzie (2014) review several empirical tests of several versions of poverty trap hypotheses to find little evidence in support of each of four separate mechanisms: a low savings equilibrium, a national big push, nutritional traps, and traps arising from lumpy investments and borrowing constraints. They note, however, that the big push evidence is both mixed and difficult to locate; the strongest evidence of traps applies to locational poverty traps—the present subject. Moreover, the studies they review miss potentially important dynamics by failing to consider interactions among these potential causes. In contrast, this chapter consid-ers interactions involving location, coordination failure, institutional constraints, and power relationships. Moreover, even at the national level, Kraay and McKenzie's figure 1 shows 17 (out of 121) countries with low incomes that are located very close to the diagonal line (their mentioned criterion for identifying a poverty trap; looking at their figure, I counted 17). Their hesitation notwithstanding, this number alone is sufficiently large to imply policy relevance for poverty traps.

17. Andrés Rodríguez-Clare (1996) derives this open-economy principle using a model in which, as in Adam Smith, a division of labor generates productivity gains and the division of labor is determined by the extent of the market. As in Alfred Mar-shall (1920) 1979, proximity to suppliers generates efficiency gains. Krugman (1995) offers a more detailed summary of this model.

18. Possible justifications for a high w_M include compensating wage differentials and efficiency wages. Analogously, the Harris-Todaro (1970) migration model predicts an excess supply of labor in an urban formal sector of an urban-rural economy. Addi-tionally, Paul Krugman (1995) notes that Nurske (1953) and Rosenstein-Rodan (1943) consider a type of unemployment that does not appear in Murphy et al. 1989: underutil-ized labor (as in clerks doing nothing). This element of effective unemployment also acts as surplus labor: in a society without a welfare state, it spreads work and income. Accordingly, the *social* marginal product of labor ($SMRP_L$) exceeds the wage, but indi-vidual firms will not hire the next worker since their own $MRP_L < w_M$. Society would benefit if they did. This source of unemployment is structural and linked to rural–urban migration, which increases the urban labor supply. Furthermore, even though labor is heterogeneous, firms cannot practice wage discrimination. They avoid hiring workers who might work for less for fear of losing more highly qualified workers.

19. The level of demand from traditional production plus only one high-wage firm would not support a sufficiently high level of output to induce the scale econ-omies that could justify paying fixed costs and w_M. This statement holds for most reasonable values of the model's parameters (Krugman 1995).

20. Chapter 3 discusses how imperfect capital markets influence H1 CAPs.

21. A fertility dynamic, in which one family's fertility decision depends on that of others (via social norms and/or expected probabilities of at least one child achieving modern-sector employment) can generate a high-fertility poverty-trap equilibrium. A low-fertility equilibrium arises when expected fertility falls below a threshold level. On fertility norms, see Dasgupta 1995 and Munshi and Myaux 2006.

22. These principles relate to an old debate concerning balanced and unbalanced development. An economy-wide big push model suggests simultaneous (balanced) investment, whereas the sectoral logic of backward and forward linkages suggests a sector-specific (unbalanced) approach (Hirschman 1958). These two arguments, however, are complementary (Krugman 1995); they offer different angles on coordination problems that generate CAPs of unequal development.

23. See Easterly 2002 for an intuitive discussion of Bangladesh textile modernization, knowledge transfer, and developmental coordination problems. See Khan 2013 on the role of the MFA.

24. Backward linkages arise when firms purchase input from upstream firms; forward linkages arise when they supply inputs to downstream firms. As Krugman (1995) points out, Marshall noted a potential for sufficiently large local markets to support efficient-scale suppliers of intermediate inputs—via backward and forward linkages.

25. Krugman (1995) states that the monopolistic competition assumption is not realistic, but it simplifies the model by eliminating the possibility of strategic behavior.

26. César Hidalgo and Ricardo Hausmann (2009) make a complementary argument using network analysis.

27. In a full model, this equation would be one component of a system of equations that specifies functions for the other terms. One could also add an equation that makes D_L a function of A_L to illustrate a direct influence of accumulated knowledge on pecuniary externalities.

28. The full model, obviously, includes other factors that affect migration equilibria.

29. This last outcome will arise even if education only signals credentials.

Chapter 5

1. Note the similarity of this statement to Harold Lasswell's (1936) definition of politics: Who gets what, when, how.

2. Consider three related concepts of power: for Mushtaq Khan, *holding power* refers to a party's (usually an organization's) ability to maintain its position, to "the capability of an individual or group to engage and survive in conflicts" (2010, 6). Khan emphasizes organizational ability to mobilize support by "identifying and rewarding the right people through formal and informal networks" (2017, 5). For Jack Knight: "To exercise power over someone or some group is to affect by some means the alternatives available to that person or group" (1992, 41).

3. Samuel Bowles and Herbert Gintis (2008) specifies a fourth property that commonly appears in the literature: Party A employs sanctions or threats of sanctions.

Ferguson 2013, chap. 4, augments this fourth condition by adding manipulative communication (which more fully represents power3; see discussion of the three domains of power in this section). Manipulative communication alters interpretations of incentives; it augments possible sanctions with tactics like shifting blame to other parties. Here is a slightly more detailed definition: A's *power* is its ability to deliberately employ sanctions or manipulative communication to influence the incentives facing some party or parties B, and/or B's understanding of such incentives, in a manner that affects B's activity in directions A believes (perhaps mistakenly) will advance its goals that B would not have otherwise taken.

4. Institutional decay shrinks the basin of attraction surrounding institutional equilibria.

5. Ferguson 2013, chap. 3, applies a game-theoretic approach to Lukes's three faces of power. On normative entrepreneurs, see Posner 2000 and Sunstein 1996.

6. The discussion in this section draws on Basu 2000b and Ferguson 2013, chap. 4.

7. Dyadic models fail to address power externalities.

8. The six formats for triadic power are based on versions of triadic relations from Simmel discussed in Wolff 1950. In principle, more than one party may exercise triadic power.

9. Formats 1–4 and 6 relate directly to concepts discussed by Simmel. Format 5 relates directly to the concept of contested exchange applied to labor markets (Bowles and Gintis 1992).

10. In such instances, B and C may already be in conflict and compete for A's favor, or their competition over A's favor may induce conflict between them.

11. In principle, one could construct a spectrum ranging from full impartiality to pure favoritism, a case that eliminates potential for mediation.

12. Arjun Jayadev and Samuel Bowles (2006), citing Toufique 1997, offer an example of a possible eighth variant that mixes dyads and triads. In Bangladesh, cooperatives have rights to fish specific inland waters, but the individual fishers lack the power to prevent outsider fishing. They sell their rights to financiers or merchants (here, a type of intermediary regarding who has sufficient connections to employ coercive tactics and do so without government complaint for such extralegal activity). A dyadic economic relationship exists between co-op members and the merchant-financiers who then have a dyadic relation with potential infringers. The two dyads constitute a triad. One might consider the fishers to be party A (the initiator), but the intermediary is the party that exercises power. Moreover, in the initial dyad, the intermediary is an agent and the fishers are principals. Typical moral hazard problems may apply.

13. Stephen Brown, "Swedish Prime Minister Löfven Loses Confidence Vote," *Politico*, September 25, 2018, https://www.politico.eu/article/swedish-prime-minister-lofven-loses-confidence-vote-sweden-democrats-election/.

14. The large efficiency wage literature includes Shapiro and Stiglitz 1984 and Bulow and Summers 1986. Bowles (1985) directly links the employment exchange to "power in exchange." Basu (2000b) draws the link with triadic power. Ferguson

2013, chap. 3, addresses relations of efficiency and fair wage arguments to power, with attention to triads and power2. For a discussion of fair wage models, segmented labor markets, and implicit bargaining power, see Ferguson 2005.

15. Roger Ransom and Richard Sutch (2001) add that merchants could have faced product market competition from other suppliers of food, farm implements, and the like, but their monopoly on credit, combined with the need for credit among small farmers, enabled them to force farmers to purchase these items from them— effectively establishing a monopoly in these markets as well.

16. Howell Raines, "George Wallace, Segregation Symbol, Dies at 79." *New York Times*, September 14, 1979, https://www.nytimes.com/1998/09/14/us/george-wallace -segregation-symbol-dies-at-79.html.

17. Kuran (1995) notes that the term "living lie" also captures the concept of suppressing oneself to give others an impression. He distinguishes preference falsification from strategic voting, an act of strategic manipulation directed toward attaining one's true goals.

18. This dynamic fits Thomas Schelling's (1978) concept of self-fulfilling expectations.

19. As a "secularized religion . . . [it] offers a ready answer to any question whatsoever. . . . In an era when metaphysical and existential certainties are in a state of crisis, when people are being uprooted and alienated and are losing their sense of what this world means, this ideology inevitably has a certain hypnotic charm. To wandering humankind it offers an immediately available home: all one has to do is accept it, and suddenly everything becomes clear once more, life takes on new meaning, and all mysteries, unanswered questions, anxiety, and loneliness vanish. Of course, one pays dearly for this low-rent home: the price is abdication of one's own reason, conscience, and responsibility, for an essential aspect of this ideology is the consignment of reason and conscience to a higher authority" (Havel 2015, 25).

20. Here, Havel implies what Peter Digeser (1992) refers to as the fourth face of power.

21. Chapter 1 discusses expressive power, using the concept from Sunstein 1996.

22. Part III returns to this key role for formal institutions that operates even in systems with weak institutions.

23. Ferguson 2013, chap. 8, distinguishes between typical social norms and socially enforced conventions, and the latter fits this case better. For present purposes, however, the concept of a social norm is sufficient.

24. The role of ideology fits Kuran's (1995) concept of how preference falsification can influence private preferences via a *social proof* heuristic in which individuals ascribe validity to ideas in proportion to their observance of consistent beliefs displayed by others. Additionally, public opinion can influence even private opinions that rely on personal experience by shaping the ideas that individuals encounter. A related review of endogenous preferences appears in Bowles 1998. Along similar lines, Anders Poulsen and Odile Poulsen (2006) offer an indirect evolutionary model of the influence of institutions on preferences.

25. Society organizes human life as the mind organizes cognition, meaning that it constructs a coherent system in a fashion that is analogous to the way the mind constructs a system of thinking out of dispersed observations; social forms created by individuals take on a life of their own (Walker 1959).

26. Nonelite individuals with power include temporary leaders of militias and the like.

27. Note that concern for reputation implies social in addition to material preferences. Concerns need not be only self-oriented, though concern for political survival typically is self-oriented, at least in the sense that a person's power is an instrument for achieving broader goals.

28. Acemoglu, Johnson, and Robinson (2005) discuss effects of the Atlantic trade on growth. For a more comprehensive treatment, see Brenner 1993.

29. I choose not to enter the debate over the extent to which the United Kingdom has a constitution. For this argument, the new political institutions of 1688 placed structural limits on the power of the English monarchs.

30. The Navigation Acts of 1651 and 1660 offer earlier examples (Acemoglu, Johnson, and Robinson 2005).

31. The core idea appears in Acemoglu, Johnson, and Robinson 2004. A less formal version with many historical examples appears in Acemoglu and Robinson 2012. The related concept of political losers as an impediment to development appears in Acemoglu and Robinson 2000.

32. Williamson 1979 discusses hold-up relations among firms.

33. Chapter 8 offers a more complete discussion of Roessler's (2011) argument. Figure 8A.1 offers a game representation of a civil war–coup trap.

34. More formally, subgame perfect equilibrium is for B to choose Not Invest and for A to choose Seize if B chooses Invest.

35. One could add probabilities of B's retaining power for actions Block and Not Block and make these probabilities (and the other variables) functions of additional variables that reflect the social, political, and economic context.

36. Acemoglu and Robinson (2000) cite Joel Mokyr (1990) on this last point.

37. Following Russia's 1856 loss in the Crimean War, which clearly demonstrated the relationship between industrialization and military power, the Russian tsars, especially Nicholas II when he took power in 1894, began promoting industrialization—too late, however, to avoid the Russian Revolution.

38. Analogously, Barrington Moore (1966) attributes the development of early- to mid-twentieth-century authoritarianism in Germany and Russia to grossly inequitable landholdings.

39. Landholders play the positions of triad parties A and C when they both hire labor and provide finance.

40. Here is a political example: In 1940, at the beginning of Hitler's invasion of the USSR, Stalin ordered peasants to burn their fields to reduce the Germans' expected benefits from invasion.

41. In such cases, prior resolutions of H4's commitment CAPs may falter, generating a new set of CAPs.

42. Western European capitalism emerged from centuries of conflict that eventually led to constraints on nongovernmental use of organized violence. Conflicts in 2018 Yemen and Syria reflect an absence of settlement.

43. Mancur Olson's (1993) stationary bandit offers a unilateral example that abstracts from issues of negotiation and enforcement across groups whose interests differ. A stationary bandit extracts at a monopoly profit level instead of preying on others, as do roving bandits. Francis Fukuyama (2014), however, citing historical examples, asserts that states rarely extract at such a monopoly level.

44. Rent distributions underlie political equilibria (Accmoglu and Robinson 2008; North et al. 2009). Economic equilibria also depend on distributions of rents. Some rents that appear inefficient when compared to hypothetical clearing markets may, nonetheless, contribute to stability in a growth-enhancing fashion (Acemoglu and Robinson 2013).

45. Second-order CAPs of credible contracting generate a similar inseparability of political and economic processes at the microlevel (Ferguson 2013, chap. 3).

Chapter 6

1. Japan held Korea as a colony from 1910 until 1945.

2. Analogously, discussing successful economic innovation in El Salvador, Ricardo Hausmann and Dani Rodrik state: "What we have in mind here is not innovation and research and development (R&D) in the sense that these terms are used in the advanced economies, but the ability to identify and generate productive activities in the Salvadoran context" (2005, 64).

3. A modified equation (4.1) could define A as policy innovations and add a term for social capital. See Ferguson 2013, chap. 9, for more on social capital and CAPs.

4. Economic performance is another (obvious) source of legitimacy.

5. African National Congress, Freedom Charter, June 26, 1955, https://www.anc1912.org.za/freedom-charter.

6. The term "steps" is a simplification. These developments can occur simultaneously, and interactions in later steps can influence earlier steps. Entrepreneurs may glean ideas from target audiences or civil servants.

7. On policy entrepreneurs, see Kingdon 2003.

8. See Greif 2006 on institutional persistence.

9. Points 1, 2, 5, 6, and most of 4 appear in Hall and Thelen 2009 and Hall 2016.

10. Peter Hall and Kathleen Thelen (2009) note four sources of institutional ambiguity: imprecise specification of rules, incomplete foresight of cognitively limited rule drafters, varying implicit assumptions about how rules operate, and the discretion of rule enforcers.

11. Macro-level punctuation may accomplish radical reform with significant restructuring of institutions—usually combining deliberate action with multiple unplanned responses. The degree to which reformers' intentions influence such outcomes depends significantly on the extent of their limited foresight and their ability to resolve CAPs, and sometimes luck.

12. Baumgartner et al.'s (2009) general punctuation hypothesis for policymaking addresses cognitive roots and permits different stable-phase duration along with context-specific institutional impact on punctuation intensity. Section 3 elaborates.

13. Arguably, punctuation dynamics, like many complex adaptive phenomena, are scale free.

14. See Baumgartner and Jones 1993; Baumgartner et al. 2009, 2011, 2018; Sabatier 1987, Sabatier and Jenkins-Smith 1993; Sabatier 1998; Sabatier and Weible 2007; Weible 2008; and Kingdon 2003. A fourth policy framework, the Institutional Analysis and Development (IAD) Framework of Elinor Ostrom (2005), receives considerable attention in Ferguson 2013, especially in chap. 8, 9, and 12.

15. Paul Cairney (2012) and Sabatier and Weible (2007) also treat these three frameworks as complementary.

16. Baumgartner et al. (2009) contrast the universality of limited cognition with institutional differences, noting that punctuation thresholds are context dependent. Jale Tosun and Samuel Workman (2018) state that the information-processing and policy image concepts of PET can apply to multiple settings. Wai Fung Lam and Kwan Nok Chan (2015) find that administrative change in Hong Kong exhibits punctuation dynamics. Chan and Shuang Zhao (2016), using data from Chinese provinces, assert that restricted information transmission in authoritarian systems generates more pronounced punctuation than in democracies. Sojin Jang, Christopher Weible, and Kyudong Park (2016) apply the ACF to South Korea. Valéry Ridde (2009) applies the MSF to Burkina Faso.

17. For simplicity, we assume one set of related issues per domain. Additionally, other analytical units appear in the literature: interest organizations (rather than advocacy coalitions) and economic sectors or specific policy issues (rather than policy domains). Advocacy coalitions, however, more directly meet the present focus on innovative ideas, and interest organizations often belong to coalitions. Policy domains apply more appropriately to this chapter's focus on H3 and H4 political constraints than do economic sectors. Chapter 9, however, addresses meso-level economic sectors.

18. Weible (2008), citing Sabatier 1987, offers a related definition: semiautonomous decision-making networks that operate within policy domains.

19. Members of policy communities operate as elites with respect to designing the details of policies, though usually not with respect to the broad directions of policy. "The communities involve bureau chiefs and officials in operating agencies, academics and consultants employed by research-and-development firms, publishers or editors of professional journals and magazines, representatives from business firms that are major suppliers of goods and services employed in the area, members of legislative staffs and legislators themselves who specialize in the subject, and other elected officials and lobbyists with interest in the policies" (Walker 1981, 79).

20. Recall that Chapter 1's discussion of mental models implies a parallel punctuation dynamic that operates at the level of individual cognition and, collectively, for institutions (as shared mental models). See also Ferguson 2013, chap. 6.

21. Baumgartner et al. (2009) assert that punctuation dynamics are *scale free*, meaning the same basic dynamic applies at different levels of aggregation (e.g., macro and meso). Punctuation reflects the power-law dynamics of complexity theory.

22. Baumgartner and Jones draw on Simon 1955, 1977, 1983, 1985; see also True, Jones, and Baumgartner 2007.

23. "Attending to problems is the sine qua non of policy making . . . a precursor of policy changes" (Baumgartner et al. 2011, 955).

24. "As issues are defined in public discourse in different ways and rise and fall in the public agenda, existing policies can be either reinforced or questioned" (Baumgartner et al. 2018, 56). Thus, relatively complex issues—such as budget allocations—exhibit higher degrees of punctuation, meaning longer stability and more dramatic changes, than do simpler issues. Distributions of policy outputs show increasing levels of kurtosis (reflecting "fat tails" and power-law dynamics) as the degree of complexity increases (Baumgartner et al. 2009).

25. For a review, see Campbell 2002.

26. See Sabatier 1987, 1993; Sabatier and Weible 2007. Because many individuals and organizations exert influence, aggregating them into coalitions simplifies analysis; shared beliefs and coordination strategies offer coherence (Jenkins-Smith et al. 2018). Advocacy coalitions also resemble Kuran's (1995) pressure groups (activists, nonactivists, lobbyists, and various informal and formal associations). Nonactivists need not agree with group goals but may associate for public acceptance or other rewards. Activists, by contrast, have more closely aligned public and private preferences. This distinction fits Weible's (2008) primary versus auxiliary members.

27. Jenkins-Smith et al. (2018, 136) note that Imre Lakatos's distinction between "hard core" axiomatic propositions and a "protective belt" of auxiliary hypothesis is a "recognizable ancestor" to the ACF concept of beliefs.

28. Jens Koed Madsen, Richard Bailey, and Toby Pilditch (2018) develop a model of echo chambers in large social networks. Even perfectly rational (Bayesian updating) agents will, despite communication among them, polarize opinion over time.

29. Baumgartner et al. develop this concept using the term *policy images*. Policy visions alter public preferences (see the discussion of preference falsification in Chapter 5).

30. A Nash bargaining model with variable power parameters can represent relations between sources of coalition power and distributed net benefits. Ferguson 2013, chap. 4, applies such a model to exercises of power1.

31. In this regard, coalition elites and policy entrepreneurs may act as normative entrepreneurs.

32. "The vast majority of policy making occurs within policy subsystems and involves negotiations among specialists" (Sabatier and Weible 2007, 193). C. Wright Mills (1956) describes an "iron triangle" (policy monopoly) of top-level military, industry, and US government officials.

33. The actions and reactions of opponents may unwittingly resolve internal coalition CAPs by motivating unified response. Adversarial coalitions often exhibit a

"devil shift" whereby each side tends to overestimate both the bad intentions and power of opponents (Sabatier and Weible 2007).

34. See James Q. Wilson's (1980) cost-benefit policy typology.

35. Chapter 8's concept of a multipolar configuration of authority can reflect a dysfunctional ruling coalition whose internal factions operate as adversarial coalitions.

36. Jenkins-Smith et al. (2018) draw these links.

37. Gupta (2014) does not utilize these types, but she notes that access to policy input was far greater in the latter period. The post-1970s transition might fit into PET.

38. Baumgartner and Jones (1993) link punctuation to waves of enthusiasm and criticism.

39. Rapid punctuation precludes coordinated response. Multiple CAPs of consolidating and implementing new arrangements follow—one reason that revolutions often fail to achieve initial objectives.

40. Herweg, Zahariadis, and Zohlnhöfer (2018) extend MSF using two stages of emergence: an agenda stage that fits Kingdon's initial conception and a decision stage into which agenda emergence is an input that enhances the role of the political stream, introduces political entrepreneurs, and responds to political institutions.

41. For Herweg et al., the MSF "negates the existence of a rational solution to a given problem" (2018, 18). Here, I would replace "rational solution" with "identifiable, unique, and optimal solution." Rationality applies to thought processes, not to solutions. Moreover, even individual substantive rationality need not imply collective rationality—because of CAPs. The MSF assumptions are, in fact, consistent with the concept of boundedly rational actors.

42. Kingdon (2003) identifies national mood, activities of organized groups, and turnover in government personnel as key political-stream variables.

43. In less institutionalized settings, relevant exchanges may include other types of favors.

44. Here is a typology of political agents, loosely based on Lohmann 2000: *open activists* publicly challenge existing arrangements; *hidden activists* publicly support and discretely challenge; *opportunists*, seeking gain, neither support nor challenge given arrangements; *parasitic beneficiaries* benefit from the status quo and follow rules, but their actions tend to erode the purpose (or spirit) of extant institutions; *supportive beneficiaries* publicly support the status quo without undermining it. All five types participate in stable-phase layering and conversion to varying degrees, reflecting different incentives. Such activity on the part of any of the first four may undermine system stability. Supportive beneficiaries, however, may counter with their own layering and conversion. As punctuation approaches, boundaries between the types shift; opportunists leap onto bandwagons. Ferguson 2015 applies this typology to prospects for radical reform during punctuation cycles of institutional systems.

45. Ferguson 2013 and 2015 relate punctuation to radical reform. On the influence of new ideas for development, see Rodrik 2014; on institutional innovation, see Mahoney and Thelen 2009.

46. In game-theoretic terms, the onset of punctuation shifts game focal points (Schelling 1960) or correlated equilibria (Aumann 1987).

47. On information cascades, see Watts 2002. On social network theory, see Jackson 2008. Ferguson 2013, chap. 11, discusses several network models, with relationships to CAPs.

48. Network position reflects key network properties, such as the degree of a node and measures of betweenness.

49. For Romer (1993), an "idea gap" impedes economic development. Introducing new ideas (nearly costless to duplicate) thus provides an inexpensive path to development. Unfortunately, this assertion ignores H1–H4 CAPs related to political context, feasibility, and implementation.

50. Most of the discussion in the remainder of this section uses concepts from Weible 2008 that address ways to apply expert opinion (as distinct from anecdotal opinion) to PET, ACF, and MSF. Here, I add reference to this text's approach and allow a possibly broad interpretation of "expert" that includes participants with substantially above-average experience (of whatever sort) addressing specific problems in specific contexts, including areas with weak formal institutions.

51. Types I and II may utilize political innovations in efforts to enhance internal organization.

52. Richard Nixon's domestic policy affairs advisor, John Ehrlichman, referring to a (later resolved) early-1970s scientific debate about ozone layer depletion, reputedly said that if scientists cannot agree, the White House will not pay attention to them (Dotto and Schiff, 61; quoted in Rowlands 1995, 45).

53. Here, Kingdon's (2003, 127) notion of "softening up" policymakers is far too limited.

Chapter 7

1. Sections 1 and 3 address these concepts.

2. Constitutional rules delineate members of a community and assign foundational decision-making authority (Ostrom 2005).

3. For a detailed discussion of these issues, see Menkhaus 2014, Malejacq 2016, and Mukhopadhyay 2014.

4. A related distinction contrasts micro- with macro-level institutions.

5. Khan, citing Knight 1992, states: "The distribution of power describes the likelihood of particular organizations 'holding out' in contests seeking to influence institutional outcomes. . . . Moreover, we know from game theory that the participants in contests and conflicts are themselves unsure of their real holding power and that is why contests and conflicts happen" (Khan 2017, 5, 8).

6. Note the relationship to a capability approach to development, Khan states: "Even if powerful groups captured productive assets and established property rights over them, they would typically not survive in competitive markets without significant additional assistance and capability building" (2010, 26).

7. This statement could imply a failure to resolve H2 coordination and H1 provision CAPs associated with structural transformation, but Khan's contrast between clientelism and precapitalist settlements implies something deeper. In terms of Robert Heilbroner's (1992) discussion of the emergence of capitalism, such societies do not possess foundations for creating markets in the factors of production.

8. This cell's characteristics resemble those of a fragile LAO.

9. Khan (2017) notes some exceptions to this transparency statement for distribution to ethnic constituencies.

10. This quadrant is similar to NWW's LAO, but distinctions are more complicated than their fragile, basic, and mature categories, and their doorstep conditions do not apply.

11. The accompanying state may exhibit characteristics of Chapter 3's discussion of Timothy Besley and Torsten Persson's (2011) S2 or S3 states, with a potential for resource rents to support longer-term stability.

12. This trade-off resembles Philip Roessler's (2011) civil war–coup trap. See Chapter 8.

13. See also Doner, Ritchie, and Slater 2005 and Whitfield and Therkildsen 2011.

14. On these points, Khan (2010) cites Khan 2000, 2008, and 2009; Doner and Ramsay 2000; and Rock 2000.

15. Nevertheless, these developments set foundations for 1980s South Asian development with more open economies (Khan 2008, 2009).

16. On Korea, Khan (2010) cites Amsden 1989, Kohli 1994, and Khan 2000; on Thailand, Khan 2008 and Phongpaichit and Baker 2009; and on West Bengal, Khan 2008.

17. For Sen (2013), Khan's framework can explain growth acceleration but not long-term maintenance.

18. Pritchett et al. (2018) note that distinct patterns of elite beliefs about the environment and strategies can help explain the contrast between the developmental outcomes for South Korea and Zimbabwe—both fit Table 7.2's quadrant A.

19. Pritchett and Werker (2012) configure the horizontal dimension slightly differently: high rent versus competitive, without the qualification "regulatory." In Chapter 9, I follow that approach.

20. Policy arrangements in quadrants 1 and 2 (e.g., the tax rate) should reflect the relative bargaining power of involved business and state actors.

21. The *impersonally enforced rule/conducive* quadrant fits developed economies with strong institutions.

Chapter 8

1. Recall that *elites* are agents who directly influence policy—public or private—within their own organizations and/or with respect to others. CEOs, for example, not only directly influence internal policies of their firms; they may also influence government policies or those of other private organizations and coalitions.

2. Depending on the question of analysis, one can model the actions of organizations as those of a single agent, with varying degrees of attention to internal distributions of power.

3. Note that the concept of disruptive capability broadens the scope of a PS beyond a focus on violence capacity (as implied in North, Wallis, and Weingast 2009 and elsewhere). This concept fits Richard Doner, Bryan Ritchie, and Dan Slater's (2005) concept of political survivability of elites. Moreover, political survival requires coalitions; leaders try to minimize the size of a coalition but can be forced to increase its size due to social conflict from elites (of relevant groups) or from a threat of disruptive mass mobilization.

4. For an insightful discussion of the Colombian civil war, see Steele 2017.

5. Multipolarity is analogous to Chapter 5's adversarial relations among insider coalitions.

6. Kelsall and vom Hau (2019) mention an intermediate category: a balanced configuration (requires some negotiation among insiders). A less parsimonious analysis could add horizontal relations among insider groups and vertical relations within them. To avoid three or more dimensions, this typology collapses these power details into the COA. An analysis of policy implementation could, however, augment any relevant quadrant with intragroup vertical power relationships.

7. Chapter 3 addresses state capacity along a single scale from weak to strong, with some distinction between fiscal and legal capacity. Imke Harbers and Abbey Steele (2019) offer a two-dimensional concept that addresses subnational variation in state provision of public goods in a manner that complements the present distinction between multipolar and unipolar COAs. Their two-dimensional typology compares the range of public goods provided (comprehensive or limited) with the territorial uniformity of such provision (high or low). Four quadrants emerge: (1) comprehensive/high—a uniform welfare state that provides many public goods and distributes them across national territory; (2) comprehensive/low—a differentiated state that provides many public goods but distributes them in different combinations in different regions; (3) limited/high—a selectively uniform state, in which the central state prioritizes a limited menu of public goods, such as public education, with much regional heterogeneity in nonprioritized goods; and (4) limited/low—a disjointed state that operates with no uniform provision and much regional variation. We expect multipolar COAs to rate low on territorial uniformity.

8. Specifically, Slater stipulates that strong elite unity requires a sufficient internal threat from a class-based social movement that demands redistribution and that "exacerbates communal tensions" (2010, 14). Slater focuses on the long-term durability (or lack thereof) of authoritarian regimes, whereas I focus on medium-term stability of PSs. The approaches are complementary because the unipolarity versus multipolarity of authoritarian regimes depends on Slater's concept of a viable protection pact.

9. Using an endogenous growth theory approach, Hausmann et al. (2005) focus on identifying whether growth fails because of low returns to investment, low private appropriability, or low access to finance and, for each, the key sources of distortion

366   Notes to Chapter 8

from market and/or government failure. Here, each distortion is a type of CAP. My approach also considers constraints on political development and interactions between the political context within a type of PS and the corresponding difficulty of addressing any given type of distortion.

10. Lindsay Whitfield and Ole Therkildsen (2011) and Doner et al. (2005) apply this principle to the emergence of industrial policy in South Korea and Taiwan. Since elites rely on coalitional support to maintain their positions, a key question is what constraints does such need place on their actions (Whitfield and Therkildsen 2011).

11. Elites face the politician's dilemma (Geddes 1994): conflict between needs of one's own political survival and longer-run goals of economic performance and regime stability (Whitfield and Therkildsen 2011, 17).

12. Recall from Chapter 2, that procedural accountability involves public oversight in the selection, tenure, and behavior of public officials, as well as creating avenues for input, whereas substantive accountability means responding to general public interests.

13. For a large, diverse country, national averages conceal much variation. At a subnational level, different states have distinctly different meso-level PSs, and there is variation across specific policy domains. India's courts and national elections, for example, function better than many other public services. Chapter 9 addresses meso-level interactions in more detail.

14. Roessler discusses exclusion from governing regimes without reference to PSs; he implies that former coalition partners and their ethnic groups moved from insiders to outsiders. Using data on 35 countries and 220 ethnic groups over the years 1946–2005, Roessler's empirical analysis supports two hypotheses: First, "Ethnic exclusion substitutes civil war risk for coup risk" (Roessler 2011, 302). Second, rulers more likely exclude groups with access to the state's coercive mechanisms (army, police), doing so at a higher risk of civil war. African leaders were four times more likely to purge former anticolonial partners than other government officials. Apparently, addressing an immediate H4 commitment CAP was worth the risk of subsequent conflict.

15. This second item reflects a key condition posed by Doner et al. (2005): the influence of an external threat on systemic vulnerability. Citing Riker 1962, the authors note that political survival for leaders requires forming coalitions, which leaders try to keep as small as possible, but credible threats of disruptive mass mobilization or external invasion can motivate coalition enlargement.

16. Rwanda's "Vision 2020" has served as "the only hymn sheet to which everyone needs to abide" (Chemouni 2017, 10; cited by Yanguas 2017). The RPF has faced no significant challenge from external factions; potential challenges from below have been preempted or diffused via participatory processes (Chemouni 2017, 32). The SF, at least via cooptation, also includes the small Batwa ethnic group and security personnel, along with representatives of foreign donors. The longevity of this PS likely depends on the extent to which the RPF leadership can forge a Rwandan national identity that crosses ethnic boundaries.

17. Again, these may be regarded as poles along a spectrum.

18. These three prerequisites appear in Doner et al. (2005), though their third item includes only external existential threats. Slater (2010), however, focuses on internal threats.

19. A developmental state features "organizational complexes in which expert and coherent bureaucratic agencies collaborate with organized private sectors to spur national economic transformation" (Doner et al. 2005, 328). They develop Weberian bureaucracies, along with substantive state–private sector linkages (Ibid., 334). Path A bears some resemblance to Timothy Besley and Torsten Persson's (2011) *common interest state*, which possesses coherent political institutions, develops state capacity, and uses fiscal resources for common interests, such as national defense.

20. Both countries received military aid from the United States, but not enough to meet domestic demands, especially civilian. Moreover, the 1973 US withdrawal of troops from Asia exacerbated the prospect of external threat.

21. A large literature supports the notion that concentrated landholding is a barrier to economic and political development (e.g., Moore 1966). Additional motivation for land reform in both countries arose from government fear of communist sympathies because China and North Korea had both recently conducted their own versions of land reform.

22. South Korea had little ethnic fractionalization, a condition that eased establishing unipolarity and public support.

23. See Doner et al. 2005 and You 2013.

24. In Slater's (2010) terms, South Korea had not possessed all necessary conditions for long-term authoritarian ordering of power. By 1987, elites were not unified in support of the regime. Yet, the transition to democracy facilitated an alternative type of unipolarity (which may be currently unraveling).

25. Romain Malejaq (2016) develops a typology of weak and failed states, most of which could fit within Q3 because the presence of active warlords suggests both multipolarity and a narrow SF. The typology compares resources available to the state with those available to warlords, high or low for each. A high/high combination, for example, implies parallel regions of power: the state controls some areas and different warlords control others, as in Afghanistan in the 1990s. In contrast, the low/low combination signifies rival islands of territorial control that continuously engage in nonconventional warfare—possibly the absence of a PS or an unstable Q3 arrangement that also fits North et al.'s (2009) fragile LAO.

26. The Pol Pot regime's misguided attempts to increase agricultural production via collectivization might appear to indicate a terribly misguided attempt to follow path C, but lacking restraints on his power, Pol Pot's extermination of opponents—real and imagined—fits path D.

Chapter 9

1. For Denmark, average annual per capita income growth from 1870 to 2003 was 1.94%, from 1890 to 1915, 1.93%; and from 1980 to 2003, 1.91%. (Author's calculation

using data from World Bank Development Indicators, https://datacatalog.worldbank
.org/dataset/world-development-indicators).

2. Table 9.1 is a slightly adjusted version of Pritchett et al. 2018, fig. 1.11, which
was adapted from Pritchett and Werker 2012.

3. Table 9.2 modifies Pritchett et al. 2018, fig. 1.14.

4. Enforceable formal contracts also rely on actions, not identities. For deals,
however, the specification of relevant actions primarily relies on informal institutions and personal networks. On Tajikistan, see Taylor Beckwith-Ferguson, "(Hitch)
Hiking the Pamirs," Blog post, August 20, 2019, http://www.taylorbf.com/blog
/hitchhiking-the-pamirs/.

5. This combination can also apply to unenforced formal procedures. Ironically,
informal ordered deals (e.g., bribes) can offer more predictable outcomes.

6. Recall from Chapter 7 that Pritchett et al.'s *deal* possesses "*characteristics* or
actions of specific entities which do not spill over with any precedential value to any
other future transaction between other entities" (2018, 24).

7. Similar assertions about the developmental potential of rent sharing appear in
Acemoglu and Robinson 2008 and in North, Wallis, and Weingast 2009. See Besley
and Persson 2011 on taxes and growth.

8. Much of this logic, with a similar game of strategic interactions among three
parties, appears in Razo 2008, 37. Later, we consider whether "no action" implies dis-
honored deals.

9. No single enforcer has enough power to deter D. Credible enforcement relies on
overlapping protection networks that emerge from private rent-sharing agreements
between selected asset holders and powerful officials or regime supporters. Various
Hs contract with several enforcers, some of whom protect more than one deal. The
applicable rent share (bR) offers enforcers a stake in restraining D. Armando Razo
(2008) uses social network analysis to apply this argument to the 1870–1910 Díaz dictatorship in Mexico, which he calls a *limited dictatorship*.

10. For simplicity, this discussion ignores discounting future values.

11. $\partial R/\partial g > 0$; $\partial R/\partial \theta > 0$.

12. $\partial \gamma/\partial \theta_{t-1} > 0$; $\partial \gamma/\partial B_{SF} > 0$; $\partial \gamma/\partial T > 0$.

13. $\partial F/\partial g_t < 0$; $\partial F/\partial \theta_{t-1} < 0$; $\partial F/\partial \zeta_t > 0$.

14. This discussion's focus on seizing revenue abstracts from the possibility of
D's seizing existing assets in the form of physical capital, land, or point-source re-
sources. If H has no assurance of non-seizure at the outset, we have path D. This
model, while a simplification, offers insight into the distinction between paths C and
D. Alternatively, the model could represent situations with foreign-owned point-
source resources—nondomestic enforcers—whom D does not want to antagonize.
Likewise, large landholders may have militias that D would rather not antagonize.
Additional games could model these trade-offs.

15. In words, H's fallback earnings must be less than H's expected revenue (including bribes), which is less than H's after-tax income, which must be less than the
cost D faces if punished, which must be less than the ratio of bribe revenue to the

per-unit cost to E of punishing D. One could solve this condition for minimum and maximum values of t, b, and R in terms of the other variables.

16. This scenario applies to a variation of Figure 9.1, where (9.1) and (9.2) fail; F and $v \to 0$ (an informal sector H has few alternatives); (9.3) either holds or not, depending on random fluctuation in R (or other factors); and $C_D \to 0$, reflecting no reliance on D for initiating a deal.

17. With Q4's narrow SF, Chapter 8's path A prerequisite I—that is, a need to retain at least minimal loyalty among broad masses by delivering benefits—fails. For simplicity, this discussion ignores H2 CAPs, which play a far greater role in Q2.

18. Path A fits David Booth and Frederick Golooba-Mutebi's (2012) concept of developmental patrimonialism: the ruling elite acquires an interest in, and a capability for, centrally managing economic rents to enhance its own and others' long-run incomes rather than maximizing short-run gains.

19. Yet in these circumstances, open competition can lead to unpredictable and inconsistent government behavior as it strives to maintain some balance between foreign and domestic firms. Given the existing PS, a government has little ability to discipline private firms. Ensuing disorder could undermine investor confidence (Behuria and Goodfellow 2018).

20. The Malaysian Chinese Association and Malaysian Indian Congress, representing business elites, joined a multiparty coalition, "the alliance," in 1952. They traded economic favors for supporting Malay privileges (Ritchie 2005). The breadth of the Malaysian SF during this period is, however, debatable. It was broad ethnically but narrow in terms of economic groupings. Labor and small enterprises were, respectively, repressed and ignored (Ibid.). This combination fits Khan's concept of weak vertical opposition. I retain the label "broad SF" because the ethnic base motivated widespread redistribution policies for most of the period (diminishing toward the end).

21. For a summary of these trends, see Sen and Tyce 2018.

22. This summary draws heavily from Sen and Tyce 2018.

23. Sen and Tyce (2018) say the PS moved to Khan's vulnerable authoritarian coalition.

24. Section 1's unipolar discussion ignores this distinction because both selective and universal public goods benefit selective patrons, and Section 2's discussion mentions this distinction but does not model it.

25. This text does not attempt to explain the origins of specific types of PSs, but in societies with little institutional development, resource curses often generate significant factional conflict, rendering Q3 status a likely outcome of prior history. Given Q3's multipolarity, even a significant external threat may not generate sufficient mutual understanding to prompt elite coordination. If such understanding does develop, the COA becomes unipolar and the PS moves to Q4.

26. In terms of Chapter 3's fiscal capacity model, Q1 fits the redistributive state with a relatively low probability of high-value public goods ($\varphi < 0.5$). Q4 path C may have a slightly higher value, though with more focus on club goods (a modified

Chapter 3 model could add this distinction). For Q2 path B, $\varphi > 0.5$, and path A reflects a common interest state.

27. In terms of Figure 9.2, the $v_{\text{RESC}} + F$ line moves rightward and $R(1 - t - b)$ moves leftward, potentially eliminating prospects for meeting condition (9.3).

28. The fractured nature of the macro-level PS allows some regional variation.

Conclusion

1. Early in the process of writing the manuscript, David Booth pointed this out to me.

2. My reading of Cartwright and Hardie is a fortuitous outcome of observing a policy class cotaught by my colleagues Doug Hess (political science) and Monty Roper (anthropology).

Chapter 5 Appendixes

1. This summary draws from Basu 2000a, 234–38. Bhaduri and Basu both also discuss innovation under these conditions, a topic not pursued in this Appendix.

2. Kaushik Basu (2000a), summarizing Bhaduri's model, notes this same principle. Lenders (landlords or merchants) often prefer lending to borrowers with whom they have some personalistic relationship (e.g., landlord-tenant). Personal knowledge about the borrower also presents a barrier to entry (Bottomley 1964), which then allows charging a monopoly interest rate and reduces the tenant's ability to escape from the relationship. This logic provides a possible explanation for observed interest rate premiums in rural developing areas and the high interest rates that appear in the debt-trap model.

3. For Samuel Bacharach and Edward Lawler (1981), party A's bargaining power increases with party B's dependence on A: the more B depends on A, the greater A's bargaining power.

4. These arrangements can, by addressing moral hazard, push out the production possibilities frontier, facilitating greater returns. In principle, both parties could gain, either could be held to an initial utility (likely subsistence for tenants), or either could be pushed to lower utility (Braverman and Stiglitz 1982, 707–8).

5. This figure closely imitates Timur Kuran's (1995, 70) fig. 4.5. A similar diagram with similar expectational logic (though not applied to preference falsification) appears in Schelling 1978, fig. 1, 104.

6. More complicated adjustments could alter α and β or a and b.

Chapter 6 Appendix

1. The negative sign before α implies continuously increasing vulnerability to shocks, a simplifying assumption.

2. A more complicated model could make d_t, l_t, γ_t, and ϕ_t functions of relevant variables.

Chapter 8 Appendix

1. This civil war–coup trap game is based on logic from Roessler 2011.

2. A more complicated model could distinguish between elites and followers in each coalition.

3. For simplicity, this treatment does not address an intermediate case of completely ignoring excluded factions, but similar logic could apply. In such a case, B has very little power and so poses no threat, and the cost to A of repressing B is greater than 0.

4. A more complicated model (like that in Chapter 3) would show the precise allocation between g and v and could allow for B (when included in the SF) to peacefully take power in t_2 (wins an election) with probability γ. The X_A and X_B functions would need to account for γ, along with any differences in B's allocation between g and v, and the impact of σ on B's distribution of v. Another complication might specify different (polarized) coalition valuations of g by designating specific value terms α_A and α_B, a change that would enhance the importance of γ.

5. This last assumption abstracts from an RC's trade-offs between g and v. Chapter 3 and Appendix 3A discuss this trade-off in more detail, making both terms endogenous. In terms of Chapter 3, this treatment assumes that α has a (fixed) intermediate value, meaning that an incumbent coalition always has an incentive to use some, but not all, available revenue for g.

6. Besley and Persson (2011) make this point.

7. Even if combat pay involves a higher wage than that paid in, say, the manufacturing sector, the tax revenue used to pay the army and other expenses depends on income (y), which depends on economic development.

8. For simplicity, I have assumed that Θ is constant over the periods considered.

References

Abdulai, Abdul-Gafaru, and Sam Hickey. 2016. "The Politics of Development Under Competitive Clientelism: Insights from Ghana's Education Sector." *African Affairs* 115 (458): 44–72.

Acemoglu, Daron, Simon Johnson, and James Robinson. 2002. "Reversal of Fortune: Geography and Institutions in the Making of the Modern World Income Distribution." *Quarterly Journal of Economics* 118:1231–94.

———. 2004. "Institutions as the Fundamental Cause of Long-Run Growth." NBER Working Paper 10481. National Bureau of Economic Research, Cambridge, MA. https://www.nber.org/papers/w10481.pdf.

———. 2005. "The Rise of Europe: Atlantic Trade, Institutional Change and Economic Growth." *American Economic Review* 95:546–79.

Acemoglu, Daron A., and James A. Robinson. 2000. "Repression or Democratization." *European Economic Review* 44:683–93.

———. 2006. *Economic Origins of Dictatorship and Democracy*. Cambridge: Cambridge University Press.

———. 2008. "Persistence of Power, Elites, and Institutions." *American Economic Review* 98 (1): 267–93.

———. 2012. *Why Nations Fail: The Origins of Power, Prosperity, and Poverty*. New York: Crown Business.

———. 2013. "Economics Versus Politics: Pitfalls of Policy Advice." *Journal of Economic Perspectives* 27 (2): 173–92.

Aghion, Philippe, Eve Caroli, and Cecilia García-Peñalosa. 1999. "Inequality and Economic Growth: The Perspective of the New Growth Theories." *Journal of Economic Literature* 37 (4): 1615–60.

Akerlof, George A. 1970. "The Market for 'Lemons': Quality Uncertainty and the Market Mechanism." *Quarterly Journal of Economics* 84 (3): 488–500.

———. 1982. "Labor Contracts as Partial Gift Exchange." *Quarterly Journal of Economics* 97 (4): 543–69.

Akerlof, George A., and Rachel E. Kranton. 2000. "Economics and Identity." *Quarterly Journal of Economics* 115 (3): 715–52.

———. 2005. "Identity and the Economics of Organizations." *Journal of Economic Perspectives* 19 (1): 9–32.

———. 2010. *Identity Economics: How Our Identities Shape Our Work, Wages, and Well-Being.* Princeton, NJ: Princeton University Press.

Alesina, Alberto, Reza Baqir, and William Easterly. 1999. "Public Goods and Ethnic Divisions." *Quarterly Journal of Economics* 114 (4): 1243–84.

Alesina, Alberto, and Edward Glaeser. 2004. *Fighting Poverty in the US and Europe: A World of Difference.* Oxford, UK: Oxford University Press.

Alkire, Sabina, and James Foster. 2011. "Counting and Multidimensional Poverty Measurement." *Journal of Public Economics* 95 (7): 476–87.

Alkire, Sabina, and María Emma Santos. 2010. "Acute Multidimensional Poverty: A New Index for Developing Countries." UNDP Human Development Report Office Background Paper 2010/11. United Nations Development Programme, Geneva, Switzerland. http://hdr.undp.org/sites/default/files/hdrp_2010_11.pdf.

Almond, Douglas, Kenneth Y. Chay, and Michael Greenstone. 2007. "Civil Rights, the War on Poverty, and Black-White Convergence in Infant Mortality in the Rural South and in Mississippi." MIT Department of Economics Working Paper 07-04. Massachusetts Institute of Technology, Cambridge, MA.

Alvaredo, Facundo, Anthony Atkinson, Thomas Piketty, and Emmanuel Saez. 2013. "The Top 1 Percent in International and Historical Perspective." *Journal of Economic Perspectives* 27 (3): 3–20.

———. 2016. "The World Wealth and Income Database." World Inequality Database. http://www.wid.world.

Alvaredo, Facundo, Lucas Chancel, Thomas Piketty, Emmanuel Saez, and Gabriel Zucman. 2018. "The Elephant Curve of Global Inequality and Growth." *American Economic Association Papers and Proceedings* 108:103–8.

Amsden, Alice. 1989. *Asia's Next Giant: South Korea and Late Industrialization.* Oxford, UK: Oxford University Press.

Andrews, Matt, Lant Pritchett, and Michael Woolcock. 2013. "Escaping Capability Traps Through Problem Driven Iterative Adaptation (PDIA)." *World Development* 51:234–44.

Aoki, Masahiko. 2010. "Between Game Theory and Institutional Studies: The Dual-Dualities of the Institutional Process." SSRN, https://www.ssrn.com/index.cfm/en/.

———. 2011. "Institutions as Cognitive Media Between Strategic Interactions and Individual Beliefs." *Journal of Economic Behavior and Organization* 79:20–34.

Arrow, Kenneth J. 1962. "The Economic Implications of Learning by Doing." *Review of Economic Studies* 29 (3): 155–73.

Arthur, W. Brian. 1994. *Increasing Returns and Path Dependence in the Economy*. Ann Arbor: University of Michigan Press.

Atkinson, Anthony B., and Thomas Piketty, eds. 2010. *Top Incomes: A Global Perspective*. Oxford, UK: Oxford University Press.

Atkinson, Anthony, Thomas Piketty, and Emmanuel Saez. 2011. "Top Incomes in the Long Run of History." *Journal of Economic Literature* 49 (1): 3–71.

Aumann, Robert J. 1987. "Correlated Equilibrium as an Expression of Bayesian Rationality." *Econometrica* 55 (1): 1–18.

Australian Agency for International Development (AusAID). 2011. "Framework for Working in Fragile and Conflict-Affected States: Guidance for Staff." Canberra: AusAID. https://dfat.gov.au/about-us/publications/Documents/aid-fragile -conflict-affected-states-staff-guidance.pdf.

Bacharach, Samuel B., and Edward J. Lawler. 1981. *Bargaining: Power, Tactics and Outcomes*. San Francisco: Jossey-Bass.

Bachrach, Peter, and Morton S. Baratz. 1962. "Two Faces of Power." *American Political Science Review* 56 (4): 947–52.

Banerjee, Abhijit V., Paul J. Gertler, and Maitreesh Ghatak. 2002. "Empowerment and Efficiency: Tenancy Reform in West Bengal." *Journal of Political Economy* 110 (2): 239–80.

Banerjee, Abhijit V., and Lakshmi Iyer. 2005. "History, Institutions, and Economic Performance: The Legacy of Colonial Land Tenure Systems in India." *American Economic Review* 95 (4): 1190–1213.

Bardhan, Pranab. 2005. *Scarcity, Conflicts, and Cooperation: Essays in the Political and Institutional Economics of Development*. Cambridge, MA: MIT Press.

Bardhan, Pranab, and Dilip Mookherjee. 2017. "Clientelistic Politics and Economic Development: An Overview." Prepared for the Economic Development and Institutions (EDI) research network. http://people.bu.edu/dilipm/wkpap/EDIclientsurv May17Fin.pdf.

Basu, Kaushik. 1999. "Child Labor: Cause, Consequence, and Cure, with Remarks on International Labor Standards." *Journal of Economic Literature* 37 (3): 1083–1119.

———. 2000a. *Analytical Development Economics: The Less Developed Economy Revisited*. Second Printing. Cambridge, MA: MIT Press.

———. 2000b. *Prelude to Political Economy: A Study of the Social and Political Foundations of Economics*. Oxford, UK: Oxford University Press.

———. 2006. "Gender and Say: A Model of Household Behavior with Endogenously Determined Balance of Power." *The Economic Journal* 116 (511): 558–80.

———. 2011. *Beyond the Invisible Hand: Groundwork for a New Economics*. Princeton, NJ: Princeton University Press.

Basu, Kaushik, and Joseph Stiglitz, eds. 2016. *Inequality and Growth: Patterns and Policy*. Vol. 2: *Regions and Regularities*. New York: Palgrave Macmillan.

Baumgartner, Frank R., Christian Breunig, Christoffer Green-Pedersen, Bryan D. Jones, Peter B. Mortensen, Michiel Nuytemans, and Stefaan Walgrave. 2009.

"Punctuated Equilibrium in Comparative Perspective." *American Journal of Political Science* 53 (3): 603–20.

Baumgartner, Frank R., and Bryan D. Jones. 1993. *Agendas and Instability in American Politics*. Chicago: University of Chicago Press.

Baumgartner, Frank R., Bryan D. Jones, and Peter B. Mortensen. 2017. "Punctuated-Equilibrium Theory: Explaining Stability and Change in Public Policymaking." In *Theories of the Policy Process*, 4th ed., edited by Paul A. Sabatier and Christopher M. Weible, 55–101. Boulder, CO: Westview.

Baumgartner, Frank, Bryan Jones, and John Wilkerson. 2011. "Comparative Studies of Policy Dynamics." *Comparative Political Science* 44 (8): 947–72.

Becker, Gary. 1971. *The Economics of Discrimination*. 2nd ed. Chicago: University of Chicago Press.

Beckwith-Ferguson, Taylor. 2019. "(Hitch)Hiking the Pamirs." http://www.taylorbf.com/blog/hitchhiking-the-pamirs/.

Behuria, Pritish, and Tom Goodfellow. 2018. "The Disorder of 'Miracle Growth' in Rwanda: Understanding the Limitations of Transitions to Open Ordered Development." In *Deals and Development: The Political Dynamics of Growth Episodes*, edited by Lant Pritchett, Kunal Sen, and Eric Werker, 217–49. Oxford, UK: Oxford University Press.

Berg, Andrew, Jonathan D. Ostry, and Jeromin Zettelmeyer. 2012. "What Makes Growth Sustained?" *Journal of Development Economics* 98 (2): 149–66.

Besley, Timothy, and Torsten Persson. 2011. *Pillars of Prosperity: The Political Economics of Development Clusters*. Princeton, NJ: Princeton University Press.

Bhaduri, Amit. 1973. "A Study in Agricultural Backwardness Under Semi-Feudalism." *The Economic Journal* 83 (329): 120–37.

———. 1977. "On the Formation of Usurious Interest Rates in Backwards Agriculture." *Cambridge Journal of Economics* 1:341–52.

Birkland, Thomas. 2011. *An Introduction to the Policy Process: Theories, Concepts and Models of Public Policymaking*. 3rd ed. Armonk, NY: M. E. Sharpe.

Booth, David. 2015. "What Next for Political Settlements Theory and African Development?" Paper presented at the African Studies Association annual meeting, San Diego, CA, November 2.

Booth, David, and Frederick Golooba-Mutebi. 2012. "Developmental Patrimonialism? The Case of Rwanda." *African Affairs* 111 (444): 379–403.

Bottomley, A. 1964. "Interest Rate Determination in Underdeveloped Rural Areas." *American Journal of Agricultural Economics* 57:279–91.

Bowles, Samuel. 1985. "The Production Process in a Competitive Economy: Walrasian, Neo-Hobbesian, and Marxian Models." *American Economic Review* 75 (1): 16–36.

———. 1998. "Endogenous Preferences: The Cultural Consequences of Markets and Other Economic Institutions." *Journal of Economic Literature* 36 (1): 75–111.

———. 2004. *Microeconomics: Behavior, Institutions, and Evolution*. Princeton, NJ: Princeton University Press.

———. 2006. "Institutional Poverty Traps." In *Poverty Traps*, edited by Samuel Bowles, Steven N. Durlauf, and Karla Hoff, 116–38. Princeton, NJ: Princeton University Press.

———. 2017. *The Moral Economy: Why Good Incentives Are No Substitute for Good Citizens*. New Haven, CT: Yale University Press.

Bowles, Samuel, Steven N. Durlauf, and Karla Hoff, eds. 2006. *Poverty Traps*. Princeton, NJ: Princeton University Press.

Bowles, Samuel, and Herbert Gintis. 1992. "Power and Wealth in a Competitive Capitalist Economy." *Philosophy and Public Affairs* 21 (4): 324–53.

———. 1993. "The Revenge of *Homo Economicus*: Contested Exchange and the Revival of Political Economy." *Journal of Economic Perspectives* 7 (1): 83–102.

———. 2008. "Power." In *The New Palgrave Dictionary of Economics*, 2nd ed., edited by Steven Durlauf and Lawrence E. Blume, 6:565–70. New York: Palgrave Macmillan.

Bowles, Samuel, Herbert Gintis, and Melissa Osborne Groves, eds. 2005. *Unequal Chances: Family Background and Economic Success*. Princeton, NJ: Princeton University Press.

Braverman, Avashay, and Joseph Stiglitz. 1982. "Sharecropping and the Interlinking of Agrarian Markets." *American Economic Review* 72:695–715.

Brenner, Robert. 1993. *Merchants and Revolution: Commercial Change, Political Conflict, and London's Overseas Traders, 1550–1653*. Princeton, NJ: Princeton University Press.

Breschi, Stefano, and Francesco Lissoni. 2001. "Knowledge Spillovers and Local Innovation Systems: A Critical Survey." *Industrial and Corporate Change* 10 (4): 975–1005.

Brown, Archie. 2009. *The Rise and Fall of Communism*. Oxford, UK: Oxford University Press.

Bukenya, Badru, and Sam Hickey. 2018. "Dominance and Deals in Africa: How Politics Shapes Uganda's Transition from Growth to Transformation." In *Deals and Development: The Political Dynamics of Growth Episodes*, edited by Lant Pritchett, Kunal Sen, and Eric Werker, 183–216. Oxford, UK: Oxford University Press.

Bulow, Jeremy I., and Lawrence H. Summers. 1986. "A Theory of Dual Labor Markets with Applications to Industrial Policy, Discrimination and Keynesian Unemployment." *Journal of Labor Economics* 4 (3): 376–414.

Cairney, Paul. 2012. *Understanding the Policy Process*. New York: Palgrave Macmillan.

Campbell, John L. 2002. "Ideas, Politics, and Public Policy." *Annual Review of Sociology* 28:21–38.

Cardenas, Mauricio. 2010. "State Capacity in Latin America." *Economia* 10 (2): 1–45.

Cartwright, Nancy, and Jeremy Hardie. 2012. *Evidence-Based Policy*. Oxford, UK: Oxford University Press.

Chan, Kwan Nok, and Shuang Zhao. 2016. "Punctuated Equilibrium and the Information Disadvantage of Authoritarianism: Evidence from the People's Republic of China." *Policy Studies Journal* 44 (2): 134–55.

Chattopadhyay, Raghabendra, and Esther Duflo. 2004. "Women as Policy Makers: Evidence from a Randomized Policy Experiment in India." *Econometrica* 72 (5): 1409–43.

Chau, Nancy H., and Ravi Kanbur. 2013. "On Footloose Industries and Labor Disputes with Endogenous Information Asymmetry." *Review of Development Economics* 17 (2): 319–41.

Chaudhuri, Shubham, and Martin Ravallion. 2006. "Partially Awakened Giants: Uneven Growth in China and India." World Bank Policy Research Working Paper 4069. SSRN, https://www.ssrn.com/index.cfm/en/.

Chemouni, Benjamin. 2017. "The Politics of Core Public Sector Reform in Rwanda." ESID Working Paper 88. Effective States and Inclusive Development Research Centre, University of Manchester, UK. http://www.effective-states.org/wp-content/uploads/working_papers/final-pdfs/esid_wp_88_chemouni.pdf.

Coase, Ronald H. 1937. "The Nature of the Firm." *Economia* IV:386–405.

Coffé, Hilde, and Benny Geys. 2005. "Institutional Performance and Social Capital: An Application to the Local Government Level." *Journal of Urban Affairs* 27 (5): 485–501.

Cohen, Michael D., James G. March, and Johan P. Olsen. 1972. "A Garbage Can Model of Organizational Choice." *Administrative Science Quarterly* 17 (1): 1–25.

Cole, Matthew A., and Eric Neumayer. 2006. "The Impact of Poor Health on Factor Productivity." *Journal of Development Studies* 42 (6): 918–38.

Conley, Timothy G., and Christopher R. Udry. 2010. "Learning About a New Technology: Pineapple in Ghana." *American Economic Review* 100 (1): 35–69.

Conlisk, John. 1996. "Why Bounded Rationality?" *Journal of Economic Literature* 34 (2): 669–700.

Crawford, Sue, and Elinor Ostrom. 1995. "A Grammar of Institutions." *American Political Science Review* 89 (3): 582–600.

Currie, Janet. 2011. "Inequality at Birth: Some Causes and Consequences." *American Economic Review* 101 (3): 1–22.

Cyert, Richard M., and James G. March. 1963. *A Behavioral Theory of the Firm*. Englewood Cliffs, NJ: Prentice-Hall.

Dahl, Robert. 1957. "The Concept of Power." *Behavioral Science* 2:201–15.

Dasgupta, Partha. 1995. "The Population Problem: Theory and Evidence." *Journal of Economic Literature* 33:1879–1902.

Deaton, A. 2002. "Policy Implications of the Gradient of Health and Wealth." *Health Affairs* 21 (2): 13–30.

———. 2003. "Health, Inequality, and Economic Development." *Journal of Economic Literature* 41 (1): 113–58.

———. 2013. *The Great Escape: Health, Wealth, and the Origins of Inequality*. Princeton, NJ: Princeton University Press.

Deininger, Klaus. 2004. "Land Policies and Land Reform." Washington, DC: World Bank.

Dell, Melissa. 2010. "The Persistent Effects of Peru's Mining *Mita*." *Econometrica* 78 (6): 1863–1903.

Denzau, Arthur T., and Douglass C. North. 1994. "Shared Mental Models: Ideologies and Institutions." *Kyklos* 47 (1): 3–31.

Department for International Development (DFID). 2010a. "Building Peaceful States and Societies: A DFID Practice Paper." DFID, London. http://www.gsdrc.org /docs/open/con75.pdf.

———. 2010b. "The Politics of Poverty: Elites, Citizens and States; Findings from Ten Years of DFID-Funded Research on Governance and Fragile States, 2001–2010." DFID, London. https://www.oecd.org/derec/unitedkingdom/48688822.pdf.

Di John, Jonathan, and James Putzel. 2009. "Political Settlements: Issues Paper." Governance and Social Development Resource Centre, University of Birmingham, UK. http://www.gsdrc.org/docs/open/eirs7.pdf.

Diao, Xinshen, Margaret McMillan, and Dani Rodrik. 2017. "The Recent Growth Boom in Developing Economies: A Structural-Change Perspective." NBER Working Paper 23132. National Bureau of Economic Research, Cambridge, MA. https://drodrik .scholar.harvard.edu/files/dani-rodrik/files/recent_growth_boom_in_ldcs.pdf.

Digeser, Peter. 1992. "The Fourth Face of Power." *Journal of Politics* 54 (4): 977–1007.

Dixit, Avinash, Susan Skeath, and David Reiley. 2015. *Games of Strategy.* 4th ed. New York: Norton.

Dixit, Avinash, and Joseph Stiglitz. 1977. "Monopolistic Competition and Optimum Product Diversity." *American Economic Review* 67 (3): 297–308.

Doeringer, Peter B., and Michael J. Piore. 1985. *Internal Labor Markets and Manpower Analysis.* Armonk, NY: M. E. Sharpe.

Doner, Richard F., and Ansil Ramsay. 2000. "Rent-Seeking and Economic Development in Thailand." In *Rents, Rent-Seeking and Economic Development: Theory and Evidence in Asia*, edited by Mushtaq H. Khan and Jomo Kwame Sundaram, 1451–81. Cambridge: Cambridge University Press.

Doner, Richard F., Bryan K. Ritchie, and Dan Slater. 2005. "Systemic Vulnerability and the Origins of Developmental States: Northeast and Southeast Asia in Comparative Perspective." *International Organization* 59:327–61.

Dotto, Lydia, and Harold Schiff. 1978. *The Ozone War.* New York: Doubleday.

Downs, Anthony. 1972. "Up and Down with Ecology: The Issue-Attention Cycle." *Public Interest* 28:38–50.

Duflo, Esther. 2003. "Grandmothers and Granddaughters: Old-Age Pensions and Intrahousehold Allocations in South Africa." *World Bank Economic Review* 17 (1): 1–25.

Durlauf, Steven. 2006. "Groups, Social Influence and Inequality." In *Poverty Traps*, edited by Samuel Bowles, Steven N. Durlauf, and Karla Hoff, 141–75. Princeton, NJ: Princeton University Press.

Easterly, William. 2002. *The Elusive Quest for Growth: Economists' Adventures and Misadventures in the Tropics.* Cambridge, MA: MIT Press.

———. 2007. "Inequality Does Cause Underdevelopment." *Journal of Development Economics* 84:755–86.

Edelman, Murray. 1964. *The Symbolic Uses of Politics.* Urbana: University of Illinois Press.

Eichengreen, Barry, Donghyun Park, and Kwanho Shin. 2013. "Growth Slowdowns Redux: New Evidence on the Middle-Income Trap." NBER Working Paper 18673. National Bureau of Economic Research, Cambridge, MA. https://www.nber.org/papers/w18673.pdf.

Engerman, Stanley L., and Kenneth L. Sokoloff. 2002. "Factor Endowments, Inequality, and Paths of Development Among New World Economies." *Economía* 3 (1): 41–109.

———. 2005. "The Evolution of Suffrage Institutions in the Americas." *Journal of Economic History* 65 (4): 891–921.

———. 2006. "The Persistence of Poverty in the Americas: The Role of Institutions." In *Poverty Traps*, edited by Samuel Bowles, Steven N. Durlauf, and Karla Hoff, 43–78. Princeton, NJ: Princeton University Press.

Evans, Peter, Dietrich Rueschemeyer, and Theda Skocpol, eds. 2015. *Bringing the State Back In.* Cambridge: Cambridge University Press.

Fehr, Ernst, and Urs Fischbacher. 2002. "Why Social Preferences Matter—The Impact of Non-Selfish Motives on Competition, Cooperation and Incentives." *The Economic Journal* 112 (478): C1–C33.

Fehr, Ernst, and Simon Gächter. 1998. "Reciprocity and Economics: The Economic Implications of *Homo Reciprocans.*" *European Economic Review* 42 (3–5): 845–59.

———. 2000. "Fairness and Retaliation: The Economics of Reciprocity." *Journal of Economic Perspectives* 14 (3): 159–81.

———. 2002. "Altruistic Punishment in Humans." *Nature* 415:137–40.

Fehr, Ernst, Simon Gächter, and Georg Kirchsteiger. 1996. "Reciprocal Fairness and Noncompensating Wage Differentials." *Journal of Institutional and Theoretical Economics* 152 (4): 608–40.

Feldman, Martha S. 1989. *Order Without Design: Information Production and Policy Making.* Stanford, CA: Stanford University Press.

Ferguson, William D. 2005. "Fair Wages, Worker Motivation, and Implicit Bargaining Power in Segmented Labor Markets." *Journal of Institutional and Theoretical Economics* 161 (1): 126–54.

———. 2013. *Collective Action and Exchange: A Game-Theoretic Approach to Contemporary Political Economy.* Stanford, CA: Stanford University Press.

———. 2015. "The Political Economy of Collective Action and Radical Reform: A Proposed Conceptual Framework." Grinnell College. SSRN, https://www.ssrn.com/index.cfm/en/.

Fioretos, Ofeo, Julia Lynch, and Adam Steinhouse. 2016. *The Oxford Handbook of Historical Institutionalism.* New York: Oxford University Press.

Fogel, Robert William, and Stanley L. Engerman. 1974. *Time on a Cross: The Economics of American Negro Slavery.* New York: Little Brown.

Foner, Eric. 1998. *Reconstruction: America's Unfinished Revolution, 1863–1867.* New York: Harper Collins.

Fujiwara, Thomas. 2015. "Voting Technology, Political Responsiveness, and Infant Health: Evidence from Brazil." *Econometrica* 83 (2): 423–64.

Fukuyama, Francis. 2013. "What Is Governance?" *Governance* 26 (3): 347–68.

———. 2014. *Political Order and Political Decay: From Industrialization to the Globalization of Democracy.* New York: Farrar, Straus and Giroux.

Gallup, John, and Jeffrey Sachs. 2001. "The Economic Burden of Malaria." *American Journal of Tropical Medicine and Hygiene* 64 (1): 85–96.

Galor, Oded, and Joseph Zeira. 1993. "Income Distribution and Macroeconomics." *Review of Economic Studies* 60 (1): 35–52.

Geddes, Barbara. 1994. *Politician's Dilemma: Building State Capacity in Latin America.* Berkeley: University of California Press.

Gintis, Herbert. 2009. *The Bounds of Reason.* Princeton, NJ: Princeton University Press.

———. 2017. *Individuality and Entanglement: The Moral and Material Bases of Social Life.* Princeton, NJ: Princeton University Press.

Gowda, Rajeev, and E. Sridharan. 2012. "Reforming India's Party Financing and Election Expenditure Laws." *Election Law Journal* 11 (2): 226–40.

Greif, Avner. 2006. *Institutions and the Path to the Modern Economy: Lessons from Medieval Trade.* Cambridge: Cambridge University Press.

Grossman, Gene, and Elhanan Helpman. 1990. "Comparative Advantage and Long-Run Growth." *American Economic Review* 80:796–815.

Groves, Melissa Osborne. 2005. "Personality and the Intergenerational Transmission of Economic Status." In *Unequal Chances: Family Background and Economic Success*, edited by Samuel Bowles, Herbert Gintis, and Melissa Osborne Groves, 208–231. Princeton, NJ: Princeton University Press.

Gupta, Kuhika. 2014. "A Comparative Policy Analysis of Coalition Strategies: Case Studies of Nuclear Energy and Forest Management in India." *Journal of Comparative Policy Analysis: Research and Practice* 16 (4): 356–72.

Gustavsson, Magnus, and Henrick Jordahl. 2008. "Inequality and Trust in Sweden: Some Inequalities Are More Harmful Than Others." *Journal of Public Economics* 92 (1–2): 348–65.

Gyimah-Boadi, E., and H. Kwasi Prempeh. 2012. "Oil, Politics, and Ghana's Democracy." *Journal of Democracy* 23 (3): 94–108.

Hacker, Jacob S., and Paul Pierson. 2014. "After the 'Master Theory': Downs, Schattschneider, and the Rebirth of Policy-Focused Analysis." *Perspectives on Politics* 12 (3): 643–62.

Hall, Anthony. 2008. "Brazil's *Bolsa Família*: A Double-Edged Sword?" *Development and Change* 39 (5): 799–822.

Hall, Peter A. 2005. "Preference Formation as a Political Process: The Case of Monetary Union in Europe." In *Preferences and Situations: Points of Intersection Between Rational Choice and Historical Institutionalism*, edited by Ira Katznelson and Barry Weingast, 129–60. New York: Russell Sage.

———. 2010. "Historical Institutionalism in Rationalist and Sociological Perspective." In *Explaining Institutional Change: Ambiguity, Agency, and Power*, edited by James Mahoney and Kathleen Thelen, 204–24. Cambridge: Cambridge University Press.

———. 2016. "Politics as Process Structured in Space and Time." In *The Oxford Handbook of Historical Institutionalism*, edited by Ofeo Fioretos, Julia Lynch, and Adam Steinhouse, 31–50. New York: Oxford University Press.

Hall, Peter A., and Kathleen Thelen. 2009. "Institutional Change in Varieties of Capitalism." *Socio-Economic Review* 7:7–34.

Hall, Richard L., and Alan V. Deardorff. 2006. "Lobbying as Legislative Subsidy." *American Political Science Review* 100 (1): 69–84.

Harari, Yuval Noah. 2015. *Sapiens: A Brief History of Humankind*. New York: Random.

Harbers, Imke, and Abbey Steele. 2019. "The Subnational State: A Typology for Cross-National Comparison." (Mimeo) Department of Political Science, University of Amsterdam.

Harris, John R., and Michael P. Todaro. 1970. "Migration, Unemployment and Development: A Two-Sector Analysis." *American Economic Review* 60 (1): 126–42.

Hausmann, Ricardo, Lant Pritchett, and Dani Rodrik. 2005. "Growth Accelerations." NBER Working Paper 10566. National Bureau of Economic Research, Cambridge, MA. https://www.nber.org/papers/w10566.pdf.

Hausmann, Ricardo, and Dani Rodrik. 2005. "Discovering El Salvador's Production Potential." *Economía* 6 (1): 43–102.

Hausmann, Ricardo, Dani Rodrik, and Andrés Velasco. 2005. "Growth Diagnostics." The Growth Lab, Center for International Development at Harvard University. https://growthlab.cid.harvard.edu/files/growthlab/files/growth-diagnostics.pdf.

Havel, Václav. 2015. *The Power of the Powerless: Citizens Against the State in Central Eastern Europe*. Edited by John Keane. New York: Routledge.

Hayek, Friedrich A. 1945. "The Use of Knowledge in Society." *American Economic Review* 35 (4): 519–30.

He, Ququhong, Ying Pan, and Sudipta Sarangi. 2018. "Lineage-Based Heterogeneity and Cooperative Behavior in Rural China." *Journal of Comparative Economics* 46:248–69.

Heckman, James J. 2007. "The Economics, Technology, and Neuroscience of Human Capability Formation." *Proceedings of the National Academy of Sciences* 104 (33): 13250–55.

Heilbroner, Robert. 1992. *The Worldly Philosophers: The Lives, Times, and Ideas of the Great Economic Thinkers*. New York: Simon and Schuster.

———. 1993. *21st Century Capitalism*. New York: Norton.

Herrendorf, Berthold, Richard Rogerson, and Ákos Valentinyi. 2013. "Growth and Structural Transformation." NBER Working Paper 18996. National Bureau of Economic Research, Cambridge, MA. https://www.nber.org/papers/w18996.pdf.

Hertz, Thomas. 2005. "Rags, Riches, and Race: The Intergenerational Economic Mobility of Black and White Families in the United States." In *Unequal Chances:*

Family Background and Economic Success, edited by Samuel Bowles, Herbert Gintis, and Melissa Osborne Groves, 165–91. Princeton, NJ: Princeton University Press.

Herweg, Nicole, Nikolaos Zahariadis, and Reimut Zohlnhöfer. 2018. "The Multiple Streams Framework: Foundations, Refinements, and Empirical Applications." In *Theories of the Policy Process*, 4th ed., edited by Christopher M. Weible and Paul A. Sabatier, 17–53. New York: Routledge.

Hickey, Sam, and Angelo Izama. 2016. "The Politics of Governing Oil in Uganda: Going Against the Grain?" *African Affairs* 116 (462): 163–85.

Hidalgo, César A., and Ricardo Hausmann. 2009. "The Building Blocks of Economic Complexity." *Proceedings of the National Academy of Sciences* 106 (26): 10570–75.

Hirschman, Albert O. 1958. *The Strategy of Economic Development*. New Haven, CT: Yale University Press.

———. 1970. *Exit, Voice and Loyalty: Responses to Decline in Firms, Organizations, and States*. Cambridge, MA: Harvard University Press.

Hobson, John. (1902) 2005. *Imperialism: A Study*. New York: Cosimo.

Hoff, Karla, and Joseph E. Stiglitz. 2016. "Striving for Balance in Economics: Towards a Theory of the Social Determination of Behavior." *Journal of Economic Behavior and Organization* 126:25–57.

"How Do You Reform a Country Where Gunmen Torch Ebola Clinics?" 2019. *The Economist* (August 3).

Hseih, Chang-Tai, and Peter J. Klenow. 2009. "Misallocation and Manufacturing TFP in China and India." *Quarterly Journal of Economics* 124 (4): 1403–48.

International Food Policy Research Institute (IFPRI). 2007. *The World's Most Deprived*. Washington, DC.

———. 2014. *2013 Global Food Policy Report*. Washington, DC: IFPRI.

Jackson, Matthew O. 2008. *Social and Economic Networks*. Princeton, NJ: Princeton University Press.

Jacobs, Jane. 1984. *Cities and the Wealth of Nations*. New York: Vintage.

Jang, Sojin, Christopher M. Weible, and Kyudong Park. 2016. "Policy Processes in South Korea Through the Lens of the Advocacy Coalition Framework." *Journal of Asian Public Policy* 9 (3): 274–90.

Jayadev, Arjun, and Samuel Bowles. 2006. "Guard Labor." *Journal of Development Economics* 79:328–48.

Jenkins-Smith, Hank, Daniel Nohrstedt, Christopher Weible, and Karin Ingold. 2018. "The Advocacy Coalition Framework: An Overview of the Research Program." In *Theories of the Policy Process*. 4th ed. Edited by Christopher M. Weible and Paul A. Sabatier, 135–72. New York: Routledge.

Jones, Bryan D., and Frank R. Baumgartner. 2005. *The Politics of Attention: How Government Prioritizes Problems*. Chicago: University of Chicago Press.

Jordahl, Henrik. 2007. "Inequality and Trust." IFN Working Paper 715. Research Institute of Industrial Economics.

Kahneman, Daniel. 2003. "Maps of Bounded Rationality: Psychology for Behavioral Economics." *American Economic Review* 93 (5): 1449–75.

———. 2011. *Thinking, Fast and Slow.* New York: Farrar, Straus and Giroux.

Kar, Sabyasachi, Lant Pritchett, Selim Raihan, and Kunal Sen. 2013. "The Dynamics of Economic Growth: A Visual Handbook of Growth Rates, Regimes, Transitions and Volatility." Effective States and Inclusive Development Research Centre, University of Manchester, UK. https://growthlab.cid.harvard.edu/files/growthlab/files/handbook.pdf.

Kar, Sabyasachi, and Kunal Sen. 2016. *The Political Economy of India's Growth Episodes.* London: Palgrave Macmillan.

Karlan, Dean, Robert Osei, Isaac Osei-Akoto, and Christopher Udry. 2014. "Agricultural Decisions After Relaxing Credit and Risk Constraints." *Quarterly Journal of Economics,* 597–652.

Katznelson, Ira, and Barry Weingast, eds. 2005. *Preferences and Situations: Points of Intersection Between Rational Choice and Historical Institutionalism.* New York: Russell Sage.

Kelsall, Tim, and Matthias vom Hau. 2019. "Beyond Institutions: A Political Settlements Approach to Development." *IBEI Working Paper* 56. Institut Barcelona d'Estudis Internacionals.

Keohane, Robert O. 1982. "The Demand for International Regimes." *International Organization* 36 (2): 325–55.

Keynes, John Maynard. (1936) 1964. *The General Theory of Employment, Interest, and Money.* New York: Harcourt, Brace, and World.

Khan, Mushtaq H. 2000. "Rent-Seeking as Process." In *Rents, Rent-Seeking and Economic Development: Theory and Evidence in Asia,* edited by Mushtaq H. Khan and Jomo Kwame Sundaram, 70–144. Cambridge: Cambridge University Press.

———. 2008. "Vulnerabilities in Market-Led Growth Strategies and Challenges for Governance." Research Paper Series on Governance for Growth. School of Oriental and African Studies, University of London. https://eprints.soas.ac.uk/9963/1/Vulnerabilities_internet.pdf.

———. 2009. "Learning, Technology Acquisition and Governance Challenges in Developing Countries." Research Paper Series on Governance for Growth. School of Oriental and African Studies, University of London. https://eprints.soas.ac.uk/9967/1/Learning_and_Technology_Acquisition_internet.pdf.

———. 2010. "Political Settlements and the Governance of Growth-Enhancing Institutions." Unpublished Working Paper. School of Oriental and African Studies, University of London. https://eprints.soas.ac.uk/9968/1/Political_Settlements_internet.pdf.

———. 2013. "Bangladesh: Economic Growth in a Vulnerable LAO." In *In the Shadow of Violence: Politics, Economics, and the Problems of Development,* edited by Douglass C. North, John Joseph Wallis, Steven B. Webb, and Barry R. Weingast, 24–69. Cambridge: Cambridge University Press.

————. 2017. "Introduction: Political Settlements and the Analysis of Institutions." *African Affairs*, 1–20.

Khan, Mushtaq H., and Jomo Kwame Sundaram. 2000. *Rents, Rent-Seeking and Economic Development: Theory and Evidence in Asia.* Cambridge: Cambridge University Press.

Kingdon, John W. 2003. *Agendas, Alternatives, and Public Policies.* 2nd ed. New York: Longman.

Klasen, Stephan, and Claudia Wink. 2003. "'Missing Women': Revisiting the Debate." *Feminist Economics* 9 (2–3): 263–99.

Knight, Frank H. 1965. *Risk, Uncertainty, and Profit.* New York: Harper and Row.

Knight, Jack. 1992. *Institutions and Social Conflict.* Cambridge: Cambridge University Press.

Kohli, Atul. 1994. "Where Do High Growth Political Economies Come From? The Japanese Lineage of Korea's Developmental State." *World Development* 22 (9): 1269–93.

Kraay, Aart, and David McKenzie. 2014. "Do Poverty Traps Exist? Assessing the Evidence." *Journal of Economic Perspectives* 28 (3): 127–48.

Kremer, Michael. 1993. "The O-Ring Theory of Economic Development." *Quarterly Journal of Economics* 108 (3): 551–75.

Krugman, Paul. 1981. "Trade Accumulation and Uneven Development." *Journal of Development Economics* 8:149–61.

————. 1991. "Increasing Returns and Economic Geography." *Journal of Political Economy* 99:183–99.

————. 1995. *Development, Geography, and Economic Theory: The Ohlin Lectures.* Cambridge, MA: MIT Press.

Kuhn, Thomas. 1962. *The Structure of Scientific Revolutions.* Chicago: Chicago University Press.

Kuran, Timur. 1995. *Private Truths, Public Lies: The Social Consequences of Preference Falsification.* Cambridge, MA: Harvard University Press.

Kuznets, Simon. 1955. "Economic Growth and Income Inequality." *American Economic Review* 45 (1): 1–28.

Lakatos, Imre. 1978. *The Methodology of Scientific Research Programmes.* Cambridge: Cambridge University Press.

Lam, Wai Fung, and Kwan Nok Chan. 2015. "How Authoritarianism Intensifies Punctuated Equilibrium: The Dynamics of Policy Attention in Hong Kong." *Governance: An International Journal of Policy, Administration, and Institutions* 28 (4): 549–70.

Lande, Carl H. 1967. "The Philippine Political Party System." *Journal of Southeast Asian History* 8 (1): 19–39.

Lane, Nathan. 2017. "Manufacturing Revolutions: Industrial Policy and Networks in South Korea." Institute for International Economic Studies, Stockholm. http://eh.net/eha/wp-content/uploads/2017/08/Lane.pdf.

Lasswell, Harold. 1936. *Politics: Who Gets What, When, How.* New York: McGraw-Hill.

Lasswell, Harold, and Abraham Kaplan. 1950. *Power and Society: A Framework for Political Inquiry.* New Haven, CT: Yale University Press.

Laws, Edward. 2012. "Political Settlements, Elite Pacts, and Governments of National Unity: A Conceptual Study." DLP Background Paper. Development Leadership Program, University of Birmingham, UK. https://res.cloudinary.com/dlprog /image/upload/background-paper-10-political-settlements-elite-pacts-and -governments-of-national-unity-a-conceptual-study.

Laws, Edward, and Adrian Leftwich. 2014. "Political Settlements." DLP Concept Brief. Development Leadership Program, University of Birmingham, UK. https://res .cloudinary.com/dlprog/image/upload/wkyZUlQEYmCzBzWvcNPt6VKCVAy KhkkCph8jTWiW.pdf.

Levy, Brian. 2013. "Seeking the Elusive Developmental Knife Edge: Zambia and Mozambique—A Tale of Two Countries." In *In the Shadow of Violence: Politics, Economics, and the Problems of Development,* edited by Douglass C. North, John Joseph Wallis, Steven B. Webb, and Barry R. Weingast, 112–148. Cambridge: Cambridge University Press.

———. 2014. *Working with the Grain: Integrating Governance and Growth in Development Strategies.* Oxford, UK: Oxford University Press.

Lewis, W. Arthur. 1954. "Economic Development with Unlimited Supplies of Labour." *The Manchester School* 22 (2): 139–91.

———. 1957. "International Competition in Manufactures." *American Economic Review* 47 (2): 578–87.

Lin, Justin Yifu. 2012. *New Structural Economics: A Framework for Rethinking Development and Policy.* Washington, DC: The World Bank.

Lipset, Seymour Martin. 1959. "Some Social Requisites of Democracy: Economic Development and Political Legitimacy." *American Political Science Review* 53 (1): 69–105.

Lohmann, Susanne. 1994. "The Dynamics of Information Cascades: The Monday Demonstrations in Leipzig, East Germany, 1989–91." *World Politics* 47 (1), 42–101.

———. 2000. "Collective Action Cascades: An Informational Rationale for the Power in Numbers." *Journal of Economic Surveys* 14 (5): 655–84.

Lowry, Ritchie P. 1964. "Leadership Interaction, Group Consciousness, and Social Change." *Pacific Sociological Review* 7 (1): 22–29.

Lukas, Georg. [1920] 1967. *History and Class Consciousness.* Translated by Rodney Livingstone. London: Merlin Press.

Lukes, Steven. 1974. *Power: A Radical View.* New York: Macmillan.

Madsen, Jens Koed, Richard Bailey, and Toby Pilditch. 2018. "Large Networks of Rational Agents Form Persistent Echo Chambers." *Scientific Reports* 8 (1): 12391.

Mahoney, Christine, and Frank Baumgartner. 2015. "Partners in Advocacy: Lobbyists and Government Officials in Washington." *Journal of Politics* 77 (1): 202–15.

Mahoney, James, and Dietrich Rueschemeyer, eds. 2003. *Comparative Historical Analysis in the Social Sciences.* Cambridge: Cambridge University Press.

Mahoney, James, and Kathleen Thelen. 2009. "A Theory of Gradual Institutional Change." In *Explaining Institutional Change: Ambiguity, Agency, and Power*, edited by James Mahoney and Kathleen Thelen, 1–38. Cambridge: Cambridge University Press.

Malejacq, Romain. 2016. "Warlords, Intervention, and State Consolidation: A Typology of Political Orders in Weak and Failed States." *Security Studies* 25 (1): 85–110.

Mankiw, N. Gregory, David Romer, and David N. Weil. 1992. "A Contribution to the Empirics of Economic Growth." *Quarterly Journal of Economics* 107 (2): 221–40.

Marshall, Alfred. (1920) 1979. *Principles of Economics*. 8th ed. London: Macmillan.

Marx, Karl. 1965. *Pre-Capitalist Economic Formations*. Translated by Jack Cohen. Edited and with an introduction by E. J. Hobsbawm. New York: International Publishers. Originally published as Grundrisse der Kritik der politischen Ökonomie (Rohentwurf). Moscow: Verlag für Fremdsprachige Literatur, 1939.

Marx, Karl, and Friedrich Engels. (1848) 1998. *The Communist Manifesto*. New York: Signet Classic.

Mazumder, Bhashkar. 2005. "The Apple Falls Even Closer to the Tree Than We Thought: New and Revised Estimates of the Intergenerational Inheritance of Earnings." In *Unequal Chances: Family Background and Economic Success*, edited by Samuel Bowles, Herbert Gintis, and Melissa Osborne Groves, 80–99. Princeton, NJ: Princeton University Press.

McCaig, Brian, and Nina Pavcnik. 2013. "Moving Out of Agriculture: Structural Change in Vietnam." NBER Working Paper 19616. National Bureau of Economic Research, Cambridge, MA. https://www.nber.org/papers/w19616.pdf.

McGavock, Tamara. 2017. "The Short End of the Deal? Crisis, Dropout, and Sibling Inequality." Working paper, Grinnell College.

McMillan, Margaret, Dani Rodrik, and Íñigo Verduzco-Gallo. 2014. "Globalization, Structural Change, and Productivity Growth, with an Update on Africa." *World Development* 63:11–32.

Menkhaus, Ken. 2014. "State Failure, State-Building, and Prospects for a 'Functional Failed State' in Somalia." *Annals of the American Academy of Political and Social Science* 656 (1): 154–72.

Milanovic, Branko. 2016. *Global Inequality: A New Approach for the Age of Globalization*. Cambridge, MA: Harvard University Press.

Milgrom, Paul, and John Roberts. 1992. *Economics, Organization and Management*. Englewood Cliffs, NJ: Prentice Hall.

Mills, C. Wright. 1956. *The Power Elite*. Oxford, UK: Oxford University Press.

Ministry of Finance and Economic Planning. 2011. "Vision 2020 Progress and Way Forward." Republic of Rwanda.

Mokyr, Joel. 1990. *The Lever of Riches: Technological Creativity and Economic Progress*. Oxford, UK: Oxford University Press.

Montinola, Gabriella. 2013. "Change and Continuity in a Limited Access Order: The Philippines." In *In the Shadow of Violence: Politics, Economics, and the Problems of*

Development, edited by Douglass C. North, John Joseph Wallis, Steven B. Webb, and Barry R. Weingast, 149–97. Cambridge: Cambridge University Press.

Moore, Barrington. 1966. *Social Origins of Dictatorship and Democracy.* Boston: Beacon Press.

Mukhopadhyay, Dipali. 2014. *Warlords, Strongman Governors, and the State in Afghanistan.* Cambridge: Cambridge University Press.

Munshi, Kaivan, and Jacques Myaux. 2006. "Social Norms and the Fertility Transition." *Journal of Development Economics* 80:1–38.

Murphy, Kevin M., Andrei Shleifer, and Robert W. Vishny. 1989. "Industrialization and the Big Push." *Journal of Political Economy* 97 (5): 1003–26.

Musacchio, Aldo, and Eric Werker. 2016. "Mapping Frontier Economies." *Harvard Business Review* 95 (12): 40–7.

Neffke, Frank. 2017. "Coworker Complementarity." SPRU Working Paper Series 2017-05. Science Policy Research Unit, University of Sussex, Brighton, UK.

Nelson, Richard R., and Paul M. Romer. 1996. "Science, Economic Growth, and Public Policy." *Challenge* 39 (2): 9–21.

Nordhaus, William, D. 2000. "New Directions in National Economic Accounting." *American Economic Review* 90 (2): 259–63.

North, Douglass C. 1990. *Institutions, Institutional Change and Economic Performance.* Cambridge: Cambridge University Press.

North, Douglass C., John Joseph Wallis, Steven B. Webb, and Barry R. Weingast, eds. 2013. *In the Shadow of Violence: Politics, Economics, and the Problems of Development.* Cambridge: Cambridge University Press.

North, Douglass C., John Joseph Wallis, and Barry R. Weingast. 2009. *Violence and Social Orders: A Conceptual Framework for Interpreting Recorded Human History.* Cambridge: Cambridge University Press.

Nurske, Ragnar. 1953. *Problems of Capital Formation in Underdeveloped Countries.* New York: Oxford University Press.

O'Donnell, Guillermo. 1993. "On the State, Democratization and Some Conceptual Problems: A Latin American View with Glances at Some Post-Communist Countries." *World Development* 21 (8): 1355–69.

O'Donnell, Guillermo, and Philippe C. Schmitter. 1986. *Transitions from Authoritarian Rule.* Baltimore: Johns Hopkins University Press.

Okun, Arthur. M. 1975. *Equality and Efficiency: The Big Tradeoff.* Washington, DC: Brookings Institution.

Oleinik, Anton. 2016. *The Invisible Hand of Power: An Economic Theory of Gatekeeping.* New York: Routledge.

Olson, Mancur. 1971. *The Logic of Collective Action: Public Goods and the Theory of Groups.* 2nd ed. Cambridge, MA: Harvard University Press.

———. 1993. "Dictatorship, Democracy, and Development." *American Political Science Review* 87 (3): 567–76.

Osei, Robert Darko, Charles Ackah, George Domfe, and Michael Danquah. 2018. "Political Settlements and Structural Change: Why Growth Has Not Been Transformational in Ghana." In *Deals and Development: The Political Dynamics of Growth Episodes*, edited by Lant Pritchett, Kunal Sen, and Eric Werker, 159–82. Oxford, UK: Oxford University Press.

Ostrom, Elinor. 1990. *Governing the Commons: The Evolution of Institutions for Collective Action*. Cambridge, UK: Cambridge University Press.

———. 1998. "A Behavioral Approach to the Rational Choice Theory of Collective Action: Presidential Address, American Political Science Association, 1997." *American Political Science Review* 92 (1): 1–22.

———. 2000. "Collective Action and the Evolution of Social Norms." *Journal of Economic Perspectives* 14 (3): 137–58.

———. 2005. *Understanding Institutional Diversity*. Princeton, NJ: Princeton University Press.

———. 2010. "Beyond Markets and States: Polycentric Governance of Complex Economic Systems." *American Economic Review* 100 (3): 641–72.

Ostry, Jonathan, and François Bourguignon. 2016. "Inequality and the Fragility of Growth." In *Inequality and Growth: Patterns and Policy*. Vol. 2: *Regions and Regularities*, edited by Kaushik Basu and Joseph Stiglitz, 136–62. New York: Palgrave MacMillan.

Oxfam. 2019. "Public Good or Private Wealth?" Oxfam Briefing Paper. Oxford, UK: Oxfam International. https://oxfamilibrary.openrepository.com/bitstream/handle/10546/620599/bp-public-good-or-private-wealth-210119-en.pdf?utm_source=indepth.

Pande, Rohini. 2003. "Can Mandated Political Representation Increase Policy Influence for Disadvantaged Minorities? Theory and Evidence from India." *American Economic Review* 93 (4): 1132–51.

Peter, Laurence J. 1976. *The Peter Plan: A Proposal for Survival*. New York: William Morrow.

Phongpaichit, Pasuk, and Chris Baker. 2009. *Thaksin*. 2nd ed. Chiang Mai, Thailand: Silkworm Books.

Pierson, Paul. 1993. "When Effect Becomes Cause: Policy Feedback and Political Change." *World Politics* 45 (4): 595–628.

Piketty, Thomas. 2014. *Capital in the Twenty-First Century*. Translated by Arthur Goldhammer. Cambridge, MA: Belknap Press of Harvard University Press.

Posner, Eric. 2000. *Laws and Social Norms*. Cambridge, MA: Harvard University Press.

Poteete, Amy, Marco Janssen, and Elinor Ostrom. 2010. *Working Together: Collective Action, the Commons, and Multiple Methods in Practice*. Princeton, NJ: Princeton University Press.

Poulsen, Anders, and Odile Poulsen. 2006. "Endogenous Preferences and Social-Dilemma Institutions." *Journal of Institutional and Theoretical Economics* 162 (4): 627–60.

Pritchett, Lant, Kunal Sen, and Eric Werker, eds. 2018. *Deals and Development: The Political Dynamics of Growth Episodes*. Oxford, UK, Oxford University Press.

Pritchett, Lant, and Eric Werker. 2012. "Developing the Guts of a GUT (Grand Unified Theory): Elite Commitment and Inclusive Growth." ESID Working Paper Series 16/12. Effective States and Inclusive Development Research Centre, University of Manchester, UK.

Psacharopoulos, George, and Harry A. Patrinos. 1994. "Indigenous People and Poverty in Latin America." *Finance and Development* 31:41.

Quattrone, George A., and Amos Tversky. 1988. "Contrasting Rational and Psychological Analyses of Political Choice." *American Political Science Review* 82 (3): 719–36.

Rajan, Raghuram G. 2010. *Fault Lines: How Hidden Fractures Still Threaten the World Economy.* Princeton, NJ: Princeton University Press.

Ranis, Gustav, and John C. H. Fei. 1961. "A Theory of Economic Development." *American Economic Review* 51 (4): 533–65.

Ransom, Roger L., and Richard Sutch. 2001. *One Kind of Freedom: The Economic Consequences of Emancipation.* Cambridge: Cambridge University Press.

Rawls, John. 1999. *A Theory of Justice.* Rev. ed. Cambridge, MA: Harvard University Press.

Razo, Armando. 2008. *Social Foundations of Limited Dictatorship: Networks and Private Protection During Mexico's Early Industrialization.* Stanford, CA: Stanford University Press.

Reyntjens, Filip. 2013. *Political Governance in Post-Genocide Rwanda.* Cambridge: Cambridge University Press.

Ricardo, David. (1815) 2010. "An Essay on the Influence of a Low Price of Corn on the Profits of Stock." Whitefish, MT: Kessinger.

Ridde, Valéry. 2009. "Policy Implementation in an African State: An Extension of Kingdon's Multiple-Streams Approach." *Public Administration* 87 (4): 938–54.

Riker, William H. 1962. *The Theory of Political Coalitions.* New Haven, CT: Yale University Press.

Ritchie, Bryan K. 2005. "Coalitional Politics, Economic Reform, and Technological Upgrading in Malaysia." *World Development* 33 (5): 745–61.

Roc, Nancy. 2008. "Haiti-Environment: From the 'Pearl of the Antilles' to Desolation." Report commissioned by Fundación para las Relaciones Internacionales y el Diálogo Exterior, Madrid. https://projects.ncsu.edu/project/amazonia/Roc.pdf.

Rock, David J. 2000. *Argentina, 1516–1987: From Spanish Colonization to the Falklands War.* Berkeley: University of California Press.

Rodríguez-Clare, Andrés. 1996. "The Division of Labor and Economic Development." *Journal of Development Economics* 49:3–32.

Rodrik, Dani. 2013. "Structural Change, Fundamentals, and Growth: An Overview." Rev. version. Institute for Advanced Study, Princeton, NJ. https://drodrik .scholar.harvard.edu/files/dani-rodrik/files/structural-change-fundamentals -and-growth-an-overview_revised.pdf.

———. 2014. "When Ideas Trump Interests: Preferences, Worldviews, and Policy Innovations." *Journal of Economic Perspectives* 28 (1): 189–208.

———. 2016. "Premature Deindustrialization." *Journal of Economic Growth* 21 (1): 1–33.

Roessler, Philip. 2011. "The Enemy Within: Personal Rule, Coups, and Civil War in Africa." *World Politics* 63 (2): 300–46.

———. 2017. *Ethnic Politics and State Power in Africa: The Logic of the Coup–Civil War Trap.* Cambridge: Cambridge University Press.

Rogan, Eugene. 2015. *The Fall of the Ottomans: The Great War in the Middle East.* New York: Basic Books.

Romer, Paul. 1990. "Endogenous Technological Change." *Journal of Political Economy* 98 (5): S71–S102.

———. 1993. "Idea Gaps and Object Gaps in Economic Development." *Journal of Monetary Economics* 32 (3): 543–73.

Rosenstein-Rodan, Paul N. 1943. "Problems of Industrialisation of Eastern and South-Eastern Europe." *The Economic Journal* 53 (210/211): 202–11.

Rowlands, Ian H. 1995. *The Politics of Global Atmospheric Change.* Manchester, UK: Manchester University Press.

Sabatier, Paul A. 1987. "Knowledge, Policy-Oriented Learning, and Policy Change: An Advocacy Coalition Framework." *Knowledge: Creation, Diffusion, Utilization* 8 (4): 649–92.

———. 1998. "The Advocacy Coalition Framework: Revisions and Relevance for Europe." *Journal of European Public Policy* 5 (1): 98–130.

———, ed. 2007. *Theories of the Policy Process.* 2nd ed. Boulder, CO: Westview.

Sabatier, Paul A. and Hank Jenkins-Smith. 1993. *Policy Change and Learning: An Advocacy Coalition Approach.* Boulder, CO: Westview.

———. 1999. "The Advocacy Coalition Framework: An Assessment." In *Theories of the Policy Process*, edited by Paul A. Sabatier, 117–66. Boulder, CO: Westview.

Sabatier, Paul A., and Christopher M. Weible. 2007. "The Advocacy Coalition Framework: Innovations and Clarifications." In *Theories of the Policy Process*, 2nd. ed., edited by Paul A. Sabatier, 189–220. Boulder, CO: Westview.

———, eds. 2014. *Theories of the Policy Process.* 3rd ed. Boulder, CO: Westview.

Saez, Emmanuel, and Gabriel Zucman. 2016. "Wealth Inequality in the United States Since 1913: Evidence from Capitalized Income Tax Data." *Quarterly Journal of Economics* 131 (2): 519–78.

Schattschneider, E. E. 1960. *The Semi-Sovereign People.* New York: Holt, Rinehart, and Winston.

Schelling, Thomas C. 1960. *The Strategy of Conflict.* Cambridge, MA: Harvard University Press.

———. 1978. *Micromotives and Macrobehavior.* New York: Norton.

Schiavone, Aldo. 2002. *The End of the Past.* Translated by Margery J. Schneider. Cambridge MA: Harvard University Press.

Schofield, Heather. 2014. "The Economic Costs of Low Caloric Intake: Evidence from India." Paper Presented at the Center for Global Development, Harvard

University, Cambridge, MA. https://www.cgdev.org/sites/default/files/Schofield,
%20Calories%20and%20Productivity,%202014.01.27(new).pdf.

Sen, Amartya. 1990. "More Than 100 Million Women Are Missing." *New York Review of Books*, December 20. https://www.nybooks.com/articles/1990/12/20/more-than-100-million-women-are-missing/.

———. 1992. *Inequality Reexamined*. Oxford, UK: Clarendon Press.

———. 1999. *Development as Freedom*. Oxford, UK: Oxford University Press.

———. 2003. "Missing Women—Revisited: Reduction in Female Mortality Has Been Counterbalanced by Sex Selective Abortions." *British Medical Journal* 327 (7427): 1297.

Sen, Kunal. 2013. "The Political Dynamics of Economic Growth." *World Development* 47:71–86. http://isiarticles.com/bundles/Article/pre/pdf/16651.pdf.

Sen, Kunal, Sabyasachi Kar, and Jagadish Prasad Sahu. 2018. "The Stroll, the Trot, and the Sprint of the Elephant: Understanding Indian Growth Episodes." In *Deals and Development: The Political Dynamics of Growth Episodes*, edited by Lant Prichett, Kunal Sen, and Eric Werker, 250–84. Oxford, UK, Oxford University Press.

Sen, Kunal, and Matthew Tyce. 2018. "The Politics of Structural (De)Transformation: The Unravelling of Malaysia and Thailand's Dualistic Deals Strategies." In *Deals and Development: The Political Dynamics of Growth Episodes*, edited by Lant Prichett, Kunal Sen, and Eric Werker, 285–338. Oxford, UK: Oxford University Press.

Shapiro, Carl, and Joseph A. Stiglitz. 1984. "Equilibrium Unemployment as a Worker Discipline Device." *American Economic Review* 75 (3): 433–44.

Shuman, Howard, and Stanley Presser. 1981. "The Attitude-Action Connection and the Issue of Gun Control." *The Annals of the American Academy of Political and Social Science* 455 (1): 40–47.

Simbulan, Dante C. 2005. *The Modern Principalia: The Historical Evolution of the Philippine Ruling Oligarchy*. Quezon City: The University of Philippines Press.

Simmel, Georg. 1902. "The Number of Members as Determining the Sociological Form of the Group: II." *American Journal of Sociology* 8:158–196.

———. 1971. *On Individuality and Social Forms*. Selected Writings, Edited with an Introduction by Donald N. Levine. Chicago: University of Chicago Press.

Simon, Herbert. 1955. "A Behavioral Model of Rational Choice." *Quarterly Journal of Economics* 69 (1): 99–118.

———. 1977. *The New Science of Management Decision*. 3rd rev. ed. Englewood Cliffs, NJ: Prentice-Hall.

———. 1983. *Reason in Human Affairs*. Oxford, UK: Blackwell.

———. 1985. *Models of Bounded Rationality*. Cambridge, MA: MIT Press.

Singelmann, Joachim. 1978. *From Agriculture to Services: The Transformation of Industrial Employment*. Beverly Hills, CA: Sage.

Slater, Dan. 2010. *Ordering Power: Contentious Politics and Authoritarian Leviathans in Southeast Asia*. Cambridge: Cambridge University Press.

Smedley, Brian D., Adrienne Y. Stith, and Alan R. Nelson, eds. 2002. *Unequal Treatment: Confronting Racial and Ethnic Disparities in Health Care.* Washington, DC: National Academies Press.

Snowdon, Brian, Howard Vane, and Peter Wynarczyk. 1994. *A Modern Guide to Macroeconomics: An Introduction to Competing Schools of Thought.* Aldershot, UK: Edward Elgar.

Sobel, Joel. 2005. "Interdependent Preferences and Reciprocity." *Journal of Economic Literature* 43 (2): 392–426.

Solow, Robert N. 1957. "Technical Change and the Aggregate Production Function." *The Review of Economics and Statistics* 39 (3): 312–20.

Steele, Abbey. A. 2017. *Democracy and Displacement in Colombia's Civil War.* Ithaca, NY: Cornell University Press.

Stigler, George. 1989. "Two Notes on the Coase Theorem." *Yale Law Journal* 9:631–33.

Stiglitz, Joseph. 1987. "The Causes and Consequences of the Dependence of Quality on Price." *Journal of Economic Literature* 25 (1): 1–48.

———. 1999. "Interest Rates, Risk, and Imperfect Markets: Puzzles and Policies." *Oxford Review of Economic Policy* 15 (2): 59–76.

———. 2000. "Formal and Informal Institutions." In *Social Capital: A Multifaceted Perspective,* edited by Partha Dasgupta and Ismail Serageldin, 59–70. Washington, DC: World Bank.

Streeck, Wolfgang, and Kathleen Thelen. 2005. "Introduction: Institutional Change in Advanced Political Economies." In *Beyond Continuity: Institutional Change in Advanced Capitalist Economies,* edited by Wolfgang Streeck and Kathleen Thelen, 1–39. Oxford, UK: Oxford University Press.

Sunstein, Cass. 1996. "Social Norms and Social Roles." *Columbia Law Review* 96 (4): 903–68.

Szreter, Simon. 1988. "The Importance of Social Intervention in Britain's Mortality Decline c. 1850–1914: A Re-interpretation of the Role of Public Health." *Social History of Medicine* 1:1–38.

Taylor, Michael. 1982. *Community, Anarchy, and Liberty.* Cambridge, UK: Cambridge University Press.

Thelen, Kathleen. 2003. "How Institutions Evolve: Insights from Comparative Institutional Analysis." In *Comparative Historical Analysis in the Social Sciences,* edited by James Mahoney and Dietrich Rueschemeyer, 208–40. Cambridge: Cambridge University Press.

Tilly, Charles. 1985. "War Making and State Making as Organized Crime." In *Bringing the State Back In,* edited by Peter Evans, Dietrich Rueschemeyer, and Theda Skocpol, 169–91. Cambridge: Cambridge University Press.

Todaro, Michael P., and Stephen C. Smith. 2015. *Economic Development.* 12th ed. New York: Pearson.

Tosun, Jale, and Samuel Workman. 2018. "Struggle and Triumph in Fusing Policy Process and Comparative Research." In *Theories of the Policy Process,* 4th ed., edited by Christopher M. Weible and Paul A. Sabatier, 329–62. New York: Routledge.

Toufique, Kazi Ali. 1997. "Some Observations on Power and Property Rights in the Inland Fisheries of Bangladesh." *World Development* 25 (3): 457–67.

Tropman, John E., Milan J. Dluhy, and Roger M. Lind, eds. *New Strategic Perspectives on Social Policy.* New York: Pergamon.

True, James L., Bryan D. Jones, and Frank. R. Baumgartner. 2007. "Punctuated-Equilibrium Theory: Explaining Stability and Change in Public Policymaking." In *Theories of the Policy Process*, 2nd ed., edited by Paul A. Sabatier, 155–87. Boulder, CO: Westview.

Udry, Christopher. 1996. "Gender, Agricultural Production, and the Theory of the Household." *Journal of Political Economy* 104:1010–46.

UNAIDS. 2012. *Global Report: UNAIDS Report on the Global AIDS Epidemic.* Geneva, Switzerland: Joint United Nations Program on HIV/AIDS.

United Nations. 2015. *The Millennium Development Goals Report 2015.* New York: United Nations.

United Nations Development Programme (UNDP). 2013. *2012–2013 Annual Report: Supporting Global Progress.* New York: UNDP. http://www.undp.org/content /undp/en/home/librarypage/corporate/annual-report-2013.html.

Walker, E. V. 1959. "Simmel's Sociology of Power: The Architecture of Politics." In *Georg Simmel, 1858–1918: A Collection of Essays with Translations and a Bibliography*, edited by Kurt H. Wolff. Columbus OH: Ohio State University Press.

Walker, Jack L. 1981. "The Diffusion of Knowledge, Policy Communities and Agenda Setting: The Relationship of Knowledge and Power." In *New Strategic Perspectives on Social Policy*, edited by John E. Tropman, Milan J. Dluhy, and Roger M. Lind, 75–96. New York: Pergamon.

Watts, Duncan J. 2002. "A Simple Model of Global Cascades in Random Networks." *Proceedings of the National Academy of Sciences* 99 (9): 5766–71.

Weber, Max. 1978. *Economy and Society: An Outline of Interpretive Sociology.* Berkeley: University of California Press.

Weible, Christopher. 2008. "Expert-Based Information and Policy Subsystems: A Review and Synthesis." *Policy Studies Journal* 36 (4): 615–35.

Weible, Christopher M., and Paul A. Sabatier, eds. 2018. *Theories of the Policy Process.* 4th ed. New York: Routledge.

Weitz, Raanan. 1971. *From Peasant to Farmer: A Revolutionary Strategy for Development.* New York: Columbia University Press.

Whaites, Alan. 2008. "States in Development: Understanding State-Building." DFID Working Paper. Department for International Development Working Paper, London. https://webarchive.nationalarchives.gov.uk/+/http://www.dfid.gov.uk /Documents/publications/State-in-Development-Wkg-Paper.pdf.

Whitfield, Lindsay, and Ole Therkildsen. 2011. "What Drives States to Support the Development of Productive Sectors? Strategies Ruling Elites Pursue for Political Survival and Their Policy Implications." DIS Working Paper 201. Danish Institute for International Studies, Copenhagen. https://www.diis.dk/files/media/publications /import/wp2011-15-what-drives-states_web.pdf.

Wilkinson, Richard, and Kate Pickett. 2009. *The Spirit Level: Why More Equal Societies Almost Always Do Better.* London: Allen Lane.

Williams, Martin J. 2018. "Beyond State Capacity: Bureaucratic Performance, Policy Implementation, and Reform." Blavatnik School of Government, Oxford University. https://martinjwilliamsdotcom.files.wordpress.com/2018/08/williams_beyondstatecapacity_180716.pdf.

Williamson, Oliver. 1979. "Transaction-Cost Economics: The Governance of Contractual Relations." *Journal of Law and Economics* 22 (2): 233–61.

Wilson, James Q. 1980. *American Government: Institutions and Policies.* Lexington, MA: D. C. Heath.

"Winning the Endgame: A Global Attack on Long-Neglected Tropical Diseases Is Succeeding." 2017. *The Economist* (April 22):51.

Wolff, Kurt H. 1950. *The Sociology of Georg Simmel.* New York: Free Press.

World Bank. 2010. *World Development Indicators 2010.* "Table 2.7: Poverty Rates at National Poverty Lines." Washington, DC: International Bank for Reconstruction and Development/The World Bank.

———. 2017. *World Development Report 2017: Governance and the Law.* Washington, DC: International Bank for Reconstruction and Development/The World Bank.

———. 2018. *World Development Indicators.* Washington, DC: The World Bank.

World Inequality Lab. 2018. "World Inequality Report 2018: Executive Summary." World Inequality Database. https://wir2018.wid.world/.

Wright, Gavin. 2013. *Sharing the Prize: The Economics of the Civil Rights Revolution in the American South.* Cambridge MA: Belknap Press of Harvard University Press.

Yanguas, Pablo. 2017. "Varieties of State-Building in Africa: Elites, Ideas and the Politics of Public Sector Reform." ESID Working Paper 89. Effective States and Inclusive Development Research Centre, University of Manchester, UK.

You, Jong-Sung. 2013. "Transition from a Limited Access Order to an Open Access Order: The Case of South Korea." In *In the Shadow of Violence: Politics, Economics, and the Problems of Development,* edited by Douglass C. North, John Joseph Wallis, Steven B. Webb, and Barry R. Weingast, 293–327. Cambridge: Cambridge University Press.

Zahariadis, Nikolaos. 2007. "The Multiple Streams Framework: Structure, Limitations, Prospects." In *Theories of the Policy Process,* 2nd ed., edited by Paul A. Sabatier, 65–92. Boulder, CO: Westview.

Index